CHIEF
MODERN POETS
OF
BRITAIN AND AMERICA

A FIFTH EDITION OF

Chief Modern Poets of England and America

CHIEF MODERN POETS OF BRITAIN AND AMERICA

VOLUME II

Poets of America

Selected and Edited by

GERALD DEWITT SANDERS
JOHN HERBERT NELSON
M. L. ROSENTHAL

THE MACMILLAN COMPANY
COLLIER-MACMILLAN LIMITED, LONDON

Credits and Acknowledgments

The editors are indebted to the publishers and agents and, in a number of instances, to the authors who are listed here for their generosity and cooperation in permitting us to reprint material for which they control the copyright. For these favors, we here record our thanks.

Athenaeum Publishers: "The Elementary Scene' appears in *The Woman at the Washington Zoo* by Randall Jarrell. Copyright © 1960 by Randall Jarrell. Reprinted by permission of Athenaeum Publishers.

Appleton-Century-Crofts, Inc.: "The Flower-Fed Buffaloes," "Rain," and "Nancy Hanks, Mother of Abraham Lincoln" from *Going-to-the-Stars* by Vachel Lindsay, copyright 1926, D. Appleton & Company, are reprinted by permission of D. Appleton & Company.

Brandt & Brandt: "The Window," copyright 1946 by Conrad Aiken. Reprinted by permission of Brandt & Brandt.

Corinth Books, Inc.: "Maximus, to Himself" and "Maximus, to Gloucester, Letter 19" from *The Maximus Poems* by Charles Olson, copyright © 1960 by Corinth Books/Jargon Books.

iv

Doubleday & Company, Inc.: "My Papa's Waltz," copyright 1942 by Hearst Magazines, Inc.; "Dolor," copyright 1943 by Modern Poetry Association, Inc.; "Big Wind," copyright 1947 by The United Chapters of Phi Beta Kappa; "The Shape of the Fire," copyright 1947 by Theodore Roethke; "Orchids," copyright 1948 by Theodore Roethke; "The Visitant," copyright 1950 by Theodore Roethke; "Meditation at Oyster River," copyright © 1960 by Beatrice Roethke as Administratrix of the Estate of Theodore Roethke; "The Thing," copyright © 1963 by Beatrice Roethke as Administratrix of the Estate of Theodore Roethke; and "Give Way, Ye Gates," all from *The Collected Poems of Theodore Roethke*, are reprinted by permission of Doubleday & Company, Inc.

Duell, Sloan & Pearce, Inc.: Sonnets I and XV from *And in the Human Heart* by Conrad Aiken are reprinted by permission of Duell, Sloan & Pearce, Inc.

Mrs. Norma Millay Ellis: "Passer Mortuus," "Elegy," "Wild Swans," "Pity Me Not because the Light of Day," "Dirge Without Music," "Sonnet to Gath," "Hearing Your Words, and Not a Word among Them," "O Sleep Forever in the Latmian Cave," "See Where Capella with Her Golden Kids," "The Strawberry Shrub," by Edna St. Vincent Millay, are reprinted by permission of Mrs. Norma Millay Ellis.

Farrar, Straus & Cudahy, Inc.: "Words for Hart Crane" and "Skunk Hour" from *Life Studies* by Robert Lowell, copyright 1959 by Robert Lowell, are reprinted by permission of the publishers, Farrar, Straus & Cudahy, Inc.

Farrar, Straus & Giroux, Inc.: "For George Santayana" and "Memories of West Street" from *Life Studies*, copyright © 1958, 1959 by Robert Lowell; "Water" and "The Lesson" from *For the Union Dead*, copyright © 1962, 1964 by Robert Lowell; and "The Opposite House" from *Near the Ocean*, copyright © 1963, 1965, 1966, 1967 by Robert Lowell, reprinted with the permission of Farrar, Straus & Giroux, Inc.

The Four Seas Co.: "The Morning Song of Senlin" from *The Charnel Rose*, copyright 1918 by Conrad Aiken, is reprinted by permission of The Four Seas Co.

Grove Press, Inc.: "Oread," "Orchard," "Pear Tree," "The Helmsman," "Heat," and "Erige Cor Tuum ad Me in Caelum," by Hilda Doolittle; "Often I Am Permitted to Return to a Meadow" from *The Opening of the Field* by Robert Duncan, copyright © 1960 by Robert Duncan; and "The Kingfishers" and "The Moon Is the Number 18" from *The Distances/Poems* by Charles Olson, copyright © 1950, 1951, 1953, 1960, by Charles Olson, are reprinted by permission of Grove Press, Inc.

Faces" from *Smoke and Steel* by Carl Sandburg, copyright 1920 by Harcourt, Brace & World, Inc. Reprinted by permission of the publishers.

"Washington Monument by Night" from *Slabs of the Sunburnt West* by Carl Sandburg, copyright 1922 by Harcourt, Brace & World, Inc., copyright 1950 by Carl Sandburg. Reprinted by permission of the publishers.

Section I from *The People, Yes*, by Carl Sandburg, copyright 1936 by Harcourt, Brace & World, Inc. Reprinted by permission of the publishers.

Harper & Row, Publishers: "Daddy," "Fever 103°," "Death & Co.,' all copyright © 1963 by Ted Hughes, and "Ariel," copyright © 1965 by Ted Hughes, all from *Ariel* by Sylvia Plath, are reprinted by permission of Harper & Row, Publishers.

"What Is Paradise" and "'Twas Like a Maelstrom" by Emily Dickinson from *Bolts of Melody*, edited by Mabel Loomis Todd and Millicent Todd Bingham. Copyright 1945 by Millicent Todd Bingham, reprinted by permission of Harper & Row.

"God's World" from *Renascence and Other Poems*, published by Harper & Brothers (copyright 1917 by Edna St. Vincent Millay), "The Philosopher" from *A Few Figs from Thistles*, published by Harper & Brothers (copyright 1922 by Edna St. Vincent Millay), "Elegy Before Death" and "Song of a Second April" from *Second April*, published by Harper & Brothers (copyright 1921 by Edna St. Vincent Millay), "Euclid Alone Has Looked on Beauty Bare" from *The Harp Weaver and Other Poems*, published by Harper & Brothers (copyright 1920, 1921, 1922, 1923 by Edna St. Vincent Millay), "On the Wide Heath" from *Wine from These Grapes*, published by Harper & Brothers (copyright 1934 by Edna St. Vincent Millay), and Sonnets XI and XXX from *Fatal Interview*, published by Harper & Brothers (copyright 1931 by Edna St. Vincent Millay), by Edna St. Vincent Millay, are reprinted by permission of Harper & Row and of the author.

Harvard University Press: Poems by Emily Dickinson included in this volume are reprinted by permission of the President and Fellows of Harvard College and the Trustees of Amherst College from *The Poems of Emily Dickinson*, edited by Thomas H. Johnson, The Belknap Press of Harvard University Press, Cambridge, Mass., copyright 1951 and 1955 by the President and Fellows of Harvard College.

Holt, Rinehart and Winston, Inc.: The selections in this volume from *Complete Poems of Robert Frost*, copyright 1923, 1928, 1930, 1949 by Holt, Rinehart and Winston, Inc., copyright 1936, 1942,

5555

1951, 1956 by Robert Frost, and "The Draft Horse" from *In the Clearing*, copyright © 1962 by Robert Frost, are reprinted by permission of Holt, Rinehart and Winston, Inc.

Selections from *Chicago Poems* and *Cornhuskers* by Carl Sandburg are reprinted by permission of Holt, Rinehart & Winston.

Houghton Mifflin Company: The selections from *Poems 1924–1933*, copyright 1925, 1926, 1928, 1932, 1933 by Archibald MacLeish, are reprinted by permission of and arrangement with Houghton Mifflin Company, the authorized publishers.

"2nd Air Force" and "The Death of the Ball Turret Gunner" from *Little Friend, Little Friend*, copyright 1945 by Randell Jarrell, are reprinted by permission of the author.

Alfred A. Knopf, Inc.: The selections in this volume by Wallace Stevens are reprinted from *Collected Poems*, copyright 1923, 1931, 1935, 1936, 1937, 1947, 1950, 1954 by Wallace Stevens, by permission of Alfred A. Knopf, Inc.

"The Snow Men," copyright 1923 by Wallace Stevens and renewed 1951, is reprinted by permission of Alfred A. Knopf, Inc., from *Collected Poems of Wallace Stevens*.

"The Souls of Women at Night," copyright © 1957 by Elsie Stevens and Holly Stevens, is reprinted by permission of Alfred A. Knopf, Inc., from *Collected Poems of Wallace Stevens*.

"Philomela," "Janet Waking," and "Dead Boy" from *Selected Poems* by John Crowe Ransom, copyright 1927, 1945 by Alfred A. Knopf, Inc.; and "Vision by Sweetwater" from *Two Gentlemen in Bonds*, copyright 1927 by Alfred A. Knopf, Inc., are reprinted by permission of Alfred A. Knopf, Inc.

"Bells for John Whiteside's Daughter," "Here Lies a Lady," "Miss Euphemia," "Emily Hardcastle, Spinster," and "Inland City" from *Chills and Fever*, copyright 1924 by John Crowe Ransom; and "Blue Girls," "Somewhere Is Such a Kingdom," and "The Equilibrists" from *Two Gentlemen in Bonds*, copyright 1927 by Alfred A. Knopf, Inc., are reprinted by permission of Alfred A. Knopf, Inc.

"Two Views of a Cadaver Room" copyright © 1960 by Sylvia Plath, is reprinted by permission of Alfred A. Knopf, Inc., from *The Colossus and Other Poems* by Sylvia Plath.

Little, Brown & Co.: "I Got So I Could Take His Name," copyright 1929 by Martha Dickinson Bianchi, © 1957 by Mary L. Hampson; " 'Twas Warm at First Like Us," copyright 1929 by Martha Dickinson Bianchi, © 1957 by Mary L. Hampson; and "This Quiet Dust," copyright 1914, 1942 by Martha Dickinson Bianchi, from Emily Dickinson's *Poems*, reprinted by permission of Little, Brown & Company.

Liveright Publishing Corporation: The selections in this volume by Hart Crane are from *The Collected Poems of Hart Crane* and are reprinted by permission of Liveright, Publishers, New York. Copy right, 1933, Liveright, Inc.

Horace Liveright, Inc.: "Priapus and the Pool" and "The Wedding" from *Priapus and the Pool and Other Poems,* copyright 1925 by Conrad Aiken; "Evening," "Fragment Thirty-six," and "Lethe" from *Collected Poems of H. D.,* copyright 1925 by Boni and Liveright, Inc.; and "The Tree," "Ballad of the Goodly Fere," "An Immorality," "A Virginal," and "The Study in Aesthetics" from *Personae* of Ezra Pound, copyright 1926 by Boni & Liveright, are reprinted by permission of Horace Liveright, Inc.

The Macmillan Company: "Abraham Lincoln Walks at Midnight" by Vachel Lindsay, from *Collected Poems* (copyright 1914 by The Macmillan Company, renewed 1942 by Elizabeth C. Lindsey); "Bryan, Bryan, Bryan, Bryan" from *Collected Poems* by Vachel Lindsay (copyright 1920 by The Macmillan Company, renewed 1948 by Elizabeth C. Lindsay); and selections from *General William Booth Enters into Heaven* (copyright 1913), *The Congo* (copyright 1914), *The Chinese Nightingale* (copyright 1917), *The Golden Whales of California* (copyright 1920), and *Collected Poems* (copyright 1913, 1914, 1916, 1917, 1919, 1920, 1923, 1925) by Vachel Lindsay are reprinted by permission of The Macmillan Company.

"The Steeplejack" and "The Hero" from *Collected Poems* by Marianne Moore (copyright 1951 by Marianne Moore); "The Jerboa," "Poetry," "Critics and Connoisseurs," "The Monkeys," "Peter," "A Grave," "Snakes, Mongooses," "To a Steamroller," "To a Snail," "Silence" from *Collected Poems* by Marianne Moore (copyright 1935 by Marianne Moore); "What Are Years," "He 'Digesteth Harde Yron,'" and "Bird-Witted" from *Collected Poems* by Marianne Moore (copyright 1944 by Marianne Moore); and "Nevertheless," "The Mind is an Enchanting Thing," and "The Wood Weasel" from *Collected Poems* by Marianne Moore (copyright 1944 by Marianne Moore) are reprinted by permission of The Macmillan Company.

Selections from *Captain Craig* (copyright 1902), *The Man Against the Sky* (copyright 1916), *The Three Taverns* (copyright 1920), *Avon's Harvest* (copyright 1921), *Dionysus in Doubt* (copyright 1925), and *Collected Poems* (copyright 1916, 1917, 1920, 1921) by Edwin Arlington Robinson; "Cassandra" and "Eros Turannos" from *Collected Poems* by Edwin Arlington Robinson (copyright 1916 by E. A. Robinson, renewed 1944 by Ruth Nivison); "Lost Anchors" from *Collected Poems* by Edwin Arlington Robinson (copyright 1921 by E. A. Robinson, renewed 1949 by Ruth Nivison); and "The Sheaves" and

"As It Looked Then" from *Collected Poems* by Edwin Arlington Robinson (copyright 1925 by E. A. Robinson, renewed 1952 by Ruth Nivison and Barbara R. Holt) are reprinted by permission of The Macmillan Company.

The selections by Edgar Lee Masters are reprinted by permission of the author and of Mrs. Ellen Masters.

The selections by Howard Nemerov are reprinted by permission of the author.

New Directions Publishing Corporation: "Sestina: Altaforte," 'Portrait d'une Femme," "The Return," "The Alchemist," "April," "The Coming of War: Actaeon," "Hugh Selwyn Mauberley," Brennbaum," "Mauberley" X, "Hugh Selwyn Mauberley 1920," and "Homage to Sextus Propertius" from Ezra Pound, *Personae*, copyright 1926 by Ezra Pound; and Cantos I, XIII, XLV, XLVII, and LXXXI (40 lines) from *The Cantos of Ezra Pound*, copyright 1934, 1937, 1940, 1948, are reprinted by permission of New Directions Publishing Corporation.

The selections of William Carlos Williams from *The Collected Earlier Poems of William Carlos Williams*, copyright 1938, 1951 by William Carlos Williams; *The Collected Later Poems of William Carlos Williams*, copyright 1944, 1950 by William Carlos Williams; *Paterson*, I, Preface, III, ii, and V, ii, copyright 1949, © 1958 by William Carlos Williams; and "Asphodel, That Greeny Flower," Book I, from *Pictures from Brueghel and Other Poems*, copyright 1954 by William Carlos Williams, are reprinted by permission of New Directions Publishing Corporation.

"An Interlude" by Robert Duncan, from *Bending the Bow*, © 1968 by Robert Duncan; "Strains of Sight," "After a Passage in Baudelaire," "Shelley's *Arethusa* Set to New Measures," from *Roots and Branches*, © 1964 by Robert Duncan, are reprinted by permission of New Directions Publishing Corporation.

Oxford University Press, Inc.: "South End" from *Collected Poems* by Conrad Aiken is reprinted by permission of Oxford University Press, Inc.

"The Roc" and "Vast Light" from *Great Praises*, © Richard Eberhart 1957; and "For a Lamb," "The Groundhog," "In a Hard Intellectual Light," "The Soul Longs to Return," "Two Loves," "When Doris Danced," "The Fury of Aerial Bombardment," and "The Horse Chestnut" from *Collected Poems 1930–1960*, © Richard Eberhart 1960, are reprinted by permission of Oxford University Press, Inc.

"The Pool" by H. D. is reprinted by permission of Norman Holmes Pearson.

Random House, Inc.: "Auto Wreck," "Buick," "The Dome of

The selections from *Collected Poems of Kenneth Fearing* are reprinted by permission of Random House, Inc., and of the author.

Charles Scribner's Sons: The selections from *Selected Poems* and *Preludes for Memnon* by Conrad Aiken; and from *The Children of the Night* and *The Town Down the River* by E. A. Robinson are reprinted by permission of Charles Scribner's Sons.

Preface to the Fifth Edition

British and American poetry of this century no longer needs defending. The age of Yeats has produced work equal in beauty and brilliance to that of any of the other great literary periods of our language. Rich in experimentation, this age has also been rich in the revitalization of poetic traditions. Moreover, throughout its tumultuous history there has run a quiet, pure stream of lyricism undefiled that has its source in the early beginnings of English poetry.

This anthology, intended for students, aims to give a balanced view of the many-sided modern achievement. The superb daring of a Pound or Eliot on the one hand, and the more conventionally contained power of a Frost or Stevens or Muir on the other, are, with many other contrasting values, essential to our poetic scene. Since its first, pioneering edition in 1929, *Chief Modern Poets of England and America* has sought to represent this scene in some depth by selecting a reasonable number of outstanding poets and giving enough of the best work of each to provide a meaningful context for any one poem. The advantages for study and appreciation over the usual anthology practice of providing a few feasts and a vast number of passing nibbles should, we hope, be clear.

In our selection of poets and poems, the primary standard has been excellence, with some attention to current informed opinion and to various further considerations useful to intelligent study. Thus the inclusion of Emily Dickinson and Gerard Manley Hopkins, though it violates the principle of representing only poets whose main achievement is of this century, seems necessary because they came into their own only in our age. They "lived before their time"—their poetry is more truly ours than that of many writers still living. Again, since Yeats so dominates the age, it is especially valuable to gain a ground sense of his development over a long career during which his whole method and way of thinking changed dynamically. Lawrence is significant not only in his own right but also because of his great influence on later poets, and it is historically important to see Auden as a spokesman of several moods of the 1930's and 1940's. Other poets, such as

Housman, Millay, and Betjeman, are figures of the age whose popular appeal—we speak of writing far above the level of the *merely* popular— is one real imperative. Our great regret is that although we provide a sampling of poets who have only recently come to the fore, our over- all purpose and our space limitations force us to exclude some whose work is comparable with that represented.

As in earlier editions, British and American writers appear separately. In each part, we print the poets in order of their birth and the poems in order of their first book publication, whose date we note after each poem. Hopkins and Dickinson were not, except insignificantly, pub- lished in their lifetimes, and so we have made an exception with them and arranged their work in the order, so far as can be determined, of composition. Where there are two dates, the first is that of composition, the second of original book publication. For a poem untitled by its author, we use the first line or opening phrase, placed in square brackets, as the title. When the author himself uses a first line as title, we follow him in the matter of quotation marks.

In general, our text is that of the most recent editions of the poets, although in some instances earlier versions seem preferable and have been retained. A notable example is Marianne Moore's "Poetry," a poem that like many others of hers has undergone considerable revision over the years. The version we use here is that of the *Collected Poems* (1951), which Miss Moore drastically alters in her *Complete Poems* (1967) by reducing it to the first three lines—though she does give the whole longer text in her notes at the back of the book, thus implying, perhaps, that she is teasing her readers by reminding them that she, after all, is mistress of her own work and quite free to balance *two* versions in the air if she wishes. Which is the better version? We choose the longer one, but at the same time accept the fact that the poetic process never really closes itself off, and that an understanding of this is essential to realizing what poems actually are.

W. H. Auden presents similar problems. As with Miss Moore, we find it a wrench to accept his omissions at times. Thus, in *The Collected Shorter Poems* (1966), he drops the eloquent original stanzas 2–4 in the third part of "In Memory of W. B. Yeats." He has, however, made some less debatable changes in the poem as well, and it would hardly do to treat his revisions selectively within a single piece. We do, though, for historical as well as critical reasons, retain a few poems he leaves out of his latest collection. For the same reasons, we have re- luctantly decided to use the text established by Thomas H. Johnson, as a result of his study of the manuscripts, for our Emily Dickinson selections. Although it seems likely that she would have revised her punctuation and capitalization for publication, this revision never in fact took place. Her mysterious dashes and eccentric capitals leave certain readings open that a more fixed system would obscure, and if that system is not hers, we do better to let every reader be his own interpreter. An anthology is, at best, a springboard to interest in a writer's whole development, and not a tyrannical reduction—this is the best teaching and studying hint we can give.

This obvious point of critical emphasis is one key to the problem of choosing the "best" versions of poems. Although a living poet will usually prepare and proofread his books with loving care, he does not always do so. If the poet is no longer living, of course, his text will be transmitted by someone who has taken on the task—perhaps his wife, perhaps another writer, perhaps a friend or a professional scholar or even some unnamed person. Recent years have seen a proliferation of new editions of varying dependability; one wonders whether earlier editions of certain poets did not, every so often, depend on insights or information that have simply vanished.

We have tried, in the light of these facts, to use intelligent judgment in preparing this edition. Sometimes we have thought it useful to choose an earlier version of a revised poem because of considerations like those provoked by Marianne Moore's "Poetry." Sometimes we have done so because an earlier version (or rejected poem) embodies qualities that first won the poet his recognition, though he himself may have turned against those qualities. We hope that the dates of first book publication provided after each of the poems, and the brief sections of bibliographical and biographical information after each volume, will help lead individual students to explore at least some poets in the perspective of their whole development.

Brief critical introductions precede the British and the American sections of this book. In each instance we intend the introduction neither as a definitive statement for the student nor an obstruction to the teacher, but merely as a series of suggestions toward rapport with the poets.

Contents

VOLUME II

Poets of America

Introduction: Modern American Poetry

Modern American poetry began to emerge in the last century whenever the idiom became familiar and the tone was derived from an immediate state of mind rather than from English literary models. The beginning of Emerson's "Hamatreya" is as modern as anything in Robert Frost:

> Bulkeley, Hunt, Willard, Hosmer, Meriam, Flint,
> Possessed the land which rendered to their toil
> Hay, corn, roots, hemp, flax, apples, wool and wood.

Emerson does not sustain this tone throughout the poem. Nor does any poet born before the Civil War, except Whitman and Emily Dickinson, approach its special kind of immediacy in the whole body of his work. Whitman does so very often—

> Where are you off to, lady? For I see you,
> You splash in the water there, yet stay stock still in your room.
>
> (*Song of Myself*)

But Whitman, with his stylistic eccentricities and his expansive rhetoric, is not yet of this century, though certainly he is its greatest poetic forerunner. Emily Dickinson is far more naturally a spokesman for the existential moment—that is, for the sense that the true matter of a poem is the feel and body of the awareness it presents. That sense, even more than a free approach to meter, stanza, and theme, is the heart of what we call "modern." Therefore, we may think of her as our first twentieth-century American poet, especially as she did not really come into her own until long after her death in 1886. Look at simple poems like "A Bird Came Down the Walk" and "A Narrow Fellow in the Grass," perfect examples of the way in which she keeps concrete pictures or figures of speech in the foreground throughout a poem yet makes the subjective awareness around the hard image her true concern. The wit, the concentration, and the subordination of syntax, rhyme, and sound to the developing tone all have a contemporary edge for us also.

I more than once at Noon

Have passed, I thought, a Whip lash
Unbraiding in the Sun
When stooping to secure it
It wrinkled, and was gone. . . .

Look, too, at a poem like " 'Twas like a Maelstrom, with a notch," in which we have a series of similes for the unstated "It"—an experience whose crucial moral character we can only surmise by way of its mounting imagery of terror, guilt, and then an infinitely regretted "reprieve." Ezra Pound's famous definition of an image as "an intellectual and emotional complex in an instant of time" has never been more piercingly illustrated than by this poem.

To speak so surely to the essence of an emotion is the purest of poetic tasks. The pressures of her life upon her natural gifts seem to have produced a miraculous, spontaneous outpouring of hundreds of brief, moving poems from Miss Dickinson. Later, when the new American poetry became a recognizable movement, cultivation of a style paced by the rhythms and turns of folk speech became more deliberate. The best work of Masters, Lindsay, Sandburg, Robinson, Frost, and Williams presents an infinite variety of effects and voices within this general movement. Poetic achievement is not, of course, just a matter of talking well, or even talking well in dialect; yet the good poet has an ear for what he hears in the world around him, and the way he uses it can be deeply involved in the values of his poetry. The poet has to know how to use it, and where to begin and where to end. Sandburg's love affair with American speech and folk wisdom, for instance, is at once one of the glories and one of the scandals of our poetry: a glory because he records them so faithfully and spiritedly; a scandal because he came gradually to love them for their own sake rather than as elements only incidental, however important, to the making of poems that stand up in their own right. He triumphs when the voice is native and the poem is the main thing, in sardonic pieces like "Balloon Faces" and "The Lawyers Know Too Much," in the occasional lyrical heights of The People, Yes (always interesting, but not always interesting as poetry), in that colloquially elegiac mood that so many American poets have expressed so well—see his "Cool Tombs," for instance, or Masters's "The Hill," or Fearing's "Memo"—and sometimes in the work that exalts the people's struggles and heroes, such as "Osawatomie."

Sandburg's populist and Socialist background strongly colors his use of the vernacular. The work of Masters and Lindsay, especially the latter, has its political and social motivations also. The former poet made his great reputation with his Spoon River Anthology, at least superficially an "exposé" of provincial American morals and manners closely akin to the fiction of Sherwood Anderson and Sinclair Lewis. A series of monologues by various inhabitants of Spoon River, the book has its muckraking side in such pieces as "Daisy Fraser" and "Editor Whedon." But many of the monologues are much less tough-minded, even sentimental—"Lucinda Matlock," with its praise of the antique virtues needed to make people love life; "Anne Rutledge," with its idealization (like Sandburg's) of the meaning of Lincoln; the rather sententious "Petit, the Poet." Lindsay, on the other hand, made a singing music of religious and political passions deep in the American blood:

In a nation of one hundred fine, mob-hearted, lynching, relenting, repenting
  millions,
There are plenty of sweeping, singing, stinging, gorgeous things to shout
  about,
And knock your old blue devils out.

("Bryan, Bryan, Bryan, Bryan")

In "The Congo," his best-known work, Lindsay sinks himself deep into a chant which he calls "a study of the Negro race." It is easy to see now that it leans too heavily on obnoxious racial stereotypes; the opening section is even named "Their Basic Savagery." But Lindsay did not mean it this way. He had a Rousseauan conception, not quite of the noble savage, but of the vital savage in touch with the demonic and, ultimately, the divine forces of life. In this poem, particularly at first, he catches the syncopation of Afro-American music, and his language is appropriately racy and exuberant. He could write more formally and conventionally, and do it rather well—witness "Abraham Lincoln Walks at Midnight" and "The Eagle That Is Forgotten," both poems that derive their passion from the *mystique* of the democratic political tradition. But he realized himself with tne fever and ecstasy of transported vision. His best work is invested with the evangelical fervor to which America has been recurrently subject.

The voice in E. A. Robinson's poetry is far subtler, usually, than that of any of the other poets so far mentioned, except, on occasion, that of Emily Dickinson. Her perceptions were every bit as subtle, but her statements were arrows that went heartbreakingly to the mark. Robinson gives us something else—statements that are imbued with the opacity, the deceptiveness of things. He is often most interested in the irony and pity of individual lives, generally lives that are somehow marked by failure. "Richard Cory" and "Flammonde" are bold enough in outline to escape ambiguity, yet both are, characteristically, *about* ambiguous lives whose meaning never will be altogether clear. When we turn to something like "Eros Turannos," we see Robinson when he was nearest to greatness, his mind playing over and over the treacherous surfaces of human lives, in this case a marriage that has fallen into the abyss. He resembles Henry James here in his curiosity about what lies behind the social mask of character, and in his dark hints about sexuality, loyalty, and man's terrible will to defeat himself. Robinson belonged to a group of Americans obsessed with nostalgia for a simpler nobility to cope with the demands of life.

Robinson thus takes us deep into the "psychology" of a changing America and of the conflicts between certain lingering chivalric ideals and the rise of a more ruthless, impersonal structure of values than the past knew. Robert Frost, too, is engaged by these themes, but his more local, New England emphasis and his ability to present the physical presence of people and scenes rather conceal the fact. No one has evoked the pastoral side of a region with such authority as Frost; no one has better pictured country life in all its reality. Nor has anyone better pictured the barrenness and the terror such life can hold. "The Hill Wife," "Home-Burial," "An Old Man's Winter Night," "A Servant to Servants," "The Witch of Coös" embody a dread of the ultimate brutality of existence that belies the idyllic surface impressions of Frost's happier poetry. Within the limits of a quite conventional verse technique, Frost has grown a body of poetry remarkably powerful in its sensuous repossession of one kind of American experience that throws all the rest of American life into complex, critical perspective.

Perhaps the most striking difference between Frost and William Carlos Williams as "localist" poets lies in the amazing liberation of Williams's poetic form. His verse never drowses, never goes off into ponderosities as do Robinson's and Frost's, at times, under the hypnosis of the iambic pentameter line. In "Spring and All," "To Elsie," or "The Crowd at the Ball Game" we see poetic form handled most cleanly and functionally. In the first of these we have an irregular series of longer (but not very long) stanzas and two-line stanzas; the second is made up of three-line stanzas; the third of two-line units. The line length varies according to the sequence of thought and feeling, the poet maintaining just enough pattern to keep a general over-all sense of structure and of the discipline of compressed form, while he relies on his extraordinary ear and sense of timing to establish a deeper underlying rhythm. In these as in most of his other poems, there is a stronger urban feeling, and a more cosmopolitan viewpoint, than in Frost. Williams's characteristic locale is the area around Rutherford and Paterson, New Jersey, a region intimately linked with New York City, on the one hand, and with the great factory- and railroad-dominated as well as the farming areas of what he calls "the ribbed end of North Jersey." At the same time, Williams is often just as much a "nature poet" as Frost.

Trees, flowers, landscapes are the subjects of a great many of his poems —he displays an intense, mysterious, often violent empathy for them that is doubtless connected with his primitivist love of vitality for its own sake. Like many another modern writer, he has looked to the undereducated and the deprived classes for their latent, unrealized power. His theme again and again, particularly in the long *Paterson* sequence, has been the need for America to discover a voice of her own so that she can create a civilization both indigenous and related to the great European tradition.

Here Williams is very close to Pound and Eliot. All three are explicitly critics of a civilization they believe has gone radically wrong, and though Williams has insisted on finding a poetic line and diction that are intrinsically American, he shares with the other two their revulsion against what has happened to our manners and values and their castigation of the whole tendency of Western society to discard traditions without wishing to create new values worthy of civilization. Williams has even gone a certain way with Pound's criticism of the money and banking systems as the root of our disorders, though never with Pound's more extreme advocacy of Italian Fascism and certain kindred ideas. Both writers are among the great lyrical and rhetorical poets of this century. Both have whatever it is in poetry that corresponds to "absolute pitch" in music. And both make of their commitment to aesthetic values ("pure beauty") a standard by which the age can be judged. Pound's *Hugh Selwyn Mauberley* finds that modern Anglo-American society has stripped the artist of his status and substituted commercialism for every kind of integrity and faith. The "he" of the first poem is presented as a modern Odysseus who has tried to restore the sense of the sublime to England and failed, and the succeeding poems of the sequence describe what has happened to the great traditions in detail. The *Cantos* elaborate on this conception of the true poet as a modern Odysseus with an epic mission who, in the course of his wanderings, passes through the desolation of the modern world and rediscovers certain moments and figures of the past that are touchstones of meaning for the present: the wise Confucius and his disciples, the *caveat* of the medieval Church against usury, the great names of heroic myth and literature, the ancient vision of an earthly paradise. Brilliant incantatory poems like "The Return" and "The Alchemist," and the equally brilliant translations from the Chinese and the Latin and other languages mean for Pound not only the making of beautiful poems but also the rediscovery of continuities with other cultures.

Pound's strong sense of the social relevance of what most people consider unworldly, and his messianic demand for a "hard" poetry, organic in form, without "emotional slither" or verbosity or enslavement to the "beat of the metronome," was an enormously important factor in the rise of the poetry of this century. This poetry has emphasized the image and the necessity of making a poem thoroughly alive in every respect, moment by moment and line by line, free of the patness of "magazine verse." Modern poetry had been tending in these directions by the end of the first decade of this century, a fact which helps account for Yeats's responsiveness to Pound's criticism of his poems when they first met, and for Eliot's experimentation along similar lines before he was "discovered" by Pound. What Emily Dickinson had done almost instinctively now became conscious method. Eliot's "The Love Song of J. Alfred Prufrock," "Gerontion," and *The Waste Land* are perhaps our most extraordinary examples in English of the application of the "new" principles.

The poet's own voice is almost never directly heard in these poems. "Prufrock" is a figure in a dramatic monologue of a new sort, a purposeful reverie in which the speaker takes a hypothetical listener through a journey among images, psychological impressions, remembered moments, literary echoes, in search of the meaning of his own failure to meet the adult challenge of life. The old man of "Gerontion" is a more symbolic figure—he too has failed to meet the challenge, but he embodies the defeat of a whole culture, its loss of creative integrity and, especially, of religious faith. Both "Gerontion" and *The Waste Land* are close to the spirit of Pound's *Mauberley*. *The Waste Land* even takes us through a similar review of contemporary society. But Eliot's poem is completely "presentative"; that is, instead of stating an abstract "message" it projects a host of effects and voices to evoke and suggest what it has to say, so that—as with "Prufrock" and "Gerontion"—our first impression is of an unrelated *mélange* of momentarily spectacular, moving, and comic passages. Gradually, however, the order of the poem emerges: the broad canvas of "The Burial of the Dead," introducing the general theme of cultural sterility, the major symbolic figures of the poem in the Tarot pack of the fortune teller (herself a representative of the meaningless, commercial manipulation of what were once sacred meanings), the Inferno-like vision of modern city life as a living death; the two closeups of "A Game of Chess," showing that the upper and lower classes alike suffer from the failure to love and communicate concern; the many instances of the triumph of uncontrolled lust in a world without moral or aesthetic perspective in "The Fire Sermon"; the implied call for a devout and heroic commitment, rather than submission to the pointlessness of a life without such commitment, in the elegy for Phlebas the Phoenician called "Death by Water"; and the imagery of promised redemption through following the Hindu message in

"What the Thunder Said." Eliot's virtuosity is dazzling throughout this sequence. He combines precise and evocative imagery, exquisite lyricism, high and low comic effects, startlingly dramatic moments, parody both serious and witty, in a display of mastery of his art all the more impressive because so many varied tones and styles are bent to the service of the driving spirit behind the whole work. Eliot's ultimate stress is a religious one—this is his sharpest distinction from Williams and Pound, with whom he shares so many root attitudes otherwise. Very likely this fact is intimately related to the struggle his poems seem constantly to carry on against a profound, depressed disgust with life.

Eliot's influence on later poets is pervasive—a matter of tonal values, of a precise and fastidious sense of the possibilities of phrasing, and of an intricate yet instinctive feeling for the dynamics of structure. But if there is a modern movement of deliberate experimentation based as much on a theory of poetry as on the inner pressure of a specific artistic problem, it derives mainly from Pound and Williams. Thus, the sequences of Eliot from *The Waste Land* to *Four Quartets* are sustained, interlocking works, verbal mobiles that are interesting and alive and at the same time have a well-defined progression from beginning to end. A sequence, however, is not necessarily a firm structure. It consists of several poems, at once independent of one another and interdependent through their relation to a central motivation and energy, and it may constitute a continuing rather than a closed process. Pound's *Cantos* and Williams's *Paterson* are much more open in this way than are Eliot's sequences, and their impact on the poetry of writers such as Charles Olson and Robert Duncan is quite evident.

Even in their shorter pieces, whether or not they are parts of sequences, these writers seem often more interested in the process than in the finished work, though both have shown that they can produce poems that hold up beautifully in the traditional manner. Each, too, is quite able to write a poem stripped down to its essential point of focus, but very often we find them feeding a good deal of special information and theoretical perspective into the poem, as Pound does in the *Cantos* and Williams does at times in *Paterson*. The method has its dangers but is a way of establishing a context with many overtones of association and significance.

But we have jumped ahead in time. Let us return to an earlier moment, the time when Wallace Stevens, Marianne Moore, H. D. (Hilda Doolittle), and E. E. Cummings began to flourish. We generally think of these poets as very much a part, in their several ways, of the modern movement of American poetry "led" by Pound and Eliot. As with the latter two poets, all four have cultivated a perfectionism of style that is a proliferation of the special speaking voice of each. Cummings is the most experimental—exploding words and sentences, working out typographical patterns so that at times his poems are visual jokes or pictures of a mood much more than they are the design of *sounds* we expect a poem to be. Yet he is often the most conventional of poets in what he has to say (romantic love poems, poems on mutability or in praise of youth and feminine beauty, satires against philistinism) and even in the basic forms he employs. Many of his poems, for instance, are sonnets, open or disguised by the rearrangement of lines. Bohemian, pacifist, and political conservative at the same time, Cummings presents the same curious fusion of pure poetry and tendentiousness as do Pound and Eliot. He veers easily into sentimentality and often repeats himself, but his work contains some of the freshest, most concentrated lyricism of our century, and his forays into the American idiom are triumphs of humor as well as of poetic power.

Marianne Moore and Wallace Stevens are less obviously experimental than Cummings, whose methods have been compared (though the resemblance is only superficial) with those of European Dadaism and Futurism. Miss Moore is, poetically, an elegant conversationalist who constructs out of detailed observation a set of principles at once hardheaded and ladylike. Small animals and plants that survive not by aggressiveness but by special devices for resistance and endurance—the armadillo, the porcupine, the chambered nautilus, the "wood-weasel" or skunk—are among the subjects dearest to her. They suit her advocacy of the unsensationally functional in all aspects of life. (See her "Poetry" for a striking application of this view to the art of poetry, which she defends because it has, "after all, a place for the genuine," and because it reveals the realities at the heart of imagination.) Yeats once described as an aristocratic ideal the uniting of "passion and precision"; Miss Moore makes them pragmatic and democratic ideals as well. But the pleasures her methods of advocacy afford, that delightful fastidiousness and pungency, which never lapse into either mere gentility or mere "charm," should no more conceal her darker strands of thought and feeling than Frost's pastoralism should conceal his.

Wallace Stevens, too, contains these depths within a high-spirited style that sometimes appears to be pure dandyism, sometimes an exquisite spoofing of all ideology and all art. Like Williams, he believes in the healing and revealing power of art—paradoxically, the purer the art the more meaningful its expression of the truly human. The viewpoint is fundamental to his secular humanism and to his constant speculations on the relation between imagination and reality. It underlies his tricky arguments in "Sunday Morning" and "Peter Quince at the Clavier" to the effect that the intensities of experience and the repetitions of nature—the return of the birds each spring, the renewal of gardens each year, the constant replacement of youthful beauty by the "maidens" of newer generations—are the closest we shall ever come to eternity. Out of our own experience, deprivations, and observation of cyclical nature we project the "truths" of myth and faith, and in art we learn to play with these motifs and search out our ideal visions of the self. How bitterly deceptive all this may be Stevens confesses in a poem like "The Emperor of Ice-Cream"; how impossible for the human spirit to avoid such projections he shows in a poem like "The Idea of Order at Key West." But always in his work there is the richest overlay of sound, an exuberance of language, and a wit alert to all its possibilities. Among younger American poets, Richard Wilbur has best learned from Stevens and Miss Moore to cultivate these gifts.

H. D. has given a body of poems which, taken together, represent precisely the Imagist ideal put forward by Pound and others of a poetry centered on a single sensuous effect or a single emotion, concrete, unredundant, an effect in action. Like Pound and the other early Imagists, she did not, of course, allow herself to be bound in all her work within the confines of this narrow if necessary discipline. (That is, the Imagist movement seemed a necessary stage in the liberation of modern verse from sentimentality, mere self-indulgence, and post-Tennysonian rhetoric.) She has also given us a small body of erotic and mystical poetry that is lovely, if not quite as immediate, in its own way. In this latter phase of her work she seems as independent of the general drift of our modern poetry as Conrad Aiken, who has always reserved to himself the right to resist the special tendencies of the Pound–Eliot movement and to cultivate a more "old-fashioned" sort of lyricism and impressionism. His modernity consists more in the kind of awareness he reveals and in the general resilience of fibre in his versification than in his particular poetic methods, although he is a skilful craftsman who knows how to depart from conventional rhythms and line patterns without getting out of touch with his over-all design. In certain ways Aiken and Edna St. Vincent Millay resemble one another, particularly in their shorter, simpler poems. Rarely, it is true, does he have the popular touch that her feminine voice possessed—ardent, often anguished, often very much of the brittle 'twenties, like the novels of Fitzgerald or the early poetry of Cummings, and a little careless of the sustaining of effects. But Aiken's "Music I heard with you was more than music" and Millay's "Song of a Second April" or "Love is not all; it is not meat nor drink" are remarkably alike in their essentials, and both writers are "natural" poets in love with language. Their easy skill may be compared, again, with that of the versatile Archibald MacLeish. And it may be compared and contrasted with that of John Crowe Ransom, whose elegiac, highly disciplined verse, with its aristocratic Southern allusions and ironies, strikes the ear with a finely intellectualized grace and sweetness.

An interesting feature of the whole movement of modern poetry has been that, while from its beginnings it has appeared to struggle toward the kind of "purity" we associate with, say, Imagism—that is, a freedom from sentimentality and rhetoric and an assertion of intensity itself, whether of emotion or sensation, as a value independent of political, religious, or moral considerations—it has nevertheless been steeped in the dominant issues of the period. As a result, our poetry, despite its high aesthetic standards, has been profoundly, even violently, involved in the intellectual and social struggles of the age. The most successful poetry has been that which could transcend those struggles not so much by ignoring them as by remaining art even while wrestling with them. One reason for the authority of Pound, Williams, and Eliot has been their triumph in certain poems over the problems this has entailed. The political poetry of figures like Millay and MacLeish, on the other hand, has often seemed to go against the grain of their natural talents, and the overinsistence of so much of Robinson Jeffers's work on pointing certain anti-machine-age morals for the times has greatly marred his reputation as one of our finest narrative and descriptive poets. The late 1920's and the 1930's, of course, were in the United States and England a time for the exploration of revolutionary perspectives on our society, and it is striking to see the uses to which the elegiac and also mordantly sardonic voice of Kenneth Fearing were bent during this period.

Hart Crane, who died in 1932 at the age of thirty-three, and therefore still seems one of our "younger poets," was close to the same impulse when he wrote "The Bridge," which attempts to find a guiding spiritual symbolism for an industrial society in one of its great engineering artifacts. Nevertheless, it is a sequence whose speaking sensibility, like that in *The Waste Land* and in the *Cantos*, is seeking to define the poet's self, both in purely personal terms and in relation to the world he knows. As in those works, the pressures upon the protagonist are psychological as well as social. The speaker measures himself against the ideal of wholeness and radiant meaning apotheosized in the Brooklyn Bridge. As he does so, the play of contrasts between his rather depressed view of himself and the possibilities he envisions gives the sequence a perhaps unintended poignancy. In other poems Crane's "social" perspectives enter only obliquely—for instance, in his identification in "Chaplinesque" with Charlie Chaplin's comically gallant little tramp, or in his passing reference to the harm done by city life to the psyche, in "Repose of Rivers." It is the wound of sentient life that is his main subject, and at the same time his will—a characteristically Romantic motif—to triumph over that wound (though in a poem like "Passage" he recognizes the impossibility of doing so).

Many of our poets have shared these perspectives of Crane's, in as many different fashions as their differences of personality and experience would suggest. Thus, Richard Eberhart has constantly set against each other an acute sense of the pity of death, an ecstatic mysticism, and a rather abstract, "Metaphysical" cast of mind. The second World War gave him ample scope for the interplay of these characteristics, but even in a poem as elementary in its theme as his famous "The Groundhog" or as private as "The Soul Longs to Return Whence It Came" they make for a powerful personal art built around the need for realization against all the odds. Randall Jarrell's emphasis is more on the vulnerability of each person, whether soldier, adult civilian, or child—especially child. Karl Shapiro throws a bright, sardonic light over our machine-made culture and its betrayals of the individual lost within it. Howard Nemerov, though a prolific poet who writes in many moods including that of a caustically satirical Liberal wit, confronts in his most serious work the absolute, inhuman terror of things very much in the spirit of Crane at his bleakest and most tragic.

It is, however, Robert Lowell and, on occasion, Sylvia Plath who seem closest to Crane's spirit among poets who have emerged since World War II. The voices in their poems are those of speakers whose private guilt, anxiety, and undirected, pent-up fury are also embodiments of their culture and its history. Lowell associates these with his Puritan, New England background and with the evils of our economic order. His violent power at first found characteristic expression in the portrayal of figures somehow involved with moral and religious burdens, particularly of a sexual nature. His *Life Studies* is a largely autobiographical sequence in which the poet uses himself frankly as the central symbol of modern life and of the prevailing neurotic condition we must all face if we are to survive and make a saner world. He is like Dylan Thomas in the stormy energy with which he makes himself his own greatest metaphor. Sylvia Plath, an exquisite lyrical artist, is at the same time driven by the thought of the Nazi death camps to a terrifying, confused double identification with both the victims and their torturers. Her combination of an exuberant imagination with certain morbidly suicidal visions became, eventually, inseparable from this double identification. Both Lowell and Sylvia Plath may be contrasted with Theodore Roethke, whose energies were more exclusively devoted to exploring his own inward states, to responding with empathy to sensuous and emotional experience, and to attempting a genial reconciliation with life in order to achieve self-transcendence.

Emily Dickinson
(1830–1886)

[SUCCESS IS COUNTED SWEETEST]

Success is counted sweetest
By those who ne'er succeed.
To comprehend a nectar
Requires sorest need.

Not one of all the purple Host
Who took the Flag today
Can tell the definition
So clear of Victory

As he defeated – dying –
On whose forbidden ear
The distant strains of triumph
Burst agonized and clear!   (1859, 1878)

[I NEVER HEAR THE WORD]

I never hear the word "escape"
Without a quicker blood,
A sudden expectation,
A flying attitude!

I never hear of prisons broad
By soldiers battered down,
But I tug childish at my bars
Only to fail again!   (c. 1859, 1891)

[I'M "WIFE"—I'VE FINISHED THAT]

I'm "wife" – I've finished that –
That other state –
I'm Czar – I'm "Woman" now –
It's safer so –

II-12

How odd the Girl's life looks
Behind this soft Eclipse –
I think that Earth feels so
To folks in Heaven – now –

This being comfort – then
That other kind – was pain –
But why compare?
I'm "Wife"! Stop there!   (c. 1860, 1890)

[COME SLOWLY—EDEN]

Come slowly – Eden!
Lips unused to Thee –
Bashful – sip thy Jessamines –
As the fainting Bee –

Reaching late his flower,
Round her chamber hums –
Counts his nectars –
Enters – and is lost in Balms.   (c. 1860, 1890)

[I TASTE A LIQUOR NEVER BREWED]

I taste a liquor never brewed –
From Tankards scooped in Pearl –
Not all the Vats upon the Rhine
Yield such an Alcohol!

Inebriate of Air – am I –
And Debauchee of Dew –
Reeling – thro endless summer days –
From inns of Molten Blue –

When "Landlords" turn the drunken Bee
Out of the Foxglove's door –
When Butterflies – renounce their "drams" –
I shall but drink the more!

Till Seraphs swing their snowy Hats –
And Saints – to windows run –
To see the little Tippler
Leaning against the – Sun –   (c. 1860, 1861)

[WHAT IS – "PARADISE"]

What is – "Paradise" –
Who live there –
Are they "Farmers" –
Do they "hoe" –
Do they know that this is "Amherst" –
And that I – am coming – too –

Do they wear "new shoes" – in "Eden" –
Is it always pleasant – there –
Won't they scold us – when we're hungry –
Or tell God – how cross we are –

You are sure there's such a person
As "a Father" – in the sky –
So if I get lost – there – ever –
Or do what the nurse calls "die" –
I shan't walk the "Jasper" – barefoot –
Ransomed folks – won't laugh at me –
Maybe – "Eden" a'nt so lonesome
As New England used to be!   (c. 1860, 1945)

[THERE'S A CERTAIN SLANT OF LIGHT]

There's a certain Slant of light,
Winter Afternoons –
That oppresses, like the Heft
Of Cathedral Tunes –

Heavenly Hurt, it gives us –
We can find no scar,
But internal difference,
Where the Meanings, are –

None may teach it – Any –
'Tis the Seal Despair –
An imperial affliction
Sent us of the Air –

When it comes, the Landscape listens –
Shadows – hold their breath –

When it goes, 'tis like the Distance
On the look of Death –   (c. 1861, 1890)

[I FELT A FUNERAL, IN MY BRAIN]

I felt a Funeral, in my Brain,
And Mourners to and fro
Kept treading – treading – till it seemed
That Sense was breaking through –

And when they all were seated,
A Service, like a Drum –
Kept beating – beating – till I thought
My Mind was going numb –

And then I heard them lift a Box
And creak across my Soul
With those same Boots of Lead, again,
Then Space – began to toll,

As all the Heavens were a Bell,
And Being, but an Ear,
And I, and Silence, some strange Race
Wrecked, solitary, here –

And then a Plank in Reason, broke,
And I dropped down, and down –
And hit a World, at every plunge,
And Finished knowing – then –   (c. 1861, 1896)

[I GOT SO I COULD TAKE HIS NAME]

I got so I could take his name –
Without – Tremendous gain –
That Stop-sensation – on my Soul –
And Thunder – in the Room –

I got so I could walk across
That Angle in the floor,
Where he turned so, and I turned – how–
And all our Sinew tore –

I got so I could stir the Box –
In which his letters grew

Without that forcing, in my breath –
As Staples – driven through –

Could dimly recollect a Grace –
I think, they call it "God" –
Renowned to ease Extremity –
When Formula, had failed –

And shape my Hands –
Petition's way,
Tho' ignorant of a word
That Ordination – utters

My Business, with the Cloud,
If any Power behind it, be,
Not subject to Despair –
It care, in some remoter way,
For so minute affair
As Misery –
Itself, too vast, for interrupting – more –   (c. 1861, 1929)

[THE SOUL SELECTS HER OWN SOCIETY]

The Soul selects her own Society –
Then – shuts the Door –
To her divine Majority –
Present no more –

Unmoved – she notes the Chariots – pausing
At her low Gate –
Unmoved – an Emperor be kneeling
Upon her Mat –

I've known her – from an ample nation –
Choose One –
Then – close the Valves of her attention –
Like Stone –   (c. 1862, 1890)

[A BIRD CAME DOWN THE WALK]

A Bird came down the Walk –
He did not know I saw –

He bit an Angleworm in halves
And ate the fellow, raw,

And then he drank a Dew
From a convenient Grass –
And then hopped sidewise to the Wall
To let a Beetle pass –

He glanced with rapid eyes
That hurried all around –
They looked like frightened Beads, I thought –
He stirrred his Velvet Head

Like one in danger, Cautious,
I offered him a Crumb
And he unrolled his feathers
And rowed him softer home –

Than Oars divide the Ocean,
Too silver for a seam –
Or Butterflies, off Banks of Noon
Leap, plashless as they swim.   (*1862, 1891*)

[*TWAS LIKE A MAELSTROM*]

'Twas like a Maelstrom, with a notch,
That nearer, every Day,
Kept narrowing its boiling Wheel
Until the Agony

Toyed coolly with the final inch
Of your delirious Hem –
And you dropt, lost,
When something broke –
And let you from a Dream –

As if a Goblin with a Gauge –
Kept measuring the Hours –
Until you felt your Second
Weigh, helpless, in his Paws –

And not a Sinew – stirred – could help,
And sense was setting numb –

When God – remembered – and the Fiend
Let go, then, Overcome –

As if your Sentence stood – pronounced –
And you were frozen led
From Dungeon's luxury of Doubt
To Gibbets, and the Dead –

And when the Film had stitched your eyes
A Creature gasped "Reprieve"!
Which Anguish was the utterest – then –
To perish, or to live?   *(c. 1862, 1945)*

[MUCH MADNESS IS DIVINEST SENSE]

Much Madness is divinest Sense –
To a discerning Eye –
Much Sense – the starkest Madness –
'Tis the Majority
In this, as All, prevail –
Assent – and you are sane –
Demur – you're straightway dangerous –
And handled with a Chain –   *(c. 1862, 1890)*

[I HEARD A FLY BUZZ]

I heard a Fly buzz – when I died –
The Stillness in the Room
Was like the Stillness in the Air –
Between the Heaves of Storm –

The Eyes around – had wrung them dry –
And Breaths were gathering firm
For that last Onset – when the King
Be witnessed – in the Room –

I willed my Keepsakes – Signed away
What portion of me be
Assignable – and then it was
There interposed a Fly –

With Blue – uncertain stumbling Buzz –
Between the light – and me –

And then the Windows failed – and then
I could not see to see – (c. 1862, 1896)

['TWAS WARM – AT FIRST – LIKE US]

'Twas warm – at first – like Us –
Until there crept upon
A Chill – like frost upon a Glass –
Till all the scene – be gone.

The Forehead copied Stone –
The Fingers grew too cold
To ache – and like a Skater's Brook -
The busy eyes – congealed –

It straightened – that was all –
It crowded Cold to Cold –
It multiplied indifference –
As Pride were all it could –

And even when with Cords –
'Twas lowered, like a Weight –
It made no Signal, nor demurred,
But dropped like Adamant. (c. 1862, 1929)

[THE HEART ASKS PLEASURE – FIRST]

The Heart asks Pleasure – first –
And then – Excuse from Pain –
And then – those little Anodynes
That deaden suffering –

And then – to go to sleep –
And then – if it should be
The will of its Inquisitor
The privilege to die – (c. 1862, 1890)

[BECAUSE I COULD NOT STOP FOR DEATH]

Because I could not stop for Death –
He kindly stopped for me –
The Carriage held but just Ourselves –
And Immortality.

We slowly drove – He knew no haste
And I had put away
My labor and my leisure too,
For His Civility –

We passed the School, where Children strove
At Recess – in the Ring –
We passed the Fields of Gazing Grain –
We passed the Setting Sun –

Or rather – He passed Us –
The Dews drew quivering and chill –
For only Gossamer, my Gown –
My Tippet – only Tulle –

We paused before a House that seemed
A Swelling of the Ground –
The Roof was scarcely visible –
The Cornice – in the Ground –

Since then – 'tis Centuries – and yet
Feels shorter than the Day
I first surmised the Horses' Heads
Were toward Eternity –   (c. 1863, 1890)

[IT DROPPED SO LOW – IN MY REGARD]

It dropped so low – in my Regard –
I heard it hit the Ground –
And go to pieces on the Stones
At bottom of my Mind –

Yet blamed the Fate that fractured – less
Than I reviled Myself,
For entertaining Plated Wares
Upon my Silver Shelf –   (c. 1863, 1896)

[THIS QUIET DUST]

This quiet Dust was Gentlemen and Ladies
And Lads and Girls –
Was laughter and ability and Sighing
And Frocks and Curls.

This Passive Place a Summer's nimble mansion
Where Bloom and Bees
Exists an Oriental Circuit
Then cease, like these –   (c. 1864, 1914)

[I STEPPED FROM PLANK TO PLANK]

I stepped from Plank to Plank
A slow and cautious way
The Stars about my Head I felt
About my Feet the Sea.

I knew not but the next
Would be my final inch –
This gave me that precarious Gait
Some call Experience.   (c. 1864, 1896)

[A NARROW FELLOW IN THE GRASS]

A narrow Fellow in the Grass
Occasionally rides –
You may have met Him – did you not
His notice sudden is –

The Grass divides as with a Comb –
A spotted shaft is seen –
And then it closes at your feet
And opens further on –

He likes a Boggy Acre
A Floor too cool for Corn –
Yet when a Boy, and Barefoot –
I more than once at Noon

Have passed, I thought, a Whip lash
Unbraiding in the Sun
When stooping to secure it
It wrinkled, and was gone –

Several of Nature's People
I know, and they know me –
I feel for them a transport
Of cordiality –

But never met this Fellow
Attended, or alone
Without a tighter breathing
And Zero at the Bone –   *(1865, 1866)*

[AS IMPERCEPTIBLY AS GRIEF]

As imperceptibly as Grief
The Summer lapsed away –
Too imperceptible at last
To seem like Perfidy –
A Quietness distilled
As Twilight long begun,
Or Nature spending with herself
Sequestered Afternoon –
The Dusk drew earlier in –
The Morning foreign shone –
A courteous, yet harrowing Grace,
As Guest, that would be gone –
And thus, without a Wing
Or service of a Keel
Our Summer made her light escape
Into the Beautiful.   *(1865, 1891)*

[THE LAST NIGHT THAT SHE LIVED]

The last Night that She lived
It was a Common Night
Except the Dying – this to Us
Made Nature different

We noticed smallest things –
Things overlooked before
By this great light upon our Minds
Italicized – as 'twere.

As We went out and in
Between Her final Room
And Rooms where Those to be alive
Tomorrow were, a Blame

That Others could exist
While She must finish quite

A Jealousy for Her arose
So nearly infinite –

We waited while She passed –
It was a narrow time –
Too jostled were Our Souls to speak
At length the notice came.

She mentioned, and forgot –
Then lightly as a Reed
Bent to the Water, struggled scarce –
Consented, and was dead –

And We – We placed the Hair –
And drew the Head erect –
And then an awful leisure was
Belief to regulate –   (c. 1866, 1890)

[THERE CAME A WIND LIKE A BUGLE]

There came a Wind like a Bugle –
It quivered through the Grass
And a Green Chill upon the Heat
So ominous did pass
We barred the Windows and the Doors
As from an Emerald Ghost –
The Doom's electric Moccasin
That very instant passed –
On a strange Mob of panting Trees
And Fences fled away
And Rivers where the Houses ran
Those looked that lived – that Day–
The Bell within the steeple wild
The flying tidings told –
How much can come
And much can go,
And yet abide the World!   (c. 1883, 1891)

[DROWNING IS NOT SO PITIFUL]

Drowning is not so pitiful
As the attempt to rise.
Three times, 'tis said, a sinking man

Comes up to face the skies,
And then declines forever
To that abhorred abode,
Where hope and he part company –
For he is grasped of God.
The Maker's cordial visage,
However good to see,
Is shunned, we must admit it,
Like an adversity.   *(1896)*

Edgar Lee Masters
(1869–1950)

THE HILL

Where are Elmer, Herman, Bert, Tom and Charley,
The weak of will, the strong of arm, the clown, the boozer, the fighter?
All, all, are sleeping on the hill.

One passed in a fever,
One was burned in a mine,
One was killed in a brawl,
One died in a jail,
One fell from a bridge toiling for children and wife—
All, all are sleeping, sleeping, sleeping on the hill.

Where are Ella, Kate, Mag, Lizzie and Edith,
The tender heart, the simple soul, the loud, the proud, the happy
    one?—
All, all, are sleeping on the hill.

One died in shameful child-birth,
One of a thwarted love,
One at the hands of a brute in a brothel,
One of a broken pride, in the search for heart's desire,
One after life in far-away London and Paris
Was brought to her little space by Ella and Kate and Mag—
All, all are sleeping, sleeping, sleeping on the hill.

Where are Uncle Isaac and Aunt Emily,
And old Towny Kincaid and Sevigne Houghton,
And Major Walker who had talked
With venerable men of the revolution?—
All, all are sleeping, on the hill.

They brought them dead sons from the war,
And daughters whom life had crushed,

And their children fatherless, crying—
All, all, are sleeping, sleeping, sleeping on the hill.

Where is Old Fiddler Jones
Who played with life all his ninety years,
Braving the sleet with bared breast,
Drinking, rioting, thinking neither of wife nor kin,
Nor gold, nor love, nor heaven?
Lo! he babbles of the fish-frys of long ago,
Of the horse-races of long ago at Clary's Grove,
Of what Abe Lincoln said
One time at Springfield. *(1915)*

PETIT, THE POET

Seeds in a dry pod, tick, tick, tick,
Tick, tick, tick, like mites in a quarrel—
Faint iambics that the full breeze wakens—
But the pine tree makes a symphony thereof.
Triolets, villanelles, rondels, rondeaus,
Ballades by the score with the same old thought:
The snows and the roses of yesterday are vanished;
And what is love but a rose that fades?
Life all around me here in the village:
Tragedy, comedy, valor, and truth,
Courage, constancy, heroism, failure—
All in the loom, and oh what patterns!
Woodlands, meadows, streams, and rivers—
Blind to all of it all my life long.
Triolets, villanelles, rondels, rondeaus,
Seeds in a dry pod, tick, tick, tick,
Tick, tick, tick, what little iambics,
While Homer and Whitman roared in the pines? *(1915)*

CARL HAMBLIN

The press of the Spoon River *Clarion* was wrecked,
And I was tarred and feathered,
For publishing this on the day the Anarchists were hanged in Chicago:
"I saw a beautiful woman with bandaged eyes
Standing on the steps of a marble temple.
Great multitudes passed in front of her,
Lifting their faces to her imploringly.

In her left hand she held a sword.
She was brandishing the sword,
Sometimes striking a child, again a laborer,
Again a slinking woman, again a lunatic.
In her right hand she held a scale;
Into the scale pieces of gold were tossed
By those who dodged the strokes of the sword.
A man in a black gown read from a manuscript:
'She is no respecter of persons.'
Then a youth wearing a red cap
Leaped to her side and snatched away the bandage.
And lo, the lashes had been eaten away
From the oozy eye-lids;
The eye-balls were seared with a milky mucus;
The madness of a dying soul
Was written on her face—
But the multitude saw why she wore the bandage." (*1915*)

EDITOR WHEDON

To be able to see every side of every question;
To be on every side, to be everything, to be nothing long;
To pervert truth, to ride it for a purpose,
To use great feelings and passions of the human family
For base designs, for cunning ends,
To wear a mask like the Greek actors—
Your eight-page paper—behind which you huddle,
Bawling through the megaphone of big type:
"This is I, the giant."
Thereby also living the life of a sneak-thief,
Poisoned with the anonymous words
Of your clandestine soul.
To scratch dirt over scandal for money,
And exhume it to the winds for revenge,
Or to sell papers,
Crushing reputations, or bodies, if need be,
To win at any cost, save your own life.
To glory in demoniac power, ditching civilization,
As a paranoiac boy puts a log on the track
And derails the express train.
To be an editor, as I was.
Then to lie here close by the river over the place
Where the sewage flows from the village,

And the empty cans and garbage are dumped,
And abortions are hidden. *(1915)*

DAISY FRASER

Did you ever hear of Editor Whedon
Giving to the public treasury any of the money he received
For supporting candidates for office?
Or for writing up the canning factory
To get people to invest?
Or for suppressing the facts about the bank,
When it was rotten and ready to break?
Did you ever hear of the Circuit Judge
Helping anyone except the "Q" railroad,
Or the bankers? Or did Rev. Peet or Rev. Sibley
Give any part of their salary, earned by keeping still,
Or speaking out as the leaders wished them to do,
To the building of the water works?
But I—Daisy Fraser who always passed
Along the streets through rows of nods and smiles,
And coughs and words such as "there she goes,"
Never was taken before Justice Arnett
Without contributing ten dollars and costs
To the school fund of Spoon River! *(1915)*

FIDDLER JONES

The earth keeps some vibration going
There in your heart, and that is you.
And if the people find you can fiddle,
Why, fiddle you must, for all your life.
What do you see, a harvest of clover?
Or a meadow to walk through to the river?
The wind's in the corn; you rub your hands
For beeves hereafter ready for market;
Or else you hear the rustle of skirts
Like the girls when dancing at Little Grove
To Cooney Potter a pillar of dust
Or whirling leaves meant ruinous drouth;
They looked to me like Red-Head Sammy
Stepping it off, to "Toor-a-Loor."
How could I till my forty acres
Not to speak of getting more,

With a medley of horns, bassoons and piccolos
Stirred in my brain by crows and robins
And the creak of a wind-mill—only these?
And I never started to plow in my life
That some one did not stop in the road
And take me away to a dance or picnic.
I ended up with forty acres;
I ended up with a broken fiddle—
And a broken laugh, and a thousand memories,
And not a single regret. (*1915*)

ANNE RUTLEDGE

Out of me unworthy and unknown
The vibrations of deathless music;
"With malice toward none, with charity for all."
Out of me the forgiveness of millions toward millions,
And the beneficent face of a nation
Shining with justice and truth.
I am Anne Rutledge who sleep beneath these weeds,
Beloved in life of Abraham Lincoln,
Wedded to him, not through union,
But through separation.
Bloom forever, O Republic,
From the dust of my bosom! (*1915*)

LUCINDA MATLOCK

I went to the dances at Chandlerville,
And played snap-out at Winchester.
One time we changed partners,
Driving home in the moonlight of middle June,
And then I found Davis.
We were married and lived together for seventy years,
Enjoying, working, raising the twelve children,
Eight of whom we lost
Ere I had reached the age of sixty.
I spun, I wove, I kept the house, I nursed the sick,
I made the garden, and for holiday
Rambled over the fields where sang the larks,
And by Spoon River gathering many a shell,
And many a flower and medicinal weed—
Shouting to the wooded hills, singing to the green valleys.

At ninety-six I had lived enough, that is all,
And passed to a sweet repose.
What is this I hear of sorrow and weariness,
Anger, discontent, and drooping hopes?
Degenerate sons and daughters,
Life is too strong for you—
It takes life to love Life. *(1915)*

THE LOST ORCHARD

Loves and sorrows of those who lose an orchard
Are less seen than the shadow shells
Of butterflies whose wings are tortured
In the perilous escape of rainy dells,
In the ecstatic flight of blinding Junes.
Save for the breath dirge of the wind-rung harebells
They have no words that ever shall be known,
Neither have they speech or tone,
Save the tones when the sun with gold galloons
Trims the blue edges of the air;
And save the quiet which quells
The music of the water drop in the well's
Water far down, where vision swoons.

These are the voices and these alone
Of the lost orchard, and its vague despair.
Branches may gnarl with scale and lift their bare
Paralysis, or the withered crone
Of loneliness breed water sprouts; or frost
Heap the dull turf over the strawberry vines;
Or rust unhinge the gates; or the fallen pear
Waste like the Cretan gold of ruined shrines
In tangled grasses; or the broken share
Be sunk in leaf mould—these are noonday signs
Of the deserted, but not of the orchard that is lost.
Silver secrets speak of the lost orchard, as the shells
Of butterflies escaped whisper the vanished wings;
Or as light shaken from the field of clover tells
Of the zephyr's irised wanderings.

A lost orchard is the memory of a friend
Wronged by life to death, who lies
Lifelike, but with unseeing eyes.

It is music made a ghost, because the end
Of life has come which made the music mean
Eyes that look and lips that thrill.
Music is no breast where wounded souls may lean,
If played when hands it signified are still.
A lost orchard is the road on which we passed
Where a house was with a candle in the night;
And we must go that way still, but at last
The house is by the roadside, but no light.

Over a lost orchard I have strayed
In March when down the wooded ravine
The behemoth wind bellowed to the glade
By the sky-blue water before the rushes were green.
While yet the acorn cups crushed under feet
Against the moss mould, yellow as smoke;
And the lanterns of wild cucumbers quenched by sleet,
And gusts of winter hung by the leafless oak;
When the crow's nest was a splotch of sticks on the sky,
And burnt out torches of feasts the sumach cone.
And I have climbed till the wind was naught but a sigh
Over the stairs of stone and the seat of stone.
And there I have seen the orchard, the apple trees
Patient in loneliness, and forgotten care;
And the grass as heavy as the Sargasso Sea's
Around the trunks, grown like a dead man's hair.
And I have returned in Spring when the nebulae
Of early blossoms whitened before it was June;
And I have seen them merge in their leafy sky
Till they became the light of the full moon.
Warm is the orchard as the stalls of the sun
At midnight, when each budded stem is dewed
With a firefly and the whispering zephyrs run
From leaf to leaf, awaking the dreams that brood
Before the gray woolens of the shadows fall
From the sleeping earth, and the lights of the orchard are wooed
From sea gray to sea green in a carnival
Change of flame, in a dawning many hued.
Till the long winds come, blowing from woodlands over
The glistening water, and meadows beyond the citrine
Sand of the hill that walls the field of clover
Nod their blossoms amid a tide of green.

Angels are never in caverns, nor presences
That speak the will to leave it lingering
About the orchard lost. Nor does the chrysalis
Lie thick in paths of the arisen wing;
Nor butterflies haunt the grasses like innocent
Desires defeated; nor the coverts mourn
With doves; nor are the wild bees rent
From habitations in old trees; nor the forlorn
Grass grow rich bespeaking humble hopes;
Nor corners of giant heliotropes
Droop so memorially; nor the stair of stone
Hold the silence that follows a footfall; nor the sky
Above the stone seat by its emptiness alone
Tell of a face and of a wondering eye;
Nor are flowers without the fruit so richly grown.

The house of the lost orchard is loneliness to the uttermost:
The chimney in the top of the elm tree,
Like the open mouth of a musing ghost
Has nothing but the void of the sky,
And the sequestered flight of the passing cloud,
Though the expectant breeze goes by
To gather smoke from the hearth long disavowed.
And under a brick of the porch the key to the fastened door
Glints out of rusts and waits
For those who won the orchard to explore
The rooms and find the unveiled Fates.

Out of the lost orchard is life that needs the orchard no more
The fence has broken places, and the gates
Swing to the passing wind. But butterflies soar
Over the tree tops to predestined mates. (*1935*)

E. A. Robinson
(1869–1935)

JOHN EVERELDOWN

"Where are you going tonight, tonight,—
    Where are you going, John Evereldown?
There's never the sign of a star in sight,
    Nor a lamp that's nearer than Tilbury Town.
Why do you stare as a dead man might?
Where are you pointing away from the light?
And where are you going tonight, tonight,—
    Where are you going, John Evereldown?"

"Right through the forest, where none can see,
    There's where I'm going, to Tilbury Town.
The men are asleep,—or awake, may be,—
    But the women are calling John Evereldown.
Ever and ever they call for me,
And while they call can a man be free?
So right through the forest, where none can see,
    There's where I'm going, to Tilbury Town."

"But why are you going so late, so late,—
    Why are you going, John Evereldown?
Though the road may be smooth and the way be straight,
    There are two long leagues to Tilbury Town.
Come in by the fire, old man, and wait!
Why do you chatter out there by the gate?
And why are you going so late, so late,—
    Why are you going, John Evereldown?"

"I follow the women wherever they call,—
    That's why I'm going to Tilbury Town.
God knows if I pray to be done with it all,
    But God is no friend to John Evereldown.
So the clouds may come and the rain may fall,

The shadows may creep and the dead men crawl,—
But I follow the women wherever they call,
  And that's why I'm going to Tilbury Town." *(1897)*

RICHARD CORY

Whenever Richard Cory went down town,
We people on the pavement looked at him:
He was a gentleman from sole to crown,
Clean favored, and imperially slim.

And he was always quietly arrayed,
And he was always human when he talked;
But still he fluttered pulses when he said,
"Good-morning," and he glittered when he walked.

And he was rich—yes, richer than a king—
And admirably schooled in every grace:
In fine, we thought that he was everything
To make us wish that we were in his place.

So on we worked, and waited for the light,
And went without the meat, and cursed the bread;
And Richard Cory, one calm summer night,
Went home and put a bullet through his head. *(1897)*

CHARLES CARVILLE'S EYES

A melancholy face Charles Carville had,
But not so melancholy as it seemed,
When once you knew him, for his mouth redeemed
His insufficient eyes, forever sad:
In them there was no life-glimpse, good or bad,
Nor joy nor passion in them ever gleamed;
His mouth was all of him that ever beamed,
His eyes were sorry, but his mouth was glad.

He never was a fellow that said much,
And half of what he did say was not heard
By many of us: we were out of touch
With all his whims and all his theories
Till he was dead, so those blank eyes of his
Might speak them. Then we heard them, every word. *(1897)*

GEORGE CRABBE

Give him the darkest inch your shelf allows,
Hide him in lonely garrets, if you will,—
But his hard, human pulse is throbbing still
With the sure strength that fearless truth endows.
In spite of all fine science disavows,
Of his plain excellence and stubborn skill
There yet remains what fashion cannot kill,
Though years have thinned the laurel from his brows.

Whether or not we read him, we can feel
From time to time the vigor of his name
Against us like a finger for the shame
And emptiness of what our souls reveal
In books that are as altars where we kneel
To consecrate the flicker, not the flame. *(1897)*

CREDO

I cannot find my way: there is no star
In all the shrouded heavens anywhere;
And there is not a whisper in the air
Of any living voice but one so far
That I can hear it only as a bar
Of lost, imperial music, played when fair
And angel fingers wove, and unaware,
Dead leaves to garlands where no roses are.

No, there is not a glimmer, nor a call,
For one that welcomes, welcomes when he fears,
The black and awful chaos of the night;
For through it all—above, beyond it all—
I know the far-sent message of the years,
I feel the coming glory of the Light. *(1897)*

MINIVER CHEEVY

Miniver Cheevy, child of scorn,
  Grew lean while he assailed the seasons;
He wept that he was ever born,
  And he had reasons.

Miniver loved the days of old
  When swords were bright and steeds were prancing;
The vision of a warrior bold
  Would set him dancing.

Miniver sighed for what was not,
  And dreamed, and rested from his labors;
He dreamed of Thebes and Camelot,
  And Priam's neighbors.

Miniver mourned the ripe renown
  That made so many a name so fragrant;
He mourned Romance, now on the town,
  And Art, a vagrant.

Miniver loved the Medici,
  Albeit he had never seen one;
He would have sinner incessantly
  Could he have been one.

Miniver cursed the commonplace
  And eyed a khaki suit with loathing;
He missed the mediæval grace
  Of iron clothing.

Miniver scorned the gold he sought,
  But sore annoyed was he without it;
Miniver thought, and thought, and thought,
  And thought about it.

Miniver Cheevy, born too late,
  Scratched his head and kept on thinking;
Miniver coughed, and called it fate,
  And kept on drinking. *(1910)*

FOR A DEAD LADY

No more with overflowing light
Shall fill the eyes that now are faded,
Nor shall another's fringe with night
Their woman-hidden world as they did.
No more shall quiver down the days
The flowing wonder of her ways,

Whereof no language may requite
The shifting and the many-shaded.

The grace, divine, definitive,
Clings only as a faint forestalling;
The laugh that love could not forgive
Is hushed, and answers to no calling;
The forehead and the little ears
Have gone where Saturn keeps the years;
The breast where roses could not live
Has done with rising and with falling.

The beauty, shattered by the laws
That have creation in their keeping,
No longer trembles at applause,
Or over children that are sleeping;
And we who delve in beauty's lore
Know all that we have known before
Of what inexorable cause
Makes Time so vicious in his reaping. (*1910*)

FLAMMONDE

The man Flammonde, from Gods knows where.
With firm address and foreign air,
With news of nations in his talk
And something royal in his walk,
With glint of iron in his eyes,
But never doubt, nor yet surprise,
Appeared, and stayed, and held his head
As one by kings accredited.

Erect, with his alert repose
About him, and about his clothes,
He pictured all tradition hears
Of what we owe to fifty years.
His cleansing heritage of taste
Paraded neither want nor waste;
And what he needed for his fee
To live, he borrowed graciously.

He never told us what he was,
Or what mischance, or other cause,

Had banished him from better days
To play the Prince of Castaways.
Meanwhile he played surpassing well
A part, for most, unplayable;
In fine, one pauses, half afraid
To say for certain that he played.

For that, one may as well forego
Conviction as to yes or no;
Nor can I say just how intense
Would then have been the difference
To several, who, having striven
In vain to get what he was given,
Would see the stranger taken on
By friends not easy to be won.

Moreover, many a malcontent
He soothed and found munificent;
His courtesy beguiled and foiled
Suspicion that his years were soiled;
His mien distinguished any crowd,
His credit strengthened when he bowed;
And women, young and old, were fond
Of looking at the man Flammonde.

There was a woman in our town
On whom the fashion was to frown;
But while our talk renewed the tinge
Of a long-faded scarlet fringe,
The man Flammonde saw none of that,
And what he saw we wondered at—
That none of us, in her distress,
Could hide or find our littleness.

There was a boy that all agreed
Had shut within him the rare seed
Of learning. We could understand,
But none of us could lift a hand.
The man Flammonde appraised the youth,
And told a few of us the truth;
And thereby, for a little gold,
A flowered future was unrolled.

There were two citizens who fought
For years and years, and over nought;
They made life awkward for their friends,
And shortened their own dividends.
The man Flammonde said what was wrong
Should be made right; nor was it long
Before they were again in line,
And had each other in to dine.

And these I mention are but four
Of many out of many more.
So much for them. But what of him—
So firm in every look and limb?
What small satanic sort of kink
Was in his brain? What broken link
Withheld him from the destinies
That came so near to being his?

What was he, when we came to sift
His meaning, and to note the drift
Of incommunicable ways
That make us ponder while we praise?
Why was it that his charm revealed
Somehow the surface of a shield?
What was it that we never caught?
What was he, and what was he not?

How much it was of him we met
We cannot ever know; nor yet
Shall all he gave us quite atone
For what was his, and his alone;
Nor need we now, since he knew best,
Nourish an ethical unrest:
Rarely at once will nature give
The power to be Flammonde and live.

We cannot know how much we learn
From those who never will return,
Until a flash of unforeseen
Remembrance falls on what has been.
We've each a darkening hill to climb;
And this is why, from time to time

In Tilbury Town, we look beyond
Horizons for the man Flammonde. *(1916)*

CASSANDRA

I heard one who said: "Verily,
    What word have I for children here?
Your Dollar is your only Word,
    The wrath of it your only fear.

"You build it altars tall enough
    To make you see, but you are blind;
You cannot leave it long enough
    To look before you or behind.

"When Reason beckons you to pause,
    You laugh and say that you know best;
But what it is you know, you keep
    As dark as ingots in a chest.

"You laugh and answer, 'We are young;
    O leave us now, and let us grow.'—
Not asking how much more of this
    Will Time endure or Fate bestow.

"Because a few complacent years
    Have made your peril of your pride,
Think you that you are to go on
    Forever pampered and untried?

"What lost eclipse of history,
    What bivouac of the marching stars,
Has given the sign for you to see
    Millenniums and last great wars?

"What unrecorded overthrow
    Of all the world has ever known,
Or ever been, has made itself
    So plain to you, and you alone!

"Your Dollar, Dove and Eagle make
    A Trinity that even you
Rate higher than you rate yourselves;
    It pays, it flatters, and it's new

"And though your very flesh and blood
   Be what your Eagle eats and drinks,
You'll praise him for the best of birds,
   Not knowing what the Eagle thinks.

"The power is yours, but not the sight;
   You see not upon what you tread;
You have the ages for your guide,
   But not the wisdom to be led.

"Think you to tread forever down
   The merciless old verities?
And are you never to have eyes
   To see the world for what it is?

"Are you to pay for what you have
   With all you are?"—no other word
We caught, but with a laughing crowd
   Moved on. None heeded, and few heard. *(1916)*

EROS TURANNOS

She fears him, and will always ask
   What fated her to choose him;
She meets in his engaging mask
   All reasons to refuse him;
But what she meets and what she fears
Are less than are the downward years,
Drawn slowly to the foamless weirs
   Of age, were she to lose him.

Between a blurred sagacity
   That once had power to sound him,
And Love, that will not let him be
   The Judas that she found him,
Her pride assuages her almost,
As if it were alone the cost.—
He sees that he will not be lost,
   And waits and looks around him.

A sense of ocean and old trees
   Envelops and allures him;
Tradition, touching all he sees,
   Beguiles and reassures him;

And all her doubts of what he says
Are dimmed with what she knows of days—
Till even prejudice delays
   And fades, and she secures him.

The falling leaf inaugurates
   The reign of her confusion;
The pounding wave reverberates
   The dirge of her illusion;
And home, where passion lived and died,
Becomes a place where she can hide,
While all the town and harbor side
   Vibrate with her seclusion.

We tell you, tapping on our brows,
   The story as it should be,—
As if the story of a house
   Were told, or ever could be;
We'll have no kindly veil between
Her visions and those we have seen,—
As if we guessed what hers have been,
   Or what they are or would be.

Meanwhile we do no harm; for they
   That with a god have striven,
Not hearing much of what we say,
   Take what the god has given;
Though like waves breaking it may be,
Or like a changed familiar tree,
Or like a stairway to the sea
   Where down the blind are driven.   *(1916)*

THE UNFORGIVEN

When he, who is the unforgiven,
Beheld her first, he found her fair:
No promise ever dreamt in heaven
Could then have lured him anywhere
That would have been away from there;
And all his wits had lightly striven,
Foiled with her voice, and eyes, and hair.

There's nothing in the saints and sages
To meet the shafts her glances had,

Or such as hers have had for ages
To blind a man till he be glad,
And humble him till he be mad.
The story would have many pages,
And would be neither good nor bad.

And, having followed, you would find him
Where properly the play begins;
But look for no red light behind him—
No fumes of many-colored sins,
Fanned high by screaming violins.
God knows what good it was to blind him,
Or whether man or woman wins.

And by the same eternal token,
Who knows just how it will all end?—
This drama of hard words unspoken,
This fireside farce, without a friend
Or enemy to comprehend
What augurs when two lives are broken,
And fear finds nothing left to mend.

He stares in vain for what awaits him,
And sees in Love a coin to toss;
He smiles, and her cold hush berates him
Beneath his hard half of the cross;
They wonder why it ever was;
And she, the unforgiving, hates him
More for her lack than for her loss.

He feeds with pride his indecision,
And shrinks from what will not occur,
Bequeathing with infirm derision
His ashes to the days that were,
Before she made him prisoner;
And labors to retrieve the vision
That he must once have had of her.

He waits, and there awaits an ending,
And he knows neither what nor when;
But no magicians are attending
To make him see as he saw then,
And he will never find again
The face that once had been the rending
Of all his purpose among men.

He blames her not, nor does he chide her,
And she has nothing new to say;
If he were Bluebeard he could hide her,
But that's not written in the play,
And there will be no change to-day;
Although, to the serene outsider,
There still would seem to be a way. *(1916)*

BEWICK FINZER

Time was when his half million drew
   The breath of six per cent;
But soon the worm of what-was-not
   Fed hard on his content;
And something crumbled in his brain
   When his half million went.

Time passed, and filled along with his
   The place of many more;
Time came, and hardly one of us
   Had credence to restore,
From what appeared one day, the man
   Whom we had known before.

The broken voice, the withered neck,
   The coat worn out with care,
The cleanliness of indigence,
   The brilliance of despair,
The fond imponderable dreams
   Of affluence,—all were there.

Poor Finzer, with his dreams and schemes,
   Fares hard now in the race,
With heart and eye that have a task
   When he looks in the face
Of one who might so easily
   Have been in Finzer's place.

He comes unfailing for the loan
   We give and then forget;
He comes, and probably for years
   Will he be coming yet,—
Familiar as an old mistake,
   And futile as regret. *(1916)*

THE MAN AGAINST THE SKY

Between me and the sunset, like a dome
Against the glory of a world on fire,
Now burned a sudden hill,
Bleak, round, and high, by flame-lit height made higher,
With nothing on it for the flame to kill
Save one who moved and was alone up there
To loom before the chaos and the glare
As if he were the last god going home
Unto his last desire.

Dark, marvelous, and inscrutable he moved on
Till down the fiery distance he was gone,
Like one of those eternal, remote things
That range across a man's imaginings
When a sure music fills him and he knows
What he may say thereafter to few men,—
The touch of ages having wrought
An echo and a glimpse of what he thought
A phantom or a legend until then;
For whether lighted over ways that save,
Or lured from all repose,
If he go on too far to find a grave,
Mostly alone he goes.

Even he, who stood where I had found him,
On high with fire all round him,
Who moved along the molten west,
And over the round hill's crest
That seemed half ready with him to go down,
Flame-bitten and flame-cleft,
As if there were to be no last thing left
Of a nameless unimaginable town,—
Even he who climbed and vanished may have taken
Down to the perils of a depth not known,
From death defended though by men forsaken,
The bread that every man must eat alone;
He may have walked while others hardly dared
Look on to see him stand where many fell;
And upward out of that, as out of hell,
He may have sung and striven
To mount where more of him shall yet be given,
Bereft of all retreat,

To sevenfold heat,—
As on a day when three in Dura shared
The furnace, and were spared
For glory by that king of Babylon
Who made himself so great that God, who heard,
Covered him with long feathers, like a bird.

Again, he may have gone down easily,
By comfortable altitudes, and found,
As always, underneath him solid ground
Whereon to be sufficient and to stand
Possessed already of the promised land,
Far stretched and fair to see:
A good sight, verily,
And one to make the eyes of her who bore him
Shine glad with hidden tears.
Why question of his ease of who before him,
In one place or another where they left
Their names as far behind them as their bones,
And yet by dint of slaughter, toil and theft,
And shrewdly sharpened stones,
Carved hard the way for his ascendency
Through deserts of lost years?
Why trouble him now who sees and hears
No more than what his innocence requires,
And therefore to no other height aspires
Than one at which he neither quails nor tires?
He may do more by seeing what he sees
Than others eager for iniquities;
He may, by seeing all things for the best,
Incite futurity to do the rest.

Or with an even likelihood,
He may have met with atrabilious eyes
The fires of time on equal terms and passed
Indifferently down, until at last
His only kind of grandeur would have been,
Apparently, in being seen.
He may have had for evil or for good
No argument; he may have had no care
For what without himself went anywhere
To failure or to glory, and least of all
For such a stale, flamboyant miracle;

He may have been the prophet of an art
Immovable to old idolatries;
He may have been a player without a part,
Annoyed that even the sun should have the skies
For such a flaming way to advertise;
He may have been a painter sick at heart
With Nature's toiling for a new surprise;
He may have been a cynic, who now, for all
Of anything divine that his effete
Negation may have tasted,
Saw truth in his own image, rather small,
Forbore to fever the ephemeral,
Found any barren height a good retreat
From any swarming street,
And in the sun saw power superbly wasted;
And when the primitive old-fashioned stars
Came out again to shine on joys and wars
More primitive, and all arrayed for doom,
He may have proved a world a sorry thing
In his imagining,
And life a lighted highway to the tomb.

Or, mounting with infirm unsearching tread,
His hopes to chaos led,
He may have stumbled up there from the past,
And with an aching strangeness viewed the last
Abysmal conflagration of his dreams,—
A flame where nothing seems
To burn but flame itself, by nothing fed;
And while it all went out,
Not even the faint anodyne of doubt
May then have eased a painful going down
From pictured heights of power and lost renown,
Revealed at length to his outlived endeavor
Remote and unapproachable forever;
And at his heart there may have gnawed
Sick memories of a dead faith foiled and flawed
And long dishonored by the living death
Assigned alike by chance
To brutes and hierophants;
And anguish fallen on those he loved around him
May once have dealt the last blow to confound him,
And so have left him as death leaves a child,

Who sees it all too near;
And he who knows no young way to forget
May struggle to the tomb unreconciled.
Whatever suns may rise or set
There may be nothing kinder for him here
Than shafts and agonies;
And under these
He may cry out and stay on horribly;
Or, seeing in death too small a thing to fear,
He may go forward like a stoic Roman
Where pangs and terrors in his pathway lie,—
Or, seizing the swift logic of a woman,
Curse God and die.

Or maybe there, like many another one
Who might have stood aloft and looked ahead,
Black-drawn against wild red,
He may have built, unawed by fiery gules
That in him no commotion stirred,
A living reason out of molecules
Why molecules occurred,
And one for smiling when he might have sighed
Had he seen far enough,
And in the same inevitable stuff
Discovered an odd reason too for pride
In being what he must have been by laws
Infrangible and for no kind of cause.
Deterred by no confusion or surprise
He may have seen with his mechanic eyes
A world without a meaning, and had room,
Alone amid magnificence and doom,
To build himself an airy monument
That should, or fail him in his vague intent,
Outlast an accidental universe—
To call it nothing worse—
Or, by the burrowing guile
Of Time disintegrated and effaced,
Like once-remembered mighty trees go down
To ruin, of which by man may now be traced
No part sufficient even to be rotten,
And in the book of things that are forgotten
Is entered as a thing not quite worth while.
He may have been so great

That satraps would have shivered at his frown,
And all he prized alive may rule a state
No larger than a grave that holds a clown;
He may have been a master of his fate,
And of his atoms,—ready as another
In his emergence to exonerate
His father and his mother;
He may have been a captain of a host,
Self-eloquent and ripe for prodigies,
Doomed here to swell by dangerous degrees,
And then give up the ghost.
Nahum's great grasshoppers were such as these,
Sun-scattered and soon lost.

Whatever the dark road he may have taken,
This man who stood on high
And faced alone the sky,
Whatever drove or lured or guided him,—
A vision answering a faith unshaken,
An easy trust assumed of easy trials,
A sick negation born of weak denials,
A crazed abhorrence of an old condition,
A blind attendance on a brief ambition,—
Whatever stayed him or derided him,
His way was even as ours;
And we, with all our wounds and all our powers,
Must each await alone at his own height
Another darkness or another light;
And there, of our poor self dominion reft,
If inference and reason shun
Hell, Heaven, and Oblivion,
May thwarted will (perforce precarious,
But for our conservation better thus)
Have no misgiving left
Of doing yet what here we leave undone?
Or if unto the last of these we cleave,
Believing or protesting we believe
In such an idle and ephemeral
Florescence of the diabolical,—
If, robbed of two fond old enormities,
Our being had no onward auguries,
What then were this great love of ours to say
For launching other lives to voyage again

A little farther into time and pain,
A little faster in a futile chase
For a kingdom and a power and a Race
That would have still in sight
A manifest end of ashes and eternal night?
Is this the music of the toys we shake
So loud,—as if there might be no mistake
Somewhere in our indomitable will?
Are we no greater than the noise we make
Along one blind atomic pilgrimage
Whereon by crass chance billeted we go
Because our brains and bones and cartilage
Will have it so?
If this we say, then let us all be still
About our share in it, and live and die
More quietly thereby.

Where was he going, this man against the sky?
You know not, nor do I.
But this we know, if we know anything:
That we may laugh and fight and sing
And of our transience here make offering
To an orient Word that will not be erased,
Or, save in incommunicable gleams
Too permanent for dreams,
Be found or known.
No tonic and ambitious irritant
Of increase or of want
Has made an otherwise insensate waste
Of ages overthrown
A ruthless, veiled, implacable foretaste
Of other ages that are still to be
Depleted and rewarded variously
Because a few, by fate's economy,
Shall seem to move the world the way it goes;
No soft evangel of equality,
Safe-cradled in a communal repose
That huddles into death and may at last
Be covered well with equatorial snows—
And all for what, the devil only knows—
Will aggregate an inkling to confirm
The credit of a sage or of a worm,
Or tell us why one man in five

Should have a care to stay alive
While in his heart he feels no violence
Laid on his humor and intelligence
When infant Science makes a pleasant face
And waves again that hollow toy, the Race;
No planetary trap where souls are wrought
For nothing but the sake of being caught
And sent again to nothing will attune
Itself to any key of any reason
Why man should hunger through another season
To find out why 'twere better late than soon
To go away and let the sun and moon
And all the silly stars illuminate
A place for creeping things,
And those that root and trumpet and have wings,
And herd and ruminate,
Or dive and flash and poise in rivers and seas,
Or by their loyal tails in lofty trees
Hang screeching lewd victorious derision
Of man's immortal vision.

Shall we, because Eternity records
Too vast an answer for the time-born words
We spell, whereof so many are dead that once
In our capricious lexicons
Were so alive and final, hear no more
The Word itself, the living word
That none alive has ever heard
Or ever spelt,
And few have ever felt
Without the fears and old surrenderings
And terrors that began
When Death let fall a feather from his wings
And humbled the first man?
Because the weight of our humility,
Wherefrom we gain
A little wisdom and much pain,
Falls here too sore and there too tedious,
Are we in anguish or complacency,
Not looking far enough ahead
To see by what mad couriers we are led
Along the roads of the ridiculous,
To pity ourselves and laugh at faith

And while we curse life bear it?
And if we see the soul's dead end in death,
Are we to fear it?
What folly is here that has not yet a name
Unless we say outright that we are liars?
What have we seen beyond our sunset fires
That lights again the way by which we came?
Why pay we such a price, and one we give
So clamoringly, for each racked empty day
That leads one more last human hope away,
As quiet fiends would lead past our crazed eyes
Our children to an unseen sacrifice?
If after all that we have lived and thought,
All comes to Nought,—
If there be nothing after Now,
And we be nothing anyhow,
And we know that,—why live?
'Twere sure but weaklings' vain distress
To suffer dungeons where so many doors
Will open on the cold eternal shores
That look sheer down
To the dark tideless floods of Nothingness
Where all who know may drown. (*1916*)

THE MILL

The miller's wife had waited long,
    The tea was cold, the fire was dead;
And there might yet be nothing wrong
    In how he went and what he said:
"There are no millers any more,"
    Was all that she had heard him say;
And he had lingered at the door
    So long that it seemed yesterday.

Sick with a fear that had no form
    She knew that she was there at last;
And in the mill there was a warm
    And mealy fragrance of the past.
What else there was would only seem
    To say again what he had meant;
And what was hanging from a beam
    Would not have heeded where she went.

And if she thought it followed her,
   She may have reasoned in the dark
That one way of the few there were
   Would hide her and would leave no mark:
Black water, smooth above the weir
   Like starry velvet in the night,
Though ruffled once, would soon appear
   The same as ever to the sight. *(1920)*

MR. FLOOD'S PARTY

Old Eben Flood, climbing alone one night
Over the hill between the town below
And the forsaken upland hermitage
That held as much as he should ever know
On earth again of home, paused warily.
The road was his with not a native near;
And Eben, having leisure, said aloud,
For no man else in Tilbury Town to hear:

"Well, Mr. Flood, we have the harvest moon
Again, and we may not have many more;
The bird is on the wing, the poet says,
And you and I have said it here before.
Drink to the bird." He raised up to the light
The jug that he had gone so far to fill,
And answered huskily: "Well, Mr. Flood,
Since you propose it, I believe I will."

Alone, as if enduring to the end
A valiant armor of scarred hopes outworn,
He stood there in the middle of the road
Like Roland's ghost winding a silent horn.
Below him, in the town among the trees,
Where friends of other days had honored him,
A phantom salutation of the dead
Rang thinly till old Eben's eyes were dim.

Then, as a mother lays her sleeping child
Down tenderly, fearing it may awake,
He set the jug down slowly at his feet
With trembling care, knowing that most things break;
And only when assured that on firm earth

It stood, as the uncertain lives of men
Assuredly did not, he paced away,
And with his hand extended paused again:

"Well, Mr. Flood, we have not met like this
In a long time; and many a change has come
To both of us, I fear, since last it was
We had a drop together. Welcome home!"
Convivially returning with himself,
Again he raised the jug up to the light;
And with an acquiescent quaver said:
"Well, Mr. Flood, if you insist, I might.

"Only a very little, Mr. Flood—
For auld lang syne. No more, sir; that will do."
So, for the time, apparently it did,
And Eben evidently thought so too;
For soon amid the silver loneliness
Of night he lifted up his voice and sang,
Secure, with only two moons listening,
Until the whole harmonious landscape rang—

"For auld lang syne." The weary throat gave out,
The last word wavered, and the song was done.
He raised again the jug regretfully
And shook his head, and was again alone.
There was not much that was ahead of him,
And there was nothing in the town below—
Where strangers would have shut the many doors
That many friends had opened long ago. (*1921*)

LOST ANCHORS

Like a dry fish flung inland far from shore,
There lived a sailor, warped and ocean-browned,
Who told of an old vessel, harbor-drowned
And out of mind a century before,
Where divers, on descending to explore
A legend that had lived its way around
The world of ships, in the dark hulk had found
Anchors, which had been seized and seen no more.

Improving a dry leisure to invest
Their misadventure with a manifest

Analogy that he may read who runs,
The sailor made it old as ocean grass—
Telling of much that once had come to pass
With him, whose mother should have had no sons. (*1921*)

THE SHEAVES

Where long the shadows of the wind had rolled,
Green wheat was yielding to the change assigned;
And as by some vast magic undivined
The world was turning slowly into gold.
Like nothing that was ever bought or sold
It waited there, the body and the mind;
And with a mighty meaning of a kind
That tells the more the more it is not told.

So in a land where all days are not fair,
Fair days went on till on another day
A thousand golden sheaves were lying there,
Shining and still, but not for long to stay—
As if a thousand girls with golden hair
Might rise from where they slept and go away. (*1925*)

AS IT LOOKED THEN

In a sick shade of spruce, moss-webbed, rock-fed,
Where, long unfollowed by sagacious man,
A scrub that once had been a pathway ran
Blindly from nowhere and to nowhere led,
One might as well have been among the dead
As half way there alive; so I began
Like a malingering pioneer to plan
A vain return—with one last look ahead.

And it was then that like a spoken word
Where there was none to speak, insensibly
A flash of blue that might have been a bird
Grew soon to the calm wonder of the sea—
Calm as a quiet sky that looked to be
Arching a world where nothing had occurred. (*1925*)

KARMA

Christmas was in the air and all was well
With him, but for a few confusing flaws

In divers of God's images. Because
A friend of his would neither buy nor sell,
Was he to answer for the axe that fell?
He pondered; and the reason for it was,
Partly, a slowly freezing Santa Claus
Upon the corner, with his beard and bell.

Acknowledging an improvident surprise,
He magnified a fancy that he wished
The friend whom he had wrecked were here again.
Not sure of that, he found a compromise;
And from the fulness of his heart he fished
A dime for Jesus who had died for men.   *(1925)*

WHY HE WAS THERE

Much as he left it when he went from us
Here was the room again where he had been
So long that something of him should be seen,
Or felt—and so it was. Incredulous,
I turned about, loath to be greeted thus,
And there he was in his old chair, serene
As ever, and as laconic and as lean
As when he lived, and as cadaverous.

Calm as he was of old when we were young,
He sat there gazing at the pallid flame
Before him. "And how far will this go on?"
I thought. He felt the failure of my tongue,
And smiled: "I was not here until you came;
And I shall not be here when you are gone."   *(1925)*

Robert Frost
(1874–1963)

STORM FEAR

When the wind works against us in the dark,
And pelts with snow
The lower chamber window on the east,
And whispers with a sort of stifled bark,
The beast,
"Come out! Come out!"—
It costs no inward struggle not to go,
Ah, no!
I count our strength,
Two and a child,
Those of us not asleep subdued to mark
How the cold creeps as the fire dies at length,—
How drifts are piled,
Dooryard and road ungraded,
Till even the comforting barn grows far away,
And my heart owns a doubt
Whether 'tis in us to arise with day
And save ourselves unaided.   *(1913)*

MOWING

There was never a sound beside the wood but one,
And that was my long scythe whispering to the ground.
What was it it whispered? I knew not well myself;
Perhaps it was something about the heat of the sun,
Something, perhaps, about the lack of sound—
And that was why it whispered and did not speak.
It was no dream of the gift of idle hours,
Or easy gold at the hand of fay or elf:
Anything more than the truth would have seemed too weak
To the earnest love that laid the swale in rows,
Not without feeble-pointed spikes of flowers
(Pale orchises), and scared a bright green snake.

The fact is the sweetest dream that labor knows.
My long scythe whispered and left the hay to make. *(1913)*

RELUCTANCE

Out through the fields and the woods
  And over the walls I have wended;
I have climbed the hills of view
  And looked at the world, and descended;
I have come by the highway home,
  And lo, it is ended.

The leaves are all dead on the ground,
  Save those that the oak is keeping
To ravel them one by one
  And let them go scraping and creeping
Out over the crusted snow,
  When others are sleeping.

And the dead leaves lie huddled and still,
  No longer blown hither and thither;
The last lone aster is gone;
  The flowers of the witch-hazel wither;
The heart is still aching to seek,
  But the feet question "Whither?"

Ah, when to the heart of man
  Was it ever less than a treason
To go with the drift of things,
  To yield with a grace to reason,
And bow and accept the end
  Of a love or a season? *(1913)*

THE PASTURE

I'm going out to clean the pasture spring;
I'll only stop to rake the leaves away
(And wait to watch the water clear, I may):
I sha'n't be gone long.—You come too.

I'm going out to fetch the little calf
That's standing by the mother. It's so young,
It totters when she licks it with her tongue.
I sha'n't be gone long.—You come too. *(1914)*

MENDING WALL

Something there is that doesn't love a wall,
That sends the frozen-ground-swell under it,
And spills the upper boulders in the sun;
And makes gaps even two can pass abreast.
The work of hunters is another thing:
I have come after them and made repair
Where they have left not one stone on a stone,
But they would have the rabbit out of hiding,
To please the yelping dogs. The gaps I mean,
No one has seen them made or heard them made,
But at spring mending-time we find them there.
I let my neighbor know beyond the hill;
And on a day we meet to walk the line
And set the wall between us once again.
We keep the wall between us as we go.
To each the boulders that have fallen to each.
And some are loaves and some so nearly balls
We have to use a spell to make them balance:
"Stay where you are until our backs are turned!"
We wear our fingers rough with handling them.
Oh, just another kind of outdoor game,
One on a side. It comes to little more:
There where it is we do not need the wall:
He is all pine and I am apple orchard.
My apple trees will never get across
And eat the cones under his pines, I tell him.
He only says, "Good fences make good neighbors."
Spring is the mischief in me, and I wonder
If I could put a notion in his head:
"Why do they make good neighbors? Isn't it
Where there are cows? But here there are no cows.
Before I built a wall I'd ask to know
What I was walling in or walling out,
And to whom I was like to give offence.
Something there is that doesn't love a wall,
That wants it down." I could say "Elves" to him,
But it's not elves exactly, and I'd rather
He said it for himself. I see him there
Bringing a stone grasped firmly by the top
In each hand, like an old-stone savage armed.
He moves in darkness as it seems to me,

Not of woods only and the shade of trees.
He will not go behind his father's saying,
And he likes having thought of it so well
He says again, "Good fences make good neighbors." (*1914*)

A SERVANT TO SERVANTS

I didn't make you know how glad I was
To have you come and camp here on our land.
I promised myself to get down some day
And see the way you lived, but I don't know!
With a houseful of hungry men to feed
I guess you'd find. . . . It seems to me
I can't express my feelings any more
Than I can raise my voice or want to lift
My hand (oh, I can lift it when I have to).
Did ever you feel so? I hope you never.
It's got so I don't even know for sure
Whether I *am* glad, sorry, or anything.
There's nothing but a voice-like left inside
That seems to tell me how I ought to feel,
And would feel if I wasn't all gone wrong.
You take the lake. I look and look at it.
I see it's a fair, pretty sheet of water,
I stand and make myself repeat out loud
The advantages it has, so long and narrow,
Like a deep piece of some old running river
Cut short off at both ends. It lies five miles
Straight away through the mountain notch
From the sink window where I wash the plates,
And all our storms come up toward the house,
Drawing the slow waves whiter and whiter and whiter.
It took my mind off doughnuts and soda biscuit
To step outdoors and take the water dazzle
A sunny morning, or take the rising wind
About my face and body and through my wrapper,
When a storm threatened from the Dragon's Den,
And a cold chill shivered across the lake.
I see it's a fair, pretty sheet of water,
Our Willoughby! How did you hear of it?
I expect, though, everyone's heard of it.
In a book about ferns? Listen to that!
You let things more like feathers regulate

Your going and coming. And you like it here?
I can see how you might. But I don't know!
It would be different if more people came,
For then there would be business. As it is,
The cottages Len built, sometimes we rent them,
Sometimes we don't. We've a good piece of shore
That ought to be worth something, and may yet.
But I don't count on it as much as Len.
He looks on the bright side of everything,
Including me. He thinks I'll be all right
With doctoring. But it's not medicine—
Lowe is the only doctor's dared to say so—
It's rest I want—there, I have said it out—
From cooking meals for hungry hired men
And washing dishes after them—from doing
Things over and over that just won't stay done.
By good rights I ought not to have so much
Put on me, but there seems no other way.
Len says one steady pull more ought to do it.
He says the best way out is always through.
And I agree to that, or in so far
As that I can see no way out but through—
Leastways for me—and then they'll be convinced.
It's not that Len don't want the best for me.
It was his plan our moving over in
Beside the lake from where that day I showed you
We used to live—ten miles from anywhere.
We didn't change without some sacrifice,
But Len went at it to make up the loss.
His work's a man's, of course, from sun to sun,
But he works when he works as hard as I do—
Though there's small profit in comparisons.
(Women and men will make them all the same.)
But work ain't all. Len undertakes too much.
He's into everything in town. This year
It's highways, and he's got too many men
Around him to look after that make waste.
They take advantage of him shamefully,
And proud, too, of themselves for doing so.
We have four here to board, great good-for-nothings,
Sprawling about the kitchen with their talk
While I fry their bacon. Much they care!
No more put out in what they do or say

Than if I wasn't in the room at all.
Coming and going all the time, they are:
I don't learn what their names are, let alone
Their characters, or whether they are safe
To have inside the house with doors unlocked.
I'm not afraid of them, though, if they're not
Afraid of me. There's two can play at that.
I have my fancies: it runs in the family.
My father's brother wasn't right. They kept him
Locked up for years back there at the old farm.
I've been away once—yes, I've been away.
The State Asylum. I was prejudiced;
I wouldn't have sent anyone of mine there;
You know the old idea—the only asylum
Was the poorhouse, and those who could afford,
Rather than send their folks to such a place,
Kept them at home; and it does seem more human.
But it's not so: the place is the asylum.
There they have every means proper to do with,
And you aren't darkening other people's lives—
Worse than no good to them, and they no good
To you in your condition; you can't know
Affection or the want of it in that state.
I've heard too much of the old-fashioned way.
My father's brother, he went mad quite young.
Some thought he had been bitten by a dog.
Because his violence took on the form
Of carrying his pillow in his teeth;
But it's more likely he was crossed in love,
Or so the story goes. It was some girl.
Anyway all he talked about was love.
They soon saw he would do someone a mischief
If he wa'n't kept strict watch of, and it ended
In father's building him a sort of cage,
Or room within a room, of hickory poles,
Like stanchions in the barn, from floor to ceiling,—
A narrow passage all the way around.
Anything they put in for furniture
He'd tear to pieces, even a bed to lie on.
So they made the place comfortable with straw,
Like a beast's stall, to ease their consciences.
Of course they had to feed him without dishes.
They tried to keep him clothed, but he paraded

With his clothes on his arm—all of his clothes.
Cruel—it sounds. I'spose they did the best
They knew. And just when he was at the height,
Father and mother married, and mother came,
A bride, to help take care of such a creature,
And accommodate her young life to his.
That was what marrying father meant to her.
She had to lie and hear love things made dreadful
By his shouts in the night. He'd shout and shout
Until the strength was shouted out of him,
And his voice died down slowly from exhaustion.
He'd pull his bars apart like bow and bowstring,
And let them go and make them twang until
His hands had worn them smooth as any oxbow.
And then he'd crow as if he thought that child's play
The only fun he had. I've heard them say, though,
They found a way to put a stop to it.
He was before my time—I never saw him;
But the pen stayed exactly as it was
There in the upper chamber in the ell,
A sort of catch-all full of attic clutter.
I often think of the smooth hickory bars.
It got so I would say—you know, half fooling—
"It's time I took my turn upstairs in jail"—
Just as you will till it becomes a habit.
No wonder I was glad to get away.
Mind you, I waited till Len said the word.
I didn't want the blame if things went wrong.
I was glad though, no end, when we moved out,
And I looked to be happy, and I was,
As I said, for a while—but I don't know!
Somehow the change wore out like a prescription.
And there's more to it than just window-views
And living by a lake. I'm past such help—
Unless Len took the notion, which he won't,
And I won't ask him—it's not sure enough.
I'spose I've got to go the road I'm going:
Other folks have to, and why shouldn't I?
I almost think if I could do like you,
Drop everything and live out on the ground—
But it might be, come night, I shouldn't like it,
Or a long rain. I should soon get enough,
And be glad of a good roof overhead.

I've lain awake thinking of you, I'll warrant,
More than you have yourself, some of these nights.
The wonder was the tents weren't snatched away
From over you as you lay in your beds.
I haven't courage for a risk like that.
Bless you, of course, you're keeping me from work,
But the thing of it is, I need to *be* kept.
There's work enough to do—there's always that;
But behind's behind. The worst that you can do
Is set me back a little more behind.
I sha'n't catch up in this world, anyway.
I'd *rather* you'd not go unless you must. (*1914*)

THE DEATH OF THE HIRED MAN

Mary sat musing on the lamp-flame at the table
Waiting for Warren. When she heard his step,
She ran on tip-toe down the darkened passage
To meet him in the doorway with the news
And put him on his guard. "Silas is back."
She pushed him outward with her through the door
And shut it after her. "Be kind," she said.
She took the market things from Warren's arms
And set them on the porch, then drew him down
To sit beside her on the wooden steps.

"When was I ever anything but kind to him?
But I'll not have the fellow back," he said.
"I told him so last haying, didn't I?
If he left then, I said, that ended it.
What good is he? Who else will harbor him
At his age for the little he can do?
What help he is there's no depending on.
Off he goes always when I need him most.
He thinks he ought to earn a little pay,
Enough at least to buy tobacco with,
So he won't have to beg and be beholden.
'All right,' I say, 'I can't afford to pay
Any fixed wages, though I wish I could.'
'Someone else can.' 'Then someone else will have to.'
I shouldn't mind his bettering himself
If that was what it was. You can be certain,
When he begins like that, there's someone at him
Trying to coax him off with pocket-money,—

In haying time, when any help is scarce.
In winter he comes back to us. I'm done."

"Sh! not so loud: he'll hear you," Mary said.

"I want him to: he'll have to soon or late."

"He's worn out. He's asleep beside the stove.
When I came up from Rowe's I found him here,
Huddled against the barn-door fast asleep,
A miserable sight, and frightening, too—
You needn't smile—I didn't recognize him—
I wasn't looking for him—and he's changed.
Wait till you see."

                    "Where did you say he'd been?"

"He didn't say. I dragged him to the house,
And gave him tea and tried to make him smoke.
I tried to make him talk about his travels.
Nothing would do: he just kept nodding off."

"What did he say? Did he say anything?"

"But little."

            "Anything? Mary, confess
He said he'd come to ditch the meadow for me."

"Warren!"

            "But did he? I just want to know."

"Of course he did. What would you have him say?
Surely you wouldn't grudge the poor old man
Some humble way to save his self-respect.
He added, if you really care to know,
He meant to clear the upper pasture, too.
That sounds like something you have heard before?
Warren, I wish you could have heard the way
He jumbled everything. I stopped to look
Two or three times—he made me feel so queer—
To see if he was talking in his sleep.
He ran on Harold Wilson—you remember—

The boy you had in haying four years since.
He's finished school, and teaching in his college.
Silas declares you'll have to get him back.
He says they two will make a team for work:
Between them they will lay this farm as smooth!
The way he mixed that in with other things.
He thinks young Wilson a likely lad, though daft
On education—you know how they fought
All through July under the blazing sun,
Silas up on the cart to build the load,
Harold along beside to pitch it on."

"Yes, I took care to keep well out of earshot."

"Well, those days trouble Silas like a dream.
You wouldn't think they would. How some things linger!
Harold's young college boy's assurance piqued him.
After so many years he still keeps finding
Good arguments he sees he might have used.
I sympathize. I know just how it feels
To think of the right thing to say too late.
Harold's associated in his mind with Latin.
He asked me what I thought of Harold's saying
He studied Latin like the violin
Because he liked it—that an argument!
He said he couldn't make the boy believe
He could find water with a hazel prong—
Which showed how much good school had ever done him.
He wanted to go over that. But most of all
He thinks if he could have another chance
To teach him how to build a load of hay—"

"I know, that's Silas' one accomplishment.
He bundles every forkful in its place,
And tags and numbers it for future reference,
So he can find and easily dislodge it
In the unloading. Silas does that well.
He takes it out in bunches like big birds' nests.
You never see him standing on the hay
He's trying to lift, straining to lift himself."

"He thinks if he could teach him that, he'd be
Some good perhaps to someone in the world.
He hates to see a boy the fool of books.

Poor Silas, so concerned for other folk,
And nothing to look backward to with pride,
And nothing to look forward to with hope,
So now and never any different."

Part of a moon was falling down the west,
Dragging the whole sky with it to the hills.
Its light poured softly in her lap. She saw
And spread her apron to it. She put out her hand
Among the harp-like morning-glory strings,
Taut with the dew from garden bed to eaves,
As if she played unheard some tenderness
That wrought on him beside her in the night.
"Warren," she said, "he has come home to die:
You needn't be afraid he'll leave you this time."

"Home," he mocked gently.

                              "Yes, what else but home?
It all depends on what you mean by home.
Of course he's nothing to us, any more
Than was the hound that came a stranger to us
Out of the woods, worn out upon the trail."

"Home is the place where, when you have to go there,
They have to take you in."

                              "I should have called it
Something you somehow haven't to deserve."

Warren leaned out and took a step or two,
Picked up a little stick, and brought it back
And broke it in his hand and tossed it by.
"Silas has better claim on us you think
Than on his brother? Thirteen little miles
As the road winds would bring him to his door.
Silas has walked that far no doubt today.
Why didn't he go there? His brother's rich,
A somebody—director in the bank."

"He never told us that."

                              "We know it though."

"I think his brother ought to help, of course.
I'll see to that if there is need. He ought of right
To take him in, and might be willing to—
He may be better than appearances.
But have some pity on Silas. Do you think
If he had any pride in claiming kin
Or anything he looked for from his brother,
He'd keep so still about him all this time?"

"I wonder what's between them."

                        "I can tell you.
Silas is what he is—we wouldn't mind him—
But just the kind that kinsfolk can't abide.
He never did a thing so very bad.
He don't know why he isn't quite as good
As anybody. Worthless though he is,
He won't be made ashamed to please his brother."

"I can't think Si ever hurt anyone."

"No, but he hurt my heart the way he lay
And rolled his old head on that sharp-edged chair-back.
He wouldn't let me put him on the lounge.
You must go in and see what you can do.
I made the bed up for him there tonight.
You'll be surprised at him—how much he's broken.
His working days are done; I'm sure of it."

"I'd not be in a hurry to say that."

"I haven't been. Go, look, see for yourself.
But, Warren, please remember how it is:
He's come to help you ditch the meadow.
He has a plan. You mustn't laugh at him.
He may not speak of it, and then he may.
I'll sit and see if that small sailing cloud
Will hit or miss the moon."

                      It hit the moon.
Then there were three there, making a dim row,
The moon, the little silver cloud, and she.

Warren returned—too soon, it seemed to her,

Slipped to her side, caught up her hand and waited.

"Warren?" she questioned.

        "Dead," was all he answered.   *(1914)*

AFTER APPLE-PICKING

My long two-pointed ladder's sticking through a tree
Toward heaven still,
And there's a barrel that I didn't fill
Beside it, and there may be two or three
Apples I didn't pick upon some bough.
But I am done with apple-picking now.
Essence of winter sleep is on the night,
The scent of apples: I am drowsing off.
I cannot rub the strangeness from my sight
I got from looking through a pane of glass
I skimmed this morning from the drinking trough
And held against the world of hoary grass.
It melted, and I let it fall and break.
But I was well
Upon my way to sleep before it fell,
And I could tell
What form my dreaming was about to take.
Magnified apples appear and disappear,
Stem end and blossom end,
And every fleck of russet showing clear.
My instep arch not only keeps the ache,
It keeps the pressure of a ladder-round.
I feel the ladder sway as the boughs bend.
And I keep hearing from the cellar bin
The rumbling sound
Of load on load of apples coming in.
For I have had too much
Of apple-picking: I am overtired
Of the great harvest I myself desired.
There were ten thousand thousand fruit to touch,
Cherish in hand, lift down, and not let fall.
For all
That struck the earth,
No matter if not bruised or spiked with stubble,
Went surely to the cider-apple heap
As of no worth.

[handwritten annotations: transitional stately / sleep-repose-rest / activity ripples / his blow]

One can see what will trouble
This sleep of mine, whatever sleep it is.
Were he not gone,
The woodchuck could say whether it's like his
Long sleep, as I describe its coming on,
Or just some human sleep. *(1914)*

THE ROAD NOT TAKEN

[handwritten annotation: Speculations of how people feel]

Two roads diverged in a yellow wood,
And sorry I could not travel both
And be one traveler, long I stood
And looked down one as far as I could
To where it bent in the undergrowth;

Then took the other, as just as fair,
And having perhaps the better claim,
Because it was grassy and wanted wear;
Though as for that the passing there
Had worn them really about the same,

[handwritten annotation: Reluctance to make decision]

And both that morning equally lay
In leaves no step had trodden black.
Oh, I kept the first for another day!
Yet knowing how way leads on to way,
I doubted if I should ever come back.

[handwritten annotation: what one knows / decision yet]

I shall be telling this with a sigh
Somewhere ages and ages hence:
Two roads diverged in a wood, and I—
I took the one less traveled by,
And that has made all the difference. *(1916)*

A PATCH OF OLD SNOW

There's a patch of old snow in a corner
  That I should have guessed
Was a blow-away paper the rain
  Had brought to rest

It is speckled with grime as if
  Small print overspread it,
The news of a day I've forgotten—
  If I ever read it. *(1916)*

BIRCHES X

When I see birches bend to left and right
Across the lines of straighter darker trees,
I like to think some boy's been swinging them.
But swinging doesn't bend them down to stay
As ice-storms do. Often you must have seen them
Loaded with ice a sunny winter morning
After a rain. They click upon themselves
As the breeze rises, and turn many-colored
As the stir cracks and crazes their enamel.
Soon the sun's warmth makes them shed crystal shells
Shattering and avalanching on the snow-crust—
Such heaps of broken glass to sweep away
You'd think the inner dome of heaven had fallen.
They are dragged to the withered bracken by the load,
And they seem not to break; though once they are bowed
So low for long, they never right themselves:
You may see their trunks arching in the woods
Years afterwards, trailing their leaves on the ground
Like girls on hands and knees that throw their hair
Before them over their heads to dry in the sun.
But I was going to say when Truth broke in
With all her matter-of-fact about the ice-storm
I should prefer to have some boy bend them
As he went out and in to fetch the cows—
Some boy too far from town to learn baseball,
Whose only play was what he found himself,
Summer or winter, and could play alone.
One by one he subdued his father's trees
By riding them down over and over again
Until he took the stiffness out of them,
And not one but hung limp, not one was left
For him to conquer. He learned all there was
To learn about not launching out too soon
And so not carrying the tree away
Clear to the ground. He always kept his poise
To the top branches, climbing carefully
With the same pains you use to fill a cup
Up to the brim, and even above the brim.
Then he flung outward, feet first, with a swish,
Kicking his way down through the air to the ground.
So was I once myself a swinger of birches.

And so I dream of going back to be.
It's when I'm weary of considerations,
And life is too much like a pathless wood
Where your face burns and tickles with the cobwebs
Broken across it, and one eye is weeping
From a twig's having lashed across it open.
I'd like to get away from earth awhile
And then come back to it and begin over.   *reincarnation*
May no fate willfully misunderstand me
And half grant what I wish and snatch me away
Not to return. Earth's the right place for love:
I don't know where it's likely to go better.
I'd like to go by climbing a birch tree,
And climb black branches up a snow-white trunk
Toward heaven, till the tree could bear no more,
But dipped its top and set me down again.
That would be good both going and coming back.
One could do worse than be a swinger of birches.   *(1916)*

THE HILL WIFE

LONELINESS

Her Word

One ought not to have to care
    So much as you and I
Care when the birds come round the house
    To seem to say good-by;

Or care so much when they come back
    With whatever it is they sing;
The truth being we are as much
    Too glad for the one thing

As we are too sad for the other here—
    With birds that fill their breasts
But with each other and themselves
    And their built or driven nests.

HOUSE FEAR

Always—I tell you this they learned—
Always at night when they returned
To the lonely house from far away

To lamps unlighted and fire gone gray,
They learned to rattle the lock and key
To give whatever might chance to be
Warning and time to be off in flight:
And preferring the out- to the in-door night,
They learned to leave the house-door wide
Until they had lit the lamp inside.

THE SMILE

Her Word

I didn't like the way he went away.
That smile! It never came of being gay.
Still he smiled—did you see him?—I was sure!
Perhaps because we gave him only bread
And the wretch knew from that that we were poor.
Perhaps because he let us give instead
Of seizing from us as he might have seized.
Perhaps he mocked at us for being wed,
Or being very young (and he was pleased
To have a vision of us old and dead).
I wonder how far down the road he's got.
He's watching from the woods as like as not.

THE OFT-REPEATED DREAM

She had no saying dark enough
    For the dark pine that kept
Forever trying the window-latch
    Of the room where they slept.

The tireless but ineffectual hands
    That with every futile pass
Made the great tree seem as a little bird
    Before the mystery of glass!

It never had been inside the room,
    And only one of the two
Was afraid in an oft-repeated dream
    Of what the tree might do.

THE IMPULSE

It was too lonely for her there,
    And too wild,

And since there were but two of them,
And no child,

And work was little in the house,
She was free,
And followed where he furrowed field,
Or felled tree.

She rested on a log and tossed
The fresh chips,
With a song only to herself
On her lips.

And once she went to break a bough
Of black alder.
She strayed so far she scarcely heard
When he called her—

And didn't answer—didn't speak—
Or return.
She stood, and then she ran and hid
In the fern.

He never found her, though he looked
Everywhere,
And he asked at her mother's house
Was she there.

Sudden and swift and light as that
The ties gave,
And he learned of finalities
Besides the grave.   (1916)

TWO WITCHES

1

THE WITCH OF COÖS

I stayed the night for shelter at a farm
Behind the mountain, with a mother and son,
Two old-believers. They did all the talking.

MOTHER. Folks think a witch who has familiar spirits
She could call up to pass a winter evening,

But won't, should be burned at the stake or something.
Summoning spirits isn't "Button, button,
Who's got the button," I would have them know.

SON. Mother can make a common table rear
And kick with two legs like an army mule.

MOTHER. And when I've done it, what good have I done?
Rather than tip a table for you, let me
Tell you what Ralle the Sioux Control once told me.
He said the dead had souls, but when I asked him
How could that be—I thought the dead were souls,
He broke my trance. Don't that make you suspicious
That there's something the dead are keeping back?
Yes, there's something the dead are keeping back.

SON. You wouldn't want to tell him what we have
Up attic, mother?

MOTHER. Bones—a skeleton.

SON. But the headboard of mother's bed is pushed
Against the attic door: the door is nailed.
It's harmless. Mother hears it in the night
Halting perplexed behind the barrier
Of door and headboard. Where it wants to get
Is back into the cellar where it came from.

MOTHER. We'll never let them, will we, son! We'll never!

SON. It left the cellar forty years ago
And carried itself like a pile of dishes
Up one flight from the cellar to the kitchen,
Another from the kitchen to the bedroom,
Another from the bedroom to the attic,
Right past both father and mother, and neither stopped it.
Father had gone upstairs; mother was downstairs.
I was a baby: I don't know where I was.

MOTHER. The only fault my husband found with me—
I went to sleep before I went to bed,
Especially in winter when the bed
Might just as well be ice and the clothes snow.
The night the bones came up the cellar-stairs

Toffile had gone to bed alone and left me,
But left an open door to cool the room off
So as to sort of turn me out of it.
I was just coming to myself enough
To wonder where the cold was coming from,
When I heard Toffile upstairs in the bedroom
And thought I heard him downstairs in the cellar.
The board we had laid down to walk dry-shod on
When there was water in the cellar in spring
Struck the hard cellar bottom. And then someone
Began the stairs, two footsteps for each step,
The way a man with one leg and a crutch,
Or a little child, comes up. It wasn't Toffile: .
It wasn't anyone who could be there.
The bulkhead double-doors were double-locked
And swollen tight and buried under snow.
The cellar windows were banked up with sawdust
And swollen tight and buried under snow.
It was the bones. I knew them—and good reason.
My first impulse was to get to the knob
And hold the door. But the bones didn't try
The door; they halted helpless on the landing,
Waiting for things to happen in their favor.
The faintest restless rustling ran all through them.
I never could have done the thing I did
If the wish hadn't been too strong in me
To see how they were mounted for this walk.
1 had a vision of them put together
Not like a man, but like a chandelier.
So suddenly I flung the door wide on him.
A moment he stood balancing with emotion,
And all but lost himself. (A tongue of fire
Flashed out and licked along his upper teeth.
Smoke rolled inside the sockets of his eyes.)
Then he came at me with one hand outstretched,
The way he did in life once; but this time
I struck the hand off brittle on the floor,
And fell back from him on the floor myself.
The finger-pieces slid in all directions.
(Where did I see one of those pieces lately?
Hand me my button-box—it must be there.)
1 sat up on the floor and shouted, "Toffile,
It's coming up to you." It had its choice

Of the door to the cellar or the hall.
It took the hall door for the novelty,
And set off briskly for so slow a thing,
Still going every which way in the joints, though,
So that it looked like lightning or a scribble,
From the slap I had just now given its hand.
I listened till it almost climbed the stairs
From the hall to the only finished bedroom,
Before I got up to do anything;
Then ran and shouted, "Shut the bedroom door,
Toffile, for my sake!" "Company?" he said,
"Don't make me get up; I'm too warm in bed."
So lying forward weakly on the handrail
I pushed myself upstairs, and in the light
(The kitchen had been dark) I had to own
I could see nothing. "Toffile, I don't see it.
It's with us in the room, though. It's the bones."
"What bones?" "The cellar bones—out of the grave."
That made him throw his bare legs out of bed
And sit up by me and take hold of me.
I wanted to put out the light and see
If I could see it, or else mow the room,
With our arms at the level of our knees,
And bring the chalk-pile down. "I'll tell you what—
It's looking for another door to try.
The uncommonly deep snow has made him think
Of his old song, *The Wild Colonial Boy*,
He always used to sing along the tote road.
He's after an open door to get outdoors.
Let's trap him with an open door up attic."
Toffile agreed to that, and sure enough,
Almost the moment he was given an opening,
The steps began to climb the attic stairs.
I heard them. Toffile didn't seem to hear them.
"Quick!" I slammed to the door and held the knob.
"Toffile, get nails." I made him nail the door shut,
And push the headboard of the bed against it.
Then we asked was there anything
Up attic that we'd ever want again.
The attic was less to us than the cellar.
If the bones liked the attic, let them have it.
Let them stay in the attic. When they sometimes
Come down the stairs at night and stand perplexed

Behind the door and headboard of the bed,
Brushing their chalky skull with chalky fingers,
With sounds like the dry rattling of a shutter,
That's what I sit up in the dark to say—
To no one any more since Toffile died.
Let them stay in the attic since they went there.
I promised Toffile to be cruel to them
For helping them be cruel once to him.

SON. We think they had a grave down in the cellar.

MOTHER. We know they had a grave down in the cellar.

SON. We never could find out whose bones they were.

MOTHER. Yes, we could too, son. Tell the truth for once.
They were a man's his father killed for me.
I mean a man he killed instead of me.
The least I could do was to help dig their grave.
We were about it one night in the cellar.
Son knows the story: but 'twas not for him
To tell the truth, suppose the time had come.
Son looks surprised to see me end a lie
We'd kept all these years between ourselves
So as to have it ready for outsiders.
But tonight I don't care enough to lie—
I don't remember why I ever cared.
Toffile, if he were here, I don't believe
Could tell you why he ever cared himself. . . .

She hadn't found the finger-bone she wanted
Among the buttons poured out in her lap.
I verified the name next morning: Toffile.
The rural letter box said Toffile Lajway.

2

THE PAUPER WITCH OF GRAFTON

Now that they've got it settled whose I be,
I'm going to tell them something they won't like:
They've got it settled wrong, and I can prove it.
Flattered I must be to have two towns fighting
To make a present of me to each other.
They don't dispose me, either one of them,

To spare them any trouble. Double trouble's
Always the witch's motto anyway.
I'll double theirs for both of them—you watch me.
They'll find they've got the whole thing to do over,
That is, if facts is what they want to go by.
They set a lot (now don't they?) by a record
Of Arthur Amy's having once been up
For Hog Reeve in March Meeting here in Warren.
I could have told them any time this twelvemonth
The Arthur Amy I was married to
Couldn't have been the one they say was up
In Warren at March Meeting for the reason
He wa'n't but fifteen at the time they say.
The Arthur Amy I was married to
Voted the only times he ever voted,
Which wasn't many, in the town of Wentworth
One of the times was when 'twas in the warrant
To see if the town wanted to take over
The tote road to our clearing where we lived.
I'll tell you who'd remember—Heman Lapish.
Their Arthur Amy was the father of mine.
So now they've dragged it through the law courts once
I guess they'd better drag it through again.
Wentworth and Warren's both good towns to live in,
Only I happen to prefer to live
In Wentworth from now on; and when all's said,
Right's right, and the temptation to do right
When I can hurt someone by doing it
Has always been too much for me, it has.
I know of some folks that'd be set up
At having in their town a noted witch:
But most would have to think of the expense
That even I would be. They ought to know
That as a witch I'd often milk a bat
And that'd be enough to last for days.
It'd make my position stronger, think,
If I was to consent to give some sign
To make it surer that I was a witch?
It wa'n't no sign, I s'pose, when Mallice Huse
Said that I took him out in his old age
And rode all over everything on him
Until I'd had him worn to skin and bones,
And if I'd left him hitched unblanketed
In front of one Town Hall, I'd left him hitched

In front of every one in Grafton County.
Some cried shame on me not to blanket him,
The poor old man. It would have been all right
If someone hadn't said to gnaw the posts
He stood beside and leave his trade mark on them,
So they could recognize them. Not a post
That they could hear tell of was scarified.
They made him keep on gnawing till he whined.
Then that same smarty someone said to look—
He'd bet Huse was a cribber and had gnawed
The crib he slept in—and as sure's you're born
They found he'd gnawed the four posts of his bed,
All four of them to splinters. What did that prove?
Not that he hadn't gnawed the hitching posts
He said he had besides. Because a horse
Gnaws in the stable ain't no proof to me
He don't gnaw trees and posts and fences too.
But everybody took it for a proof.
I was a strapping girl of twenty then.
The smarty someone who spoiled everything
Was Arthur Amy. You know who he was.
That was the way he started courting me.
He never said much after we were married,
But I mistrusted he was none too proud
Of having interfered in the Huse business.
I guess he found he got more out of me
By having me a witch. Or something happened
To turn him round. He got to saying things
To undo what he'd done and make it right,
Like, "No, she ain't come back from kiting yet.
Last night was one of her nights out. She's kiting.
She thinks when the wind makes a night of it
She might as well herself." But he liked best
To let on he was plagued to death with me:
If anyone had seen me coming home
Over the ridgepole, 'stride of a broomstick,
As often as he had in the tail of the night,
He guessed they'd know what he had to put up with.
Well, I showed Arthur Amy signs enough
Off from the house as far as we could keep
And from barn smells you can't wash out of plowed ground
With all the rain and snow of seven years;
And I don't mean just skulls of Rogers' Rangers

On Moosilauke, but woman signs to man,
Only bewitched so I would last him longer.
Up where the trees grow short, the mosses tall,
I made him gather me wet snow berries
On slippery rocks beside a waterfall.
I made him do it for me in the dark.
And he liked everything I made him do.
I hope if he is where he sees me now
He's so far off he can't see what I've come to.
You *can* come down from everything to nothing.
All is, if I'd a-known when I was young
And full of it, that this would be the end,
It doesn't seem as if I'd had the courage
To make so free and kick up in folks' faces.
I might have, but it doesn't seem as if. *(1923)*

FIRE AND ICE

Some say the world will end in fire,
Some say in ice.
From what I've tasted of desire
I hold with those who favor fire.
But if it had to perish twice,
I think I know enough of hate
To say that for destruction ice
Is also great
And would suffice. *(1923)*

DUST OF SNOW

The way a crow
Shook down on me
The dust of snow
From a hemlock tree

Has given my heart
A change of mood
And saved some part
Of a day I had rued. *(1923)*

STOPPING BY WOODS ON A SNOWY EVENING

Whose woods these are I think I know.
His house is in the village though;

He will not see me stopping here
To watch his woods fill up with snow.

My little horse must think it queer
To stop without a farmhouse near
Between the woods and frozen lake
The darkest evening of the year.

— accentuate the solitariveness of frost.

He gives his harness bells a shake
To ask if there is some mistake.
The only other sound's the sweep
Of easy wind and downy flake.

frost wonders what he doing there

The woods are lovely, dark and deep,
But I have promises to keep,
And miles to go before I sleep,
And miles to go before I sleep.   *(1923)*

THE ONSET

Always the same, when on a fated night
At last the gathered snow lets down as white
As may be in dark woods, and with a song
It shall not make again all winter long
Of hissing on the yet uncovered ground,
I almost stumble looking up and round,
As one who overtaken by the end
Gives up his errand, and lets death descend
Upon him where he is, with nothing done
To evil, no important triumph won,
More than if life had never been begun.

Yet all the precedent is on my side:
I know that winter death has never tried
The earth but it has failed: the snow may heap
In long storms an undrifted four feet deep
As measured against maple, birch, and oak,
It cannot check the peeper's silver croak;
And I shall see the snow all go down hill
In water of a slender April rill
That flashes tail through last year's withered brake
And dead weeds, like a disappearing snake.
Nothing will be left white but here a birch,
And there a clump of houses with a church.   *(1923)*

GOOD-BY AND KEEP COLD

This saying good-by on the edge of the dark
And cold to an orchard so young in the bark
Reminds me of all that can happen to harm
An orchard away at the end of the farm
All winter, cut off by a hill from the house.
I don't want it girdled by rabbit and mouse,
I don't want it dreamily nibbled for browse
By deer, and I don't want it budded by grouse.
(If certain it wouldn't be idle to call
I'd summon grouse, rabbit, and deer to the wall
And warn them away with a stick for a gun.)
I don't want it stirred by the heat of the sun.
(We made it secure against being, I hope,
By setting it out on a northerly slope.)
No orchard's the worse for the wintriest storm;
But one thing about it, it mustn't get warm.
"How often already you've had to be told,
Keep cold, young orchard. Good-by and keep cold.
Dread fifty above more than fifty below."
I have to be gone for a season or so.
My business awhile is with different trees,
Less carefully nourished, less fruitful than these,
And such as is done to their wood with an ax—
Maples and birches and tamaracks.
I wish I could promise to lie in the night
And think of an orchard's arboreal plight
When slowly (and nobody comes with a light)
Its heart sinks lower under the sod.
But something has to be left to God. *(1923)*

NOT TO KEEP

They sent him back to her. The letter came
Saying . . . And she could have him. And before
She could be sure there was no hidden ill
Under the formal writing, he was there,
Living. They gave him back to her alive—
How else! They are not known to send the dead—
And not disfigured visibly. His face?
His hands? She had to look, to look and ask,

"What is it, dear?" And she had given all
And still she had all—*they* had—they the lucky!
Wasn't she glad now? Everything seemed won,
And all the rest for them permissible ease.
She had to ask, "What was it, dear?"
                            "Enough,
Yet not enough. A bullet through and through,
High in the breast. Nothing but what good care
And medicine and rest, and you a week,
Can cure me of to go again." The same
Grim giving to do over for them both.
She dared no more than ask him with her eyes
How was it with him for a second trial.
And with his eyes he asked her not to ask.
They had given him back to her, but not to keep.   *(1923)*

A HILLSIDE THAW

To think to know the country and not know
The hillside on the day the sun lets go
Ten million silver lizards out of snow!
As often as I've seen it done before
I can't pretend to tell the way it's done.
It looks as if some magic of the sun
Lifted the rug that bred them on the floor
And the light breaking on them made them run.
But if I thought to stop the wet stampede,
And caught one silver lizard by the tail,
And put my foot on one without avail,
And threw myself wet-elbowed and wet-kneed
In front of twenty others' wriggling speed,—
In the confusion of them all aglitter,
And birds that joined in the excited fun
By doubling and redoubling song and twitter,
I have no doubt I'd end by holding none.

It takes the moon for this. The sun's a wizard
By all I tell; but so's the moon a witch.
From the high west she makes a gentle cast
And suddenly, without a jerk or twitch,
She has her spell on every single lizard.
I fancied when I looked at six o'clock
The swarm still ran and scuttled just as fast.

The moon was waiting for her chill effect.
I looked at nine: the swarm was turned to rock
In every lifelike posture of the swarm,
Transfixed on mountain slopes almost erect.
Across each other and side by side they lay.
The spell that so could hold them as they were
Was wrought through trees without a breath of storm
To make a leaf, if there had been one, stir.
It was the moon's: she held them until day,
One lizard at the end of every ray.
The thought of my attempting such a stay! *(1923)*

ACCEPTANCE

When the spent sun throws up its rays on cloud
And goes down burning into the gulf below,
No voice in nature is heard to cry aloud
At what has happened. Birds, at least, must know
It is the change to darkness in the sky.
Murmuring something quiet in her breast,
One bird begins to close a faded eye;
Or overtaken too far from his nest,
Hurrying low above the grove, some waif
Swoops just in time to his remembered tree.
At most he thinks or twitters softly, "Safe!
Now let the night be dark for all of me.
Let the night be too dark for me to see
Into the future. Let what will be, be." *(1928)*

A MINOR BIRD

I have wished a bird would fly away,
And not sing by my house all day;

Have clapped my hands at him from the door
When it seemed as if I could bear no more.

The fault must partly have been in me.
The bird was not to blame for his key.

And of course there must be something wrong
In wanting to silence any song. *(1928)*

ONCE BY THE PACIFIC

The shattered water made a misty din.
Great waves looked over others coming in,
And thought of doing something to the shore
That water never did to land before.
The clouds were low and hairy in the skies,
Like locks blown forward in the gleam of eyes.
You could not tell, and yet it looked as if
The shore was lucky in being backed by cliff,
The cliff in being backed by continent;
It looked as if a night of dark intent
Was coming, and not only a night, an age.
Someone had better be prepared for rage.
There would be more than ocean-water broken
Before God's last *Put out the Light* was spoken. *(1928)*

ACQUAINTED WITH THE NIGHT

I have been one acquainted with the night.
I have walked out in rain—and back in rain.
I have outwalked the furthest city light.

I have looked down the saddest city lane.
I have passed by the watchman on his beat
And dropped my eyes, unwilling to explain.

I have stood still and stopped the sound of feet
When far away an interrupted cry
Came over houses from another street,

But not to call me back or say good-by;
And further still at an unearthly height,
One luminary clock against the sky

Proclaimed the time was neither wrong nor right.
I have been one acquainted with the night. *(1928)*

THE INVESTMENT

Over back where they speak of life as staying
("You couldn't call it living, for it ain't"),

There was an old, old house renewed with paint,
And in it a piano loudly playing.

Out in the ploughed ground in the cold a digger,
Among unearthed potatoes standing still,
Was counting winter dinners, one a hill,
With half an ear to the piano's vigor.

All that piano and new paint back there,
Was it some money suddenly come into?
Or some extravagance young love had been to?
Or old love on an impulse not to care—

Not to sink under being man and wife,
But get some color and music out of life?   (*1928*)

THE ARMFUL

For every parcel I stoop down to seize,
I lose some other off my arms and knees,
And the whole pile is slipping, bottles, buns,
Extremes too hard to comprehend at once,
Yet nothing I should care to leave behind.
With all I have to hold with, hand and mind
And heart, if need be, I will do my best
To keep their building balanced at my breast.
I crouch down to prevent them as they fall;
Then sit down in the middle of them all.
I had to drop the armful in the road
And try to stack them in a better load.   (*1928*)

ON LOOKING UP BY CHANCE
AT THE CONSTELLATIONS

You'll wait a long, long time for anything much
To happen in heaven beyond the floats of cloud
And the Northern Lights that run like tingling nerves.
The sun and moon get crossed, but they never touch,
Nor strike out fire from each other, nor crash out loud.
The planets seem to interfere in their curves,
But nothing ever happens, no harm is done.
We may as well go patiently on with our life,
And look elsewhere than to stars and moon and sun

For the shocks and changes we need to keep us sane.
It is true the longest drouth will end in rain,
The longest peace in China will end in strife.
Still it wouldn't reward the watcher to stay awake
In hopes of seeing the calm of heaven break
On his particular time and personal sight.
That calm seems certainly safe to last tonight.   *(1928)*

TWO TRAMPS IN MUD TIME

Out of the mud two strangers came
And caught me splitting wood in the yard.
And one of them put me off my aim
By hailing cheerily "Hit them hard!"
I knew pretty well why he dropped behind
And let the other go on a way.
I knew pretty well what he had in mind:
He wanted to take my job for pay.

Good blocks of beech it was I split,
As large around as the chopping block;
And every piece I squarely hit
Fell splinterless as a cloven rock.
The blows that a life of self-control
Spares to strike for the common good
That day, giving a loose to my soul,
I spent on the unimportant wood.

The sun was warm but the wind was chill.
You know how it is with an April day
When the sun is out and the wind is still,
You're one month on in the middle of May.
But if you so much as dare to speak,
A cloud comes over the sunlit arch,
A wind comes off a frozen peak,
And you're two months back in the middle of March.

A bluebird comes tenderly up to alight
And turns to the wind to unruffle a plume,
His song so pitched as not to excite
A single flower as yet to bloom.
It is snowing a flake: and he half knew
Winter was only playing possum

Except in color he isn't blue,
But he wouldn't advise a thing to blossom.

The water for which we may have to look
In summertime with a witching-wand,
In every wheelrut's now a brook,
In every print of a hoof a pond.
Be glad of water, but don't forget
The lurking frost in the earth beneath
That will steal forth after the sun is set
And show on the water its crystal teeth.

The time when most I loved my task
These two must make me love it more
By coming with what they came to ask.
You'd think I never had felt before
The weight of an ax-head poised aloft,
The grip on earth of outspread feet,
The life of muscles rocking soft
And smooth and moist in vernal heat.

Out of the woods two hulking tramps
(From sleeping God knows where last night,
But not long since in the lumber camps).
They thought all chopping was theirs of right.
Men of the woods and lumberjacks,
They judged me by their appropriate tool.
Except as a fellow handled an ax,
They had no way of knowing a fool.

Nothing on either side was said.
They knew they had but to stay their stay
And all their logic would fill my head:
As that I had no right to play
With what was another man's work for gain.
My right might be love but theirs was need.
And where the two exist in twain
Theirs was the better right—agreed.

But yield who will to their separation,
My object in living is to unite
My avocation and my vocation
As my two eyes make one in sight.

actuality — love & need don't go together usually in life.

sacrifice for the ultimate future, for heaven etc

the prob. situation isn't solved by this moral abstraction of

Only where love and need are one,
And the work is play for mortal stakes,
Is the deed ever really done
For Heaven and the future's sakes. (1936)

ON THE HEART'S BEGINNING TO CLOUD THE MIND

Something I saw or thought I saw
In the desert at midnight in Utah,
Looking out of my lower berth
At moonlit sky and moonlit earth.
The sky had here and there a star;
The earth had a single light afar,
A flickering, human pathetic light,
That was maintained against the night,
It seemed to me, by the people there,
With a God-forsaken brute despair.
It would flutter and fall in half an hour
Like the last petal off a flower.
But my heart was beginning to cloud my mind.
I knew a tale of a better kind.
That far light flickers because of trees.
The people can burn it as long as they please:
And when their interests in it end,
They can leave it to someone else to tend.
Come back that way a summer hence,
I should find it no more no less intense.
I pass, but scarcely pass no doubt,
When one will say, "Let us put it out."
The other without demur agrees.
They can keep it burning as long as they please;
They can put it out whenever they please.
One looks out last from the darkened room
At the shiny desert with spots of gloom
That might be people and are but cedar,
Have no purpose, have no leader,
Have never made the first move to assemble,
And so are nothing to make her tremble.
She can think of places that are not thus
Without indulging a "Not for us!"
Life is not so sinister-grave.
Matter of fact has made them brave.
He is husband, she is wife.

She fears not him, they fear not life.
They know where another light has been
And more than one to theirs akin,
But earlier out for bed tonight,
So lost on me in my surface flight.

This I saw when waking late,
Going by at a railroad rate,
Looking through wreaths of engine smoke
Far into the lives of other folk.   *(1936)*

DESERT PLACES

Snow falling and night falling fast, oh, fast
In a field I looked into going past,
And the ground almost covered smooth in snow,
But a few weeds and stubble showing last.

The woods around it have it—it is theirs.
All animals are smothered in their lairs.
I am too absent-spirited to count;
The loneliness includes me unawares.

And lonely as it is that loneliness
Will be more lonely ere it will be less—
A blanker whiteness of benighted snow
With no expression, nothing to express.

They cannot scare me with their empty spaces
Between stars—on stars where no human race is.
I have it in me so much nearer home
To scare myself with my own desert places.   *(1936)*

THE STRONG ARE SAYING NOTHING

The soil now gets a rumpling soft and damp,
And small regard to the future of any weed.
The final flat of the hoe's approval stamp
Is reserved for the bed of a few selected seed.

There is seldom more than a man to a harrowed piece.
Men work alone, their lots plowed far apart,
One stringing a chain of seed in an open crease,
And another stumbling after a halting cart

To the fresh and black of the squares of early mould
The leafless bloom of a plum is fresh and white;
Though there's more than a doubt if the weather is not too cold
For the bees to come and serve its beauty aright.

Wind goes from farm to farm in wave on wave,
But carries no cry of what is hoped to be.
There may be little or much beyond the grave,
But the strong are saying nothing until they see. *(1936)*

DESIGN

I found a dimpled spider, fat and white,
On a white heal-all, holding up a moth
Like a white piece of rigid satin cloth—
Assorted characters of death and blight
Mixed ready to begin the morning right,
Like the ingredients of a witches' broth—
A snow-drop spider, a flower like a froth,
And dead wings carried like a paper kite.

What had that flower to do with being white,
The wayside blue and innocent heal-all?
What brought the kindred spider to that height,
Then steered the white moth thither in the night?
What but design of darkness to appall?—
If design govern in a thing so small. *(1936)*

THERE ARE ROUGHLY ZONES

We sit indoors and talk of the cold outside.
And every gust that gathers strength and heaves
Is a threat to the house. But the house has long been tried.
We think of the tree. If it never again has leaves,
We'll know, we say, that this was the night it died.
It is very far north, we admit, to have brought the peach.
What comes over a man, is it soul or mind—
That to no limits and bounds he can stay confined?
You would say his ambition was to extend the reach
Clear to the Arctic of every living kind.
Why is his nature forever so hard to teach
That though there is no fixed line between wrong and right,
There are roughly zones whose laws must be obeyed?

There is nothing much we can do for the tree tonight,
But we can't help feeling more than a little betrayed
That the northwest wind should rise to such a height
Just when the cold went down so many below.
The tree has no leaves and may never have them again.
We must wait till some months hence in the spring to know.
But if it is destined never again to grow,
It can blame this limitless trait in the hearts of men.   *(1936)*

PROVIDE, PROVIDE

The witch that came (the withered hag)
To wash the steps with pail and rag,
Was once the beauty Abishag,

The picture pride of Hollywood.
Too many fall from great and good
For you to doubt the likelihood.

Die early and avoid the fate.
Or if predestined to die late,
Make up your mind to die in state.

Make the whole stock exchange your own!
If need be occupy a throne,
Where nobody can call *you* crone.

Some have relied on what they knew;
Others on simply being true.
What worked for them might work for you.

No memory of having starred
Atones for later disregard,
Or keeps the end from being hard.

Better to go down dignified
With boughten friendship at your side
Than none at all. Provide, provide!   *(1936)*

THE GIFT OUTRIGHT

The land was ours before we were the land's.
She was our land more than a hundred years

Before we were her people. She was ours
In Massachusetts, in Virginia,
But we were England's, still colonials,
Possessing what we still were unpossessed by,
Possessed by what we now no more possessed.
Something we were withholding made us weak
Until we found out that it was ourselves
We were withholding from our land of living,
And forthwith found salvation in surrender.
Such as we were we gave ourselves outright
(The deed of gift was many deeds of war)
To the land vaguely realizing westward,
But still unstoried, artless, unenhanced,
Such as she was, such as she would become.   *(1942)*

THE SUBVERTED FLOWER

She drew back; he was calm:
"It is this that had the power."
And he lashed his open palm
With the tender-headed flower.
He smiled for her to smile,
But she was either blind
Or willfully unkind.
He eyed her for a while
For a woman and a puzzle.
He flicked and flung the flower,
And another sort of smile
Caught up like finger tips
The corners of his lips
And cracked his ragged muzzle.
She was standing to the waist
In goldenrod and brake,
Her shining hair displaced.
He stretched her either arm
As if she made it ache
To clasp her—not to harm;
As if he could not spare
To touch her neck and hair.
"If this has come to us
And not to me alone—"
So she thought she heard him say;
Though with every word he spoke

His lips were sucked and blown
And the effort made him choke
Like a tiger at a bone.
She had to lean away.
She dared not stir a foot,
Lest movement should provoke
The demon of pursuit
That slumbers in a brute.
It was then her mother's call
From inside the garden wall
Made her steal a look of fear
To see if he could hear
And would pounce to end it all
Before her mother came.
She looked and saw the shame:
A hand hung like a paw,
An arm worked like a saw
As if to be persuasive,
An ingratiating laugh
That cut the snout in half,
An eye become evasive.
A girl could only see
That a flower had marred a man,
But what she could not see
Was that the flower might be
Other than base and fetid:
That the flower had done but part,
And what the flower began
Her own too meager heart
Had terribly completed.
She looked and saw the worst.
And the dog or what it was,
Obeying bestial laws,
A coward save at night,
Turned from the place and ran.
She heard him stumble first
And use his hands in flight.
She heard him bark outright.
And oh, for one so young
The bitter words she spit
Like some tenacious bit
That will not leave the tongue.
She plucked her lips for it,

And still the horror clung.
Her mother wiped the foam
From her chin, picked up her comb
And drew her backward home. *(1942)*

DIRECTIVE

Back out of all this now too much for us,
Back in a time made simple by the loss
Of detail, burned, dissolved, and broken off
Like graveyard marble sculpture in the weather,
There is a house that is no more a house
Upon a farm that is no more a farm
And in a town that is no more a town.
The road there, if you'll let a guide direct you
Who only has at heart your getting lost,
May seem as if it should have been a quarry—
Great monolithic knees the former town
Long since gave up pretence of keeping covered.
And there's a story in a book about it:
Besides the wear of iron wagon wheels
The ledges show lines ruled southeast northwest,
The chisel work of an enormous Glacier
That braced his feet against the Arctic Pole.
You must not mind a certain coolness from him
Still said to haunt this side of Panther Mountain.
Nor need you mind the serial ordeal
Of being watched from forty cellar holes
As if by eye pairs out of forty firkins.
As for the woods' excitement over you
That sends light rustle rushes to their leaves,
Charge that to upstart inexperience.
Where were they all not twenty years ago?
They think too much of having shaded out
A few old pecker-fretted apple trees.
Make yourself up a cheering song of how
Someone's road home from work this once was,
Who may be just ahead of you on foot
Or creaking with a buggy load of grain.
The height of the adventure is the height
Of country where two village cultures faded
Into each other. Both of them are lost.
And if you're lost enough to find yourself

By now, pull in your ladder road behind you
And put a sign up CLOSED to all but me.
Then make yourself at home. The only field
Now left's no bigger than a harness gall.
First there's the children's house of make believe,
Some shattered dishes underneath a pine,
The playthings in the playhouse of the children.
Weep for what little things could make them glad.
Then for the house that is no more a house,
But only a belilaced cellar hole,
Now slowly closing like a dent in dough.
This was no playhouse but a house in earnest.
Your destination and your destiny's
A brook that was the water of the house,
Cold as a spring as yet so near its source,
Too lofty and original to rage.
(We know the valley streams that when aroused
Will leave their tatters hung on barb and thorn.)
I have kept hidden in the instep arch
Of an old cedar at the waterside
A broken drinking goblet like the Grail
Under a spell so the wrong ones can't find it,
So can't get saved, as Saint Mark says they mustn't.
(I stole the goblet from the children's playhouse.)
Here are your waters and your watering place.
Drink and be whole again beyond confusion.   *(1947)*

THE DRAFT HORSE

With a lantern that wouldn't burn
In too frail a buggy we drove
Behind too heavy a horse
Through a pitch-dark limitless grove.

And a man came out of the trees
And took our horse by the head
And reaching back to his ribs
Deliberately stabbed him dead.

The ponderous beast went down
With a crack of a broken shaft.
And the night drew through the trees
In one long invidious draft.

The most unquestioning pair
That ever accepted fate
And the least disposed to ascribe
Any more than we had to to hate,

We assumed that the man himself
Or someone he had to obey
Wanted us to get down
And walk the rest of the way.   *(1962)*

Carl Sandburg
(1878–1967)

CHICAGO

Hog Butcher for the World,
Tool Maker, Stacker of Wheat,
Player with Railroads and the Nation's Freight Handler;
Stormy, husky, brawling,
City of the Big Shoulders:

They tell me you are wicked and I believe them, for I have seen your
    painted women under the gas lamps luring the farm boys.
And they tell me you are crooked and I answer: Yes, it is true I have
    seen the gunman kill and go free to kill again.
And they tell me you are brutal and my reply is: On the faces of
    women and children I have seen the marks of wanton hunger.
And having answered so I turn once more to those who sneer at this
    my city, and I give them back the sneer and say to them:
Come and show me another city with lifted head singing so proud to
    be alive and coarse and strong and cunning.
Flinging magnetic curses amid the toil of piling job on job, here is a
    tall bold slugger set vivid against the little soft cities;
Fierce as a dog with tongue lapping for action, cunning as a savage
    pitted against the wilderness,
            Bareheaded,
            Shoveling,
            Wrecking,
            Planning,
            Building, breaking, rebuilding,
Under the smoke, dust all over his mouth, laughing with white teeth,
Under the terrible burden of destiny laughing as a young man laughs,
Laughing even as an ignorant fighter laughs who has never lost a battle,
Bragging and laughing that under his wrist is the pulse, and under his
    ribs the heart of the people,
                    Laughing!
Laughing the stormy, husky, brawling laughter of Youth, half-naked,

sweating, proud to be Hog Butcher, Tool Maker, Stacker of Wheat,
Player with Railroads and Freight Handler to the Nation. (*1916*)

LOST

Desolate and lone
All night long on the lake
Where fog trails and mist creeps,
The whistle of a boat
Calls and cries unendingly,
Like some lost child
In tears and trouble
Hunting the harbor's breast
And the harbor's eyes (*1916*)

CABOOSE THOUGHTS

It's going to come out all right—do you know?
The sun, the birds, the grass—they know.
They get along—and we'll get along.

Some days will be rainy and you will sit waiting
And the letter you wait for won't come,
And I will sit watching the sky tear off gray and gray
And the letter I wait for won't come.

There will be ac-ci-dents.
I know ac-ci-dents are coming.
Smash-ups, signals wrong, washouts, trestles rotten,
Red and yellow ac-ci-dents.
But somehow and somewhere the end of the run
The train gets put together again
And the caboose and the green tail lights
Fade down the right of way like a new white hope.

I never heard a mockingbird in Kentucky.
Spilling its heart in the morning.

I never saw the snow on Chimborazo.
It's a high white Mexican hat, I hear.

I never had supper with Abe Lincoln,
Nor a dish of soup with Jim Hill.
But I've been around.

I know some of the boys here who can go a little.
I know girls good for a burst of speed any time.

I heard Williams and Walker
Before Walker died in the bughouse.

I knew a mandolin player
Working in a barber shop in an Indiana town,
And he thought he had a million dollars.

I knew a hotel girl in Des Moines.
She had eyes; I saw her and said to myself
The sun rises and the sun sets in her eyes.
I was her steady and her heart went pit-a-pat.
We took away the money for a prize waltz at a Brotherhood dance.
She had eyes; she was safe as the bridge over the Mississippi at Burling-
   ton; I married her.

Last summer we took the cushions going west.
Pike's Peak is a big old stone, believe me.
It's fastened down; something you can count on.

It's going to come out all right—do you know?
The sun, the birds, the grass—they know.
They get along—and we'll get along. *(1918)*

PRAYERS OF STEEL

Lay me on an anvil, O God.
Beat me and hammer me into a crowbar.
Let me pry loose old walls.
Let me lift and loosen old foundations.

Lay me on an anvil, O God.
Beat me and hammer me into a steel spike.
Drive me into the girders that hold a skyscraper together.
Take red-hot rivets and fasten me into the central girders.
Let me be the great nail holding a skyscraper through blue nights into
   white stars. *(1918)*

COOL TOMBS

When Abraham Lincoln was shoveled into the tombs, he forgot the
   copperheads and the assassin . . . in the dust, in the cool tombs.

And Ulysses Grant lost all thought of con men and Wall Street, cash
and collateral turned ashes . . . in the dust, in the cool tombs.
Pocahontas' body, lovely as a poplar, sweet as a red haw in November
or a pawpaw in May, did she wonder? does she remember? . . . in
the dust, in the cool tombs?
Take any streetful of people buying clothes and groceries, cheering a
hero or throwing confetti and blowing tin horns . . . tell me if the
lovers are losers . . . tell me if any get more than the lovers . . . in
the dust . . . in the cool tombs. *(1918)*

DEATH SNIPS PROUD MEN

Death is stronger than all the governments because the governments
are men and men die and then death laughs: Now you see 'em, now
you don't.

Death is stronger than all proud men and so death snips proud men on
the nose, throws a pair of dice and says: Read 'em and weep.

Death sends a radiogram every day: When I want you I'll drop in—
and then one day he comes with a master-key and lets himself in and
says: We'll go now.

Death is a nurse mother with big arms: 'Twon't hurt you at all; it's
your time now; you just need a long sleep, child; what have you had
anyhow better than sleep? *(1920)*

LOSERS

If I should pass the tomb of Jonah
I would stop there and sit for a while;
Because I was swallowed one time deep in the dark
And came out alive after all.

If I pass the burial spot of Nero
I shall say to the wind, "Well, well!"—
I who have fiddled in a world on fire,
I who have done so many stunts not worth doing.

I am looking for the grave of Sinbad too.
I want to shake his ghost-hand and say,
"Neither of us died very early, did we?"

And the last sleeping-place of Nebuchadnezzar—
When I arrive there I shall tell the wind:

"You ate grass; I have eaten crow—
Who is better off now or next year?"

Jack Cade, John Brown, Jesse James,
There too I could sit down and stop for a while.
I think I could tell their headstones:
"God, let me remember all good losers."

I could ask people to throw ashes on their heads
In the name of that sergeant at Belleau Woods,
Walking into the drumfires, calling his men,
"Come on, you ... Do you want to live forever?" (*1920*)

SANDHILL PEOPLE

I took away three pictures.
One was a white gull forming a half mile arch from the pines toward
Waukegan.
One was a whistle in the little sandhills, a bird crying either to the
sunset gone or the dusk come.
One was three spotted waterbirds, zigzagging, cutting scrolls and jags,
writing a bird Sanscrit of wing points, half over the sand, half over
the water, a half-love for the sea, a half-love for the land.

I took away three thoughts.
One was a thing my people call "love," a shut-in river hunting the sea,
breaking white falls between tall clefs of hill country.
One was a thing my people call "silence," the wind running over the
butter faced sand-flowers, running over the sea, and never heard
of again.
One was a thing my people call "death," neither a whistle in the little
sandhills, nor a bird Sanscrit of wing points, yet a coat all the stars
and seas have worn, yet a face the beach wears between sunset and
dusk. (*1920*)

MIST FORMS

The sheets of night mist travel a long valley.
I know why you came at sundown in a scarf mist.
What was it we touched asking nothing and asking all?
How many times can death come and pay back what we saw?

In the oath of the sod, the lips that swore,
In the oath of night mist, nothing and all,
A riddle is here no man tells, no woman. (*1920*)

FOUR PRELUDES ON PLAYTHINGS OF THE WIND

"The past is a bucket of ashes"

1

The woman named Tomorrow
sits with a hairpin in her teeth
and takes her time
and does her hair the way she wants it
and fastens at last the last braid and coil
and puts the hairpin where it belongs
and turns and drawls: Well, what of it?
My grandmother, Yesterday, is gone.
What of it? Let the dead be dead.

2

The doors were cedar
and the panel strips of gold
and the girls were golden girls
and the panels read and the girls chanted:
    We are the greatest city,
    the greatest nation:
    nothing like us ever was.
The doors are twisted on broken hinges.
Sheets of rain swish through on the wind
    where the golden girls ran and the panels read:
    We are the greatest city,
    the greatest nation,
    nothing like us ever was.

3

It has happened before.
Strong men put up a city and got
    a nation together,
And paid singers to sing and women
    to warble: We are the greatest city,
        the greatest nation,
        nothing like us ever was.

And while the singers sang
and the strong men listened
and paid the singers well

and felt good about it all,
 there were rats and lizards who listened
 ... and the only listeners left now
 ... are ... the rats ... and the lizards.

And there are black crows
crying, "Caw, caw,"
bringing mud and sticks
building a nest
over the words carved
on the doors where the panels were cedar
and the strips on the panels were gold
and the golden girls came singing:
 We are the greatest city,
 the greatest nation:
 nothing like us ever was.

The only singers now are crows crying, "Caw, caw,"
And the sheets of rain whine in the wind and doorways.
And the only listeners now are ... the rats ... and the lizards

4

The feet of the rats
scribble on the doorsills;
the hieroglyphs of the rat footprints
chatter the pedigrees of the rats
and babble of the blood
and gabble of the breed
of the grandfathers and the great-grandfathers
of the rats.

And the wind shifts
and the dust on a doorsill shifts
and even the writing of the rat footprints
tells us nothing, nothing at all
about the greatest city, the greatest nation
where the strong men listened
and the women warbled: Nothing like us ever was. (*1920*)

THE LAWYERS KNOW TOO MUCH

The lawyers, Bob, know too much.
They are chums of the books of old John Marshall.

They know it all, what a dead hand wrote,
A stiff dead hand and its knuckles crumbling,
The bones of the fingers a thin white ash.
　　The lawyers know
　　a dead man's thoughts too well.

In the heels of the higgling lawyers, Bob,
Too many slippery ifs and buts and howevers,
Too much hereinbefore provided whereas,
Too many doors to go in and out of.

　　　When the lawyers are through
　　　What is there left, Bob?
　　　Can a mouse nibble at it
　　　And find enough to fasten a tooth in?

　　　Why is there always a secret singing
　　　When a lawyer cashes in?
　　　Why does a hearse horse snicker
　　　Hauling a lawyer away?

The work of a bricklayer goes to the blue.
The knack of a mason outlasts a moon.
The hands of a plasterer hold a room together.
The land of a farmer wishes him back again.
　　Singers of songs and dreamers of plays
　　Build a house no wind blows over.
The lawyers—tell me why a hearse horse snickers
　　hauling a lawyer's bones.   (*1920*)

OSAWATOMIE

I don't know how he came,
shambling, dark, and strong.

He stood in the city and told men:
My people are fools, my people are young and strong, my people must
　　learn, my people are terrible workers and fighters.
Always he kept on asking: Where did that blood come from?

They said: You for the fool killer,
　　　　you for the booby hatch

and a necktie party.
They hauled him into jail.
They sneered at him and spit on him,
And he wrecked their jails,
Singing, "God damn your jails,"
And when he was most in jail
Crummy among the crazy in the dark
Then he was most of all out of jail
Shambling, dark, and strong,
Always asking: Where did that blood come from?
They laid hands on him
And the fool killers had a laugh
And the necktie party was a go, by God.
They laid hands on him and he was a goner.
They hammered him to pieces and he stood up.
They buried him and he walked out of the grave, by God,
Asking again: Where did that blood come from?   (*1920*)

THREES

I was a boy when I heard three red words
a thousand Frenchmen died in the streets
for: Liberty, Equality, Fraternity—I asked
why men die for words.

I was older; men with mustaches, sideburns,
lilacs, told me the high golden words are:
Mother, Home, and Heaven—other older men with
face decorations said: God, Duty, Immortality
—they sang these threes slow from deep lungs.

Years ticked off their say-so on the great clocks
of doom and damnation, soup and nuts: meteors flashed
their say-so: and out of great Russia came three
dusky syllables workmen took guns and went out to die
for: Bread, Peace, Land.

And I met a marine of the U.S.A., a leatherneck with
a girl on his knee for a memory in ports circling the
earth and he said: Tell me how to say three things
and I always get by—gimme a plate of ham and eggs
—how much?—and—do you love me, kid?   (*1920*)

A. E. F.

There will be a rusty gun on the wall, sweetheart,
The rifle grooves curling with flakes of rust.
A spider will make a silver string nest in the darkest, warmest corner
of it.
The trigger and the range-finder, they too will be rusty.
And no hands will polish the gun, and it will hang on the wall.
Forefingers and thumbs will point absently and casually toward it.
It will be spoken among half-forgotten, wished-to-be-forgotten things.
They will tell the spider: Go on, you're doing good work. (*1920*)

BALLOON FACES

The balloons hang on wires in the Marigold Gardens.
They spot their yellow and gold, they juggle their blue and red, they
float their faces on the face of the sky.
Balloon face eaters sit by hundreds reading the eat cards, asking, "What
shall we eat?"—and the waiters, "Have you ordered?" they are sixty
balloon faces sifting white over the tuxedos.
Poets, lawyers, ad men, mason contractors, smart-alecks discussing
"educated jackasses," here they put crabs into their balloon faces.
Here sit the heavy balloon face women lifting crimson lobsters into
their crimson faces, lobsters out of Sargossa sea bottoms.
Here sits a man cross-examining a woman, "Where were you last night?
What do you do with all your money? Who's buying your shoes
now, anyhow?"
So they sit eating whitefish, two balloon faces swept on God's night
wind.
And all the time the balloon spots on the wires, a little mile of festoons,
they play their own silence play of film yellow and film gold, bubble
blue and bubble red.
The wind crosses the town, the wind from the west side comes to the
banks of marigolds boxed in the Marigold Gardens.
Night moths fly and fix their feet in the leaves and eat and are seen
by the eaters.
The jazz outfit sweats and the drums and the saxophones reach for the
ears of the eaters.
The chorus brought from Broadway works at the fun and the slouch of
their shoulders, the kick of their ankles, reach for the eyes of the
eaters.
These girls from Kokomo and Peoria, these hungry girls, since they are
paid-for, let us look on and listen, let us get their number.

Why do I go again to the balloons on the wires, something for nothing,
kin women of the half-moon, dream women?
And the half-moon swinging on the wind crossing the town—these two,
the half-moon and the wind—this will be about all, this will be
about all.

Eaters, go to it: your mazuma pays for it all; it's a knockout, a classy
knockout—and payday always comes.
The moths in the marigolds will do for me, the half-moon, the wishing
wind and the little mile of balloon spots on wires—this will be about
all, this will be about all. (*1920*)

WASHINGTON MONUMENT BY NIGHT

1

The stone goes straight.
A lean swimmer dives into night sky,
Into half-moon mist.

2

Two trees are coal black.
This is a great white ghost between.
It is cool to look at.
Strong men, strong women, come here.

3

Eight years is a long time
To be fighting all the time.

The republic is a dream.
Nothing happens unless first a dream.

5

The wind bit hard at Valley Forge one Christmas.
Soldiers tied rags on their feet.
Red footprints wrote on the snow . . .
. . . and stone shoots into stars here
. . . into half-moon mist tonight.

6

Tongues wrangled dark at a man.
He buttoned his overcoat and stood alone.
In a snowstorm, red hollyberries, thoughts, he stood alone.

7

Women said: He is lonely
... fighting ... fighting ... eight years ...

8

The name of an iron man goes over the world.
It takes a long time to forget an iron man.

9

. . . .
. . . .   (1922)

From THE PEOPLE, YES : 1

From the four corners of the earth,
from corners lashed in wind
and bitten with rain and fire,
from places where the winds begin
and fogs are born with mist children,
tall men from tall rocky slopes came
and sleepy men from sleepy valleys,
their women tall, their women sleepy,
with bundles and belongings,
with little ones babbling, "Where to now?
    what next?"

The people of the earth, the family of man,
wanted to put up something proud to look at,
a tower from the flat land of earth
on up through the ceiling into the top of the sky.

    And the big job got going,
    the caissons and pilings sunk,
    floors, walls and winding staircases
    aimed at the stars high over,
    aimed to go beyond the ladders of the moon.

    And God Almighty could have struck them dead
    or smitten them deaf and dumb.

    And God was a whimsical fixer.
    God was an understanding Boss

with another plan in mind,
And suddenly shuffled all the languages,
    changed the tongues of men
    so they all talked different
And the masons couldn't get what the hodcarriers said,
The helpers handed the carpenters the wrong tools,
Five hundred ways to say, "W h o a r e y o u?"
Changed ways of asking, "Where do we go from here?"
Or of saying, "Being born is only the beginning,"
Or, "Would you just as soon sing as make that noise?"
Or, "What you don't know won't hurt you."
And the material-and-supply men started disputes
With the hauling gangs and the building trades
And the architects tore their hair over the blueprints
And the brickmakers and the mule skinners talked back
To the straw bosses who talked back to the superintendents
And the signals got mixed; the men who shovelled the bucket
Hooted the hoisting men—and the job was wrecked.

Some called it the Tower of Babel job
And the people gave it many other names.
The wreck of it stood as a skull and a ghost,
a memorandum hardly begun,
swaying and sagging in tall hostile winds,
held up by slow friendly winds. *(1936)*

Vachel Lindsay
(1879–1931)

GENERAL WILLIAM BOOTH ENTERS INTO HEAVEN

(To be sung to the tune of "The Blood of the Lamb"
with indicated instrument.)

1

(Bass drum beaten loudly.)
Booth led boldly with his big bass drum—
(Are you washed in the blood of the Lamb?)
The Saints smiled gravely and they said: "He's come."
(Are you washed in the blood of the Lamb?)
Walking lepers followed, rank on rank,
Lurching bravos from the ditches dank,
Drabs from the alleyways and drug fiends pale—
Minds still passion-ridden, soul-powers frail:—
Vermin-eaten saints with moldy breath,
Unwashed legions with the ways of Death—
(Are you washed in the blood of the Lamb?)

(Banjos.)
Every slum had sent its half-a-score
The round world over. (Booth had groaned for more.)
Every banner that the wide world flies
Bloomed with glory and transcendent dyes.
Big-voiced lasses made their banjos bang;
Tranced, fanatical they shrieked and sang:—
"Are you washed in the blood of the Lamb?"
Hallelujah! It was queer to see
Bull-necked convicts with that land make free.
Loons with trumpets blowed a blare, blare, blare
On, on upward thro' the golden air!
(Are you washed in the blood of the Lamb?)

(Bass drum slower and softer.)
Booth died blind and still by faith he trod,
Eyes still dazzled by the ways of God.

Booth led boldly, and he looked the chief,
Eagle countenance in sharp relief,
Beard a-flying, air of high command
Unabated in that holy land.

(*Sweet flute music.*)
Jesus came from out the court-house door,
Stretched his hands above the passing poor.
Booth saw not, but led his queer ones there
Round and round the mighty court-house square.
Then, in an instant all that blear review
Marched on spotless, clad in raiment new.
The lame were straightened, withered limbs uncurled
And blind eyes opened on a new, sweet world.

(*Bass drum louder.*)
Drabs and vixens in a flash made whole!
Gone was the weasel-head, the snout, the jowl!
Sages and sibyls now, and athletes clean,
Rulers of empires, and of forests green!

(*Grand chorus of all instruments. Tambourines to the foreground.*)
The hosts were sandalled, and their wings were fire!
(Are you washed in the blood of the Lamb?)
But their noise played havoc with the angel-choir.
(Are you washed in the blood of the Lamb?)
Oh, shout Salvation! It was good to see
Kings and Princes by the Lamb set free.
The banjos rattled and the tambourines
Jing-jing-jingled in the hands of Queens.

(*Reverently sung, no instruments.*)
And when Booth halted by the curb for prayer
He saw his Master thro' the flag-filled air.
Christ came gently with a robe and crown
For Booth the soldier, while the throng knelt down.
He saw King Jesus. They were face to face,
And he knelt a-weeping in that holy place.
Are you washed in the blood of the Lamb?   (*1913*)

THE EAGLE THAT IS FORGOTTEN

(John P. Altgeld. Born December 30, 1847; Died March 12, 1902)

Sleep softly . . . eagle forgotten . . . under the stone.
Time has its way with you there, and the clay has its own.

"We have buried him now," thought your foes, and in secret rejoiced.
They made a brave show of their mourning, their hatred unvoiced.
They had snarled at you, barked at you, foamed at you day after day.
Now you were ended. They praised you, . . . and laid you away.

The others that mourned you in silence and terror and truth,
The widow bereft of her crust, and the boy without youth,
The mocked and the scorned and the wounded, the lame and the poor
That should have remembered forever, . . . remember no more.

Where are those lovers of yours, on what name do they call,
The lost, that in armies wept over your funeral pall?
They call on the names of a hundred high-valiant ones;
A hundred white eagles have risen the sons of your sons;
The zeal in their wings is a zeal that your dreaming began,
The valor that wore out your soul in the service of man.

Sleep softly, . . . eagle forgotten, . . . under the stone,
Time has its way with you there, and the clay has its own.
Sleep on, O brave-hearted, O wise man, that kindled the flame—
To live in mankind is far more than to live in a name,
To live in mankind, far, far more . . . than to live in a name.   (*1913*)

THE CONGO

A STUDY OF THE NEGRO RACE

I. THEIR BASIC SAVAGERY

Fat black bucks in a wine-barrel room,
Barrel-house kings, with feet unstable,
Sagged and reeled and pounded on the table,   *A deep roll-*
Pounded on the table,   *ing bass.*
Beat an empty barrel with the handle of a broom,
Hard as they were able,
Boom, boom, Boom,
With a silk umbrella and the handle of a broom,
Boomlay, boomlay, boomlay, Boom.
Then I had religion, Then I had a vision.
I could not turn from their revel in derision.
Then i saw the Congo, creeping through the black,   *More*
Cutting through the forest with a golden track.   *deliberate.*
Then along that riverbank   *Solemnly*
A thousand miles   *chanted.*

Tattooed cannibals danced in files;
Then I heard the boom of the blood-lust song
And a thigh-bone beating on a tin-pan gong.   *A rapidly*
And "BLOOD" screamed the whistles and the fifes of the   *piling cli-*
    warriors,   *max of*
"BLOOD" screamed the skull-faced, lean witch-doctors,   *speed and*
"Whirl ye the deadly voo-doo rattle,   *racket.*
Harry the uplands,
Steal all the cattle,
Rattle-rattle, rattle-rattle,
Bing.
Boomlay, boomlay, boomlay, BOOM,"
A roaring, epic, rag-time tune   *With a*
From the mouth of the Congo   *philosophic*
To the Mountains of the Moon.   *pause.*
Death is an Elephant,
Torch-eyed and horrible,   *Shrilly and*
Foam-flanked and terrible.   *with a*
BOOM, steal the pygmies,   *heavily ac-*
BOOM, kill the Arabs,   *cented*
BOOM, kill the white men,   *metre.*
Hoo, Hoo, Hoo.
Listen to the yell of Leopold's ghost   *Like the*
Burning in Hell for his hand-maimed host.   *wind in the*
Hear how the demons chuckle and yell   *chimney.*
Cutting his hands off, down in Hell.
Listen to the creepy proclamation,
Blown through the lairs of the forest-nation,
Blown past the white-ants' hill of clay,
Blown past the marsh where the butterflies play:
"Be careful what you do,
Or Mumbo-Jumbo, God of the Congo,   *All the "o" sounds*
And all the other   *very golden.*
Gods of the Congo,   *Heavy accents very*
Mumbo-Jumbo will hoo-doo you,   *heavy. Light accents*
Mumbo-Jumbo will hoo-doo you,   *very light. Last line*
Mumbo-Jumbo will hoo-doo you."   *whispered.*

II. THEIR IRREPRESSIBLE HIGH SPIRITS

Wild crap-shooters with a whoop and a call   *Rather*
Danced the juba in their gambling hall   *shrill and*
And laughed fit to kill, and shook the town,   *high.*
And guyed the policemen and laughed them down

With a boomlay, boomlay, boomlay, BOOM.   *Read ex-*
THEN I SAW THE CONGO, CREEPING THROUGH THE BLACK,   *actly as in*
CUTTING THROUGH THE FOREST WITH A GOLDEN TRACK.   *first section.*
A negro fairyland swung into view,   *Lay em-*
A minstrel river   *phasis on*
Where dreams come true.   *the deli-*
The ebony palace soared on high   *cate ideas.*
Through the blossoming trees to the evening sky.   *Keep as*
The inlaid porches and casements shone   *light-footed*
With gold and ivory and elephant-bone.   *as   possible*
And the black crowd laughed till their sides were sore
At the baboon butler in the agate door,
And the well-known tunes of the parrot band
That trilled on the bushes of that magic land.

A troupe of skull-faced witch-men came   *With*
Through the agate doorway in suits of flame,   *pomposity.*
Yea, long-tailed coats with a gold-leaf crust
And hats that were covered with diamond-dust.
And the crowd in the court gave a whoop and a call
And danced the juba from wall to wall.
But the witch-men suddenly stilled the throng   *With a great delibera-*
With a stern cold glare, and a stern old song:— *tion and ghostliness.*
"Mumbo-Jumbo will hoo-doo you." . . .
Just then from the doorway, as fat as shotes,   *With overwhelming assur-*
Came the cake-walk princes in their long   *ance, good cheer, and pomp*
    red coats,
Canes with a brillant lacquer shine,
And tall silk hats that were red as wine.
And they pranced with their butterfly partners there,   *With grow-*
Coal-black maidens with pearls in their hair,   *ing speed*
Knee-skirts trimmed with the jassamine sweet,   *and sharply*
And bells on their ankles and little black feet.   *marked*
And the couples railed at the chant and the frown   *dance-*
Of the witch-men lean, and laughed them down.   *rhythm.*
(Oh, rare was the revel, and well worth while
That made those glowering witch-men smile.)

The cake-walk royalty then began
To walk for a cake that was tall as a man
To the tune of "Boomlay, boomlay, BOOM,"
While the witch-men laughed, with a sinister air,   *With a*
And sang with the scalawags prancing there:—   *touch of*
"Walk with care, walk with care,   *negro*

Or Mumbo-Jumbo, God of the Congo,
And all of the other Gods of the Congo,
Mumbo-Jumbo will hoo-doo you.
Beware, beware, walk with care,
Boomlay, boomlay, boomlay, boom.
Boomlay, boomlay, boomlay, boom.
Boomlay, boomlay, boomlay, boom.
Boomlay, boomlay, boomlay,
Boom."

*dialect, and
as rapidly
as possible
toward
the end.*

(Oh, rare was the revel, and well worth while
That made those glowering witch-men smile.)

*Slow, philo-
sophic calm.*

III. THE HOPE OF THEIR RELIGION

A good old negro in the slums of the town
Preached at a sister for her velvet gown.
Howled at a brother for his low-down ways,
His prowling, guzzling, sneak-thief days.
Beat on the Bible till he wore it out
Starting the jubilee revival shout.
And some had visions, as they stood on chairs,
And sang of Jacob, and the golden stairs,
And they all repented, a thousand strong,
From their stupor and savagery and sin and wrong,
And slammed with their hymn books till they shook
    the room
With "Glory, glory, glory,"
And "Boom, boom, Boom."

*Heavy bass.
With a
literal imi-
tation of
camp-meet-
ing racket,
and trance.*

THEN I SAW THE CONGO, CREEPING THROUGH THE BLACK,
CUTTING THROUGH THE FOREST WITH A GOLDEN TRACK.
And the gray sky opened like a new-rent veil
And showed the Apostles with their coats of mail.
In bright white steel they were seated round
And their fire-eyes watched where the Congo wound
And the twelve Apostles, from their thrones on high,
Thrilled all the forest with their heavenly cry:—
"Mumbo-Jumbo will die in the jungle;
Never again will he hoo-doo you,
Never again will he hoo-doo you."

*Exactly as
in the first
section.
Begin with
terror and
power, end
with joy.*

*Sung to the tune of
"Hark, ten thousand
harps and voices."*

Then along that river, a thousand miles,
The vine-snared trees fell down in files.
Pioneer angels cleared the way
For a Congo paradise, for babes at play,
For sacred capitals, for temples clean.

*With
growing de-
liberation
and joy.*

Gone were the skull-faced witch-men lean.
There, where the wild ghost-gods had wailed
A million boats of the angels sailed
With oars of silver, and prows of blue
And silken pennants that the sun shone through.
'Twas a land transfigured, 'twas a new creation.
Oh, a singing wind swept the negro nation
And on through the backwoods clearing flew:—
"Mumbo-Jumbo is dead in the jungle.
Never again will he hoo-doo you.
Never again will he hoo-doo you."

*In a rather
high key—
as delicately
as possible.*

*To the tune of
"Hark, ten thousand
harps and voices."*

Redeemed were the forests, the beasts and the men,
And only the vulture dared again
By the far, lone mountains of the moon
To cry, in the silence, the Congo tune:—
"Mumbo-Jumbo will hoo-doo you,
Mumbo-Jumbo will hoo-doo you,
Mumbo . . . Jumbo . . . will . . . hoo-doo
 . . . you." *(1914)*

*Dying down into a
penetrating terrified
whisper.*

THE LEADEN-EYED

Let not young souls be smothered out before
They do quaint deeds and fully flaunt their pride.
It is the world's one crime its babes grow dull,
Its poor are ox-like, limp and leaden-eyed.
Not that they starve, but starve so dreamlessly,
Not that they sow, but that they seldom reap,
Not that they serve, but have no gods to serve,
Not that they die, but that they die like sheep.   *(1914)*

ABRAHAM LINCOLN WALKS AT MIDNIGHT

(IN SPRINGFIELD, ILLINOIS)

It is portentous, and a thing of state
That here at midnight, in our little town
A mourning figure walks, and will not rest,
Near the old court-house pacing up and down,

Or by his homestead, or in shadowed yards
He lingers where his children used to play,

Or through the market, on the well-worn stones
He stalks until the dawn-stars burn away.

A bronzed, lank man! His suit of ancient black,
A famous high top-hat and plain worn shawl
Make him the quaint great figure that men love,
The prairie-lawyer, master of us all.

He cannot sleep upon his hillside now.
He is among us:—as in times before!
And we who toss and lie awake for long
Breathe deep, and start, to see him pass the door.

His head is bowed. He thinks on men and kings.
Yea, when the sick world cries, how can he sleep?
Too many peasants fight, they know not why,
Too many homesteads in black terror weep.

The sins of all the war-lords burn his heart.
He sees the dreadnaughts scouring every main.
He carries on his shawl-wrapped shoulders now
The bitterness, the folly and the pain.

He cannot rest until a spirit-dawn
Shall come;—the shining hope of Europe free:
The league of sober folk, the Workers' Earth,
Bringing long peace to Cornland, Alp and Sea.

It breaks his heart that kings must murder still,
That all his hours of travail here for men
Seem yet in vain. And who will bring white peace
That he may sleep upon his hill again? (*1914*)

THE UNPARDONABLE SIN

This is the sin against the Holy Ghost:—
To speak of bloody power as right divine,
And call on God to guard each vile chief's house,
And for such chiefs, turn men to wolves and swine:—

To go forth killing in White Mercy's name,
Making the trenches stink with spattered brains,

Tearing the nerves and arteries apart,
Sowing with flesh the unreaped golden plains.

In any Church's name, to sack fair towns,
And turn each home into a screaming sty,
To make the little children fugitive,
And have their mothers for a quick death cry,—

This is the sin against the Holy Ghost:
This is the sin no purging can atone:—
To send forth rapine in the name of Christ:—
To set the face and make the heart a stone. *(1914)*

BRYAN, BRYAN, BRYAN, BRYAN

THE CAMPAIGN OF EIGHTEEN NINETY-SIX, AS VIEWED AT THE TIME BY A SIXTEEN-YEAR-OLD, ETC.

1

In a nation of one hundred fine, mob-hearted, lynching, relenting, repenting millions,
There are plenty of sweeping, swinging, stinging, gorgeous things to shout about,
And knock your old blue devils out.

I brag and chant of Bryan, Bryan, Bryan,
Candidate for president who sketched a silver Zion,
The one American Poet who could sing outdoors,
He brought in tides of wonder, of unprecedented splendor,
Wild roses from the plains, that made hearts tender,
All the funny circus silks
Of politics unfurled,
Bartlett pears of romance that were honey at the cores,
And torchlights down the street, to the end of the world.

There were truths eternal in the gab and tittle-tattle.
There were real heads broken in the fustian and the rattle.
There were real lines drawn:
Not the silver and the gold,
But Nebraska's cry went eastward against the dour and old,
The mean and cold.

It was eighteen ninety-six, and I was just sixteen
And Altgeld ruled in Springfield, Illinois,
When there came from the sunset Nebraska's shout of joy:

In a coat like a deacon, in a black Stetson hat
He scourged the elephant plutocrats
With barbed wire from the Platte.
The scales dropped from their mighty eyes.
They saw that summer's noon
A tribe of wonders coming
To a marching tune.

Oh, the longhorns from Texas,
The jay hawks from Kansas,
The plop-eyed bungaroo and giant giassicus,
The varmint, chipmunk, bugaboo,
The horned-toad, prairie-dog and ballyhoo,
From all the newborn states arow,
Bidding the eagles of the west fly on,
Bidding the eagles of the west fly on.
The fawn, prodactyl and thing-a-ma-jig,
The rakaboor, the hellangone,
The whangdoodle, batfowl and pig,
The coyote, wild-cat and grizzly in a glow,
In a miracle of health and speed, the whole breed abreast,
They leaped the Mississippi, blue border of the West,
From the Gulf to Canada, two thousand miles long:—
Against the towns of Tubal Cain,
Ah,—sharp was their song.
Against the ways of Tubal Cain, too cunning for the young,
The longhorn calf, the buffalo and wampus gave tongue.

These creatures were defending things Mark Hanna never dreamed.
The moods of airy childhood that in desert dews gleamed,
The gossamers and whimsies,
The monkeyshines and didoes
Rank and strange
Of the canyons and the range,
The ultimate fantastics
Of the far western slope,
And of prairie schooner children
Born beneath the stars,
Beneath falling snows,
Of the babies born at midnight
In the sod huts of lost hope,
With no physician there,
Except a Kansas prayer,
With the Indian raid a howling through the air.

And all these in their helpless days
By the dour East oppressed,
Mean paternalism
Making their mistakes for them,
Crucifying half the West,
Till the whole Atlantic coast
Seemed a giant spiders' nest.

And these children and their sons
At last rode through the cactus,
A cliff of mighty cowboys
On the lope,
With gun and rope.
And all the way to frightened Maine the old East heard them call,
And saw our Bryan by a mile lead the wall
Of men and whirling flowers and beasts,
The bard and the prophet of them all.
Prairie avenger, mountain lion,
Bryan, Bryan, Bryan, Bryan,
Gigantic troubadour, speaking like a siege gun,
Smashing Plymouth Rock with his boulders from the West,
And just a hundred miles behind, tornadoes piled across the sky,
Blotting out sun and moon,
A sign on high.

Headlong, dazed and blinking in the weird green light,
The scalawags made moan,
Afraid to fight.

2

When Bryan came to Springfield, and Altgeld gave him greeting,
Rochester was deserted, Divernon was deserted,
Mechanicsburg, Riverton, Chickenbristle, Cotton Hill,
Empty: for all Sangamon drove to the meeting—
In silver-decked racing cart,
Buggy, buckboard, carryall,
Carriage, phaeton, whatever would haul,
And silver-decked farm-wagons gritted, banged and rolled,
With the new tale of Bryan by the iron tires told.

The State House loomed afar,
A speck, a hive, a football,

A captive balloon!
And the town was all one spreading wing of bunting, plumes, and
    sunshine,
Every rag and flag, and Bryan picture sold,
When the rigs in many a dusty line
Jammed our streets at noon,
And joined the wild parade against the power of gold.

We roamed, we boys from High School,
With mankind,
While Springfield gleamed,
Silk-lined.
Oh, Tom Dines, and Art Fitzgerald,
And the gangs that they could get!
I can hear them yelling yet.
Helping the incantation,
Defying aristocracy,
With every bridle gone,
Ridding the world of the low down mean,
Bidding the eagles of the West fly on,
Bidding the eagles of the West fly on,
We were bully, wild and woolly,
Never yet curried below the knees.
We saw flowers in the air,
Fair as the Pleiades, bright as Orion,
—Hopes of all mankind,
Made rare, resistless, thrice refined.
Oh, we bucks from every Springfield ward!
Colts of democracy—
Yet time-winds out of Chaos from the star-fields of the Lord.

The long parade rolled on. I stood by my best girl.
She was a cool young citizen, with wise and laughing eyes.
With my necktie by my ear, I was stepping on my dear,
But she kept like a pattern, without a shaken curl.

She wore in her hair a brave prairie rose.
Her gold chums cut her, for that was not the pose.
No Gibson Girl would wear it in that fresh way.
But we were fairy Democrats, and this was our day.

The earth rocked like the ocean, the sidewalk was a deck.
The houses for the moment were lost in the wide wreck.

And the bands played strange and stranger music as they trailed along.
Against the ways of Tubal Cain,
Ah, sharp was their song!
The demons in the bricks, the demons in the grass,
The demons in the bank-vaults peered out to see us pass,
And the angels in the trees, the angels in the grass,
The angels in the flags, peered out to see us pass.
And the sidewalk was our chariot, and the flowers bloomed higher,
And the street turned to silver and the grass turned to fire,
And then it was but grass, and the town was there again,
A place for women and men.

3

Then we stood where we could see
Every band,
And the speaker's stand.
And Byran took the platform.
And he was introduced.
And he lifted his hand
And cast a new spell.
Progressive silence fell
In Springfield,
In Illinois,
Around the world.
Then we heard these glacial boulders across the prairie rolled:
"The people have a right to make their own mistakes. . . .
You shall not crucify mankind
Upon a cross of gold."

And everybody heard him—
In the streets and State House yard.
And everybody heard him
In Springfield,
In Illinois,
Around and around and around the world,
That danced upon its axis
And like a darling broncho whirled.

4

July, August, suspense.
Wall Street lost to sense.
August, September, October,
More suspense,
And the whole East down like a wind-smashed fence.

Then Hanna to the rescue,
Hanna of Ohio,
Rallying the roller-tops,
Rallying the bucket-shops.
Threatening drouth and death,
Promising manna,
Rallying the trusts against the bawling flannelmouth;
Invading misers' cellars,
Tin-cans, socks,
Melting down the rocks,
Pouring out the long green to a million workers,
Spondulix by the mountain-load, to stop each new tornado
And beat the cheapskate, blatherskite,
Populistic, anarchistic,
Deacon—desperado.

5

Election night at midnight:
Boy Bryan's defeat.
Defeat of western silver.
Defeat of the wheat.
Victory of letterfiles
And plutocrats in miles
With dollar signs upon their coats,
Diamond watchchains on their vests
And spats on their feet.
Victory of custodians,
Plymouth Rock,
And all that inbred landlord stock.
Victory of the neat.
Defeat of the aspen groves of Colorado valleys,
The blue bells of the Rockies,
And blue bonnets of old Texas,
By the Pittsburgh alleys.
Defeat of alfalfa and the Mariposa lily.
Defeat of the Pacific and the long Mississippi.
Defeat of the young by the old and silly.
Defeat of tornadoes by the poison vats supreme.
Defeat of my boyhood, defeat of my dream.

6

Where is McKinley, that respectable McKinley,
The man without an angle or a tangle,
Who soothed down the city man and soothed down the farmer,

The German, the Irish, the Southerner, the Northerner,
Who climbed every greasy pole, and slipped through every crack;
Who soothed down the gambling hall, the bar-room, the church,
The devil vote, the angel vote, the neutral vote,
The desperately wicked, and their victims on the rack,
The gold vote, the silver vote, the brass vote, the lead vote,
Every vote? . . .

Where is McKinley, Mark Hanna's McKinley,
His slave, his echo, his suit of clothes?
Gone to join the shadows, with the pomps of that time,
And the flame of that summer's prairie rose.

Where is Cleveland whom the Democratic platform
Read from the party in a glorious hour,
Gone to join the shadows with pitchfork Tillman,
And sledge-hammer Altgeld who wrecked his power.

Where is Hanna, bulldog Hanna,
Low-browed Hanna, who said: "Stand pat"?
Gone to his place with old Pierpont Morgan.
Gone somewhere . . . with lean rat Platt.

Where is Roosevelt, the young dude cowboy,
Who hated Bryan, then aped his way?
Gone to join the shadows with mighty Cromwell
And tall King Saul, till the Judgment day.

Where is Altgeld, brave as the truth,
Whose name the few still say with tears?
Gone to join the ironies with Old John Brown,
Whose fame rings loud for a thousand years.

Where is that boy, that Heaven-born Bryan,
That Homer Bryan, who sang from the West?
Gone to join the shadows with Altgeld the Eagle,
Where the kings and the slaves and the troubadours rest.

(*August 1919, 1920*)

WHEN THE MISSISSIPPI FLOWED IN INDIANA

Inscribed to Bruce Campbell, who read "Tom Sawyer" with
me in the old house

Beneath Time's roaring cannon
Many walls fall down.

But though the guns break every stone,
Level every town:—
Within our Grandma's old front hall
Some wonders flourish yet:—
The Pavement of Verona,
Where stands young Juliet;
The roof of Blue-beard's palace,
And Kubla Khan's wild ground;
The cave of young Aladdin,
Where the jewel-flowers were found;
And the garden of old Sparta
Where little Helen played;
The grotto of Miranda
That Prospero arrayed;
And the cave, by the Mississippi,
Where Becky Thatcher strayed.

On that Indiana stairway
Gleams Cinderella's shoe.
Upon that mighty mountainside
Walks Snow-white in the dew.
Upon that grassy hillside
Trips shining Nicolette:—
That stairway of remembrance
Time's cannon will not get—
That chattering slope of glory
Our little cousins made,
That hill by the Mississippi
Where Becky Thatcher strayed.

Spring beauties on that cliffside,
Love in the air,
While the soul's deep Mississippi
Sweeps on, forever fair.
And he who enters in the cave,
Nothing shall make afraid,
The cave by the Mississippi
Where Tom and Becky strayed.   (*1920*)

THE FLOWER-FED BUFFALOES

The flower-fed buffaloes of the spring
In the days of long ago,
Ranged where the locomotives sing

And the prairie flowers lie low:
The tossing, blooming, perfumed grass
Is swept away by the wheat,
Wheels and wheels and wheels spin by
In the spring that still is sweet.
But the flower-fed buffaloes of the spring
Left us, long ago.
They gore no more, they bellow no more,
They trundle around the hills no more:
With the Blackfeet, lying low.
With the Pawnees, lying low,
Lying low. (*1926*)

RAIN

Each storm-soaked flower has a beautiful eye.
And this is the voice of the stone-cold sky:
"Only boys keep their cheeks dry.
Only boys are afraid to cry.
Men thank God for tears,
Alone with the memory of their dead,
Alone with lost years." (*1926*)

NANCY HANKS, MOTHER OF ABRAHAM LINCOLN

*Out of the eater came forth meat; and out of the strong came forth sweet-
ness.*—Judges 14:14

A sweet girl graduate, lean as a fawn,
The very whimsy of time,
Read her class poem Commencement Day—
A trembling filigree rhyme.

The pansy that blooms on the window sill,
Blooms in exactly the proper place;
And she nodded just like a pansy there,
And her poem was all about bowers and showers,
Sugary streamlet and mossy rill,
All about daisies on dale and hill—
And she was the mother of Buffalo Bill.

Another girl, a cloud-drift sort,
Dreamlit, moonlit, marble-white,

Light-footed saint on the pilgrim shore,
The best since New England fairies began,
Was the mother of Barnum, the circus man.

A girl from Missouri, snippy and vain,
As frothy a miss as any you know,
A wren, a toy, a pink silk bow,
The belle of the choir, she drove insane
Missouri deacons and all the sleek,
Her utter tomfoolery made men weak,
Till they could not stand and they could not speak.
Oh, queen of fifteen and sixteen,
Missouri sweetened beneath her reign—
And she was the mother of bad Mark Twain.

Not always are lions born of lions,
Roosevelt sprang from a palace of lace;
On the other hand is the dizzy truth:
Not always is beauty born of beauty.
Some treasures wait in a hidden place.
All over the world were thousands of belles
In far-off eighteen hundred and nine,
Girls of fifteen, girls of twenty,
Their mammas dressed them up a-plenty—
Each garter was bright, each stocking fine,
But for all their innocent devices,
Their cheeks of fruit and their eyes of wine,
And each voluptuous design,
And all soft glories that we trace
In Europe's palaces of lace,
A girl who slept in dust and sorrow,
Nancy Hanks, in a lost log cabin,
Nancy Hanks had the loveliest face! (1926)

Wallace Stevens
(1879–1955)

PETER QUINCE AT THE CLAVIER

1

Just as my fingers on these keys
Make music, so the selfsame sounds
On my spirit make a music, too.

Music is feeling, then, not sound;
And thus it is that what I feel,
Here in this room, desiring you,

Thinking of your blue-shadowed silk,
Is music. It is like the strain
Waked in the elders by Susanna.

Of a green evening, clear and warm,
She bathed in her still garden, while
The red-eyed elders watching, felt

The basses of their beings throb
In witching chords, and their thin blood
Pulse pizzicati of Hosanna.

2

In the green water, clear and warm,
Susanna lay.
She searched
The touch of springs,
And found
Concealed imaginings.
She sighed,
For so much melody.

Upon the bank, she stood
In the cool

Of spent emotions.
She felt, among the leaves,
The dew
Of old devotions.

She walked upon the grass,
Still quavering.
The winds were like her maids,
On timid feet,
Fetching her woven scarves,
Yet wavering.

A breath upon her hand
Muted the night.
She turned—
A cymbal crashed,
And roaring horns.

3

Soon, with a noise like tambourines,
Came her attendant Byzantines.

They wondered why Susanna cried
Against the elders by her side;

And as they whispered, the refrain
Was like a willow swept by rain.

Anon, their lamps' uplifted flame
Revealed Susanna and her shame.

And then, the simpering Byzantines
Fled, with a noise like tambourines.

4

Beauty is momentary in the mind—
The fitful tracing of a portal;
But in the flesh it is immortal.

The body dies; the body's beauty lives.
So evenings die, in their green going,
A wave, interminably flowing.
So gardens die, their meek breath scenting
The cowl of winter, done repenting.

So maidens die, to the auroral
Celebration of a maiden's choral.
Susanna's music touched the bawdy strings
Of those white elders; but, escaping,
Left only Death's ironic scraping.
Now, in its immortality, it plays
On the clear viol of her memory,
And makes a constant sacrament of praise. *(1915)*

DISILLUSIONMENT OF TEN O'CLOCK

The houses are haunted
By white night-gowns.
None are green,
Or purple with green rings,
Or green with yellow rings,
Or yellow with blue rings.
None of them are strange,
With socks of lace
And beaded ceintures.
People are not going
To dream of baboons and periwinkles.
Only, here and there, an old sailor,
Drunk and asleep in his boots,
Catches tigers
In red weather. *(1915)*

SUNDAY MORNING

1

Complacencies of the peignoir, and late
Coffee and oranges in a sunny chair,
And the green freedom of a cockatoo
Upon a rug mingle to dissipate
The holy rush of ancient sacrifice.
She dreams a little, and she feels the dark
Encroachment of that old catastrophe,
As a calm darkens among water-lights.
The pungent oranges and bright, green wings
Seem things in some procession of the dead,
Winding across wide water, without sound.
The day is like wide water, without sound,

Stilled for the passing of her dreaming feet
Over the seas, to silent Palestine,
Dominion of the blood and sepulchre.

2

Why should she give her bounty to the dead?
What is divinity if it can come
Only in silent shadows and in dreams?
Shall she not find in comforts of the sun,
In pungent fruit and bright, green wings, or else
In any balm or beauty of the earth,
Things to be cherished like the thought of heaven?
Divinity must live within herself:
Passions of rain, or moods in falling snow;
Grievings in loneliness, or unsubdued
Elations when the forest blooms; gusty
Emotions on wet roads on autumn nights;
All pleasures and all pains, remembering
The bough of summer and the winter branch.
These are the measures destined for her soul.

3

Jove in the clouds had his inhuman birth.
No mother suckled him, no sweet land gave
Large-mannered motions to his mythy mind.
He moved among us, as a muttering king,
Magnificent, would move among his hinds,
Until our blood, commingling, virginal,
With heaven, brought such requital to desire
The very hinds discerned it, in a star.
Shall our blood fail? Or shall it come to be
The blood of paradise? And shall the earth
Seem all of paradise that we shall know?
The sky will be much friendlier then than now,
A part of labor and a part of pain,
And next in glory to enduring love,
Not this dividing and indifferent blue.

4

She says, "I am content when wakened birds,
Before they fly, test the reality
Of misty fields, by their sweet questionings;

But when the birds are gone, and their warm fields
Return no more, where, then, is paradise?"
There is not any haunt of prophecy,
Nor any old chimera of the grave,
Neither the golden underground, nor isle
Melodious, where spirits gat them home,
Nor visionary south, nor cloudy palm
Remote on heaven's hill, that has endured
As April's green endures; or will endure
Like her remembrance of awakened birds,
Or her desire for June and evening, tipped
By the consummation of the swallow's wings.

5

She says, "But in contentment I still feel
The need of some imperishable bliss."
Death is the mother of beauty; hence from her,
Alone, shall come fulfilment to our dreams
And our desires. Although she strews the leaves
Of sure obliteration on our paths,
The path sick sorrow took, the many paths
Where triumph rang its brassy phrase, or love
Whispered a little out of tenderness,
She makes the willow shiver in the sun
For maidens who were wont to sit and gaze
Upon the grass, relinquished to their feet.
She causes boys to pile new plums and pears
On disregarded plate. The maidens taste
And stray impassioned in the littering leaves.

6

Is there no change of death in paradise?
Does ripe fruit never fall? Or do the boughs
Hang always heavy in that perfect sky,
Unchanging, yet so like our perishing earth,
With rivers like our own that seek for seas
They never find, the same receding shores
That never touch with inarticulate pang?
Why set the pear upon those river-banks
Or spice the shores with odors of the plum?
Alas, that they should wear our colors there,
The silken weavings of our afternoons,
And pick the strings of our insipid lutes!
Death is the mother of beauty, mystical,

Within whose burning bosom we devise
Our earthly mothers waiting, sleeplessly.

7

Supple and turbulent, a ring of men
Shall chant in orgy on a summer morn
Their boisterous devotion to the sun,
Not as a god, but as a god might be,
Naked among them, like a savage source.
Their chant shall be a chant of paradise,
Out of their blood, returning to the sky;
And in their chant shall enter, voice by voice,
The windy lake wherein their lord delights,
The trees, like serafin, and echoing hills,
That choir among themselves long afterward.
They shall know well the heavenly fellowship
Of men that perish and of summer morn.
And whence they came and whither they shall go
The dew upon their feet shall manifest.

8

She hears, upon that water without sound,
A voice that cries, "The tomb in Palestine
Is not the porch of spirits lingering.
It is the grave of Jesus, where he lay."
We live in an old chaos of the sun,
Or old dependency of day and night,
Or island solitude, unsponsored, free,
Of that wide water, inescapable.
Deer walk upon our mountains, and the quail
Whistle about us their spontaneous cries;
Sweet berries ripen in the wilderness;
And, in the isolation of the sky,
At evening, casual flocks of pigeons make
Ambiguous undulations as they sink,
Downward to darkness, on extended wings. *(1915)*

THIRTEEN WAYS OF LOOKING AT A BLACKBIRD

1

Among twenty snowy mountains,
The only moving thing
Was the eye of the blackbird.

2

I was of three minds,
Like a tree
In which there are three blackbirds.

3

The blackbird whirled in the autumn winds.
It was a small part of the pantomime.

4

A man and a woman
Are one.
A man and a woman and a blackbird
Are one.

5

I do not know which to prefer,
The beauty of inflections
Or the beauty of innuendoes,
The blackbird whistling
Or just after.

6

Icicles filled the long window
With barbaric glass.
The shadow of the blackbird
Crossed it, to and fro.
The mood
Traced in the shadow
An indecipherable cause.

7

O thin men of Haddam,
Why do you imagine golden birds?
Do you not see how the blackbird
Walks around the feet
Of the women about you?

8

I know noble accents
And lucid, inescapable rhythms;
But I know, too,
That the blackbird is involved
In what I know.

9

When the blackbird flew out of sight,
It marked the edge
Of one of many circles.

10

At the sight of blackbirds
Flying in a green light,
Even the bawds of euphony
Would cry out sharply.

11

He rode over Connecticut
In a glass coach.
Once, a fear pierced him,
In that he mistook
The shadow of his equipage
For blackbirds.

12

The river is moving.
The blackbird must be flying.

13

It was evening all afternoon.
It was snowing
And it was going to snow.
The blackbird sat
In the cedar-limbs. *(1917)*

ANECDOTE OF THE JAR

I placed a jar in Tennessee,
And round it was, upon a hill.
It made the slovenly wilderness
Surround that hill.

The wilderness rose up to it,
And sprawled around, no longer wild.
The jar was round upon the ground
And tall and of a port in air.

It took dominion everywhere.
The jar was gray and bare.

It did not give of bird or bush,
Like nothing else in Tennessee. *(1919)*

THE SNOW MAN

One must have a mind of winter
To regard the frost and the boughs
Of the pine-trees crusted with snow;

And have been cold a long time
To behold the junipers shagged with ice,
The spruces rough in the distant glitter

Of the January sun; and not to think
Of any misery in the sound of the wind,
In the sound of a few leaves,

Which is the sound of the land
Full of the same wind
That is blowing in the same bare place

For the listener, who listens in the snow,
And, nothing himself, beholds
Nothing that is not there and the nothing that is. *(1919)*

BANTAMS IN PINE-WOODS

Chieftain Iffucan of Azcan in caftan
Of tan with henna hackles, halt!

Damned universal cock, as if the sun
Was blackamoor to bear your blazing tail.

Fat! Fat! Fat! Fat! I am the personal.
Your world is you. I am my world.

You ten-foot poet among inchlings. Fat!
Begone! An inchling bristles in these pines,

Bristles, and points their Appalachian tangs,
And fears not portly Azcan nor his hoos. *(1922)*

A HIGH-TONED OLD CHRISTIAN WOMAN

Poetry is the supreme fiction, madame.
Take the moral law and make a nave of it
And from the nave build haunted heaven. Thus,
The conscience is converted into palms,
Like windy citherns hankering for hymns.
We agree in principle. That's clear. But take
The opposing law and make a peristyle,
And from the peristyle project a masque
Beyond the planets. Thus, our bawdiness,
Unpurged by epitaph, indulged at last,
Is equally converted into palms,
Squiggling like saxophones. And palm for palm,
Madame, we are where we began. Allow,
Therefore, that in the planetary scene
Your disaffected flagellants, well-stuffed,
Smacking their muzzy bellies in parade,
Proud of such novelties of the sublime,
Such tink and tank and tunk-a-tunk-tunk,
May, merely may, madame, whip from themselves
A jovial hullabaloo among the spheres.
This will make widows wince. But fictive things
Wink as they will. Wink most when widows wince. *(1922)*

THE EMPEROR OF ICE-CREAM

Call the roller of big cigars,
The muscular one, and bid him whip
In kitchen cups concupiscent curds.
Let the wenches dawdle in such dress
As they are used to wear, and let the boys
Bring flowers in last month's newspapers.
Let be be finale of seem.
The only emperor is the emperor of ice-cream.

Take from the dresser of deal,
Lacking the three glass knobs, that sheet
On which she embroidered fantails once
And spread it so as to cover her face.
If her horny feet protrude, they come
To show how cold she is, and dumb.

Let the lamp affix its beam.
The only emperor is the emperor of ice-cream. *(1922)*

EARTHY ANECDOTE

Every time the bucks went clattering
Over Oklahoma
A firecat bristled in the way.

Wherever they went,
They went clattering,
Until they swerved
In a swift, circular line
To the right,
Because of the firecat.

Or until they swerved
In a swift, circular line
To the left,
Because of the firecat.

The bucks clattered.
The firecat went leaping,
To the right, to the left,
And
Bristled in the way.

Later, the firecat closed his bright eyes
And slept. *(1923)*

THE PLOT AGAINST THE GIANT

FIRST GIRL

When this yokel comes maundering,
Whetting his hacker,
I shall run before him,
Diffusing the civilest odors
Out of geraniums and unsmelled flowers.
It will check him.

SECOND GIRL

I shall run before him,
Arching cloths besprinkled with colors

As small as fish-eggs.
The threads
Will abash him.

THIRD GIRL

Oh, la ... le pauvre!
I shall run before him,
With a curious puffing.
He will bend his ear then.
I shall whisper
Heavenly labials in a world of gutturals.
It will undo him. *(1923)*

NUANCES OF A THEME BY WILLIAMS

It's a strange courage
you give me, ancient star:

Shine alone in the sunrise
toward which you lend no part!

1

Shine alone, shine nakedly, shine like bronze,
that reflects neither my face nor any inner part
of my being, shine like fire, that mirrors nothing.

2

Lend no part to any humanity that suffuses
you in its own light.
Be not chimera of morning,
Half-man, half-star.
Be not an intelligence,
Like a widow's bird
Or an old horse. *(1923)*

SEA SURFACE FULL OF CLOUDS

1

In that November off Tehuantepec,
The slopping of the sea grew still one night
And in the morning summer hued the deck

And made one think of rosy chocolate
And gilt umbrellas. Paradisal green
Gave suavity to the perplexed machine

Of ocean, which like limpid water lay.
Who, then, in that ambrosial latitude
Out of the light evolved the moving blooms,

Who, then, evolved the sea-blooms from the clouds
Diffusing balm in that Pacific calm?
C'était mon enfant, mon bijou, mon âme.

The sea-clouds whitened far below the calm
And moved, as blooms move, in the swimming green
And in its watery radiance, while the hue

Of heaven in an antique reflection rolled
Round those flotillas. And sometimes the sea
Poured brilliant iris on the glistening blue.

2

In that November off Tehuantepec
The slopping of the sea grew still one night.
At breakfast jelly yellow streaked the deck

And made one think of chop-house chocolate
And sham umbrellas. And a sham-like green
Capped summer-seeming on the tense machine

Of ocean, which in sinister flatness lay.
Who, then, beheld the rising of the clouds
That strode submerged in that malevolent sheen,

Who saw the mortal massives of the blooms
Of water moving on the water-floor?
C'était mon frère du ciel, ma vie, mon or.

The gongs rang loudly as the windy booms
Hoo-hooed it in the darkened ocean-blooms.
The gongs grew still. And then blue heaven spread

Its crystalline pendentives on the sea
And the macabre of the water-glooms
In an enormous undulation fled.

3

In that November off Tehuantepec,
The slopping of the sea grew still one night
And a pale silver patterned on the deck

And made one think of porcelain chocolate
And pied umbrellas. An uncertain green,
Piano-polished, held the tranced machine

Of ocean, as a prelude holds and holds.
Who, seeing silver petals of white blooms
Unfolding in the water, feeling sure

Of the milk within the saltiest spurge, heard, then,
The sea unfolding in the sunken clouds?
Oh! C'était mon extase et mon amour.

So deeply sunken were they that the shrouds,
The shrouding shadows, made the petals black
Until the rolling heaven made them blue,

A blue beyond the rainy hyacinth,
And smiting the crevasses of the leaves
Deluged the ocean with a sapphire blue.

4

In that November off Tehuantepec
The night-long slopping of the sea grew still.
A mallow morning dozed upon the deck

And made one think of musky chocolate
And frail umbrellas. A too-fluent green
Suggested malice in the dry machine

Of ocean, pondering dank stratagem.
Who then beheld the figures of the clouds
Like blooms secluded in the thick marine?

Like blooms? Like damasks that were shaken off
From the loosed girdles in the spangling must.
C'était ma foi, la nonchalance divine.

The nakedness would rise and suddenly turn
Salt masks of beard and mouths of bellowing,
Would—But more suddenly the heaven rolled

Its bluest sea-clouds in the thinking green,
And the nakedness became the broadest blooms,
Mile-mallows that a mallow sun cajoled.

5

In that November off Tehuantepec
Night stilled the slopping of the sea. The day
Came, bowing and voluble, upon the deck,

Good clown. . . . One thought of Chinese chocolate
And large umbrellas. And a motley green
Followed the drift of the obese machine

Of ocean, perfected in indolence.
What pistache one, ingenious and droll,
Beheld the sovereign clouds as jugglery

And the sea as turquoise-turbaned Sambo, neat
At tossing saucers—cloudy-conjuring sea?
C'était mon esprit bâtard, l'ignominie.

The sovereign clouds came clustering. The conch
Of loyal conjuration trumped. The wind
Of green blooms turning crisped the motley hue

To clearing opalescence. Then the sea
And heaven rolled as one and from the two
Came fresh transfigurings of freshest blue.   (1924)

THE IDEA OF ORDER AT KEY WEST

She sang beyond the genius of the sea.
The water never formed to mind or voice,
Like a body wholly body, fluttering
Its empty sleeves; and yet its mimic motion
Made constant cry, caused constantly a cry,
That was not ours although we understood,
Inhuman, of the veritable ocean.

The sea was not a mask. No more was she.
The song and water were not medleyed sound
Even if what she sang was what she heard,
Since what she sang was uttered word by word.

It may be that in all her phrases stirred
The grinding water and the gasping wind;
But it was she and not the sea we heard.

For she was the maker of the song she sang.
The ever-hooded, tragic-gestured sea
Was merely a place by which she walked to sing.
Whose spirit is this? we said, because we knew
It was the spirit that we sought and knew
That we should ask this often as she sang.

If it was only the dark voice of the sea
That rose, or even colored by many waves;
If it was only the outer voice of sky
And cloud, of the sunken coral water-walled,
However clear, it would have been deep air,
The heaving speech of air, a summer sound
Repeated in a summer without end
And sound alone. But it was more than that,
More even than her voice, and ours, among
The meaningless plungings of water and the wind,
Theatrical distances, bronze shadows heaped
On high horizons, mountainous atmospheres
Of sky and sea.
                    It was her voice that made
The sky acutest at its vanishing.
She measured to the hour its solitude.
She was the single artificer of the world
In which she sang. And when she sang, the sea,
Whatever self it had, became the self
That was her song, for she was the maker. Then we,
As we beheld her striding there alone,
Knew that there never was a world for her
Except the one she sang and, singing, made.

Ramon Fernandez, tell me, if you know,
Why, when the singing ended and we turned
Toward the town, tell why the glassy lights,
The lights in the fishing boats at anchor there,
As the night descended, tilting in the air,
Mastered the night and portioned out the sea,
Fixing emblazoned zones and fiery poles,
Arranging, deepening, enchanting night.
Oh! Blessed rage for order, pale Ramon,

The maker's rage to order words of the sea,
Words of the fragrant portals, dimly-starred,
And of ourselves and of our origins,
In ghostlier demarcations, keener sounds. *(1934)*

DANCE OF THE MACABRE MICE

In the land of turkeys in turkey weather
At the base of the statue, we go round and round.
What a beautiful history, beautiful surprise!
Monsieur is on horseback. The horse is covered with mice.

This dance has no name. It is a hungry dance.
We dance it out to the tip of Monsieur's sword,
Reading the lordly language of the inscription,
Which is like zithers and tambourines combined:

The Founder of the State. Whoever founded
A state that was free, in the dead of winter, from mice?
What a beautiful tableau tinted and towering,
The arm of bronze outstretched against all evil! *(1935)*

From THE MAN WITH THE BLUE GUITAR

1

The man bent over his guitar,
A shearsman of sorts. The day was green.

They said, "You have a blue guitar,
You do not play things as they are."

The man replied, "Things as they are
Are changed upon the blue guitar."

And they said then, "But play, you must,
A tune beyond us, yet ourselves,

A tune upon the blue guitar
Of things exactly as they are."

2

I cannot bring a world quite round,
Although I patch it as I can.

I sing a hero's head, large eye
And bearded bronze, but not a man,

Although I patch him as I can
And reach through him almost to man.

If to serenade almost to man
Is to miss, by that, things as they are,

Say that it is the serenade
Of a man that plays a blue guitar.

6

A tune beyond us as we are,
Yet nothing changed by the blue guitar;

Ourselves in the tune as if in space,
Yet nothing changed, except the place

Of things as they are and only the place
As you play them, on the blue guitar,

Placed, so, beyond the compass of change,
Perceived in a final atmosphere;

For a moment final, in the way
The thinking of art seems final when

The thinking of god is smoky dew.
The tune is space. The blue guitar

Becomes the place of things as they are,
A composing of senses of the guitar.

12

Tom-tom, c'est moi. The blue guitar
And I are one. The orchestra

Fills the high hall with shuffling men
High as the hall. The whirling noise

Of a multitude dwindles, all said,
To his breath that lies awake at night.

I know that timid breathing. Where
Do I begin and end? And where

As I strum the thing, do I pick up
That which momentously declares

Itself not to be I and yet
Must be. It could be nothing else. *(1937)*

From ESTHÉTIQUE DU MAL

1

He was at Naples writing letters home
And, between his letters, reading paragraphs
On the sublime. Vesuvius had groaned
For a month. It was pleasant to be sitting there,
While the sultriest fulgurations, flickering,
Cast corners in the glass. He could describe
The terror of the sound because the sound
Was ancient. He tried to remember the phrases: pain
Audible at noon, pain torturing itself,
Pain killing pain on the very point of pain.
The volcano trembled in another ether,
As the body trembles at the end of life.

It was almost time for lunch. Pain is human.
There were roses in the cool café. His book
Made sure of the most correct catastrophe.
Except for us, Vesuvius might consume
In solid fire the utmost earth and know
No pain (ignoring the cocks that crow us up
To die). This is a part of the sublime
From which we shrink. And yet, except for us,
The total past felt nothing when destroyed.

7

How red the rose that is the soldier's wound,
The wounds of many soldiers, the wounds of all
The soldiers that have fallen, red in blood,
The soldier of time grown deathless in great size.

A mountain in which no ease is ever found,
Unless indifference to deeper death

Is ease, stands in the dark, a shadows' hill,
And there the soldier of time has deathless rest.

Concentric circles of shadows, motionless
Of their own part, yet moving on the wind,
From mystical convolutions in the sleep
Of time's red soldier deathless on his bed.

The shadows of his fellows ring him round
In the high night, the summer breathes for them
Its fragrance, a heavy somnolence, and for him,
For the soldier of time, it breathes a summer sleep,

In which his wound is good because life was.
No part of him was ever part of death.
A woman smoothes her forehead with her hand
And the soldier of time lies calm beneath that stroke.

11

Life is a bitter aspic. We are not
At the centre of a diamond. At dawn,
The paratroopers fall and as they fall
They mow the lawn. A vessel sinks in waves
Of people, as big bell-billows from its bell
Bell-bellow in the village steeple. Violets,
Great tufts, spring up from buried houses
Of poor, dishonest people, for whom the steeple,
Long since, rang out farewell, farewell, farewell.

Natives of poverty, children of malheur,
The gaiety of language is our seigneur.

A man of bitter appetite despises
A well-made scene in which paratroopers
Select adieux; and he despises this:
A ship that rolls on a confected ocean,
The weather pink, the wind in motion; and this:
A steeple that tip-tops the classic sun's
Arrangements; and the violets' exhumo.
The tongue caresses these exacerbations.
They press it as epicure, distinguishing
Themselves from its essential savor,
Like hunger that feeds on its own hungriness. (*1944*)

From THE AURORAS OF AUTUMN

1

This is where the serpent lives, the bodiless.
His head is air. Beneath his tip at night
Eyes open and fix on us in every sky.

Or is this another wriggling out of the egg,
Another image at the end of the cave,
Another bodiless for the body's slough?

This is where the serpent lives. This is his nest,
These fields, these hills, these tinted distances,
And the pines above and along and beside the sea.

This is form gulping after formlessness,
Skin flashing to wished-for disappearances
And the serpent body flashing without the skin.

This is the height emerging and its base
These lights may finally attain a pole
In the midmost midnight and find the serpent there,

In another nest, the master of the maze
Of body and air and forms and images,
Relentlessly in possession of happiness.

This is his poison: that we should disbelieve
Even that. His meditations in the ferns,
When he moved so slightly to make sure of sun,

Made us no less as sure. We saw in his head,
Black beaded on the rock, the flecked animal,
The moving grass, the Indian in his glade.

2

Farewell to an idea . . . A cabin stands,
Deserted, on a beach. It is white,
As by a custom or according to

An ancestral theme or as a consequence
Of an infinite course. The flowers against the wall
Are white, a little dried, a kind of mark

Reminding, trying to remind, of a white
That was different, something else, last year
Or before, not the white of an aging afternoon,

Whether fresher or duller, whether of winter cloud
Or of winter sky, from horizon to horizon.
The wind is blowing the sand across the floor.

Here, being visible is being white,
Is being of the solid of white, the accomplishment
Of an extremist in an exercise . . .

The season changes. A cold wind chills the beach.
The long lines of it grow longer, emptier,
A darkness gathers though it does not fall

And the whiteness grows less vivid on the wall.
The man who is walking turns blankly on the sand.
He observes how the north is always enlarging the change,

With its frigid brilliances, its blue-red sweeps
And gusts of great enkindlings, its polar green,
The color of ice and fire and solitude.

10

An unhappy people in a happy world—
Read, rabbi, the phases of this difference.
An unhappy people in an unhappy world—

Here are too many mirrors for misery.
A happy people in an unhappy world—
It cannot be. There's nothing there to roll

On the expressive tongue, the finding fang.
A happy people in a happy world—
Buffo! A ball, an opera, a bar.

Turn back to where we were when we began:
An unhappy people in a happy world.
Now, solemnize the secretive syllables.

Read to the congregation, for today
And for tomorrow, this extremity,
This contrivance of the spectre of the spheres,

Contriving balance to contrive a whole,
The vital, the never-failing genius,
Fulfilling his meditations, great and small.

In these unhappy he meditates a whole,
The full of fortune and the full of fate,
As if he lived all lives, that he might know

In hall harridan, not hushful paradise,
To a haggling of wind and weather, by these lights
Like a blaze of summer straw, in winter's nick. *(1950)*

THE SOULS OF WOMEN AT NIGHT

Now, being invisible, I walk without mantilla,
In the much-horned night, as its chief personage.
Owls warn me and with tuft-eared watches keep

Distance between me and the five-times-sensed,
In these stations, in which nothing has been lost,
Sight least, but metaphysical blindness gained,

The blindness in which seeing would be false,
A fantastic irruption. Salute you, cata-sisters,
Ancient amigas, knowing partisans—

Or is it I that, wandering, know, one-sensed,
Not one of the five, and keep a rendezvous,
Of the loftiest amour, in a human midnight? *(1957)*

William Carlos Williams
(1883–1963)

PORTRAIT OF A LADY

Your thighs are appletrees
whose blossoms touch the sky.
Which sky? The sky
where Watteau hung a lady's
slipper. Your knees
are a southern breeze—or
a gust of snow. Agh! what
sort of man was Fragonard?
—as if that answered
anything. Ah, yes—below
the knees, since the tune
drops that way, it is
one of those white summer days,
the tall grass of your ankles
flickers upon the shore—
Which shore?—
the sand clings to my lips—
Which shore?
Agh, petals maybe. How
should I know?
Which shore? Which shore?
I said petals from an appletree.   *(1913)*

EL HOMBRE

It's a strange courage
you give me ancient star:

Shine alone in the sunrise
toward which you lend no part!   *(1917)*

DANSE RUSSE

If I when my wife is sleeping
and the baby and Kathleen

are sleeping
and the sun is a flame-white disc
in silken mists
above shining trees,—
if I in my north room
dance naked, grotesquely
before my mirror
waving my shirt round my head
and singing softly to myself:
"I am lonely, lonely.
I was born to be lonely,
I am best so!"
If I admire my arms, my face,
my shoulders, flanks, buttocks
against the yellow drawn shades,—

Who shall say I am not
the happy genius of my household?   (*1917*)

THE WIDOW'S LAMENT IN SPRINGTIME

Sorrow is my own yard
where the new grass
flames as it has flamed
often before but not
with the cold fire
that closes round me this year.
Thirtyfive years
I lived with my husband.
The plumtree is white today
with masses of flowers.
Masses of flowers
load the cherry branches
and color some bushes
yellow and some red
but the grief in my heart
is stronger than they
for though they were my joy
formerly, today I notice them
and turned away forgetting.
Today my son told me
that in the meadows,
at the edge of the heavy woods

in the distance, he saw
trees of white flowers.
I feel that I would like
to go there
and fall into those flowers
and sink into the marsh near them. *(1921)*

SPRING AND ALL

By the road to the contagious hospital
under the surge of the blue
mottled clouds driven from the
northeast—a cold wind. Beyond, the
waste of broad, muddy fields
brown with dried weeds, standing and fallen

patches of standing water
the scattering of tall trees

All along the road the reddish
purplish, forked, upstanding, twiggy
stuff of bushes and small trees
with dead, brown leaves under them
leafless vines—

Lifeless in appearance, sluggish
dazed spring approaches—

They enter the new world naked,
cold, uncertain of all
save that they enter. All about them
the cold, familiar wind—

Now the grass, tomorrow
the stiff curl of wildcarrot leaf
One by one objects are defined—
It quickens: clarity, outline of leaf

But now the stark dignity of
entrance—Still, the profound change
has come upon them: rooted, they
grip down and begin to awaken *(1923)*

TO ELSIE

The pure products of America
go crazy—
mountain folk from Kentucky

or the ribbed north end of
Jersey
with its isolate lakes and

valleys, its deaf-mutes, thieves
old names
and promiscuity between

devil-may-care men who have taken
to railroading
out of sheer lust of adventure—

and young slatterns, bathed
in filth
from Monday to Saturday

to be tricked out that night
with gauds
from imaginations which have no

peasant traditions to give them
character
but flutter and flaunt

sheer rags—succumbing without
emotion
save numbed terror

under some hedge of choke-cherry
or viburnum—
which they cannot express—

Unless it be that marriage
perhaps
with a dash of Indian blood

will throw up a girl so desolate
so hemmed round
with disease or murder

that she'll be rescued by an
agent—
reared by the state and

sent out at fifteen to work in
some hard-pressed
house in the suburbs—

some doctor's family, some Elsie—
voluptuous water
expressing with broken

brain the truth about us—
her great
ungainly hips and flopping breasts

addressed to cheap
jewelry
and rich young men with fine eyes

as if the earth under our feet
were
an excrement of some sky

and we degraded prisoners
destined
to hunger until we eat filth

while the imagination strains
after deer
going by fields of goldenrod in

the stifling heat of September
Somehow
it seems to destroy us

It is only in isolate flecks that
something
is given off

No one
to witness
and adjust, no one to drive the car   *(1923)*

THE RED WHEELBARROW

so much depends
upon

a red wheel
barrow

glazed with rain
water

beside the white
chickens.   *(1923)*

AT THE BALL GAME

The crowd at the ball game
is moved uniformly

by a spirit of uselessness
which delights them—

all the exciting detail
of the chase

and the escape, the error
the flash of genius—

all to no end save beauty
the eternal—

So in detail they, the crowd,
are beautiful

for this
to be warned against

saluted and defied—
It is alive, venomous

it smiles grimly
its words cut—

The flashy female with her
mother, gets it—

The Jew gets it straight—it
is deadly, terrifying—

It is the Inquisition, the
Revolution

It is beauty itself
that lives

day by day in them
idly—

This is
the power of their faces

It is summer, it is the solstice
the crowd is

cheering, the crowd is laughing
in detail

permanently, seriously
without thought   *(1923)*

THE YACHTS

contend in a sea which the land partly encloses
shielding them from the too-heavy blows
of an ungoverned ocean which when it chooses

tortures the biggest hulls, the best man knows
to pit against its beatings, and sinks them pitilessly.
Mothlike in mists, scintillant in the minute

brilliance of cloudless days, with broad bellying sails
they glide to the wind tossing green water
from their sharp prows while over them the crew crawls

ant-like, solicitously grooming them, releasing,
making fast as they turn, lean far over and having
caught the wind again, side by side, head for the mark.

In a well guarded arena of open water surrounded by
lesser and greater craft which, sycophant, lumbering
and flittering follow them, they appear youthful, rare

as the light of a happy eye, live with the grace
of all that in the mind is feckless, free and
naturally to be desired. Now the sea which holds them

is moody, lapping their glossy sides, as if feeling
for some slightest flaw but fails completely.
Today no race. Then the wind comes again. The yachts

move, jockeying for a start, the signal is set and they
are off. Now the waves strike at them but they are too
well made, they slip through, though they take in canvas.

Arms with hands grasping seek to clutch at the prows.
Bodies thrown recklessly in the way are cut aside.
It is a sea of faces about them in agony, in despair

until the horror of the race dawns staggering the mind,
the whole sea become an entanglement of watery bodies
lost to the world bearing what they cannot hold. Broken,

beaten, desolate, reaching from the dead to be taken up
they cry out, failing, failing! their cries rising
in waves still as the skillful yachts pass over. (*1935*)

FLOWERS BY THE SEA

When over the flowery, sharp pasture's
edge, unseen, the salt ocean

lifts its form—chickory and daisies
tied, released, seem hardly flowers alone

but color and the movement—or the shape
perhaps—of restlessness, whereas

the sea is circled and sways
peacefully upon its plantlike stem (*1935*)

THE CATHOLIC BELLS

Tho' I'm no Catholic
I listen hard when the bells
in the yellow-brick tower
of their new church

ring down the leaves
ring in the frost upon them
and the death of the flowers
ring out the grackle

toward the south, the sky
darkened by them, ring in
the new baby of Mr. and Mrs.
Krantz which cannot

for the fat of its cheeks
open well its eyes, ring out
the parrot under its hood
jealous of the child

ring in Sunday morning
and old age which adds as it
takes away. Let them ring
only ring! over the oil

painting of a young priest
on the church wall advertising
last week's Novena to St.
Anthony, ring for the lame

young man in black with
gaunt cheeks and wearing a
Derby hat, who is hurrying
to 11 o'clock Mass (the

grapes still hanging to
the vines along the nearby
Concordia Halle like broken
teeth in the head of an

old man) Let them ring
for the eyes and ring for

the hands and ring for
the children of my friend

who no longer hears
them ring but with a smile
and in a low voice speaks
of the decisions of her

daughter and the proposals
and betrayals of her
husband's friends. O bells
ring for the ringing!

the beginning and the end
of the ringing! Ring ring
ring ring ring ring ring!
Catholic bells—! (*1935*)

THE DANCE

In Breughel's great picture, The Kermess,
the dancers go round, they go round and
around, the squeal and the blare and the
tweedle of bagpipes, a bugle and fiddles
tipping their bellies (round as the thick-
sided glasses whose wash they impound)
their hips and their bellies off balance
to turn them. Kicking and rolling about
the Fair Grounds, swinging their butts, those
shanks must be sound to bear up under such
rollicking measures, prance as they dance
in Breughel's great picture, The Kermess. (*1944*)

From PATERSON

FROM BOOK I: PREFACE

"*Rigor of beauty is the quest. But how will you find beauty when it is
locked in the mind past all remonstrance?*"

To make a start,
out of particulars
and make them general, rolling
up the sum, by defective means—

Sniffing the trees,
just another dog
among a lot of dogs. What
else is there? And to do?
The rest have run out—
after the rabbits.
Only the lame stands—on
three legs, Scratch front and back.
Deceive and eat. Dig
a musty bone

For the beginning is assuredly
the end—since we know nothing, pure
and simple, beyond
our own complexities.

                    Yet there is
no return: rolling up out of chaos,
a nine months' wonder, the city
the man, an identity—it can't be
otherwise—an
interpenetration, both ways. Rolling
up! obverse, reverse;
the drunk the sober; the illustrious
the gross; one. In ignorance
a certain knowledge and knowledge,
undispersed, its own undoing.

                    (The multiple seed,
packed tight with detail, soured,
is lost in the flux and the mind,
distracted, floats off in the same
scum)

Rolling up, rolling up heavy with
numbers.

                    It is the ignorant sun
rising in the slot of
hollow suns risen, so that never in this
world will a man live well in his body
save dying—and not know himself
dying; yet that is
the design. Renews himself

    thereby, in addition and subtraction,
walking up and down.

        and the craft,
subverted by thought, rolling up, let
him beware lest he turn to no more than
the writing of stale poems . . .
Minds like beds always made up,
              (more stony than a shore)
unwilling or unable.

        Rolling in, top up,
under, thrust and recoil, a great clatter:
lifted as air, boated, multicolored, a
wash of seas—
from mathematics to particulars—

        divided as the dew,
floating mists, to be rained down and
regathered into a river that flows
and encircles:

        shells and animalcules
generally and so to man,

        to Paterson. *(1946)*

FROM BOOK III, SECTION II

    Beautiful thing
        I saw you:

        Yes, said
the Lady of the House to my questioning.
Downstairs
      (by the laundry tubs)
        and she pointed,
smiling, to the basement, still smiling, and
went out and left me with you (alone in the house)
lying there, ill
      (I don't at all think that you
were ill)
      by the wall on your damp bed, your long
body stretched out negligently on the dirty sheet

Where is the pain?
                    (You put on a simper designed
not to reveal)

                    —the small window with two panes,
my eye level of the ground, the furnace odor .

                    Persephone
gone to hell, that hell could not keep with
the advancing season of pity.

                    —for I was overcome
by amazement and could do nothing but admire
and lean to care for you in your quietness—

who looked at me, smiling, and we remained
thus looking, each at the other . in silence .

You lethargic, waiting upon me, waiting for
the fire and I
          attendant upon you, shaken by your beauty

Shaken by your beauty .
                    Shaken.

—flat on your back, in a low bed (waiting)
under the mud plashed windows among the scrabrous
dirt of the holy sheets .

You showed me your legs, scarred (as a child)
by the whip .

Read. Bring the mind back (attendant upon
the page) to the day's heat. The page also is
the same beauty : a dry beauty of the page—
beaten by whips

          A tapestry hound
with his thread teeth drawing crimson from
the throat of the unicorn

          . . . a yelping of white hounds
—under a ceiling like that of San Lorenzo, the long
painted beams, straight across, that preceded

the domes and arches
           more primitive, square edged

. a docile queen, not bothered
to stick her tongue out at the moon, indifferent,
through loss, but .

                queenly,
   in bad luck, the luck of the stars, the black stars

              . the night of a mine

Dear heart
           It's all for you, my dove, my
                            changeling

      But you!
      —in your white lace dress
      "the dying swan"
and high-heeled slippers—tall
as you already were—
      till your head
through fruitful exaggeration
was reaching the sky and the
prickles of its ecstasy
      Beautiful Thing!
And the guys from Paterson
      beat up
the guys from Newark and told
them to stay the hell out
of their territory and then
socked you one
      across the nose
      Beautiful Thing
for good luck and emphasis
      cracking it
till I must believe that all
desired women have had each
      in the end
      a busted nose
and live afterward marked up
      Beautiful Thing
      for memory's sake
to be credible in their deeds

Then back to the party!
    and they maled
and femaled you jealously
    Beautiful Thing
as if to discover whence and
    by what miracle
there should escape, what?
still to be possessed, out of
    what part
    Beautiful Thing
should it look?
    or be extinguished—
Three days in the same dress
    up and down .

    I can't be half gentle enough,
half tender enough
    toward you, toward you,
inarticulate, not half loving enough

BRIGHTen
        the cor
                ner
where   you   are!

        —a flame,
    black plush, a dark flame.   (*1949*)

FROM BOOK V, SECTION II

There is a woman in our town
walks rapidly, flat bellied
in worn slacks upon the street
where I saw her.
                neither short
nor tall, nor old nor young
her
    face would attract no

adolescent. Grey eyes looked
straight before her.
            Her
                hair
was gathered simply behind the
ears under a shapeless hat.

Her
    hips were narrow, her
                legs
thin and straight. She stopped
me in my tracks—until I saw
her
    disappear in the crowd.

An inconspicuous decoration
made of sombre cloth, meant
I think to be a flower, was
pinned flat to her
        right

breast—any woman might have
done the same to
say she was a woman and warn
us of her mood. Otherwise

she was dressed in male attire,
as much as to say to hell
with you. Her
        expression was
serious, her
      feet were small.

And she was gone!

. if ever I see you again
as I have sought you
daily without success

I'll speak to you, alas
too late! ask,
What are you doing on the

streets of Paterson? a
thousand questions:
Are you married? Have you any

children? And, most important,
your NAME! which
of course she may not

give me—though
I cannot conceive it
in such a lonely and

intelligent woman

have you read anything that I have written?
It is all for you

or the birds .
or Mezz Mezzrow. . . . (*1958*)

THE HORSE SHOW

Constantly near you, I never in my entire
sixty-four years knew you so well as yesterday
or half so well. We talked. You were never
so lucid, so disengaged from all exigencies
of place and time. We talked of ourselves,
intimately, a thing never heard of between us.
How long have we waited? almost a hundred years.

You said, Unless there is some spark, some
spirit we keep within ourselves, life, a
continuing life's impossible—and it is all
we have. There is no other life, only the one.
The world of the spirits that comes afterward
is the same as our own, just like you sitting
there they come and talk to me, just the same.

They come to bother us. Why? I said. I don't
know. Perhaps to find out what we are doing.
Jealous, do you think? I don't know. I
don't know why they should want to come back.
I was reading about some men who had been
buried under a mountain, I said to her, and
one of them came back after two months,

digging himself out. It was in Switzerland,
you remember? Of course I remember. The
villagers tho't it was a ghost coming down

to complain. They were frightened. They
do come, she said, what you call
my "visions." I talk to them just as I
am talking to you. I see them plainly.

Oh if I could only read! You don't know
what adjustments I have made. All
I can do is to try to live over again
what I knew when your brother and you
were children—but I can't always succeed.
Tell me about the horse show. I have
been waiting all week to hear about it.

Mother darling, I wasn't able to get away.
Oh that's too bad. It was just a show;
they make the horses walk up and down
to judge them by their form. Oh is that
all? I tho't it was something else. Oh
they jump and run too. I wish you had been
there, I was so interested to hear about it. (*1949*)

From *ASPHODEL, THAT GREENY FLOWER: BOOK 1*

Of asphodel, that greeny flower,
     like a buttercup
          upon its branching stem—
save that it's green and wooden—
     I come, my sweet,
          to sing to you.
We lived long together
     a life filled,
          if you will,
with flowers. So that
     I was cheered
          when I came first to know
that there were flowers also
     in hell.
          Today
I'm filled with the fading memory of those flowers
     that we both loved,
          even to this poor
colorless thing—
     I saw it

when I was a child—
little prized among the living
        but the dead see,
                asking among themselves:
What do I remember
        that was shaped
                as this thing is shaped?
while our eyes fill
        with tears.
                Of love, abiding love
it will be telling
        though too weak a wash of crimson
                colors it
to make it wholly credible.
        There is something
                something urgent
I have to say to you
        and you alone
                but it must wait
while I drink in
        the joy of your approach,
                perhaps for the last time.
And so
        with fear in my heart
                I drag it out
and keep on talking
        for I dare not stop.
                Listen while I talk on
against time.
        It will not be
                for long.
I have forgot .
        and yet I see clearly enough
                something
central to the sky
        which ranges round it.
                An odor
springs from it!
        A sweetest odor!
                Honeysuckle! And now
there comes the buzzing of a bee!
        and a whole flood
                of sister memories!

Only give me time,
        time to recall them
                before I shall speak out.
Give me time,
        time.
When I was a boy
        I kept a book
                to which, from time
to time,
        I added pressed flowers
                until, after a time,
I had a good collection.
        The asphodel,
                forebodingly,
among them.
        I bring you,
                reawakened,
a memory of those flowers.
        They were sweet
                when I pressed them
and retained
        something of their sweetness
                a long time.
It is a curious odor,
        a moral odor,
                that brings me
near to you.
        The color
                was the first to go.
There had come to me
        a challenge,
                your dear self,
mortal as I was,
        the lily's throat
                to the hummingbird!
Endless wealth,
        I thought,
                held out its arms to me.
A thousand tropics
        in an apple blossom.
                The generous earth itself
gave us lief.
        The whole world

became my garden!
But the sea
which no one tends
is also a garden
when the sun strikes it
and the waves
are wakened.
I have seen it
and so have you
when it puts all flowers
to shame.
Too, there are the starfish
stiffened by the sun
and other sea wrack
and weeds. We knew that
along with the rest of it
for we were born by the sea,
knew its rose hedges
to the very water's brink
There the pink mallow grows
and in their season
strawberries
and there, later,
we went to gather
the wild plum.
I cannot say
that I have gone to hell
for your love
but often
found myself there
in your pursuit.
I do not like it
and wanted to be
in heaven. Hear me out.
Do not turn away.

I have learned much in my life
from books
and out of them
about love.
Death
is not the end of it.
There is a hierarchy

which can be attained,
        I think,
in its service.
    Its guerdon
        is a fairy flower;
a cat of twenty lives.
    If no one came to try it
        the world
would be the loser.
    It has been
        for you and me
as one who watches a storm
    come in over the water.
        We have stood
from year to year
    before the spectacle of our lives
        with joined hands.
The storm unfolds.
    Lightning
        plays about the edges of the clouds.
The sky to the north
    is placid,
        blue in the afterglow
as the storm piles up.
    It is a flower
        that will soon reach
the apex of its bloom.
    We danced,
        in our minds,
and read a book together.
    You remember?
        It was a serious book.
And so books
    entered our lives.
The sea! The sea!
    Always
        when I think of the sea
there comes to mind
    the *Iliad*
        and Helen's public fault
that bred it.
    Were it not for that
        there would have been

no poem but the world
      if we had remembered,
           those crimson petals
spilled among the stones,
      would have called it simply
           murder.
The sexual orchid that bloomed then
      sending so many
           disinterested
men to their graves
      has left its memory
           to a race of fools
or heroes
      if silence is a virtue.
           The sea alone
with its multiplicity
      holds any hope.
           The storm
has proven abortive
      but we remain
           after the thoughts it roused
to
      re-cement our lives.
           It is the mind
the mind
      that must be cured
           short of death's
intervention,
      and the will becomes again
           a garden. The poem
is complex and the place made
      in our lives
           for the poem.
Silence can be complex too,
      but you do not get far
           with silence.
Begin again.
      It is like Homer's
           catalogue of ships:
it fills up the time.
      I speak in figures,
           well enough, the dresses
you wear are figures also,

we could not meet
            otherwise. When I speak
of flowers
        it is to recall
            that at one time
we were young.
        All women are not Helen,
            I know that,
but have Helen in their hearts.
        My sweet,
            you have it also, therefore
I love you
        and could not love you otherwise.
            Imagine you saw
a field made up of women
        all silver-white.
            What should you do
but love them?
        The storm bursts
            or fades! it is not
the end of the world.
        Love is something else,
            or so I thought it,
a garden which expands
        though I knew you as a woman
            and never thought otherwise,
until the whole sea
        has been taken up
            and all its gardens.
It was the love of love,
        the love that swallows up all else,
            a grateful love,
a love of nature, of people,
        animals,
            a love engendering
gentleness and goodness
        that moved me
            and *that* I saw in you.
I should have known,
        though I did not,
            that the lily-of-the-valley
is a flower makes many ill
        who whiff it.

We had our children,
rivals in the general onslaught.
I put them aside
though I cared for them
as well as any man
could care for his children
according to my lights.
You understand
I had to meet you
after the event
and have still to meet you.
Love
to which you too shall bow
along with me—
a flower
a weakest flower
shall be our trust
and not because
we are too feeble
to do otherwise
but because
at the height of my power
I risked what I had to do,
therefore to prove
that we love each other
while my very bones sweated
that I could not cry to you
in the act.
Of asphodel, that greeny flower,
I come, my sweet,
to sing to you!
My heart rouses
thinking to bring you news
of something
that concerns you
and concerns many men. Look at
what passes for the new.
You will not find it there but in
despised poems.
It is difficult
to get the news from poems
yet men die miserably every day
for lack

of what is found there.
        Hear me out
                for I too am concerned
and every man
                who wants to die in peace in his bed
                        besides.   (*1955*)

Ezra Pound
(1885–   )

THE TREE

I stood still and was a tree amid the wood,
Knowing the truth of things unseen before;
Of Daphne and the laurel bow
And that god-feasting couple old
That grew elm-oak amid the wold.
'Twas not until the gods had been
Kindly entreated, and been brought within
Unto the hearth of their heart's home
That they might do this wonder thing;
Nathless I have been a tree amid the wood
And many a new thing understood
That was rank folly to my head before.   *(1908)*

SESTINA: ALTAFORTE   𝒳

LOQUITUR: *En* Bertrans de Born. Dante Alighieri put this man in hell for
that he was a stirrer up of strife. Eccovi! Judge ye! Have I dug him up
again? The scene is at his castle, Altaforte. "Papiols" is his jongleur. "The
Leopard," the *device* of Richard Cœur de Lion.

1

Damn it all! all this our South stinks peace.
You whoreson dog, Papiols, come! Let's to music!
I have no life save when the swords clash.
But ah! when I see the standards gold, vair, purple, opposing
And the broad fields beneath them turn crimson,
Then howl I my heart nigh mad with rejoicing.

2

In hot summer have I great rejoicing
When the tempests kill the earth's foul peace,
And the lightnings from black heav'n flash crimson,
And the fierce thunders roar me their music

II-179

And the winds shriek through the clouds mad, opposing,
And through all the riven skies God's swords clash.

3

Hell grant soon we hear again the swords clash!
And the shrill neighs of destriers in battle rejoicing,
Spiked breast to spiked breast opposing!
Better one hour's stour than a year's peace
With fat boards, bawds, wine and frail music!
Bah! there's no wine like the blood's crimson!

4

And I love to see the sun rise blood-crimson.
And I watch his spears through the dark clash
And it fills all my heart with rejoicing
And pries wide my mouth with fast music
When I see him so scorn and defy peace,
His lone might 'gainst all darkness opposing.

5

The man who fears war and squats opposing
My words for stour, hath no blood of crimson
But is fit only to rot in womanish peace
Far from where worth's won and the swords clash
For the death of such sluts I go rejoicing;
Yea, I fill all the air with my music.

6

Papiols, Papiols, to the music!
There's no sound like to swords swords opposing,
No cry like the battle's rejoicing
When our elbows and swords drip the crimson
And our charges 'gainst "The Leopard's" rush clash.
May God damn for ever all who cry "Peace!"

7

And let the music of the swords make them crimson!
Hell grant soon we hear again the swords clash!
Hell blot black for alway the thought "Peace!" (*1909*)

BALLAD OF THE GOODLY FERE

Simon Zelotes speaketh it somewhile after the Crucifixion.

Ha' we lost the goodliest fere o' all
For the priests and the gallows tree?

Aye lover he was of brawny men,
O' ships and the open sea.

When they came wi' a host to take Our Man
His smile was good to see;
"First let these go!" quo' our Goodly Fere,
"Or I'll see ye damned," says he.

Aye, he sent us out through the crossed high spears,
And the scorn of his laugh rang free;
"Why took ye not me when I walked about
Alone in the town?" says he.

Oh, we drunk his "Hale" in the good red wine
When we last made company;
No capon priest was the Goodly Fere
But a man o' men was he.

I ha' seen him drive a hundred men
Wi' a bundle o' cords swung free,
That they took the high and holy house
For their pawn and treasury.

They'll no' get him a' in a book I think,
Though they write it cunningly;
No mouse of the scrolls was the Goodly Fere
But aye loved the open sea.

If they think they ha' snared our Goodly Fere
They are fools to the last degree.
"I'll go to the feast," quo' our Goodly Fere,
"Though I go to the gallows tree."

"Ye ha' seen me heal the lame and blind,
And wake the dead," says he;
"Ye shall see one thing to master all:
'Tis how a brave man dies on the tree."

A son of God was the Goodly Fere
That bade us his brothers be.
I ha' seen him cow a thousand men.
I have seen him upon the tree.

He cried no cry when they drave the nails
And the blood gushed hot and free;

The hounds of the crimson sky gave tongue
But never a cry cried he.

I ha' seen him cow a thousand men
On the hills o' Galilee;
They whined as he walked out calm between,
Wi' his eyes like the grey o' the sea,

Like the sea that brooks no voyaging
With the winds unleashed and free,
Like the sea that he cowed at Genseret
Wi' twey words spoke' suddently.

A master of men was the Goodly Fere,
A mate of the wind and sea;
If they think they ha' slain our Goodly Fere
They are fools eternally.

I ha' seen him eat o' the honey-comb
Sin' they nailed him to the tree. *(1909)*

AN IMMORALITY

Sing we for love and idleness,
Naught else is worth the having.

Though I have been in many a land,
There is naught else in living.

And I would rather have my sweet,
Though rose-leaves die of grieving,

Than do high deeds in Hungary
To pass all men's believing. *(1912)*

A VIRGINAL

No, no! Go from me. I have left her lately.
I will not spoil my sheath with lesser brightness,
For my surrounding air hath a new lightness;
Slight are her arms, yet they have bound me straitly
And left me cloaked as with a gauze of æther;
As with sweet leaves; as with subtle clearness.

Oh, I have picked up magic in her nearness
To sheathe me half in half the things that sheathe her.
No, no! Go from me. I have still the flavour,
Soft as spring wind that's come from birchen bowers.
Green come the shoots, aye April in the branches,
As winter's wounds with her sleight hand she staunches,
Hath of the trees a likeness of the savour:
As white their bark, so white this lady's hours. *(1912)*

THE ALCHEMIST

CHANT FOR THE TRANSMUTATION OF METALS

Saîl of Claustra, Aelis, Azalais,
As you move among the bright trees;
As your voices, under the larches of Paradise
Make a clear sound,
Saîl of Claustra, Aelis, Azalais,
Raimona, Tibors, Berangèrë,
'Neath the dark gleam of the sky;
Under night, the peacock-throated,
Bring the saffron-coloured shell,
Bring the red gold of the maple,
Bring the light of the birch tree in autumn
Mirals, Cembelins, Audiarda,
     Remember this fire.
Elain, Tireis, Alcmena
'Mid the silver rustling of wheat,
Agradiva, Anhes, Ardenca,
From the plum-coloured lake, in stillness,
From the molten dyes of the water
Bring the burnished nature of fire;
Briseis, Lianor, Loica,
From the wide earth and the olive,
From the poplars weeping their amber,
By the bright flame of the fishing torch
     Remember this fire.
Midonz, with the gold of the sun, the leaf of the poplar, by the light of
  the amber,
Midonz, daughter of the sun, shaft of the tree, silver of the leaf, light
  of the yellow of the amber,
Midonz, gift of the God, gift of the light, gift of the amber of the sun,
     Give light to the metal.

Anhes of Rocacoart, Ardenca, Aemelis,
From the power of grass,
From the white, alive in the seed,
From the heat of the bud,
From the copper of the leaf in autumn,
From the bronze of the maple, from the sap in the bough;
Lianor, Ioanna, Loica,
By the stir of the fin,
By the trout asleep in the gray-green of water;
Vanna, Mandetta, Viera, Alodetta, Picarda, Manuela
From the red gleam of copper,
Ysaut, Ydone, slight rustling of leaves,
Vierna, Jocelynn, daring of spirits,
By the mirror of burnished copper,
O Queen of Cypress,
Out of Erebus, the flat-lying breadth,
Breath that is stretched out beneath the world:
Out of Erebus, out of the flat waste of air, lying beneath the world;
Out of brown leaf-brown colourless
Bring the imperceptible cool.
Elain, Tireis, Alcmena,
Quiet this metal!
Let the manes put off their terror, let them put off their aqueous bodies
with fire.
Let them assume the milk-white bodies of agate.
Let them draw together the bones of the metal.

Selvaggia, Guiscarda, Mandetta,
Rain flakes of gold on the water
Azure and flaking silver of water,
Alcyon, Phætona, Alcmena,
Pallor of silver, pale lustre of Latona,
By these, from the malevolence of the dew
Guard this alembic.
Elain, Tireis, Allodetta
Quiet this metal. (*1912?, 1920*)

PORTRAIT D'UNE FEMME

Your mind and you are our Sargasso Sea,
London has swept about you this score years
And bright ships left you this or that in fee:
Ideas, old gossip, oddments of all things,
Strange spars of knowledge and dimmed wares of price.

Great minds have sought you—lacking someone else.
You have been second always. Tragical?
No. You preferred it to the usual thing:
One dull man, dulling and uxorious,
One average mind—with one thought less, each year.
Oh, you are patient, I have seen you sit
Hours, where something might have floated up.
And now you pay one. Yes, you richly pay.
You are a person of some interest, one comes to you
And takes strange gain away:
Trophies fished up; some curious suggestion;
Fact that leads nowhere; and a tale or two,
Pregnant with mandrakes, or with something else
That might prove useful and yet never proves,
That never fits a corner or shows use,
Or finds its hour upon the loom of days:
The tarnished, gaudy, wonderful old work;
Idols and ambergris and rare inlays,
These are your riches, your great store; and yet
For all this sea-hoard of deciduous things,
Strange woods half sodden, and new brighter stuff:
In the slow float of differing light and deep,
No! there is nothing! In the whole and all,
Nothing that's quite your own.
     Yet this is you. *(1912)*

THE RETURN

See, they return; ah, see the tentative
Movements, and the slow feet,
The trouble in the pace and the uncertain
Wavering!

See, they return, one, and by one,
With fear, as half-awakened;
As if the snow should hesitate
And murmur in the wind,
    and half turn back;
These were the "Wing'd-with-Awe,"
    Inviolable,

Gods of the wingèd shoe!
With them the silver hounds,
    sniffing the trace of air!

Haie! Haie!
                These were the swift to harry;
            These the keen-scented;
            These were the souls of blood.

        Slow on the leash,
                pallid the leash-men! (*1912*)

THE STUDY IN ÆSTHETICS

The very small children in patched clothing,
Being smitten with an unusual wisdom,
Stopped in their play as she passed them
And cried up from their cobbles:

        Guarda! Ahi, guarda! ch' è be'a!

But three years after this
I heard the young Dante, whose last name I do not know—
For there are, in Sirmione, twenty-eight young Dantes and thirty-four
    Catulli;
And there had been a great catch of sardines,
And his elders
Were packing them in the great wooden boxes
For the market in Brescia, and he
Leapt about, snatching at the bright fish
And getting in both of their ways;
And in vain they commanded him to *sta fermo!*
And when they would not let him arrange
The fish in the boxes
He stroked those which were already arranged,
Murmuring for his own satisfaction
This identical phrase:

        Ch' è be'a.

And at this I was mildly abashed. (*1916*)

APRIL   X

Nympharum membra disjecta

    Three spirits came to me
    And drew me apart

To where the olive boughs *plant world again*
Lay stripped upon the ground:
Pale carnage beneath bright mist. *(1916)*

THE COMING OF WAR: ACTAEON ✗

An image of Lethe,
    and the fields
Full of faint light
    but golden,
Gray cliffs,
    and beneath them
A sea
Harsher than granite,
    unstill, never ceasing;
High forms
    with the movement of gods,
Perilous aspect;
    And one said:
"This is Actaeon."
    Actaeon of golden greaves!
Over fair meadows,
Over the cool face of that field,
Unstill, ever moving
Hosts of an ancient people,
The silent cortège. *(1916)*

From HOMAGE TO SEXTUS PROPERTIUS

1

Shades of Callimachus, Coan ghosts of Philetas
It is in your grove I would walk,
I who come first from the clear font
Bringing the Grecian orgies into Italy,
                and the dance into Italy.
Who hath taught you so subtle a measure,
        in what hall have you heard it;
What foot beat out your time-bar,
      what water has mellowed your whistles?

Out-weariers of Apollo will, as we know, continue their Martian gen-
    eralities,
    We have kept our erasers in order.

A new-fangled chariot follows the flower-hung horses;
A young Muse with young loves clustered about her
             ascends with me into the æther, . . .
And there is no high-road to the Muses.

Annalists will continue to record Roman reputations,
Celebrities from the Trans-Caucasus will belaud Roman celebrities
And expound the distentions of Empire,
But for something to read in normal circumstances?
For a few pages brought down from the forked hill unsullied?
I ask a wreath which will not crush my head.
             And there is no hurry about it;
I shall have, doubtless, a boom after my funeral,
Seeing that long standing increases all things
                 regardless of quality.

And who would have known the towers
             pulled down by a deal-wood horse;
Or of Achilles withstaying waters by Simois
Or of Hector spattering wheel-rims,
Or of Polydmantus, by Scamander, or Helenus and Deiphoibos?
Their door-yards would scarcely know them, or Paris.
Small talk O Ilion, and O Troad
             twice taken by Oetian gods,
If Homer had not stated your case!

And I also among the later nephews of this city
             shall have my dog's day,
With no stone upon my contemptible sepulchre;
My vote coming from the temple of Phoebus in Lycia, at Patara,
And in the mean time my songs will travel,
And the devirginated young ladies will enjoy them
             when they have got over the strangeness,
For Orpheus tamed the wild beasts—
             and held up the Threician river;
And Citharaon shook up the rocks by Thebes
     and danced them into a bulwark at his pleasure,
And you, O Polyphemus? Did harsh Galatea almost
Turn to your dripping horses, because of a tune, under Aetna?
We must look into the matter.
Bacchus and Apollo in favour of it,
There will be a crowd of young women doing homage to my palaver,
Though my house is not propped up by Taenarian columns from
    Laconia (associated with Neptune and Cerberus),

Though it is not stretched upon gilded beams;
My orchards do not lie level and wide
                as the forests of Phaecia,
                the luxurious and Ionian,
Nor are my caverns stuffed stiff with a Marcian vintage,
My cellar does not date from Numa Pompilius,
Nor bristle with wine jars,
Nor is it equipped with a frigidaire patent;
Yet the companions of the Muses
                will keep their collective nose in my books,
And weary with historical data, they will turn to my dance tune.

Happy who are mentioned in my pamphlets,
                the songs shall be a fine tomb-stone over their beauty.
                But against this?
Neither expensive pyramids scraping the stars in their route,
Nor houses modelled upon that of Jove in East Elis,
Nor the monumental effigies of Mausolus,
                are a complete elucidation of death.

Flame burns, rain sinks into the cracks
And they all go to rack ruin beneath the thud of the years.
Stands genius a deathless adornment,
                a name not to be worn out with the years. *(1919)*

HUGH SELWYN MAUBERLEY

[PART I]

E. P. ODE POUR L'ELECTION DE SON SEPULCHRE

For three years, out of key with his time,
He strove to resuscitate the dead art
Of poetry; to maintain "the sublime"
In the old sense. Wrong from the start—

No, hardly, but seeing he had been born
In a half savage country, out of date;
Bent resolutely on wringing lilies from the acorn;
Capaneus; trout for factitious bait;

Ἴδμεν γάρ τοι πάνθ', ὅσ' ἐνὶ Τροίῃ
Caught in the unstopped ear;
Giving the rocks small lee-way
The chopped seas held him, therefore, that year.

His true Penelope was Flaubert,
He fished by obstinate isles;
Observed the elegance of Circe's hair
Rather than the mottoes on sun-dials.

Unaffected by "the march of events,"
He passed from men's memory in *l'an trentiesme
De son eage*; the case presents
No adjunct to the Muses' diadem.

2

The age demanded an image
Of its accelerated grimace,
Something for the modern stage,
Not, at any rate, an Attic grace;

Not, not certainly, the obscure reveries
Of the inward gaze;
Better mendacities
Than the classics in paraphrase!

The "age demanded" chiefly a mould in plaster,
Made with no loss of time,
A prose kinema, not, not assuredly, alabaster
Or the "sculpture" of rhyme.

3

The tea-rose tea-gown, etc.
Supplants the mousseline of Cos,
The pianola "replaces"
Sappho's barbitos.

Christ follows Dionysus,
Phallic and ambrosial
Made way for macerations;
Caliban casts out Ariel.

All things are a flowing,
Sage Heracleitus says;
But a tawdry cheapness
Shall outlast our days.

Even the Christian beauty
Defects—after Samothrace;

We see τὸ καλόν *(the beautiful)*
Decreed in the market place.

Faun's flesh is not to us, *we don't put our gods in animals like Greeks*
Nor the saint's vision,
We have the press for wafer; *news paper*
Franchise for circumcision.

All men, in law, are equals.
Free of Pisistratus, *tyrant*
We choose a knave or an eunuch *we elect out... now instead of — them forcing themselves on us.*
To rule over us.

O bright Apollo,
τίν' ἄνδρα, τιν' ἥρωα, τίνα θεόν, *(what man, what hero, what god)*
What god, man, or hero
Shall I place a tin wreath upon!

(3 & 4 share same anger)

4

These fought in any case,
and some believing, *angry reaction to war*
         pro domo, in any case . . .

Some quick to arm,
some for adventure,
some from fear of weakness,
some from fear of censure,
some for love of slaughter, in imagination,
learning later . . .
some in fear, learning love of slaughter;

Died some, pro patria,
         non "dulce" non "et decor" . . .
walked eye-deep in hell
believing in old men's lies, then unbelieving
came home, home to a lie,
home to many deceits,
home to old lies and new infamy;
usury age-old and age-thick
and liars in public places.

Daring as never before, wastage as never before.
Young blood and high blood,
fair cheeks, and fine bodies;

fortitude as never before

frankness as never before,
disillusions as never told in the old days,
hysterias, trench confessions,
laughter out of dead bellies.

5

There died a myriad,
And of the best, among them,
For an old bitch gone in the teeth,
For a botched civilization,

Charm, smiling at the good mouth,
Quick eyes gone under earth's lid,

For two gross of broken statues,
For a few thousand battered books.

YEUX GLAUQUES

Gladstone was still respected,
When John Ruskin produced
"King's Treasuries"; Swinburne
And Rossetti still abused.

Fœtid Buchanan lifted up his voice
When that faun's head of hers
Became a pastime for
Painters and adulterers.

The Burne-Jones cartons
Have preserved her eyes;
Still, at the Tate, they teach
Cophetua to rhapsodize;

Thin like brook-water,
With a vacant gaze.
The English Rubaiyat was still-born
In those days.

The thin, clear gaze, the same
Still darts out faunlike from the half-ruin'd face,

Questing and passive. . . .
"Ah, poor Jenny's case" . . .

Bewildered that a world
Shows no surprise
At her last maquero's
Adulteries.

"SIENA MI FE'; DISFECEMI MAREMMA"

Among the pickled fœtuses and bottled bones,
Engaged in perfecting the catalogue,
I found the last scion of the
Senatorial families of Strasbourg, Monsieur Verog.

For two hours he talked of Gallifet;
Of Dowson; of the Rhymers' Club;
Told me how Johnson (Lionel) died
By falling from a high stool in a pub . .

But showed no trace of alcohol
At the autopsy, privately performed—
Tissue preserved—the pure mind
Arose toward Newman as the whiskey warmed.

Dowson found harlots cheaper than hotels;
Headlam for uplift; Image impartially imbued
With raptures for Bacchus, Terpsichore and the Church.
So spoke the author of "The Dorian Mood,"

M. Verog, out of step with the decade,
Detached from his contemporaries,
Neglected by the young,
Because of these reveries.

BRENNBAUM

The skylike limpid eyes,
The circular infant's face,
The stiffness from spats to collar
Never relaxing into grace;

The heavy memories of Horeb, Sinai and the forty years,
Showed only when the daylight fell

Level across the face
Of Brennbaum "The Impeccable."

MR. NIXON

— voice of corruption

In the cream gilded cabin of his steam yacht
Mr. Nixon advised me kindly, to advance with fewer
Dangers of delay. "Consider
       "Carefully the reviewer.

practical advice on how to cheat etc.

"I was as poor as you are;
"When I began I got, of course,
"Advance on royalties, fifty at first," said Mr. Nixon,
"Follow me, and take a column,
"Even if you have to work free.

"Butter reviewers. From fifty to three hundred
"I rose in eighteen months;
"The hardest nut I had to crack
"Was Dr. Dundas.

"I never mentioned a man but with the view
"Of selling my own works.
"The tip's a good one, as for literature
"It gives no man a sinecure.

"And no one knows, at sight, a masterpiece.
"And give up verse, my boy,
"There's nothing in it."

*   *   *

Likewise a friend of Bloughram's once advised me:
Don't kick against the pricks,
Accept opinion. The "Nineties" tried your game
And died, there's nothing in it.

10

life of the recluse artist

Beneath the sagging roof
The stylist has taken shelter,
Unpaid, uncelebrated,
At last from the world's welter

Nature receives him;
With a placid and uneducated mistress

He exercises his talents
And the soil meets his distress.

The haven from sophistications and contentions
Leaks through its thatch;
He offers succulent cooking;
The door has a creaking latch.

11

"Conservatrix of Milésien" *Women who are conservers of milesien trad.*
Habits of mind and feeling,
Possibly. But in Ealing
With the most bank-clerkly of Englishmen?

No, "Milesian" is an exaggeration.
No instinct has survived in her
Older than those her grandmother
Told her would fit her station.

12

"Daphne with her thighs in bark
"Stretches toward me her leafy hands,"—
Subjectively. In the stuffed-satin drawing-room
I await The Lady Valentine's commands,

Knowing my coat has never been
Of precisely the fashion
To stimulate, in her,
A durable passion;

Doubtful, somewhat, of the value
Of well-gowned approbation
Of literary effort,
But never of The Lady Valentine's vocation:

Poetry, her border of ideas,
The edge, uncertain, but a means of blending
With other strata
Where the lower and higher have ending;

A hook to catch the Lady Jane's attention,
A modulation toward the theatre,

Also, in the case of revolution,
A possible friend and comforter.

                    *   *   *

Conduct, on the other hand, the soul
"Which the highest cultures have nourished"
To Fleet St. where
Dr. Johnson flourished;

Beside this thoroughfare
The sale of half-hose has
Long since superseded the cultivation
Of Pierian roses.

                    ENVOI (1919)

Go, dumb-born book,
Tell her that sang me once that song of Lawes:
Hadst thou but song
As thou hast subjects known,
Then were there cause in thee that should condone
Even my faults that heavy upon me lie,
And build her glories their longevity.

Tell her that sheds
Such treasure in the air,
Recking naught else but that her graces give
Life to the moment,
I would bid them live
As roses might, in magic amber laid,
Red overwrought with orange and all made
One substance and one colour
Braving time.

Tell her that goes
With song upon her lips
But sings not out the song, nor knows
The maker of it, some other mouth
May be as fair as hers,
Might, in new ages, gain her worshippers,
When our two dusts with Waller's shall be laid,
Siftings on siftings in oblivion,
Till change hath broken down
All things save Beauty alone.   (1920)

MAUBERLEY (1920) [PART II]

"Vacuos exercet aera morsus."

Turned from the "eau-forte
Par Jaquemart"
To the strait head
Of Messalina:

"His true Penelope
Was Flaubert,"
And his tool
The engraver's.

Firmness,
Not the full smile,
His art, but an art
In profile;

Colourless
Pier Francesca,
Pisanello lacking the skill
To forge Achaia.

2

"Qu'est ce qu'ils savent de l'amour, et qu'est ce qu'ils peuvent comprendre?
S'ils ne comprennent pas la poésie, s'ils ne sentent pas la musique, qu'est
ce qu'ils peuvent comprendre de cette passion en comparaison avec laquelle
la rose est grossière et la parfum des violettes un tonnerre?"—Caid Ali.

For three years, diabolus in the scale,
He drank ambrosia,
All passes, ANANGKE prevails,
Came end, at last, to that Arcadia.

He had moved amid her phantasmagoria,
Amid her galaxies,
NUKTOS AGALMA

      *   *   *

Drifted . . . drifted precipitate,
Asking time to be rid of . . .
Of his bewilderment; to designate
His new found orchid. . . .

To be certain . . . certain . . .
(Amid ærial flowers) . . . time for arrangements—
Drifted on
To the final estrangement;

Unable in the supervening blankness
To sift TO AGATHON from the chaff
Until he found his sieve . . .
Ultimately, his seismograph:

—Given that is his "fundamental passion,"
This urge to convey the relation
Of eye-lid and cheek-bone
By verbal manifestations;

To present the series
Of curious heads in medallion—

He had passed, inconscient, full gaze,
The wide-banded irides
And botticellian sprays implied
In their diastasis;

Which anæsthesis, noted a year late,
And weighed, revealed his great affect,
(Orchid), mandate
Of Eros, a retrospect.

*   *   *

Mouths biting empty air,
The still stone dogs,
Caught in metamorphosis, were
Left him as epilogues.

"THE AGE DEMANDED"

Vide Poem 2, Page 190

For this agility chance found
Him of all men, unfit
As the red-beaked steeds of
The Cytheræan for a chain bit.

The glow of porcelain
Brought no reforming sense

To his perception
Of the social inconsequence.

Thus, if her colour
Came against his gaze,
Tempered as if
It were through a perfect glaze

He made no immediate application
Of this to relation of the state
To the individual, the month was more temperate
Because this beauty had been.

> The coral isle, the lion-coloured sand
> Burst in upon the porcelain revery:
> Impetuous troubling
> Of his imagery.

Mildness, amid the neo-Nietzschean clatter,
His sense of graduations,
Quite out of place amid
Resistance to current exacerbations,

Invitation, mere invitation to perceptivity
Gradually led him to the isolation
Which these presents place
Under a more tolerant, perhaps, examination.

By constant elimination
The manifest universe
Yielded an armour
Against utter consternation,

A Minoan undulation,
Seen, we admit, amid ambrosial circumstances
Strengthened him against
The discouraging doctrine of chances,

And his desire for survival,
Faint in the most strenuous moods,
Became an Olympian *apathein*
In the presence of selected perceptions.

A pale gold, in the aforesaid pattern,
The unexpected palms
Destroying, certainly, the artist's urge,
Left him delighted with the imaginary
Audition of the phantasmal sea-surge,

Incapable of the least utterance or composition,
Emendation, conservation of the "better tradition,"
Refinement of medium, elimination of superfluities,
August attraction or concentration.

Nothing, in brief, but maudlin confession,
Irresponse to human aggression,
Amid the precipitation, down-float
Of insubstantial manna,
Lifting the faint susurrus
Of his subjective hosannah.

Ultimate affronts to
Human redundancies;

Non-esteem of self-styled "his betters"
Leading, as he well knew,
To his final
Exclusion from the world of letters.

4

Scattered Moluccas
Not knowing, day to day,
The first day's end, in the next noon;
The placid water
Unbroken by the Simoon;

Thick foliage
Placid beneath warm suns,
Tawn fore-shores
Washed in the cobalt of oblivions;

Or through dawn-mist
The grey and rose
Of the juridical
Flamingoes;

A consciousness disjunct,
Being but this overblotted
Series
Of intermittences;

Coracle of Pacific voyages,
The unforecasted beach;
Then on an oar
Read this:

"I was
"And I no more exist;
"Here drifted
"An hedonist."

MEDALLION

Luini in porcelain!
The grand piano
Utters a profane
Protest with her clear soprano.

The sleek head emerges
From the gold-yellow frock
As Anadyomene in the opening
Pages of Reinach.

Honey-red, closing the face-oval,
A basket-work of braids which seem as if they were
Spun in King Minos' hall
From metal, or intractable amber;

The face-oval beneath the glaze,
Bright in its suave bounding-line, as,
Beneath half-watt rays,
The eyes turn topaz. (*1920*)

CANTO I

And then went down to the ship,
Set keel to breakers, forth on the godly sea, and
We set up mast and sail on that swart ship,
Bore sheep aboard her, and our bodies also
Heavy with weeping, and winds from sternward

Bore us out onward with bellying canvas,
Circe's this craft, the trim-coifed goddess.
Then sat we amidships, wind jamming the tiller,
Thus with stretched sail, we went over sea till day's end.
Sun to his slumber, shadows o'er all the ocean,
Came we then to the bounds of deepest water,
To the Kimmerian lands, and peopled cities
Covered with close-webbed mist, unpierced ever
With glitter of sun-rays
Nor with stars stretched, nor looking back from heaven
Swartest night stretched over wretched men there.
The ocean flowing backward, came we then to the place
Aforesaid by Circe.
Here did they rites, Perimedes and Eurylochus,
And drawing sword from my hip
I dug the ell-square pitkin;
Poured we libations unto each the dead,
First mead and then sweet wine, water mixed with white flour.
Then prayed I many a prayer to the sickly death's-heads;
As set in Ithaca, sterile bulls of the best
For sacrifice, heaping the pyre with goods,
A sheep to Tiresias only, black and a bell-sheep.
Dark blood flowed in the fosse,
Souls out of Erebus, cadaverous dead, of brides
Of youths and of the old who had borne much;
Souls stained with recent tears, girls tender,
Men many, mauled with bronze lance heads,
Battle spoil, bearing yet dreory arms,
These many crowded about me; with shouting,
Pallor upon me, cried to my men for more beasts;
Slaughtered the herds, sheep slain of bronze;
Poured ointment, cried to the gods,
To Pluto the strong, and praised Proserpine;
Unsheathed the narrow sword,
I sat to keep off the impetuous impotent dead,
Till I should hear Tiresias.
But first Elpenor came, our friend Elpenor,
Unburied, cast on the wide earth,
Limbs that we left in the house of Circe,
Unwept, unwrapped in sepulchre, since toils urged other.
Pitiful spirit. And I cried in hurried speech:
"Elpenor, how art thou come to this dark coast?
"Cam'st thou afoot, outstripping seamen?"

And he in heavy speech:
"Ill fate and abundant wine. I slept in Circe's ingle.
"Going down the long ladder unguarded,
"I fell against the buttress,
"Shattered the nape-nerve, the soul sought Avernus.
"But thou, O King, I bid remember me, unwept, unburied,
"Heap up mine arms, be tomb by sea-bord, and inscribed:
"*A man of no fortune, and with a name to come.*
"And set my oar up, that I swung mid fellows."

And Anticlea came, whom I beat off, and then Tiresias Theban,
Holding his golden wand, knew me, and spoke first:
"A second time? why? man of ill star,
"Facing the sunless dead and this joyless region?
"Stand from the fosse, leave me my bloody bever
"For soothsay."
          And I stepped back,
And he strong with the blood, said then: "Odysseus
"Shalt return through spiteful Neptune, over dark seas,
"Lose all companions." Then Anticlea came.
Lie quiet Divus. I mean, that is Andreas Divus,
In officina Wecheli, 1538, out of Homer.
And he sailed, by Sirens and thence outward and away
And unto Circe.
          Venerandam,
In the Cretan's phrase, with the golden crown, Aphrodite,
Cypri munimenta sortita est, mirthful, oricalchi, with golden
Girdles and breast bands, thou with dark eyelids
Bearing the golden bough of Argicida. So that: *(1917)*

Confucius (wise leader) organizes on common sense

CANTO XIII

Kung walked
          by the dynastic temple
and into the cedar grove,
          and then out by the lower river,
And with him Khieu Tchi
          and Tian the low speaking
And "we are unknown," said Kung,
"You will take up charioteering?
          Then you will become known,
"Or perhaps I should take up charioteering, or archery?

"Or the practice of public speaking?"
And Tseu-lou said, "I would put the defences in order,"
And Khieu said, "If I were lord of a province
I would put it in better order than this is."
And Tchi said, "I should prefer a small mountain temple,
"With order in the observances,
　　　　　with a suitable performance of the ritual,"
And Tian said, with his hand on the strings of his lute
The low sounds continuing
　　　　　after his hand left the strings,
And the sound went up like smoke, under the leaves,
And he looked after the sound:
　　　　　"The old swimming hole,
"And the boys flopping off the planks,
"Or sitting in the underbrush playing mandolins."
　　　　　And Kung smiled upon all of them equally.
And Thseng-sie desired to know:
　　　　　"Which had answered correctly?"
And Kung said, "They have all answered correctly,
"That is to say, each in his nature."
And Kung raised his cane against Yuan Jang,
　　　　　Yuan Jang being his elder,
For Yuan Jang sat by the roadside pretending to
　　　　　be receiving wisdom.
And Kung said
　　　　　"You old fool, come out of it,
"Get up and do something useful."
　　　　　And Kung said
"Respect a child's faculties
"From the moment it inhales the clear air,
"But a man of fifty who knows nothing
　　　　　Is worthy of no respect."
And "When the prince has gathered about him
"All the savants and artists, his riches will be fully employed."
And Kung said, and wrote on the bo leaves:
　　　　　"If a man have not order within him
"He can not spread order about him;
"And if a man have not order within him
"His family will not act with due order;
　　　　　And if the prince have not order within him
He can not put order in his dominions."
And Kung gave the words "order"
and "brotherly deference"

And said nothing of the "life after death."
And he said
      "Anyone can run to excesses,
"It is easy to shoot past the mark,
"It is hard to stand firm in the middle."

And they said: "If a man commit murder
      Should his father protect him, and hide him?"
And Kung said:
      "He should hide him."
And Kung gave his daughter to Kong-Tchang
      Although Kong-Tchang was in prison.
And he gave his niece to Nan-Young
      although Nan-Young was out of office.
And Kung said "Wang ruled with moderation,
      "In his day the State was well kept,
"And even I can remember
"A day when the historians left blanks in their writings,
"I mean for things they didn't know,
"But that time seems to be passing."
And Kung said, "Without character you will
      be unable to play on that instrument
"Or to execute the music fit for the Odes.
"The blossoms of the apricot
      blow from the east to the west,
"And I have tried to keep from falling." *(1925)*

[handwritten margin note: These weight are forms / en of right principle / lets Kung play / right music]

CANTO XLV

With *Usura*

With usura hath no man a house of good stone
each block cut smooth and well fitting
that design might cover their face,
with usura
hath no man a painted paradise on his church wall
harpes et luthes
or where virgin receiveth message
and halo projects from incision,
with usura
seeth no man Gonzaga his heirs and his concubines
no picture is made to endure nor to live with
but it is made to sell and sell quickly

with usura, sin against nature,
is thy bread ever more of stale rags
is thy bread dry as paper,
with no mountain wheat, no strong flour
with usura the line grows thick
with usura is no clear demarcation
and no man can find site for his dwelling.
Stone cutter is kept from his stone
weaver is kept from his loom
WITH USURA
wool comes not to market
sheep bringeth no gain with usura
Usura is a murrain, usura
blunteth the needle in the maid's hand
and stoppeth the spinner's cunning. Pietro Lombardo
came not by usura
Duccio came not by usura
nor Pier della Francesca; Zuan Bellin' not by usura
nor was 'La Calunnia' painted.
Came not by usura Angelico; came not Ambrogio Praedis,
Came no church of cut stone signed: *Adamo me fecit.*
Not by usura St Trophime
Not by usura Saint Hilaire,
Usura rusteth the chisel
It rusteth the craft and the craftsman
It gnaweth the thread in the loom
None learneth to weave gold in her pattern;
Azure hath a canker by usura; cramoisi is unbroidered
Emerald findeth no Memling
Usura slayeth the child in the womb
It stayeth the young man's courting
It hath brought palsey to bed, lyeth
between the young bride and her bridegroom
                              CONTRA NATURAM
They have brought whores for Eleusis
Corpses are set to banquet
at behest of usura. (*1937*)

                    CANTO XLVII

Who even dead, yet hath his mind entire!
This sound came in the dark
First must thou go the road
                    to hell

And to the bower of Ceres' daughter Proserpine,
Through overhanging dark, to see Tiresias,
Eyeless that was, a shade, that is in hell
So full of knowing that the beefy men know less than he,
Ere thou come to thy road's end.
                    Knowledge the shade of a shade,
Yet must thou sail after knowledge
Knowing less than drugged beasts. *phtheggometha
thasson*
φθεγγώμεθα θᾶσσον
          The small lamps drift in the bay
And the sea's claw gathers them.
Neptunus drinks after neap-tide.
Tamuz! Tamuz!!
The red flame going seaward.
          By this gate art thou measured.
From the long boats they have set lights in the water,
The sea's claw gathers them outward.
Scilla's dogs snarl at the cliff's base,
The white teeth gnaw in under the crag,
But in the pale night the small lamps float seaward
                    Τυ Διώνα
                    TU DIONA
Και Μοῖραι τ' Ἄδονιν
KAI MOIRAI' 'T' ADONIN
The sea is streaked red with Adonis,
The lights flicker red in small jars.
Wheat shoots rise new by the altar,
          flower from the swift seed.
Two span, two span to a woman,
Beyond that she believes not. Nothing is of any importance
To that is she bent, her intention
To that art thou called ever turning intention,
Whether by night the owl-call, whether by sap in shoot,
Never idle, by no means by no wiles intermittent
Moth is called over mountain
The bull runs blind on the sword, *naturans*
To the cave art thou called, Odysseus,
By Molü hast thou respite for a little,
By Molü art thou freed from the one bed
          that thou may'st return to another
The stars are not in her counting,
          To her they are but wandering holes.
Begin thy plowing

When the Pleiades go down to their rest,
Begin thy plowing
40 days are they under seabord,
Thus do in fields by seabord
And in valleys winding down toward the sea.
When the cranes fly high
          think of plowing.
By this gate art thou measured
Thy day is between a door and a door
Two oxen are yoked for plowing
Or six in the hill field
White bulk under olives, a score for drawing down stone,
Here the mules are gabled with slate on the hill road.
Thus was it in time.
And the small stars now fall from the olive branch,
Forked shadow falls dark on the terrace
More black than the floating martin
          that has no care for your presence,
His wing-print is black on the roof tiles
And the print is gone with his cry.
So light is thy weight on Tellus
Thy notch no deeper indented
Thy weight less than the shadow
Yet hast thou gnawed through the mountain,
          Scylla's white teeth less sharp.
Hast thou found a nest softer than cunnus
Or hast thou found better rest
Hast'ou a deeper planting, doth thy death year
Bring swifter shoot?
Hast thou entered more deeply the mountain?

The light has entered the cave. Io! Io!
The light has gone down into the cave,
Splendour on splendour!
By prong have I entered these hills:
That the grass grow from my body,
That I hear the roots speaking together,
The air is new on my leaf,
The forked boughs shake with the wind.
Is Zephyrus more light on the bough, Apeliota
more light on the almond branch?
By this door have I entered the hill.
Falleth,
Adonis falleth.

Fruit cometh after. The small lights drift out with the tide,
sea's claw has gathered them outward,
Four banners to every flower
The sea's claw draws the lamps outward.
Think thus of thy plowing
When the seven stars go down to their rest
Forty days for their rest, by seabord
And in valleys that wind down toward the sea

Καὶ Μοῖραι' τ' Ἄδονιν
KAI MOIRAI' T' ADONIN
When the almond bough puts forth its flame,
When the new shoots are brought to the altar,
Τυ Διώνα, Καὶ Μοῖραι
TU DIONA, KAI MOIRAI
Καὶ Μοῖραι' τ' Ἄδονιν
KAI MOIRAI' T' ADONIN
that hath the gift of healing,
that hath the power over wild beasts.   (*1937*)

From CANTO LXXXI

What thou lov'st well remains,
the rest is dross
What thou lov'st well shall not be reft from thee
What thou lov'st well is thy true heritage
Whose world, or mine or theirs
or is it of none?
First came the seen, then thus the palpable
Elysium, though it were in the halls of hell,
What thou lovest well is thy true heritage
What thou lov'st well shall not be reft from thee

The ant's a centaur in his dragon world.
Pull down thy vanity, it is not man
Made courage, or made order, or made grace,
Pull down thy vanity, I say pull down.
Learn of the green world what can be thy place
In scaled invention or true artistry,
Pull down thy vanity,
Paquin pull down!
The green casque has outdone your elegance.

"Master thyself, then others shall thee beare"

Pull down thy vanity
Thou art a beaten dog beneath the hail,
A swollen magpie in a fitful sun,
Half black half white
Nor knowst'ou wing from tail
Pull down thy vanity
                How mean thy hates
Fostered in falsity,
                Pull down thy vanity,
Rathe to destroy, niggard in charity,
Pull down thy vanity,
                I say pull down.

But to have done instead of not doing
                this is not vanity
To have, with decency, knocked
That a Blunt should open
                To have gathered from the air a live tradition
or from a fine old eye the unconquered flame
This is not vanity.
        Here error is all in the not done,
all in the diffidence that faltered.   *(1948)*

Hilda Doolittle (H. D.)
(1886–1961)

EVENING

The light passes
from ridge to ridge,
from flower to flower—
the hypaticas, wide-spread
under the light
grow faint—
the petals reach inward,
the blue tips bend
toward the bluer heart
and the flowers are lost.

The cornel-buds are still white,
but shadows dart
from the cornel-roots—
black creeps from root to root,
each leaf
cuts another leaf on the grass,
shadow seeks shadow,
then both leaf
and leaf-shadow are lost.   *(1916)*

HEAT

O wind, rend open the heat,
cut apart the heat,
rend it to tatters.

Fruit cannot drop
through this thick air—
fruit cannot fall into heat
that presses up and blunts

the points of pears
and rounds the grapes.

Cut the heat—
plough through it,
turning it on either side
of your path. *(1916)*

ORCHARD

I saw the first pear
as it fell—
the honey-seeking, golden-banded,
the yellow swarm
was not more fleet than I,
(spare us from loveliness)
and I fell prostrate,
crying:
you have flayed us
with your blossoms,
spare us the beauty
of fruit-trees.

The honey-seeking
paused not,
the air thundered their song,
and I alone was prostrate.

O rough-hewn
god of the orchard,
I bring an offering—
do you, alone unbeautiful,
son of the god,
spare us from loveliness:

these fallen hazel-nuts,
stripped late of their green sheaths,
grapes, red-purple,
their berries
dripping with wine,
pomegranates already broken,
and shrunken figs
and quinces untouched,
I bring you as offering. *(1916)*

PEAR TREE

Silver dust,
lifted from the earth,
higher than my arms reach,
you have mounted,
O, silver,
higher than my arms reach,
you front us with great mass;

no flower ever opened
so staunch a white leaf,
no flower ever parted silver
from such rare silver;

O, white pear,
your flower-tufts
thick on the branch
bring summer and ripe fruits
in their purple hearts.   *(1916)*

THE HELMSMAN

O be swift—
we have always known you wanted us.

We fled inland with our flocks,
we pastured them in hollows,
cut off from the wind
and the salt track of the marsh.

We worshipped inland—
we stepped past wood-flowers,
we forgot your tang,
we brushed wood-grass.

We wandered from pine-hills
through oak and scrub oak tangles,
we broke hyssop and bramble,
we caught flower and new bramble-fruit
in our hair: we laughed
as each branch whipped back,
we tore our feet in half-buried rocks
and knotted roots and acorn-cups.

We forgot—we worshipped,
we parted green from green,
we sought further thickets,
we dipped our ankles
through leaf-mold and earth,
and wood and wood-bank enchanted us—
and the feel of the clefts in the bark,
and the slope between tree and tree—
and a slender path strung field to field
and wood to wood
and hill to hill
and the forest after it.

We forgot for a moment;
tree-resin, tree-bark,
sweat of a torn branch
were sweet to the taste.

We were enchanted with the fields,
the tufts of coarse grass—
in the shorter grass—
we loved all this.

But now, our boat climbs—hesitates—drops—
climbs—hesitates—crawls back—
climbs—hesitates—
O be swift—
we have always known you wanted us.   *(1916)*

OREAD

Whirl up, sea—
whirl your pointed pines,
splash your great pines
on our rocks,
hurl your green over us,
cover us with your pools of fir.   *(1924)*

THE POOL

Are you alive?
I touch you.
You quiver like a sea-fish.

I cover you with my net.
What are you—banded one? *(1924)*

FRAGMENT THIRTY-SIX

I know not what to do: my mind is divided.—Sappho.

I know not what to do,
my mind is reft:
is song's gift best?
is love's gift loveliest?
I know not what to do,
now sleep has pressed
weight on your eyelids.

Shall I break your rest,
devouring, eager?
is love's gift best?
nay, song's the loveliest:
yet were you lost,
what rapture
could I take from song?
what song were left?

I know not what to do:
to turn and slake
the rage that burns,
with my breath burn
and trouble your cool breath?
so shall I turn and take
snow in my arms?
(is love's gift best?)
yet flake on flake
of snow were comfortless,
did you lie wondering,
wakened yet unawake.

Shall I turn and take
comfortless snow within my arms?
press lips to lips
that answer not,
press lips to flesh
that shudders not nor breaks?

Is love's gift best?
shall I turn and slake
all the wild longing?
O I am eager for you!
as the Pleiads shake
white light in whiter water
so shall I take you?

My mind is quite divided,
my minds hesitate,
so perfect matched,
I know not what to do:
each strives with each
as two white wrestlers
standing for a match,
ready to turn and clutch
yet never shake muscle nor nerve nor tendon;
so my mind waits
to grapple with my mind,
yet I lie quiet,
I would seem at rest.

I know not what to do:
strain upon strain,
sound surging upon sound
makes my brain blind;
as a wave-line may wait to fall
yet (waiting for its falling)
still the wind may take
from off its crest,
white flake on flake of foam,
that rises,
seeming to dart and pulse
and rend the light,
so my mind hesitates
above the passion
quivering yet to break,
so my mind hesitates
above my mind,
listening to song's delight.

I know not what to do:
will the sound break,

rending the night
with rift on rift of rose
and scattered light?
will the sound break at last
as the wave hesitant,
or will the whole night pass
and I lie listening awake? *(1924)*

LETHE

Nor skin nor hide nor fleece
   Shall cover you,
Nor curtain of crimson nor fine
Shelter of cedar-wood be over you,
   Nor the fir-tree
   Nor the pine.

Nor sight of whin nor gorse
   Nor river-yew,
Nor fragrance of flowering bush,
Nor wailing of reed-bird to waken you,
    Nor of linnet,
    Nor of thrush.

Nor word nor touch nor sight
   Of lover, you
Shall long through the night but for this:
The roll of the full tide to cover you
    Without question,
    Without kiss. *(1924)*

ERIGE COR TUUM AD ME IN CAELUM

(September 1940)

1

Lift up your eyes on high,
under the sky—
indeed?
watch planets swerve and lend
lustre to partner-planet,
as they serve
magnetic stress, and turn
subservient to your hands,

your will that guides
majestic cycle of obedient tides?

lift up our eyes to you?
no, God, we stare and stare,
upon a nearer thing
that greets us here,
Death, violent and near.

2

The alchemy and mystery is this,
no cross to kiss,
but a cross pointing on a compass-face,
east, west, south, north;

the secret of the ages is revealed,
the book un-sealed,
the fisherman entangled in his nets
felled where he waded
for the evening catch,
the house-door
swinging on the broken latch,
the woman with her basket on the quay,
shading her eyes to see
if the last boat
really is the last,
the house-dog lost,
the little hen escaped,
the precious hay-rick scattered,
and the empty cage,
the book of life is open,
turn and read:

the linnet picking at the wasted seed
is holy ghost,
the weed,
broken by iron axle,
is the flower
magicians bartered for. (*1957*)

Robinson Jeffers
(1887–1963)

SHINE, PERISHING REPUBLIC

While this America settles in the mould of its vulgarity, heavily thickening to empire,
And protest, only a bubble in the molten mass, pops and sighs out, and
the mass hardens,

I sadly smiling remember that the flower fades to make fruit, the fruit
rots to make earth.
Out of the mother; and through the spring exultances, ripeness and
decadence; and home to the mother.

You making haste haste on decay; not blameworthy; life is good, be it
stubbornly long or suddenly
A mortal splendor: meteors are not needed less than mountains: shine,
perishing republic.

But for my children, I would have them keep their distance from the
thickening center; corruption
Never has been compulsory, when the cities lie at the monster's feet
there are left the mountains.

And boys, be in nothing so moderate as in love of man, a clever servant,
insufferable master.
There is the trap that catches noblest spirits, that caught—they say—
God, when he walked on earth. *(1925)*

JOY

Though joy is better than sorrow, joy is not great;
Peace is great, strength is great.
Not for joy the stars burn, not for joy the vulture
Spreads her gray sails on the air

Over the mountain; not for joy the worn mountain
Stands, while years like water
Trench his long sides. "I am neither mountain nor bird
Nor star; and I seek joy."
The weakness of your breed: yet at length quietness
Will cover those wistful eyes. *(1925)*

HURT HAWKS

1

The broken pillar of the wing jags from the clotted shoulder,
The wing trails like a banner in defeat,
No more to use the sky forever but live with famine
And pain a few days: cat nor coyote
Will shorten the week of waiting for death, there is game without
   talons.
He stands under the oak-bush and waits
The lame feet of salvation; at night he remembers freedom
And flies in a dream, the dawns ruin it.
He is strong and pain is worse to the strong, incapacity is worse.
The curs of the day come and torment him
At distance, no one but death the redeemer will humble that head,
The intrepid readiness, the terrible eyes.
The wild God of the world is sometimes merciful to those
That ask mercy, not often to the arrogant.
You do not know him, you communal people, or you have forgotten
   him;
Intemperate and savage, the hawk remembers him;
Beautiful and wild, the hawks, and men that are dying, remember him.

2

I'd sooner, except the penalties, kill a man than a hawk; but the great
   redtail
Had nothing left but unable misery
From the bone too shattered for mending, the wing that trailed under
   his talons when he moved.
We had fed him six weeks, I gave him freedom,
He wandered over the foreland hill and returned in the evening, asking
   for death,
Not like a beggar, still eyed with the old
Implacable arrogance. I gave him the lead gift in the twilight. What
   fell was relaxed,

Owl-downy, soft feminine feathers; but what
Soared: the fierce rush: the night-herons by the flooded river cried fear
    at its rising
Before it was quite unsheathed from reality. *(1928)*

FIRE ON THE HILLS

The deer were bounding like blown leaves
Under the smoke in front of the roaring wave of the brushfire;
I thought of the smaller lives that were caught.
Beauty is not always lovely; the fire was beautiful, the terror
Of the deer was beautiful; and when I returned
Down the black slopes after the fire had gone by, an eagle
Was perched on the jag of a burnt pine,
Insolent and gorged, cloaked in the folded storms of his shoulders.
He had come from far off for the good hunting
With fire for his beater to drive the game; the sky was merciless
Blue, and the hills merciless black,
The sombre-feathered great bird sleepily merciless between them.
I thought, painfully, but the whole mind,
The destruction that brings an eagle from heaven is better than mercy.
    (1932)

STILL THE MIND SMILES

Still the mind smiles at its own rebellions,
Knowing all the while that civilization and the other evils
That make humanity ridiculous, remain
Beautiful in the whole fabric, excesses that balance each other
Like the paired wings of a flying bird.
Misery and riches, civilization and squalid savagery,
Mass war and the odor of unmanly peace:
Tragic flourishes above and below the normal of life.
In order to value this fretful time
It is necessary to remember our norm, the unaltered passions,
The same-colored wings of imagination,
That the crowd clips, in lonely places new-grown; the unchanged
Lives of herdsmen and mountain farms,
Where men are few, and few tools, a few weapons, and their dawns are
    beautiful.
From here for normal one sees both ways,
And listens to the splendor of God, the exact poet, the sonorous
Antistrophe of desolation to the strophe multitude. *(1933)*

CRUMBS OR THE LOAF

If one should tell them what's clearly seen
They'd not understand; if they understood they would not believe;
If they understood and believed they'd say,
"Hater of men, annihilating with a sterile enormous
Splendor our lives: where are our lives?"
A little chilled perhaps, but not hurt. But it's quite true
The invulnerable love is not bought for nothing.
It is better no doubt to give crumbs than the loaf; make fables again,
Tell people not to fear death, toughen
Their bones if possible with bitter fables not to fear life.
—And one's own, not to have pity too much;
For it seems compassion sticks longer than the other colors, in this
   bleaching cloth.   (*1933*)

LIFE FROM THE LIFELESS

Spirits and illusions have died,
The naked mind lives
In the beauty of inanimate things.

Flowers wither, grass fades, trees wilt,
The forest is burnt;
The rock is not burnt.

The deer starve, the winter birds
Die on their twigs and lie
In the blue dawns in the snow.

Men suffer want and become
Curiously ignoble; as prosperity
Made them curiously vile.

But look how noble the world is,
The lonely-flowing waters, the secret-
Keeping stones, the flowing sky.   (*1935*)

GRAY WEATHER

It is true that, older than man and ages to outlast him, the Pacific surf
Still cheerfully pounds the worn granite drum;
But there's no storm; and the birds are still, no song; no kind of excess;

Nothing that shines, nothing is dark;
There is neither joy nor grief nor a person, the sun's tooth sheathed in
    cloud,
And life has no more desires than a stone.
The stormy conditions of time and change are all abrogated, the essential
Violences of survival, pleasure,
Love, wrath and pain, and the curious desire of knowing, all perfectly
    suspended.
In the cloudy light, in the timeless quietness,
One explores deeper than the nerves or heart of nature, the womb or
    soul,
To the bone, the careless white bone, the excellence.   *(1935)*

THE PURSE-SEINE

Our sardine fishermen work at night in the dark of the moon; daylight
    or moonlight
They could not tell where to spread the net, unable to see the phos-
    phorescence of the shoals of fish.
They work northward from Monterey, coasting Santa Cruz; off New
    Year's Point or off Pigeon Point
The look-out man will see some lakes of milk-color light on the sea's
    night-purple; he points, and the helmsman
Turns the dark prow, the motorboat circles the gleaming shoal and drifts
    out her seine-net. They close the circle
And purse the bottom of the net, then with great labor haul it in.

                                          I cannot tell you
How beautiful the scene is, and a little terrible, then, when the crowded
    fish
Know they are caught, and wildly beat from one wall to the other of
    their closing destiny the phosphorescent
Water to a pool of flame, each beautiful slender body sheeted with
    flame, like a live rocket
A comet's tail wake of clear yellow flame; while outside the narrowing
Floats and cordage of the net great sea-lions come up to watch, sighing
    in the dark; the vast walls of night
Stand erect to the stars.

                          Lately I was looking from a night mountain-top
On a wide city, the colored splendor, galaxies of light: how could I help
    but recall the seine-net
Gathering the luminous fish? I cannot tell you how beautiful the city
    appeared, and a little terrible.

I thought, We have geared the machines and locked all together into
  interdependence; we have built the great cities; now
There is no escape. We have gathered vast populations incapable of free
  survival, insulated
From the strong earth, each person in himself helpless, on all dependent.
  The circle is closed, and the net
Is being hauled in. They hardly feel the cords drawing, yet they shine
  already. The inevitable mass-disasters
Will not come in our time nor in our children's, but we and our children
Must watch the net draw narrower, government take all powers—or
  revolution, and the new government
Take more than all, add to kept bodies kept souls—or anarchy, the mass-
  disasters.

                              These things are Progress;
Do you marvel our verse is troubled or frowning, while it keeps its
  reason? Or it lets go, lets the mood flow
In the manner of the recent young men into mere hysteria, splintered
  gleams, crackled laughter. But they are quite wrong.
There is no reason for amazement: surely one always knew that cultures
  decay, and life's end is death. (1937)

THE ANSWER

Then what is the answer?—Not to be deluded by dreams.
To know that great civilizations have broken down into violence, and
  their tyrants come, many times before.
When open violence appears, to avoid it with honor or choose the least
  ugly faction; these evils are essential.
To keep one's own integrity, be merciful and uncorrupted and not wish
  for evil; and not be duped
By dreams of universal justice or happiness. These dreams will not be
  fulfilled.
To know this, and to know that however ugly the parts appear the
  whole remains beautiful. A severed hand
Is an ugly thing, and man disservered from the earth and stars and his
  history . . . for contemplation or in fact . . .
Often appears atrociously ugly. Integrity is wholeness, the greatest
  beauty is
Organic wholeness, the wholeness of life and things, the divine beauty
  of the universe. Love that, not man
Apart from that, or else you will share man's pitiful confusions, or
  drown in despair when his days darken. (1937)

NOVA

That Nova was a moderate star like our good sun; it stored no doubt a
little more than it spent
Of heat and energy until the increasing tension came to the trigger-point
Of a new chemistry; then what was already flaming found a new man-
ner of flaming ten-thousandfold
More brightly for a brief time; what was a pin-point fleck on a sensitive
plate at the great telescope's
Eye-piece now shouts down the steep night to the naked eye, a nine-day
super-star.
                                        It is likely our moderate
Father the sun will sometime put off his nature for a similar glory. The
earth would share it; these tall
Green trees would become a moment's torches and vanish, the oceans
would explode into invisible steam,
The ships and the great whales fall through them like flaming meteors
into the emptied abysm, the six mile
Hollows of the Pacific sea-bed might smoke for a moment. Then the
earth would be like the pale proud moon.
Nothing but vitrified sand and rock would be left on earth. This is a
probable death-passion
For the sun's planets; we have no knowledge to assure us it may not
happen at any moment of time.

Meanwhile the sun shines wisely and warm, trees flutter green in the
wind, girls take their clothes off
To bathe in the cold ocean or to hunt love; they stand laughing in the
white foam, they have beautiful
Shoulders and thighs, they are beautiful animals, all life is beautiful.
We cannot be sure of life for one moment;
We can, by force and self-discipline, by many refusals and a few
assertions, in the teeth of fortune assure ourselves
Freedom and integrity in life or integrity in death. And we know that
the enormous invulnerable beauty of things
Is the face of God, to live gladly in its presence, and die without grief
or fear knowing it survives us. (*1937*)

WATCH THE LIGHTS FADE

Gray steel, cloud-shadow-stained,
The ocean takes the last lights of evening.

Loud is the voice and the foam lead-color,
And flood-tide devours the sands.

Here stand, like an old stone,
And watch the lights fade and hear the sea's voice.
Hate and despair take Europe and Asia,
And the sea-wind blows cold.

Night comes: night will claim all.
The world is not changed, only more naked:
The strong struggle for power and the weak
Warm their poor hearts with hate.

Night comes: come into the house,
Try around the dial for a late news-cast.
These others are America's voices: naïve and
Powerful, spurious, doom-touched.

How soon? Four years or forty?
Why should an old stone pick at the future?
Stand on your shore, old stone, be still while the
Sea-wind salts your head white. *(1941)*

THE BLOODY SIRE

It is not bad. Let them play.
Let the guns bark and the bombing-plane
Speak his prodigious blasphemies.
It is not bad, it is high time,
Stark violence is still the sire of all the world's values.

What but the wolf's tooth whittled so fine
The fleet limbs of the antelope?
What but fear winged the birds, and hunger
Jeweled with such eyes the great goshawk's head?
Violence has been the sire of all the world's values.

Who would remember Helen's face
Lacking the terrible halo of spears?
Who formed Christ but Herod and Cæsar,
The cruel and bloody victories of Caesar?
Violence, the bloody sire of all the world's values.

Never weep, let them play,
Old violence is not too old to beget new values. *(1941)*

Marianne Moore
(1887–   )

POETRY

I, too, dislike it: there are things that are important beyond all this
     fiddle.
Reading it, however, with a perfect contempt for it, one discovers in
it after all, a place for the genuine.
     Hands that can grasp, eyes
     that can dilate, hair that can rise
          if it must, these things are important not because a

high-sounding interpretation can be put upon them but because they are
     useful. When they become so derivative as to become unintelligible,
     the same thing may be said for all of us, that we
          do not admire what
          we cannot understand: the bat
               holding on upside down or in quest of something to

eat, elephants pushing, a wild horse taking a roll, a tireless wolf under
     a tree, the immovable critic twitching his skin like a horse that feels
          a flea, the base-
     ball fan, the statistician—
          nor is it valid
               to discriminate against "business documents and

school-books"; all these phenomena are important. One must make a
          distinction
     however: when dragged into prominence by half poets, the result is
          not poetry,
     nor till the poets among us can be
          "literalists of
          the imagination"—above
               insolence and triviality and can present

for inspection, "imaginary gardens with real toads in them," shall we
          have

II-227

it. In the meantime, if you demand on the one hand,
the raw material of poetry in
   all its rawness and
   that which is on the other hand
      genuine, you are interested in poetry.   *(1921)*

CRITICS AND CONNOISSEURS

There is a great amount of poetry in unconscious
   fastidiousness. Certain Ming
      products, imperial floor-coverings of coach-
wheel yellow, are well enough in their way but I have seen something
   that I like better—a
      mere childish attempt to make an imperfectly ballasted animal
         stand up,
      similar determination to make a pup
         eat his meat from the plate.

I remember a swan under the willows in Oxford,
   with flamingo-colored, maple-
      leaflike feet. It reconnoitred like a battle-
ship. Disbelief and conscious fastidiousness were
      ingredients in its
         disinclination to move. Finally its hardihood was not proof
            against its
         proclivity to more fully appraise such bits
            of food as the stream

bore counter to it; it made away with what I gave it
   to eat. I have seen this swan and
      I have seen you; I have seen ambition without
understanding in a variety of forms. Happening to stand
   by an ant-hill, I have
      seen a fastidious ant carrying a stick north, south, east, west, till
         it turned on
      itself, struck out from the flower-bed into the lawn,
         and returned to the point

from which it had started. Then abandoning the stick as
   useless and overtaxing its
      jaws with a particle of whitewash—pill-like but
heavy—it again went through the same course of procedure.
      What is
there in being able

to say that one has dominated the stream in an attitude of self-defense;
in proving that one has had the experience
   of carrying a stick? *(1924)*

PETER

Strong and slippery, built for the midnight grass-party confronted by
      four cats,
   he sleeps his time away—the detached first claw on the foreleg, which
         corresponds
   to the thumb, retracted to its tip; the small tuft of fronds
      or katydid-legs above each eye, still numbering the units in each
         group;
         the shadbones regularly set about the mouth, to droop or rise

in unison like the porcupine's quills—motionless. He lets himself be flat-
      tened out by gravity, as it were a piece of seaweed tamed and weak-
         ened by
   exposure to the sun; compelled when extended, to lie
      stationary. Sleep is the result of his delusion that one must do as
         well as one can for oneself; sleep—epitome of what is to

him as to the average person, the end of life. Demonstrate on him how
      the lady caught the dangerous southern snake, placing a forked stick
         on either
   side of its innocuous neck; one need not try to stir
      him up; his prune-shaped head and alligator eyes are not a party to
         the
         joke. Lifted and handled, he may be dangled like an eel or set

up on the forearm like a mouse; his eyes bisected by pupils of a pin's
      width, are flickeringly exhibited, then covered up. May be? I should
         say
   might have been; when he has been got the better of in a
      dream—as in a fight with nature or with cats—we all know it.
         Profound sleep is
         not with him a fixed illusion. Springing about with froglike ac-

curacy, emitting jerky cries when taken in the hand, he is himself
   again; to sit caged by the rungs of a domestic chair would be unprofit-
   able—human. What is the good of hypocrisy? It
      is permissible to choose one's employment, to abandon the wire
         nail, the
         roly-poly, when it shows signs of being no longer a pleas-

ure, to score the adjacent magazine with a double line of strokes. He can
talk, but insolently says nothing. What of it? When one is frank,
one's very
presence is a compliment. It is clear that he can see
the virtue of naturalness, that he is one of those who do not regard
the published fact as a surrender. As for the disposition

invariably to affront, an animal with claws wants to have to use
them; that eel-like extension of trunk into tail is not an accident. To
leap, to lengthen out, divide the air—to purloin, to pursue.
To tell the hen: fly over the fence, go in the wrong way in your
perturba-
tion—this is life; to do less would be nothing but dishonesty.

(1924)

A GRAVE

Man looking into the sea,
taking the view from those who have as much right to it as you have
to it yourself,
it is human nature to stand in the middle of a thing,
but you cannot stand in the middle of this;
the sea has nothing to give but a well excavated grave.
The firs stand in a procession, each with an emerald turkey foot at the
top,
reserved as their contours, saying nothing;
repression, however, is not the most obvious characteristic of the sea;
the sea is a collector, quick to return a rapacious look.
There are others besides you who have worn that look—
whose expression is no longer a protest; the fish no longer investigate
them
for their bones have not lasted:
men lower nets, unconscious of the fact that they are desecrating a
grave,
and row quickly away—the blades of the oars
moving together like the feet of water-spiders as if there were no such
thing as death.
The wrinkles progress among themselves in a phalanx—beautiful under
networks of foam,
and fade breathlessly while the sea rustles in and out of the seaweed;
the birds swim through the air at top speed, emitting catcalls as here-
tofore—

the tortoise shell scourges about the feet of the cliffs, in motion beneath
them;
and the ocean, under the pulsation of lighthouses and noise of bell
buoys,
advances as usual, looking as if it were not that ocean in which dropped
things are bound to sink—
in which if they turn and twist, it is neither with volition nor consciousness. (1924)

SNAKES, MONGOOSES, SNAKE-CHARMERS AND THE LIKE

I have a friend who would give a price for those long fingers all of one
length—
those hideous bird's claws, for that exotic asp and the mongoose—
products of the country in which everything is hard work, the country
of the grass-getter,
the torch-bearer, the dog-servant, the messenger-bearer, the holy-man.
Engrossed in this distinguished worm nearly as wild and as fierce as the
day it was caught,
he gazes as if incapable of looking at anything with a view to analysis.
"The slight snake rippling quickly through the grass,
the leisurely tortoise with its pied back,
the chameleon passing from twig to stone, from stone to straw,"
lit his imagination at one time; his admiration now converges upon this.
Thick, not heavy, it stands up from its travelling-basket,
the essentially Greek, the plastic animal all of a piece from nose to tail;
one is compelled to look at it as at the shadows of the alps
imprisoning in their folds like flies in amber, the rhythms of the skating
rink.
This animal to which from the earliest times, importance has attached,
fine as its worshippers have said—for what was it invented?
To show that when intelligence in its pure form
has embarked on a train of thought which is unproductive, it will come
back?
We do not know; the only positive thing about it is its shape; but why
protest?
The passion for setting people right is in itself an afflictive disease.
Distaste which takes no credit to itself is best. (1924)

TO A STEAM ROLLER

The illustration
is nothing to you without the application.

You lack half wit. You crush all the particles down
   into close conformity, and then walk back and forth on them.

Sparkling chips of rock
are crushed down to the level of the parent block.
   Were not "impersonal judgment in aesthetic
      matters, a metaphysical impossibility," you

might fairly achieve
it. As for butterflies, I can hardly conceive
   of one's attending upon you, but to question
      the congruence of the complement is vain, if it exists.   (*1924*)

TO A SNAIL

If "compression is the first grace of style,"
you have it. Contractility is a virtue
as modesty is a virtue.
It is not the acquisition of any one thing
that is able to adorn,
or the incidental quality that occurs
as a concomitant of something well said,
that we value in style,
but the principle that is hid:
in the absence of feet, "a method of conclusions";
"a knowledge of principles,"
in the curious phenomenon of your occipital horn.   (*1924*)

SILENCE

My father used to say,
"Superior people never make long visits,
have to be shown Longfellow's grave
or the glass flowers at Harvard.
Self-reliant like the cat—
that takes its prey to privacy,
the mouse's limp tail hanging like a shoelace from its mouth—
they sometimes enjoy solitude,
and can be robbed of speech
by speech which has delighted them.
The deepest feeling always shows itself in silence;
not in silence, but restraint."
Nor was he insincere in saying, "Make my house your inn."
Inn: are not residences.   (*1924*)

THE MONKEYS

winked too much and were afraid of snakes. The zebras, supreme in
their abnormality; the elephants with their fog-colored skin
  and strictly practical appendages
     were there, the small cats; and the parrakeet—
      trivial and humdrum on examination, destroying
     bark and portions of the food it could not eat.

I recall their magnificence, now not more magnificent
than it is dim. It is difficult to recall the ornament,
  speech, and precise manner of what one might
     call the minor acquaintances twenty
      years back; but I shall not forget him—that Gilgamesh
        among
     the hairy carnivora—that cat with the

wedge-shaped, slate-grey marks on its forelegs and the resolute tail,
astringently remarking, "They have imposed on us with their pale
  half-fledged protestations, trembling about
     in inarticulate frenzy, saying
      it is not for us to understand art; finding it
     all so difficult, examining the thing

as if it were inconceivably arcanic, as symmetrically frigid as if it had been carved out of chrysoprase
  or marble—strict with tension, malignant
     in its power over us and deeper
      than the sea when it proffers flattery in exchange for hemp,
     rye, flax, horses, platinum, timber, and fur." *(1935)*

THE STEEPLE-JACK

Dürer would have seen a reason for living
  in a town like this, with eight stranded whales
to look at; with the sweet sea air coming into your house
on a fine day, from water etched
  with waves as formal as the scales
on a fish.

One by one, in two's, in three's, the seagulls keep
  flying back and forth over the town clock,
or sailing around the lighthouse without moving their wings—

rising steadily with a slight
        quiver of the body—or flock
mewing where

a sea the purple of the peacock's neck is
        paled to greenish azure as Dürer changed
the pine green of the Tyrol to peacock blue and guinea
grey. You can see a twenty-five-
        pound lobster; and fish-nets arranged
to dry. The

whirlwind fife-and-drum of the storm bends the salt
        marsh grass, disturbs stars in the sky and the
star on the steeple; it is a privilege to see so
much confusion. Disguised by what
        might seem the opposite, the sea-
side flowers and

trees are favored by the fog so that you have
        the tropics at first hand: the trumpet vine,
foxglove, giant snapdragon, a salpiglossis that has
spots and stripes; morning-glories, gourds,
        or moon-vines trained on fishing twine
at the back door:

cattails, flags, blueberries and spiderwort,
        striped grass, lichens, sunflowers, asters, daisies—
yellow and crab-claw ragged sailors with green bracts—toad-plant,
petunias, ferns; pink lilies, blue
        ones, tigers; poppies; black sweet-peas.
The climate

is not right for the banyan, frangipani, or
        jack-fruit trees; or for exotic serpent
life. Ring lizard and snakeskin for the foot, if you see fit;
but here they've cats, not cobras, to
        keep down the rats. The diffident
little newt

with white pin-dots on black horizontal spaced-
        out bands lives here; yet there is nothing that
ambition can buy or take away. The college student
named Ambrose sits on the hillside

with his not-native books and hat
and sees boats

at sea progress white and rigid as if in
    a groove. Liking an elegance of which
the source is not bravado, he knows by heart the antique
sugar-bowl shaped summerhouse of
    interlacing slats, and the pitch
of the church

spire, not true, from which a man in scarlet lets
    down a rope as a spider spins a thread;
he might be part of a novel, but on the sidewalk a
sign says C. J. Poole, Steeple-Jack,
    in black and white; and one in red
and white says

Danger. The church portico has four fluted
    columns, each a single piece of stone, made
modester by white-wash. This would be a fit haven for
waifs, children, animals, prisoners,
    and presidents who have repaid
sin-driven

senators by not thinking about them. The
    place has a school-house, a post-office in a
store, fish-houses, hen-houses, a three-masted schooner on
the stocks. The hero, the student,
    the steeple-jack, each in his way,
is at home.

It could not be dangerous to be living
    in a town like this, of simple people,
who have a steeple-jack placing danger signs by the church
when he is gilding the solid-
    pointed star, which on a steeple
stands for hope. *(1935)*

THE HERO

Where there is personal liking we go.
    Where the ground is sour; where there are
    weeds of beanstalk height,

snakes' hypodermic teeth, or
the wind brings the "scarebabe voice"
from the neglected yew set with
the semi-precious cat's eyes of the owl—
awake, asleep, "raised ears extended to fine points," and so
on—love won't grow.

We do not like some things, and the hero
doesn't; deviating head-stones
and uncertainty;
going where one does not wish
to go; suffering and not
saying so; standing and listening where something
is hiding. The hero shrinks
as what it is flies out on muffled wings, with twin yellow
eyes—to and fro—

with quavering water-whistle note, low,
high, in basso-falsetto chirps
until the skin creeps.
Jacob when a-dying, asked
Joseph. Who are these? and blessed
both sons, the younger most, vexing Joseph. And
Joseph was vexing to some.
Cincinnatus was; Regulus; and some of our fellow
men have been, although devout,

like Pilgrim having to go slow
to find his roll; tired but hopeful—
hope not being hope
until all ground for hope has
vanished; and lenient, looking
upon a fellow creature's error with the
feelings of a mother—a
woman or a cat. The decorous frock-coated Negro
by the grotto

answers the fearless sightseeing hobo
who asks the man she's with, what's this,
what's that, where's Martha
buried, "Gen-ral Washington
there; his lady, here"; speaking
as if in a play—not seeing her; with a

sense of human dignity
and reverence for mystery, standing like the shadow
of the willow.

Moses would not be grandson to Pharaoh.
    It is not what I eat that is
    my natural meat,
    the hero says. He's not out
    seeing a sight but the rock
    crystal thing to see—the startling El Greco
    brimming with inner light—that
covets nothing that it has let go. This then you may know
as the hero. (1935)

From THE JERBOA

TOO MUCH

A Roman had an
artist, a freedman,
    contrive a cone—pine cone
    or fir cone—with holes for a fountain. Placed on
        the Prison of St. Angelo, this cone
        of the Pompeys which is known

now as the Popes', passed
for art. A huge cast
    bronze, dwarfing the peacock
    statue in the garden of the Vatican,
        it looks like a work of art made to give
        to a Pompey, or native

of Thebes. Others could
build, and understood
    making colossi and
    how to use slaves, and kept crocodiles and put
        baboons on the necks of giraffes to pick
        fruit, and used serpent magic.

They had their men tie
hippopotami
    and bring out dapple dog-
    cats to course antelopes, dikdik, and ibex;

or used small eagles. They looked on as theirs,
impalas and onigers,

the wild ostrich herd
with hard feet and bird
   necks rearing back in the
   dust like a serpent preparing to strike, cranes,
      mongooses, storks, anoas, Nile geese;
      and there were gardens for these—

combining planes, dates,
limes, and pomegranates,
   in avenues—with square
   pools of pink flowers, tame fish, and small frogs. Besides
      yarns dyed with indigo, and red cotton,
      they had a flax which they spun

into fine linen
cordage for yachtsmen.
   These people liked small things;
   they gave to boys little paired playthings such as
      nests of eggs, ichneumon and snake, paddle
      and raft, badger and camel;

and made toys for them-
selves: the royal totem;
   and toilet-boxes marked
   with the contents. Lords and ladies put goose-grease
      paint in round bone boxes—the pivoting
      lid incised with a duck-wing

or reverted duck-
head; kept in a buck
   or rhinoceros horn,
   the ground horn; and locust oil in stone locusts
      It was a picture with a fine distance;
      of drought, and of assistance

in time, from the Nile
rising slowly, while
   the pig-tailed monkey on
   slab-hands, with arched-up slack-slung gait, and the brown
      dandy looked at the jasmine two-leafed twig
      and bud, cactus-pads, and fig.

Dwarfs here and there, lent
to an evident
   poetry of frog grays,
   duck-egg greens, and eggplant blues, a fantasy
      and a verisimilitude that were
      right to those with, everywhere,

power over the poor.
The bees' food is your
   food. Those who tended flower-
   beds and stables were like the king's cane in the
      form of a hand, or the folding bedroom
      made for his mother of whom

he was fond. Princes
clad in queens' dresses,
   calla or petunia
   white, that trembled at the edge, and queens in a
      king's underskirt of fine-twilled thread like silk-
      worm gut, as bee-man and milk-

maid, kept divine cows
and bees; limestone brows,
   and gold-foil wings. They made
   basalt serpents and portraits of beetles; the
      king gave his name to them and he was named
      for them. He feared snakes, and tamed

Pharaoh's rat, the rust-
backed mongoose. No bust
   of it was made, but there
   was pleasure for the rat. Its restlessness was
      its excellence; it was praised for its wit;
      and the jerboa, like it,

a small desert rat,
and not famous, that
   lives without water, has
   happiness. Abroad seeking food, or at home
      in its burrow, the Sahara field-mouse
      has a shining silver house

of sand. O rest and
joy, the boundless sand,

the stupendous sand-spout,
no water, no palm-trees, no ivory bed,
   tiny cactus; but one would not be he
   who has nothing but plenty.   *(1935)*

WHAT ARE YEARS?

What is our innocence,
what is our guilt? All are
   naked, none is safe. And whence
is courage: the unanswered question,
the resolute doubt,—
dumbly calling, deafly listening—that
in misfortune, even death,
      encourages others
      and in its defeat, stirs

   the soul to be strong? He
sees deep and is glad, who
   accedes to mortality
and in his imprisonment rises
upon himself as
   the sea in a chasm, struggling to be
free and unable to be,
      in its surrendering
      finds its continuing.

   So he who strongly feels,
behaves. The very bird,
   grown taller as he sings, steels
his form straight up. Though he is captive,
his mighty singing
says, satisfaction is a lowly
thing, how pure a thing is joy.
      This is mortality,
      this is eternity.   *(1941)*

HE "DIGESTETH HARDE YRON"

Although the aepyornis
   or roc that lived in Madagascar, and
the moa are extinct,
the camel-sparrow, linked
   with them in size—the large sparrow

Xenophon saw walking by a stream—was and is
a symbol of justice.

This bird watches his chicks with
a maternal concentration—and he's
been mothering the eggs
at night six weeks—his legs
their only weapon of defence.
He is swifter than a horse; he has a foot hard
as a hoof; the leopard

is not more suspicious. How
could he, prized for plumes and eggs and young,
used even as a riding-beast, respect men
hiding actor-like in ostrich-skins, with the right hand
making the neck move as if alive
and from a bag the left hand

strewing grain, that ostriches
might be decoyed and killed! Yes, this is he
whose plume was anciently
the plume of justice; he
whose comic duckling head on its
great neck revolves with compass-needle nervousness
when he stands guard,

in S-like foragings as he is
preening the down on his leaden-skinned back.
The egg piously shown
as Leda's very own
from which Castor and Pollux hatched,
was an ostrich-egg. And what could have been more fit
for the Chinese lawn it

grazed on as a gift to an
emperor who admired strange birds, than this
one who builds his mud-made
nest in dust yet will wade
in lake or sea till only the head shows.

*   *   *

Six hundred ostrich-brains served
at one banquet, the ostrich-plume-tipped tent
and desert spear, jewel-

gorgeous ugly egg-shell
    goblets, eight pairs of ostriches
in harness, dramatize a meaning
always missed by the externalist.

The power of the visible
    is the invisible; as even where
no tree of freedom grows,
so-called brute courage knows.
    Heroism is exhausting, yet
it contradicts a greed that did not wisely spare
the harmless solitaire

or great auk in its grandeur;
    unsolicitude having swallowed up
all giant birds but an alert gargantuan
    little-winged, magnificently speedy running-bird.
This one remaining rebel
is the sparrow-camel.   (*1941*)

BIRD-WITTED

With innocent wide penguin eyes, three
    large fledgling mocking-birds below
the pussy-willow tree,
    stand in a row,
wings touching, feebly solemn,
till they see
        their no longer larger
        mother bringing
something which will partially
feed one of them.

Toward the high-keyed intermittent squeak
    of broken carriage-springs, made by
the three similar, meek-
    coated bird's-eye
freckled forms she comes; and when
from the beak
        of one, the still living
        beetle has dropped
out, she picks it up and puts
it in again.

Standing in the shade till they have dressed
   their thickly-filamented, pale
pussy-willow-surfaced
   coats, they spread tail
and wings, showing one by one,
the modest
      white stripe lengthwise on the
      tail and crosswise
underneath the wing, and the
accordion

is closed again. What delightful note
   with rapid unexpected flute-
sounds leaping from the throat
   of the astute
grown bird, comes back to one from
the remote
      unenergetic sun-
      lit air before
the brood was here? How harsh
the bird's voice has become.

A piebald cat observing them,
   is slowly creeping toward the trim
trio on the tree stem.
   Unused to him
the three make room—uneasy
new problem.
      A dangling foot that missed
      its grasp, is raised
and finds the twig on which it
planned to perch. The

parent darting down, nerved by what chills
   the blood, and by hope rewarded—
of toil—since nothing fills
   squeaking unfed
mouths, wages deadly combat,
and half kills
      with bayonet beak and
      cruel wings, the
intellectual cautious-
ly creeping cat. (*1941*)

NEVERTHELESS

you've seen a strawberry
    that's had a struggle; yet
    was, where the fragments met,

a hedgehog or a star-
    fish for the multitude
    of seeds. What better food

than apple seeds—the fruit
    within the fruit—locked in
    like counter-curved twin

hazelnuts? Frost that kills
    the little rubber-plant-
    leaves of *kok-saghyz*-stalks, can't

harm the roots; they still grow
    in frozen ground. Once where
    there was a prickly-pear-

leaf clinging to barbed wire,
    a root shot down to grow
    in earth two feet below;

as carrots form mandrakes
    or a ram's-horn root some-
    times. Victory won't come

to me unless I go
    to it; a grape tendril
    ties a knot in knots till

knotted thirty times—so
    the bound twig that's under-
    gone and over-gone, can't stir.

The weak overcomes its
    menace, the strong over-
    comes itself. What is there

like fortitude! What sap
　went through that little thread
　to make the cherry red!   *(1944)*

THE WOOD-WEASEL

emerges daintily, the skunk—
don't laugh—in sylvan black and white chipmunk
regalia. The inky thing
adaptively whited with glistening
goat fur, is wood-warden. In his
ermined well-cuttlefish-inked wool, he is
determination's totem. Out-
lawed? His sweet face and powerful feet go about
in chieftain's coat of Chilcat cloth.
He is his own protection from the moth,

noble little warrior. That
otter-skin on it, the living pole-cat,
smothers anything that stings. Well,—
this same weasel's playful and his weasel
associates are too. Only
wood-weasels shall associate with me.   *(1944)*

THE MIND IS AN ENCHANTING THING

　is an enchanted thing
　　like the glaze on a
　katydid-wing
　　　subdivided by sun
　　　till the nettings are legion.
　Like Gieseking playing Scarlatti;

　like the apteryx-awl
　　as a beak, or the
　kiwi's rain-shawl
　　　of haired feathers, the mind
　　　feeling its way as though blind,
　walks along with its eyes on the ground.

　It has memory's ear
　　that can hear without
　having to hear.

Like the gyroscope's fall,
truly unequivocal
because trued by regnant certainty,

it is a power of
strong enchantment. It
is like the dove-
neck animated by
sun; it is memory's eye;
it's conscientious inconsistency.

It tears off the veil; tears
the temptation, the
mist the heart wears,
from its eyes—if the heart
has a face; it takes apart
dejection. It's fire in the dove-neck's

iridescence; in the
inconsistencies
of Scarlatti.
Unconfusion submits
its confusion to proof; it's
not a Herod's oath that cannot change.   (*1944*)

John Crowe Ransom
(1888–   )

BELLS FOR JOHN WHITESIDE'S DAUGHTER

There was such speed in her little body,
And such lightness in her footfall,
It is no wonder that her brown study
Astonishes us all.

Her wars were bruited in our high window.
We looked among orchard trees and beyond,
Where she took arms against her shadow,
Or harried unto the pond

The lazy geese, like a snow cloud
Dripping their snow on the green grass,
Tricking and stopping, sleepy and proud,
Who cried in goose, Alas,

For the tireless heart within the little
Lady with rod that made them rise
From their noon apple dreams, and scuttle
Goose-fashion under the skies!

But now go the bells, and we are ready;
In one house we are sternly stopped
To say we are vexed at her brown study,
Lying so primly propped. *(1924)*

HERE LIES A LADY

Here lies a lady of beauty and high degree.
Of chills and fever she died, of fever and chills,
The delight of her husband, her aunts, an infant of three,
And of medicos marvelling sweetly on her ills.

For either she burned, and her confident eyes would blaze,
And her fingers fly in a manner to puzzle their heads—
What was she making? Why, nothing; she sat in a maze
Of old scraps of laces, snipped into curious shreds—

Or this would pass, and the light of her fire decline
Till she lay discouraged and cold as a thin stalk white and blown,
And would not open her eyes, to kisses, to wine;
The sixth of these states was her last; the cold settled down.

Sweet ladies, long may ye bloom, and toughly I hope ye may thole,
But was she not lucky? In flowers and lace and mourning,
In love and great honor we bade God rest her soul
After six little spaces of chill, and six of burning. *(1924)*

MISS EUPHEMIA

Out of her house she crept,
Which was her winter's gaol,
Hearing the rumor that now
Was the birds' common tale—
Birds for all the ladies,
And husbands at church-door—
In fine, a spring was promised
As fifty years before.

A phase of green and tender
Was on the mortal clay,
But white upon her stick went
Miss Euphemia,
To count up all her tulips
That celebrated March,
Out of the frore escaping
To the blue upper arch.

Into her house she fled,
Buffeted back to prison,
And sought the very great-chair
From which she had arisen;
Down sat in her whiteness—
Bitter how she laughed—
Opening doors to March, yet
Quaking in his draught.

Nor scarcely can she, dwindling,
Throw down a bridge of dream
For a broken lady's traverse,
Neat-footing on the beam;
She had too much of winter,
And all her ways were lost,
And she sits with us only
Till next Pentecost. *(1924)*

PHILOMELA

Procne, Philomela, and Itylus,
Your names are liquid, your improbable tale
Is recited in the classic numbers of the nightingale.
Ah, but our numbers are not felicitous,
It goes not liquidly for us.

Perched on a Roman ilex, and duly apostrophized,
The nightingale descanted unto Ovid;
She has even appeared to the Teutons, the swilled and gravid;
At Fontainebleau it may be the bird was gallicized;
Never was she baptized.

To England came Philomela with her pain,
Fleeing the hawk her husband; querulous ghost,
She wanders when he sits heavy on his roost,
Utters herself in the original again,
The untranslatable refrain.

Not to these shores she came! this other Thrace,
Environ barbarous to the royal Attic;
How could her delicate dirge run democratic,
Delivered in a cloudless boundless public place
To an inordinate race?

I pernoctated with the Oxford students once,
And in the quadrangles, in the cloisters, on the Cher,
Precociously knocked at antique doors ajar,
Fatuously touched the hems of the hierophants,
Sick of my dissonance.

I went out to Bagley Wood, I climbed the hill;
Even the moon had slanted off in a twinkling,

I heard the sepulchral owl and a few bells tinkling,
There was no more villainous day to unfulfil,
The diuturnity was still.

Up from the darkest wood where Philomela sat,
Her fairy numbers issued. What then ailed me?
My ears are called capacious but they failed me,
Her classics registered a little flat!
I rose, and venomously spat.

Philomela, Philomela, lover of song,
I am in despair if we may make us worthy,
A bantering breed sophistical and swarthy;
Unto more beautiful, persistently more young,
Thy fabulous provinces belong. (1924)

EMILY HARDCASTLE, SPINSTER

We shall come to-morrow morning, who were not to have her love;
We shall bring no face of envy, but a gift of praise and lilies
To the stately ceremonial we are not the heroes of.

Let the sisters now attend her, who are red-eyed, who are wroth;
They were younger, she was finer, for they wearied of the waiting
And they married them to merchants, being unbelievers both.

I was dapper when I dangled in my pepper-and-salt;
We were only local beauties, and we beautifully trusted
If the proud one had to tarry we would take her by default.

But right across her threshold has the Grizzled Baron come;
Let them wrap her as a princess, who'd go softly down a stairway
And seal her to the stranger for his castle in the gloom.

INLAND CITY

She lies far inland, and no stick nor stone of her
Ever has looked on the sounding sea,
And how should she speak of her swift barks and roadways
And white sloops crowding to lift and be free?

"Ye towers and steeples, and belfries and crosses,
Toll for the doomed ships passing to sea.

But ye walls and gateposts, and ye halls and gardens,
Moor in my little boats vigilantly!" (*1924*)

BLUE GIRLS

Twirling your blue skirts, travelling the sward
Under the towers of your seminary,
Go listen to your teachers old and contrary
Without believing a word.

Tie the white fillets then about your lustrous hair
And think no more of what will come to pass
Than bluebirds that go walking on the grass
And chattering on the air.

Practise your beauty, blue girls, before it fail;
And I will cry with my loud lips and publish
Beauty which all our power shall never establish,
It is so frail.

For I could tell you a story which is true;
I know a lady with a terrible tongue,
Blear eyes fallen from blue,
All her perfections tarnished—and yet it is not long
Since she was lovelier than any of you. (*1927*)

SOMEWHERE IS SUCH A KINGDOM

The famous kingdom of the birds
Has a sweet tongue and liquid words,—
The red-birds polish their notes
In their easy practised throats,—
Smooth as orators are the thrushes
Of the airy city of the bushes,—
And God reward the fierce cock wrens
Who have such suavity with their hens.

To me this has its worth
As I sit upon the earth
Lacking my winter and quiet hearth.
For I go up into a nook
With a mind burdened, or a book,
And hear no strife or quarreling
As the birds and their wives sing.

Or, so it has been today.
Yet I cannot therefore say
If the red-bird, wren, or thrush
Know when to speak and when to hush;
Though their manifest education
Be a right enunciation
And their chief excellence
A verbal elegance,
I cannot say if the wind never blows,
Nor how it sometimes goes.

This I know, that if they wrangle
Their words inevitably will jangle.
If they be hateful as men
They will be harsh as we have been.
When they go to pecking
You will soon hear shrieking,
And they who will have the law,
How those will jaw!
Girls that dream unlawful dreams
Will waken full of their own screams,
And boys that get too arrant
Will have rows with a parent,—
And when friend falls out with friend,
All songs must have quick end.

Have they not claws like knives?
Have not these gentlemen wives?

But when they croak and fleer and swear,
My dull heart I must take elsewhere;
For I will see if God has made
Otherwhere another shade
Where the men or beasts or birds
Exchange few words and pleasant words
And dare I think it is absurd
If no such beast were, no such bird?   (*1927*)

THE EQUILIBRISTS

Full of her long white arms and milky skin
He had a thousand times remembered sin.

Alone in the press of people travelled he,
Minding her jacinth and myrrh and ivory.

Mouth he remembered: the quaint orifice
From which came heat that flamed upon the kiss,
Till cold words came down spiral from the head,
Grey doves from the officious tower illsped.

Body: it was a white field ready for love.
On her body's field, with the gaunt tower above,
The lilies grew, beseeching him to take,
If he would pluck and wear them, bruise and break.

Eyes talking: Never mind the cruel words,
Embrace my flowers but not embrace the swords.
But what they said, the doves came straightway flying
And unsaid: Honor, Honor, they came crying.

Importunate her doves. Too pure, too wise,
Clambering on his shoulder, saying, Arise,
Leave me now, and never let us meet,
Eternal distance now command thy feet.

Predicament indeed, which thus discovers
Honor among thieves, Honor between lovers.
O such a little word is Honor, they feel!
But the grey word is between them cold as steel.

At length I saw these lovers fully were come
Into their torture of equilibrium:
Dreadfully had forsworn each other, and yet
They were bound each to each, and they did not forget

And rigid as two painful stars, and twirled
About the clustered night their prison world,
They burned with fierce love always to come near,
But Honor beat them back and kept them clear.

Ah, the strict lovers, they are ruined now!
I cried in anger. But with puddled brow
Devising for those gibbeted and brave
Came I descanting: Man, what would you have?

For spin your period out, and draw your breath,
A kinder saeculum begins with Death.
Would you ascend to Heaven and bodiless dwell?
Or take your bodies honorless to Hell?

In Heaven you have heard no marriage is,
No white flesh tinder to your lecheries,
Your male and female tissue sweetly shaped
Sublimed away, and furious blood escaped.

Great lovers lie in Hell, the stubborn ones
Infatuate of the flesh upon the bones;
Stuprate, they rend each other when they kiss;
The pieces kiss again—no end to this.

But still I watched them spinning, orbited nice.
Their flames were not more radiant than their ice.
I dug in the quiet earth and wrought the tomb
And made these lines to memorize their doom:—

Equilibrists lie here; stranger, tread light;
Close, but untouching in each other's sight;
Mouldered the lips and ashy the tall skull,
Let them lie perilous and beautiful. (1927)

DEAD BOY

The little cousin is dead, by foul subtraction,
A green bough from Virginia's aged tree,
And none of the county kin like the transaction,
Nor some of the world of outer dark, like me.

A boy not beautiful, not good, nor clever,
A black cloud full of storms too hot for keeping,
A sword beneath his mother's heart—yet never
Woman bewept her babe as this is weeping.

A pig with a pasty face, so I had said,
Squealing for cookies, kinned by poor pretense
With a noble house. But the little man quite dead,
I see the forbears' antique lineaments.

The elder men have strode by the box of death
To the wide flag porch, and muttering low send round

The bruit of the day. O friendly waste of breath!
Their hearts are hurt with a deep dynastic wound.

He was pale and little, the foolish neighbors say;
The first-fruits, saith the Preacher, the Lord hath taken,
But this was the old tree's late branch wrenched away,
Grieving the sapless limbs, the shorn and shaken. *(1927)*

JANET WAKING

Beautifully Janet slept
Till it was deeply morning. She woke then
And thought about her dainty-feathered hen,
To see how it had kept.

One kiss she gave her mother.
Only a small one gave she to her daddy
Who would have kissed each curl of his shining baby;
No kiss at all for her brother.

"Old Chucky, old Chucky!" she cried,
Running across the world upon the grass
To Chucky's house, and listening. But alas,
Her Chucky had died.

It was a transmogrifying bee
Came droning down on Chucky's old bald head
And sat and put the poison. It scarcely bled,
But how exceedingly

And purply did the knot
Swell with the venom and communicate
Its rigor! Now the poor comb stood up straight
But Chucky did not.

So there was Janet
Kneeling on the wet grass, crying her brown hen
(Translated far beyond the daughters of men)
To rise and walk upon it.

And weeping fast as she had breath
Janet implored us, "Wake her from her sleep!"
And would not be instructed in how deep
Was the forgetful kingdom of death *(1927)*

VISION BY SWEETWATER

Go and ask Robin to bring the girls over
To Sweetwater, said my Aunt; and that was why
It was like a dream of ladies sweeping by
The willows, clouds, deep meadowgrass, and the river.

Robin's sisters and my Aunt's lily daughter
Laughed and talked, and tinkled light as wrens
If there were a little colony all hens
To go walking by the steep turn of Sweetwater.

Let them alone, dear Aunt, just for one minute
Till I go fishing in the dark of my mind:
Where have I seen before, against the wind,
These bright virgins, robed and bare of bonnet,

Flowing with music of their strange quick tongue
And adventuring with delicate paces by the stream,—
Myself a child, old suddenly at the scream
From one of the white throats which it hid among?   *(1927)*

T. S. Eliot
(1888–1965)

THE LOVE SONG OF J. ALFRED PRUFROCK

S'io credesse che mia risposta fosse
A persona che mai tornasse al mondo,
Questa fiamma staria senza più scosse.
Ma perciocché giammai di questo fondo
Non tornò vivo alcun, s'i'odo il vero,
Senza tema d'infamia ti rispondo.

Let us go then, you and I,
When the evening is spread out against the sky
Like a patient etherised upon a table;
Let us go, through certain half-deserted streets,
The muttering retreats
Of restless nights in one-night cheap hotels
And sawdust restaurants with oyster-shells:
Streets that follow like a tedious argument
Of insidious intent
To lead you to an overwhelming question . . .
Oh, do not ask, "What is it?"
Let us go and make our visit.

In the room the women come and go
Talking of Michelangelo.

The yellow fog that rubs its back upon the window-panes,
The yellow smoke that rubs its muzzle on the window-panes,
Licked its tongue into the corners of the evening,
Lingered upon the pools that stand in drains,
Let fall upon its back the soot that falls from chimneys,
Slipped by the terrace, made a sudden leap,
And seeing that it was a soft October night,
Curled once about the house, and fell asleep.

And indeed there will be time
For the yellow smoke that slides along the street,

Rubbing its back upon the window-panes;
There will be time, there will be time
To prepare a face to meet the faces that you meet;
There will be time to murder and create,
And time for all the works and days of hands
That lift and drop a question on your plate;
Time for you and time for me,
And time yet for a hundred indecisions,
And for a hundred visions and revisions,
Before the taking of a toast and tea.

    In the room the women come and go
Talking of Michelangelo.

    And indeed there will be time
To wonder, "Do I dare?" and, "Do I dare?"
Time to turn back and descend the stair,
With a bald spot in the middle of my hair—
(They will say: "How his hair is growing thin!")
My morning coat, my collar mounting firmly to the chin,
My necktie rich and modest, but asserted by a simple pin—
(They will say: "But how his arms and legs are thin!")
Do I dare
Disturb the universe?
In a minute there is time
For decisions and revisions which a minute will reverse.

    For I have known them all already, known them all—
Have known the evenings, mornings, afternoons,
I have measured out my life with coffee spoons;
I know the voices dying with a dying fall
Beneath the music from a farther room.
    So how should I presume?

    And I have known the eyes already, known them all—
The eyes that fix you in a formulated phrase,
And when I am formulated, sprawling on a pin,
When I am pinned and wriggling on the wall,
Then how should I begin
To spit out all the butt-ends of my days and ways?
    And how should I presume?

    And I have known the arms already, known them all—
Arms that are braceleted and white and bare

(But in the lamplight, downed with light brown hair!)
Is it perfume from a dress
That makes me so digress?
Arms that lie along a table, or wrap about a shawl.
  And should I then presume?
  And how should I begin?

          *   *   *

Shall I say, I have gone at dusk through narrow streets
And watched the smoke that rises from the pipes
Of lonely men in shirt-sleeves, leaning out of windows? . . .

  I should have been a pair of ragged claws
Scuttling across the floors of silent seas.

          *   *   *

And the afternoon, the evening, sleeps so peacefully!
Smoothed by long fingers,
Asleep . . . tired . . . or it malingers,
Stretched on the floor, here beside you and me.
Should I, after tea and cakes and ices,
Have the strength to force the moment to its crisis?
But though I have wept and fasted, wept and prayed,
Though I have seen my head (grown slightly bald) brought in upon a
    platter,
I am no prophet—and here's no great matter;
I have seen the moment of my greatness flicker,
And I have seen the eternal Footman hold my coat, and snicker,
And in short, I was afraid.

  And would it have been worth it, after all,
After the cups, the marmalade, the tea,
Among the porcelain, among some talk of you and me,
Would it have been worth while,
To have bitten off the matter with a smile,
To have squeezed the universe into a ball
To roll it toward some overwhelming question,
To say: "I am Lazarus, come from the dead,
Come back to tell you all, I shall tell you all"—
If one, settling a pillow by her head,
    Should say: "That is not what I meant at all;
    That is not it, at all."

  And would it have been worth it, after all,
Would it have been worth while,

After the sunsets and the dooryards and the sprinkled streets,
After the novels, after the teacups, after the skirts that trail along the
    floor—
And this, and so much more?—
It is impossible to say just what I mean!
But as if a magic lantern threw the nerves in patterns on a
    screen:
Would it have been worth while
If one, settling a pillow or throwing off a shawl,
And turning toward the window, should say:
    "That is not it at all,
    That is not what I meant, at all."

                *   *   *

No! I am not Prince Hamlet, nor was meant to be;
Am an attendant lord, one that will do
To swell a progress, start a scene or two,
Advise the prince; no doubt, an easy tool,
Deferential, glad to be of use,
Politic, cautious, and meticulous;
Full of high sentence, but a bit obtuse;
At times, indeed, almost ridiculous—
Almost, at times, the Fool.

    I grow old . . . I grow old . . .
I shall wear the bottoms of my trousers rolled.

    Shall I part my hair behind? Do I dare to eat a peach?
I shall wear white flannel trousers, and walk upon the beach.
I have heard the mermaids singing, each to each.

    I do not think that they will sing to me.

    I have seen them riding seaward on the waves
Combing the white hair of the waves blown back
When the wind blows the water white and black.

    We have lingered in the chambers of the sea
By sea-girls wreathed with seaweed red and brown
Till human voices wake us, and we drown. *(1917)*

RHAPSODY ON A WINDY NIGHT

    Twelve o'clock.
    Along the reaches of the street

Held in a lunar synthesis,
Whispering lunar incantations
Dissolve the floors of memory
And all its clear relations
Its divisions and precisions,
Every street lamp that I pass
Beats like a fatalistic drum,
And through the spaces of the dark
Midnight shakes the memory
As a madman shakes a dead geranium

Half-past one,
The street-lamp sputtered,
The street-lamp muttered,
The street-lamp said, "Regard that woman
Who hesitates toward you in the light of the door
Which opens on her like a grin.
You see the border of her dress
Is torn and stained with sand,
And you see the corner of her eye
Twists like a crooked pin."

The memory throws up high and dry
A crowd of twisted things;
A twisted branch upon the beach
Eaten smooth, and polished
As if the world gave up
The secret of its skeleton,
Stiff and white.
A broken spring in a factory yard,
Rust that clings to the form that the strength has left
Hard and curled and ready to snap.

Half-past two,
The street-lamp said,
"Remark the cat which flattens itself in the gutter,
Slips out its tongue
And devours a morsel of rancid butter."
So the hand of the child, automatic,
Slipped out and pocketed a toy that was running along the quay.
I could see nothing behind that child's eye.
I have seen eyes in the street
Trying to peer through lighted shutters,
And a crab one afternoon in a pool,

An old crab with barnacles on his back,
Gripped the end of a stick which I held him.

Half-past three,
The lamp sputtered,
The lamp muttered in the dark.
The lamp hummed:
"Regard the moon,
La lune ne garde aucune rancune,
She winks a feeble eye,
She smiles into corners.
She smooths the hair of the grass.
The moon has lost her memory.
A washed-out smallpox cracks her face,
Her hand twists a paper rose,
That smells of dust and eau de Cologne,
She is alone
With all the old nocturnal smells
That cross and cross across her brain."
The reminiscence comes
Of sunless dry geraniums
And dust in crevices,
Smells of chestnuts in the streets,
And female smells in shuttered rooms,
And cigarettes in corridors
And cocktail smells in bars.

The lamp said,
"Four o'clock,
Here is the number on the door.
Memory!
You have the key,
The little lamp spreads a ring on the stair.
Mount,
The bed is open; the tooth-brush hangs on the wall,
Put your shoes at the door, sleep, prepare for life."

The last twist of the knife. (*1917*)

GERONTION

Thou hast nor youth nor age
But as it were an after dinner sleep
Dreaming of both.

Here I am, an old man in a dry month,
Being read to by a boy, waiting for rain.
I was neither at the hot gates
Nor fought in the warm rain
Nor knee deep in the salt marsh, heaving a cutlass,
Bitten by flies, fought.
My house is a decayed house,
And the jew squats on the window sill, the owner,
Spawned in some estaminet of Antwerp,
Blistered in Brussels, patched and peeled in London.
The goat coughs at night in the field overhead;
Rocks, moss, stonecrop, iron, merds.
The woman keeps the kitchen, makes tea,
Sneezes at evening, poking the peevish gutter.
                    I an old man,
A dull head among windy spaces.

    Signs are taken for wonders. "We would see a sign!"
The word within a word, unable to speak a word,
Swaddled with darkness. In the juvescence of the year
Came Christ the tiger

    In depraved May, dogwood and chestnut, flowering judas,
To be eaten, to be divided, to be drunk
Among whispers; by Mr. Silvero
With caressing hands, at Limoges
Who walked all night in the next room;

    By Hakagawa, bowing among the Titians;
By Madame de Tornquist, in the dark room
Shifting the candles; Fräulein von Kulp
Who turned in the hall, one hand on the door. Vacant shuttles
Weave the wind. I have no ghosts,
An old man in a draughty house
Under a windy knob.

    After such knowledge, what forgiveness? Think now
History has many cunning passages, contrived corridors
And issues, deceives with whispering ambitions,
Guides us by vanities. Think now
She gives when our attention is distracted
And what she gives, gives with such supple confusions
That the giving famishes the craving. Gives too late

What's not believed in, or if still believed,
In memory only, reconsidered passion. Gives too soon
Into weak hands, what's thought can be dispensed with
Till the refusal propagates a fear. Think
Neither fear nor courage saves us. Unnatural vices
Are fathered by our heroism. Virtues
Are forced upon us by our impudent crimes.
These tears are shaken from the wrath-bearing tree.

The tiger springs in the new year. Us he devours. Think at last
We have not reached conclusion, when I
Stiffen in a rented house. Think at last
I have not made this show purposelessly
And it is not by any concitation
Of the backward devils.
I would meet you upon this honestly.
I that was near your heart was removed therefrom
To lose beauty in terror, terror in inquisition.
I have lost my passion: why should I need to keep it
Since what is kept must be adulterated?
I have lost my sight, smell, hearing, taste, and touch:
How should I use them for your closer contact?

These with a thousand small deliberations
Protract the profit of their chilled delirium,
Excite the membrane, when the sense has cooled,
With pungent sauces, multiply variety
In a wilderness of mirrors. What will the spider do,
Suspend its operations, will the weevil
Delay? De Bailhache, Fresca, Mrs. Cammel, whirled
Beyond the circuit of the shuddering Bear
In fractured atoms. Gull against the wind, in the windy straits
Of Belle Isle, or running on the Horn,
White feathers in the snow, the Gulf claims,
And an old man driven by the Trades
To a sleepy corner.

Tenants of the house,
Thoughts of a dry brain in a dry season. (*1920*)

WHISPERS OF IMMORTALITY

Webster was much possessed by death
And saw the skull beneath the skin;

And breastless creatures under ground
Leaned backward with a lipless grin.

Daffodil bulbs instead of balls
Stared from the sockets of the eyes!
He knew that thought clings round dead limbs
Tightening its lusts and luxuries.

Donne, I suppose, was such another
Who found no substitute for sense,
To seize and clutch and penetrate;
Expert beyond experience,

He knew the anguish of the marrow
The ague of the skeleton;
No contact possible to flesh
Allayed the fever of the bone.

*   *   *

Grishkin is nice: her Russian eye
Is underlined for emphasis;
Uncorseted, her friendly bust
Gives promise of pneumatic bliss.

The couched Brazilian jaguar
Compels the scampering marmoset
With subtle effluence of cat;
Grishkin has a maisonette;

The sleek Brazilian jaguar
Does not in its arboreal gloom
Distil so rank a feline smell
As Grishkin in a drawing-room.

And even the Abstract Entities
Circumambulate her charm;
But our lot crawls between dry ribs
To keep our metaphysics warm.   (1920)

SWEENEY AMONG THE NIGHTINGALES

ὤμοι, πέπληγμαι καιρίαν πληγὴν ἔσω.

Apeneck Sweeney spreads his knees
Letting his arms hang down to laugh,

The zebra stripes along his jaw
Swelling to maculate giraffe.

The circles of the stormy moon
Slide westward toward the River Plate,
Death and the Raven drift above
And Sweeney guards the hornèd gate

Gloomy Orion and the Dog
Are veiled; and hushed the shrunken seas;
The person in the Spanish cape
Tries to sit on Sweeney's knees

Slips and pulls the table cloth
Overturns a coffee-cup,
Reorganized upon the floor
She yawns and draws a stocking up;

The silent man in mocha brown
Sprawls at the window-sill and gapes;
The waiter brings in oranges
Bananas figs and hothouse grapes;

The silent vertebrate in brown
Contracts and concentrates, withdraws;
Rachel *née* Rabinovitch
Tears at the grapes with murderous paws;

She and the lady in the cape
Are suspect, thought to be in league;
Therefore the man with heavy eyes
Declines the gambit, shows fatigue,

Leaves the room and reappears
Outside the window, leaning in,
Branches of wistaria
Circumscribe a golden grin;

The host with someone indistinct
Converses at the door apart,
The nightingales are singing near
The Convent of the Sacred Heart,

And sang within the bloody wood
When Agamemnon cried aloud,
And let their liquid siftings fall
To stain the stiff dishonored shroud. *(1920)*

THE WASTE LAND

"Nam Sibyllam quidem Cumis ego ipse oculis meis vidi in ampulla pendere, et cum illi pueri dicerent: Σίβυλλα τί θέλεις; respondebat illa: ἀποθανεῖν θέλω."

For Ezra Pound *il miglior fabbro.*

I. THE BURIAL OF THE DEAD

April is the cruellest month, breeding
Lilacs out of the dead land, mixing
Memory and desire, stirring
Dull roots with spring rain.
Winter kept us warm, covering
Earth in forgetful snow, feeding
A little life with dried tubers.
Summer surprised us, coming over the Starnbergersee
With a shower of rain; we stopped in the colonnade,
And went on in sunlight, into the Hofgarten,   10
And drank coffee, and talked for an hour.
Bin gar keine Russin, stamm' aus Litauen, echt deutsch.
And when we were children, staying at the archduke's,
My cousin's, he took me out on a sled,
And I was frightened. He said, Marie,
Marie, hold on tight. And down we went.
In the mountains, there you feel free.
I read, much of the night, and go south in the winter.

What are the roots that clutch, what branches grow
Out of this stony rubbish? Son of man,   20
You cannot say, or guess, for you know only
A heap of broken images, where the sun beats,
And the dead tree gives no shelter, the cricket no relief,
And the dry stone no sound of water. Only
There is shadow under this red rock
(Come in under the shadow of this red rock),
And I will show you something different from either
Your shadow at morning striding behind you

Or your shadow at evening rising to meet you;
I will show you fear in a handful of dust.   30

> Frisch weht der Wind
> Der Heimat zu
> Mein Irisch Kind,
> Wo weilest du?

"You gave me hyacinths first a year ago;
They called me the hyacinth girl."
—Yet when we came back, late, from the Hyacinth garden,
Your arms full, and your hair wet, I could not
Speak, and my eyes failed, I was neither
Living nor dead, and I knew nothing,
Looking into the heart of light, the silence.   40
Oed' und leer das Meer.

    Madame Sosostris, famous clairvoyante,
Had a bad cold, nevertheless
Is known to be the wisest woman in Europe,
With a wicked pack of cards. Here, said she,
Is your card, the drowned Phoenician Sailor,
(Those are pearls that were his eyes. Look!)
Here is Belladonna, the Lady of the Rocks,
The lady of situations.   50
Here is the man with three staves, and here the Wheel,
And here is the one-eyed merchant, and this card,
Which is blank, is something he carries on his back,
Which I am forbidden to see. I do not find
The Hanged Man. Fear death by water.
I see crowds of people, walking round in a ring.
Thank you. If you see dear Mrs. Equitone,
Tell her I bring the horoscope myself:
One must be so careful these days.

    Unreal City,   60
Under the brown fog of a winter dawn,
A crowd flowed over London Bridge, so many,
I had not thought death had undone so many.
Sighs, short and infrequent, were exhaled,
And each man fixed his eyes before his feet.
Flowed up the hill and down King William Street,
To where Saint Mary Woolnoth kept the hours

With a dead sound on the final stroke of nine.
There I saw one I knew, and stopped him, crying: "Stetson!
You who were with me in the ships at Mylae!   70
That corpse you planted last year in your garden,
Has it begun to sprout? Will it bloom this year?
Or has the sudden frost disturbed its bed?
Oh keep the Dog far hence, that's friend to men,
Or with his nails he'll dig it up again!
You! hypocrite lecteur!—mon semblable,—mon frère!"

II. A GAME OF CHESS

The Chair she sat in, like a burnished throne,
Glowed on the marble, where the glass
Held up by standards wrought with fruited vines
From which a golden Cupidon peeped out   80
(Another hid his eyes behind his wing)
Doubled the flames of sevenbranched candelabra
Reflecting light upon the table as
The glitter of her jewels rose to meet it,
From satin cases poured in rich profusion;
In vials of ivory and coloured glass
Unstoppered, lurked her strange synthetic perfumes,
Unguent, powdered, or liquid—troubled, confused
And drowned the sense in odours; stirred by the air
That freshened from the window, these ascended   90
In fattening the prolonged candle-flames,
Flung their smoke into the laquearia,
Stirring the pattern on the coffered ceiling.
Huge sea-wood fed with copper
Burned green and orange, framed by the coloured stone,
In which sad light a carvèd dolphin swam.
Above the antique mantel was displayed
As though a window gave upon the sylvan scene
The change of Philomel, by the barbarous king
So rudely forced; yet there the nightingale   100
Filled all the desert with inviolable voice
And still she cried, and still the world pursues,
"Jug Jug" to dirty ears.
And other withered stumps of time
Were told upon the walls; staring forms
Leaned out, leaning, hushing the room enclosed.
Footsteps shuffled on the stair.
Under the firelight, under the brush, her hair

Spread out in fiery points
Glowed into words, then would be savagely still.   110

   "My nerves are bad to-night. Yes, bad. Stay with me.
Speak to me. Why do you never speak. Speak.
    What are you thinking of? What thinking? What?
I never know what you are thinking. Think."

   I think we are in rats' alley
Where the dead men lost their bones.

"What is that noise?"
               The wind under the door.
"What is that noise now? What is the wind doing?"
               Nothing again nothing.   120
                     "Do
You know nothing? Do you see nothing? Do you remember
Nothing?"

   I remember
Those are pearls that were his eyes.
"Are you alive, or not? Is there nothing in your head?"
                               But

O O O O that Shakespeherian Rag—
It's so elegant
So intelligent   130
"What shall I do now? What shall I do?"
"I shall rush out as I am, and walk the street
With my hair down, so. What shall we do to-morrow?
What shall we ever do?"
                   The hot water at ten.
And if it rains, a closed car at four.
And we shall play a game of chess,
Pressing lidless eyes and waiting for a knock upon the door.

   When Lil's husband got demobbed, I said—
I didn't mince my words, I said to her myself,   140
HURRY UP PLEASE ITS TIME
Now Albert's coming back, make yourself a bit smart.
He'll want to know what you done with that money he gave you
To get yourself some teeth. He did, I was there.
You have them all out, Lil, and get a nice set,
He said, I swear, I can't bear to look at you.

And no more can't I, I said, and think of poor Albert,
He's been in the army four years, he wants a good time,
And if you don't give it him, there's others will, I said.
Oh is there, she said. Something o' that, I said.   150
Then I'll know who to thank, she said, and give me a straight look.
HURRY UP PLEASE ITS TIME
If you don't like it you can get on with it, I said.
Others can pick and choose if you can't.
But if Albert makes off, it won't be for lack of telling.
You ought to be ashamed, I said, to look so antique.
(And her only thirty-one.)
I can't help it, she said, pulling a long face,
It's them pills I took, to bring it off, she said.
(She's had five already, and nearly died of young George.)   160
The chemist said it would be all right, but I've never been the same.
You *are* a proper fool, I said.
Well, if Albert won't leave you alone, there it is, I said,
What you get married for if you don't want children?
HURRY UP PLEASE ITS TIME
Well, that Sunday Albert was home, they had a hot gammon,
And they asked me in to dinner, to get the beauty of it hot—
HURRY UP PLEASE ITS TIME
HURRY UP PLEASE ITS TIME
Goonight Bill. Goonight Lou. Goonight May. Goonight.   170
Ta ta. Goonight. Goonight.
Good night, ladies, good night, sweet ladies, good night, good night

III. THE FIRE SERMON

The river's tent is broken: the last fingers of leaf
Clutch and sink into the wet bank. The wind
Crosses the brown land, unheard. The nymphs are departed.
Sweet Thames, run softly, till I end my song.
The river bears no empty bottles, sandwich papers,
Silk handkerchiefs, cardboard boxes, cigarette ends
Or other testimony of summer nights. The nymphs are departed.
And their friends, the loitering heirs of City directors;   180
Departed, have left no addresses.
By the waters of Leman I sat down and wept . . .
Sweet Thames, run softly till I end my song,
Sweet Thames, run softly, for I speak not loud or long.
But at my back in a cold blast I hear
The rattle of the bones, and chuckle spread from ear to ear.
A rat crept softly through the vegetation

Dragging its slimy belly on the bank
While I was fishing in the dull canal
On a winter evening round behind the gashouse   190
Musing upon the king my brother's wreck
And on the king my father's death before him.
White bodies naked on the low damp ground
And bones cast in a little low dry garret,
Rattled by the rat's foot only, year to year.
But at my back from time to time I hear
The sound of horns and motors, which shall bring
Sweeney to Mrs. Porter in the spring.
O the moon shone bright on Mrs. Porter
And on her daughter   200
They wash their feet in soda water
Et O ces voix d'enfants, chantant dans la coupole!

     Twit twit twit
Jug jug jug jug jug jug
So rudely forc'd.
Tereu

     Unreal City
Under the brown fog of a winter noon
Mr. Eugenides, the Smyrna merchant
Unshaven, with a pocket full of currants   210
C.i.f. London: documents at sight,
Asked me in demotic French
To luncheon at the Cannon Street Hotel
Followed by a weekend at the Metropole.

     At the violet hour, when the eyes and back
Turn upward from the desk, when the human engine waits
Like a taxi throbbing waiting,
I Tiresias, though blind, throbbing between two lives,
Old man with wrinkled female breasts, can see
At the violet hour, the evening hour that strives   220
Homeward, and brings the sailor home from sea,
The typist home at teatime, clears her breakfast, lights
Her stove, and lays out food in tins.
Out of the window perilously spread
Her drying combinations touched by the sun's last rays,
On the divan are piled (at night her bed)
Stockings, slippers, camisoles, and stays.
I Tiresias, old man with wrinkled dugs

Perceived the scene, and foretold the rest—
I too awaited the expected guest.   230
He, the young man carbuncular, arrives,
A small house agent's clerk, with one bold stare,
One of the low on whom assurance sits
As a silk hat on a Bradford millionaire.
The time is now propitious, as he guesses,
The meal is ended, she is bored and tired,
Endeavours to engage her in caresses
Which still are unreproved, if undesired.
Flushed and decided, he assaults at once;
Exploring hands encounter no defence;   240
His vanity requires no response,
And makes a welcome of indifference.
(And I Tiresias have foresuffered all
Enacted on this same divan or bed;
I who have sat by Thebes below the wall
And walked among the lowest of the dead.)
Bestows one final patronising kiss,
And gropes his way, finding the stairs unlit . . .

She turns and looks a moment in the glass,
Hardly aware of her departed lover;   250
Her brain allows one half-formed thought to pass:
"Well now that's done: and I'm glad it's over."
When lovely woman stoops to folly and
Paces about her room again, alone,
She smoothes her hair with automatic hand,
And puts a record on the gramophone.

"This music crept by me upon the waters"
And along the Strand, up Queen Victoria Street.
O City city, I can sometimes hear
Beside a public bar in Lower Thames Street,   260
The pleasant whining of a mandoline
And a clatter and a chatter from within
Where fishmen lounge at noon: where the walls
Of Magnus Martyr hold
Inexplicable splendour of Ionian white and gold.

            The river sweats
            Oil and tar
            The barges drift
            With the turning tide

Red sails   270
Wide
To leeward, swing on the heavy spar.
The barges wash
Drifting logs
Down Greenwich reach
Past the Isle of Dogs.
    Weialala leia
    Wallala leialala

    Elizabeth and Leicester
Beating oars   280
The stern was formed
A gilded shell
Red and gold
The brisk swell
Rippled both shores
Southwest wind
Carried down stream
The peal of bells
White towers
    Weialala leia   290
    Wallala leialala

    "Trams and dusty trees.
Highbury bore me Richmond and Kew
Undid me. By Richmond I raised my knees
Supine on the floor of a narrow canoe."

"My feet are at Moorgate, and my heart
Under my feet. After the event
He wept. He promised 'a new start.'
I made no comment. What should I resent?"

    "On Margate Sands.   300
I can connect
Nothing with nothing.
The broken fingernails of dirty hands.
My people humble people who expect
Nothing."
    la la

    To Carthage then I came
    Burning burning burning burning

O Lord Thou pluckest me out
O Lord Thou pluckest   310

burning

IV. DEATH BY WATER

Phlebas the Phoenician, a fortnight dead,
Forgot the cry of gulls, and the deep sea swell
And the profit and loss.
                    A current under sea
Picked his bones in whispers. As he rose and fell
He passed the stages of his age and youth
Entering the whirlpool.
                    Gentile or Jew
O you who turn the wheel and look to windward,   320
Consider Phlebas, who was once handsome and tall as you.

V. WHAT THE THUNDER SAID

After the torchlight red on sweaty faces
After the frosty silence in the gardens
After the agony in stony places
The shouting and the crying
Prison and palace and reverberation
Of thunder of spring over distant mountains
He who was living is now dead
We who were living are now dying
With a little patience   330

    Here is no water but only rock
Rock and no water and the sandy road
The road winding above among the mountains
Which are mountains of rock without water
If there were water we should stop and drink
Amongst the rock one cannot stop or think
Sweat is dry and feet are in the sand
If there were only water amongst the rock
Dead mountain mouth of carious teeth that cannot spit
Here one can neither stand nor lie nor sit   340
There is not even silence in the mountains
But dry sterile thunder without rain
There is not even solitude in the mountains
But red sullen faces sneer and snarl

From doors of mudcracked houses
                    If there were water
    And no rock
    If there were rock
    And also water
    And water   350
    A spring
    A pool among the rock
    If there were the sound of water only
    Not the cicada
    And dry grass singing
    But sound of water over a rock
    Where the hermit-thrush sings in the pine trees
    Drip drop drip drop drop drop drop
    But there is no water

    Who is the third who walks always beside you?   360
    When I count, there are only you and I together
    But when I look ahead up the white road
    There is always another one walking beside you
    Gliding wrapt in a brown mantle, hooded
    I do not know whether a man or a woman
    —But who is that on the other side of you?

    What is that sound high in the air
    Murmur of maternal lamentation
    Who are those hooded hordes swarming
    Over endless plains, stumbling in cracked earth   370
    Ringed by the flat horizon only
    What is the city over the mountains
    Cracks and reforms and bursts in the violet air
    Falling towers
    Jerusalem Athens Alexandria
    Vienna London
    Unreal

    A woman drew her long black hair out tight
    And fiddled whisper music on those strings
    And bats with baby faces in the violet light   380
    Whistled, and beat their wings
    And crawled head downward down a blackened wall
    And upside down in air were towers
    Tolling reminiscent bells, that kept the hours

And voices singing out of empty cisterns and exhausted wells.

    In this decayed hole among the mountains
In the faint moonlight, the grass is singing
Over the tumbled graves, about the chapel
There is the empty chapel, only the wind's home.
It has no windows, and the door swings,   390
Dry bones can harm no one.
Only a cock stood on the rooftree
Co co rico co co rico
In a flash of lightning. Then a damp gust
Bringing rain

    Ganga was sunken, and the limp leaves
Waited for rain, while the black clouds
Gathered far distant, over Himavant.
The jungle crouched, humped in silence.
Then spoke the thunder   400
D<small>A</small>
Datta: what have we given?
My friend, blood shaking my heart
The awful daring of a moment's surrender
Which an age of prudence can never retract
By this, and this only, we have existed
Which is not to be found in our obituaries
Or in memories draped by the beneficent spider
Or under seals broken by the lean solicitor
In our empty rooms   410
D<small>A</small>
Dayadhvam: I have heard the key
Turn in the door once and turn once only
We think of the key, each in his prison
Thinking of the key, each confirms a prison
Only at nightfall, aethereal rumours
Revive for a moment a broken Coriolanus
D<small>A</small>
Damyata: The boat responded
Gaily, to the hand expert with sail and oar   420
The sea was calm, your heart would have responded
Gaily, when invited, beating obedient
To controlling hands

                    I sat upon the shore
Fishing, with the arid plain behind me

Shall I at least set my lands in order?
London Bridge is falling down falling down falling down
Poi s'ascose nel foco che gli affina
Quando fiam uti chelidon—O swallow swallow
Le Prince d'Aquitaine à la tour abolie   430
These fragments I have shored against my ruins
Why then Ile fit you. Hieronymo's mad againe.
Datta. Dayadhvam. Damyata.
 Shantih shantih shantih *(1922)*

AUTHOR'S NOTES ON THE WASTE LAND

Not only the title, but the plan and a good deal of the incidental symbolism of the poem were suggested by Miss Jessie L. Weston's book on the Grail legend: *From Ritual to Romance* (Cambridge). Indeed, so deeply am I indebted, Miss Weston's book will elucidate the difficulties of the poem much better than my notes can do; and I recommend it (apart from the great interest of the book itself) to any who think such elucidation of the poem worth the trouble. To another work of anthropology I am indebted in general, one which has influenced our generation profoundly; I mean *The Golden Bough*; I have used especially the two volumes *Adonis, Attis, Osiris*. Anyone who is acquainted with these works will immediately recognize in the poem certain references to vegetation ceremonies.

I. THE BURIAL OF THE DEAD

Line 20. Cf. *Ezekiel* II, i.
23. Cf. *Ecclesiastes* XII, v.
31. V. *Tristan und Isolde*, I, verses 5–8.
42. Id. III, verse 24.
46. I am not familiar with the exact constitution of the Tarot pack of cards, from which I have obviously departed to suit my own convenience. The Hanged Man, a member of the traditional pack, fits my purpose in two ways: because he is associated in my mind with the Hanged God of Frazer, and because I associate him with the hooded figure in the passage of the disciples to Emmaus in Part V. The Phoenician Sailor and the Merchant appear later; also the "crowds of people," and Death by Water is executed in Part IV. The Man with Three Staves (an authentic member of the Tarot pack) I associate, quite arbitrarily, with the Fisher King himself.
60. Cf. Baudelaire:
      "Fourmillante cité, cité pleine de rêves,
          Où le spectre en plein jour raccroche le passant"
63. Cf. *Inferno*, III, 55–7:
                                "sì lunga tratta
          di gente, ch'io non averei creduto

che morte tanta n'avesse disfatta."
64. Cf. *Inferno*, IV, 25–7:
"Quivi, secondo che per ascoltare,
"non avea pianto, ma' che di sospiri,
"che l'aura eterna facevan tremare."
68. A phenomenon which I have often noticed.
74. Cf. the Dirge in Webster's *White Devil*.
76. V. Baudelaire, Preface to *Fleurs du Mal*.

II. A GAME OF CHESS

77. Cf. *Antony and Cleopatra*, II, ii, l. 190.
92. Laquearia. V. *Aeneid*, I, 726:
dependent lychni laquearibus aureis incensi, et noctem flammis funalia vincunt.
98. Sylvan scene. V. Milton, *Paradise Lost*, IV, 140.
99. V. Ovid, *Metamorphoses*, VI, Philomela.
100. Cf. Part III, l. 204.
115. Cf. Part III, l. 195.
118. Cf. Webster: "Is the wind in that door still?"
126. Cf. Part I, l. 37, 48.
138. Cf. the game of chess in Middleton's *Women beware Women*

III. THE FIRE SERMON

176. V. Spenser, *Prothalamion*.
192. Cf. *The Tempest*, I, ii.
196. Cf. Marvell, *To His Coy Mistress*.
197. Cf. Day, *Parliament of Bees*:
"When of the sudden, listening, you shall hear,
"A noise of horns and hunting, which shall bring
"Actaeon to Diana in the spring,
"Where all shall see her naked skin . . ."
199. I do not know the origin of the ballad from which these lines are taken: it was reported to me from Sydney, Australia.
202. V. Verlaine, *Parsifal*.
210. The currants were quoted at a price "cost insurance and freight to London"; and the Bill of Lading, etc., were to be handed to the buyer upon payment of the sight draft.
218. Tiresias, although a mere spectator and not indeed a "character," is yet the most important personage in the poem, uniting all the rest. Just as the one-eyed merchant, seller of currants, melts into the Phoenician Sailor, and the latter is not wholly distinct from Ferdinand Prince of Naples, so all the women are one woman, and the two sexes meet in Tiresias. What Tiresias *sees*, in fact, is the substance of the poem. The whole passage from Ovid is of great anthropological interest:
". . . Cum Iunone iocos et maior vestra profecto est
Quam, quae contingit maribus," dixisse, "voluptas."

Illa negat; placuit quae sit sententia docti
Quaerere Tiresiae: venus huic erat utraque nota.
Nam duo magnorum viridi coeuntia silva
Corpora serpentum baculi violaverat ictu
Deque viro factus, mirabile, femina septem
Egerat autumnos; octavo rursus eosdem
Vidit et "est vestrae si tanta potentia plagae,"
Dixit "ut auctoris sortem in contraria mutet,
Nunc quoque vos feriam!" percussis anguibus isdem
Forma prior rediit genetivaque venit imago.
Arbiter hic igitur sumptus de lite iocosa
Dicta Iovis firmat; gravius Saturnia iusto
Nec pro materia fertur doluisse suique
Iudicis aeterna damnavit lumina nocte,
At pater omnipotens (neque enim licet inrita cuiquam
Facta dei fecisse deo) pro lumine adempto
Scire futura dedit poenamque levavit honore.

221. This may not appear as exact as Sappho's lines, but I had in mind the "longshore" or "dory" fisherman, who returns at nightfall.

253. V. Goldsmith, the song in *The Vicar of Wakefield*.

257. V. *The Tempest*, as above.

264. The interior of St. Magnus Martyr is to my mind one of the finest among Wren's interiors. See *The Proposed Demolition of Nineteen City Churches* (P. S. King & Son, Ltd.).

266. The Song of the (three) Thames-daughters begins here. From line 292 to 306 inclusive they speak in turn. V. *Götterdämmerung*, III, i: the Rhine-daughters.

279. V. Froude, *Elizabeth*, Vol. I, ch. iv, letter of De Quadra to Philip of Spain:

"In the afternoon we were in a barge, watching the games on the river. (The queen) was alone with Lord Robert and myself on the poop, when they began to talk nonsense, and went so far that Lord Robert at last said, as I was on the spot there was no reason why they should not be married if the queen pleased."

293. Cf. *Purgatorio*, V., 133:

"Ricorditi di me, che son la Pia;
"Siena mi fe', disfecemi Maremma."

307. V. St. Augustine's *Confessions*: "to Carthage then I came, where a cauldron of unholy loves sang all about mine ears."

308. The complete text of the Buddha's Fire Sermon (which corresponds in importance to the Sermon on the Mount) from which these words are taken, will be found translated in the late Henry Clarke Warren's *Buddhism in Translation* (Harvard Oriental Series). Mr. Warren was one of the great pioneers of Buddhist studies in the Occident.

309. From St. Augustine's *Confessions* again. The collocation of these two representatives of eastern and western asceticism, as the culmination of this part of the poem, is not an accident.

V. WHAT THE THUNDER SAID

In the first part of Part V three themes are employed: the journey to Emmaus, the approach to the Chapel Perilous (see Miss Weston's book) and the present decay of eastern Europe.

357. This is *Turdus aonalaschkae pallasii*, the hermit-thrush which I have heard in Quebec Province. Chapman says (*Handbook of Birds of Eastern North America*) "it is most at home in secluded woodland and thickety retreats. . . . Its notes are not remarkable for variety or volume, but in purity and sweetness of tone and exquisite modulation they are unequalled." Its "water-dripping song" is justly celebrated.

360. The following lines were stimulated by the account of one of the Antarctic expeditions (I forget which, but I think one of Shackleton's): it was related that the party of explorers, at the extremity of their strengh, had the constant delusion that there was *one more member* than could actually be counted.

367–77. Cf. Hermann Hesse, *Blick ins Chaos*: "Schon ist halb Europa, schon ist zumindest der halbe Osten Europas auf dem Wege zum Chaos, fährt betrunken im heiligen Wahn am Abgrund entlang und singt dazu, singt betrunken und hymnisch wie Dmitri Karamasoff sang. Ueber diese Lieder lacht der Bürger beleidigt, der Heilige und Seher hört sie mit Tränen."

402. "Datta, dayadhvam, damyata" (Give, sympathize, control). The fable of the meaning of the Thunder is found in the *Brihadaranyaka—Upanishad*, 5, 1. A translation is found in Deussen's *Sechzig Upanishads des Veda*, p. 489.

408. Cf. Webster, *The White Devil*, V, vi:
". . . they'll remarry
Ere the worm pierce your winding-sheet, ere the spider
Make a thin curtain for your epitaphs."

412. Cf. *Inferno*, XXXIII, 46:
"ed io sentii chiavar l'uscio di sotto
all'orribile torre."

Also F. H. Bradley, *Appearance and Reality*, p. 346. "My external sensations are no less private to myself than are my thoughts or my feelings. In either case my experience falls within my own circle, a circle closed on the outside; and, with all its elements alike, every sphere is opaque to the others which surround it. . . . In brief, regarded as an existence which appears in a soul, the whole world for each is peculiar and private to that soul."

425. V. Weston: *From Ritual to Romance;* chapter on the Fisher King.

428. V. *Purgatorio*, XXVI, 148:
" 'Ara vos prec, per aquella valor
que vos guida al som de l'escalina,
sovegna vos a temps de ma dolor.'
Poi s'ascose nel foco che gli affina."

429. V. *Pervigilium Veneris*. Cf. Philomela in Parts II and III.

430. V. Gerard de Nerval, Sonnet *El Desdichado*.
432. V. Kyd's *Spanish Tragedy*.
434. Shantih. Repeated as here, a formal ending to an Upanishad. "The Peace which passeth understanding" is our equivalent to this word.

MARINA

Quis hic locus, quae regio, quae mundi plaga?

What seas what shores what grey rocks and what islands
What water lapping the bow
And scent of pine and the woodthrush singing through the fog
What images return
O my daughter.

    Those who sharpen the tooth of the dog, meaning
Death
Those who glitter with the glory of the humming-bird, meaning
Death
Those who sit in the sty of contentment, meaning
Death
Those who suffer the ecstasy of the animals, meaning
Death

    Are become unsubstantial, reduced by a wind,
A breath of pine, and the woodsong fog
By this grace dissolved in place

    What is this face, less clear and clearer
The pulse in the arm, less strong and stronger—
Given or lent? more distant than stars and nearer than the eye

    Whispers and small laughter between leaves and hurrying feet
Under sleep, where all the waters meet.

    Bowsprit cracked with ice and paint cracked with heat.
I made this, I have forgotten
And remember.
The rigging weak and the canvas rotten
Between one June and another September.
Made this unknowing, half conscious, unknown, my own.
The garboard strake leaks, the seams need caulking.
This form, this face, this life
Living to live in a world of time beyond me; let me

Resign my life for this life, my speech for that unspoken,
The awakened, lips parted, the hope, the new ships.

What seas what shores what granite islands towards my timbers
And woodthrush calling through the fog
My daughter.   *(1930)*

BURNT NORTON

τοῦ λόγου δ'ἐόντος ξυνοῦ ζώουσιν οἱ πολλοὶ
ὡς ἰδίαν ἔχοντες φρόνησιν.—I, p. 77. Fr. 2.
ὁδὸς ἄνω κάτω μία καὶ ὡυτή.—I, p. 89. Fr. 60.
Diels: *Die Fragmente der Vorsokratiker* (Herakleitos).

1

Time present and time past
Are both perhaps present in time future,
And time future contained in time past.
If all time is eternally present
All time is unredeemable.
What might have been is an abstraction
Remaining a perpetual possibility
Only in a world of speculation.
What might have been and what has been
Point to one end, which is always present.
Footfalls echo in the memory
Down the passage which we did not take
Towards the door we never opened
Into the rose-garden. My words echo
Thus, in your mind.
                    But to what purpose
Disturbing the dust on a bowl of rose-leaves
I do not know.
              Other echoes
Inhabit the garden. Shall we follow?
Quick, said the bird, find them, find them,
Round the corner. Through the first gate,
Into our first world, shall we follow
The deception of the thrush? Into our first world.
There they were, dignified, invisible,
Moving without pressure, over the dead leaves,
In the autumn heat, through the vibrant air,
And the bird called, in response to

The unheard music hidden in the shrubbery,
And the unseen eyebeam crossed, for the roses
Had the look of flowers that are looked at.
There they were as our guests, accepted and accepting.
So we moved, and they, in a formal pattern,
Along the empty alley, into the box circle,
To look down into the drained pool.
Dry the pool, dry concrete, brown edged,
And the pool was filled with water out of sunlight,
And the lotos rose, quietly, quietly,
The surface glittered out of heart of light,
And they were behind us, reflected in the pool.
Then a cloud passed, and the pool was empty.
Go, said the bird, for the leaves were full of children,
Hidden excitedly, containing laughter.
Go, go, go, said the bird: human kind
Cannot bear very much reality.
Time past and time future
What might have been and what has been
Point to one end, which is always present

2

Garlic and sapphires in the mud
Clot the bedded axle-tree.
The trilling wire in the blood
Sings below inveterate scars
And reconciles forgotten wars.
The dance along the artery
The circulation of the lymph
Are figured in the drift of stars
Ascend to summer in the tree
We move above the moving tree
In light upon the figured leaf
And hear upon the sodden floor
Below, the boarhound and the boar
Pursue their pattern as before
But reconciled among the stars.

At the still point of the turning world. Neither flesh nor fleshless;
Neither from nor towards; at the still point, there the dance is,
But neither arrest nor movement. And do not call it fixity,
Where past and future are gathered. Neither movement from nor to-
wards,

Neither ascent nor decline. Except for the point, the still point,
There would be no dance, and there is only the dance.
I can only say, *there* we have been: but I cannot say where.
And I cannot say, how long, for that is to place it in time.

   The inner freedom from the practical desire,
The release from action and suffering, release from the inner
And the outer compulsion, yet surrounded
By a grace of sense, a white light still and moving,
Erhebung without motion, concentration
Without elimination, both a new world
And the old made explicit, understood
In the completion of its partial ecstasy,
The resolution of its partial horror.
Yet the enchainment of past and future
Woven in the weakness of the changing body,
Protects mankind from heaven and damnation
Which flesh cannot endure.
                Time past and time future
Allow but a little consciousness.
To be conscious is not to be in time
But only in time can the moment in the rose-garden,
The moment in the arbour where the rain beat,
The moment in the draughty church at smokefall
Be remembered; involved with past and future.
Only through time time is conquered.

3

Here is a place of disaffection
Time before and time after
In a dim light: neither daylight
Investing form with lucid stillness
Turning shadow into transient beauty
With slow rotation suggesting permanence
Nor darkness to purify the soul
Emptying the sensual with deprivation
Cleansing affection from the temporal.
Neither plenitude nor vacancy. Only a flicker
Over the strained time-ridden faces
Distracted from distraction by distraction
Filled with fancies and empty of meaning
Tumid apathy with no concentration
Men and bits of paper, whirled by the cold wind

That blows before and after time,
Wind in and out of unwholesome lungs
Time before and time after.
Eructation of unhealthy souls
Into the faded air, the torpid
Driven on the wind that sweeps the gloomy hills of London,
Hampstead and Clerkenwell, Campden and Putney,
Highgate, Primrose and Ludgate. Not here
Not here the darkness, in this twittering world.

    Descend lower, descend only
Into the world of perpetual solitude,
World not world, but that which is not world,
Internal darkness, deprivation
And destitution of all property,
Desiccation of the world of sense,
Evacuation of the world of fancy,
Inoperancy of the world of spirit;
This is the one way, and the other
Is the same, not in movement
But abstention from movement; while the world moves
In appetency, on its metalled ways
Of time past and time future.

4

Time and the bell have buried the day,
The black cloud carries the sun away.
Will the sunflower turn to us, will the clematis
Stray down, bend to us; tendril and spray
Clutch and cling?
Chill
Fingers of yew be curled
Down on us? After the kingfisher's wing
Has answered light to light, and is silent, the light is still
At the still point of the turning world.

5

Words move, music moves
Only in time; but that which is only living
Can only die. Words, after speech, reach
Into the silence. Only by the form, the pattern,
Can words or music reach
The stillness, as a Chinese jar still

Moves perpetually in its stillness.
Not the stillness of the violin, while the note lasts,
Not that only, but the co-existence,
Or say that the end precedes the beginning,
And the end and the beginning were always there
Before the beginning and after the end.
And all is always now. Words strain,
Crack and sometimes break, under the burden,
Under the tension, slip, slide, perish,
Decay with imprecision, will not stay in place,
Will not stay still. Shrieking voices
Scolding, mocking, or merely chattering,
Always assail them. The Word in the desert
Is most attacked by voices of temptation,
The crying shadow in the funeral dance,
The loud lament of the disconsolate chimera.

   The detail of the pattern is movement,
As in the figure of the ten stairs.
Desire itself is movement
Not in itself desirable;
Love is itself unmoving,
Only the cause and end of movement,
Timeless, and undesiring
Except in the aspect of time
Caught in the form of limitation
Between un-being and being.
Sudden in a shaft of sunlight
Even while the dust moves
There rises the hidden laughter
Of children in the foliage
Quick now, here, now, always—
Ridiculous the waste sad time
Stretching before and after.   (1936)

Conrad Aiken
(1889–   )

[MUSIC I HEARD WITH YOU]

Music I heard with you was more than music,
And bread I broke with you was more than bread;
Now that I am without you, all is desolate;
All that was once so beautiful is dead.

Your hands once touched this table and this silver,
And I have seen your fingers hold this glass.
These things do not remember you, belovèd,—
And yet your touch upon them will not pass.

For it was in my heart you moved among them,
And blessed them with your hands and with your eyes;
And in my heart they will remember always,—
They knew you once, O beautiful and wise.   (*1916*)

MORNING SONG *from* SENLIN

It is morning, Senlin says, and in the morning
When the light drips through the shutters like the dew,
I arise, I face the sunrise,
And do the things my fathers learned to do.
Stars in the purple dusk above the rooftops
Pale in a saffron mist and seem to die,
And I myself on a swiftly tilting planet
Stand before a glass and tie my tie.

Vine leaves tap my window,
Dew-drops sing to the garden stones,
The robin chirps in the chinaberry tree
Repeating three clear tones.

It is morning. I stand by the mirror
And tie my tie once more,

While waves far off in a pale rose twilight
Crash on a white sand shore.
I stand by a mirror and comb my hair:
How small and white my face!—
The green earth tilts through a sphere of air
And bathes in a flame of space.

There are houses hanging above the stars
And stars hung under a sea . . .
And a sun far off in a shell of silence
Dapples my walls for me . . .

It is morning, Senlin says, and in the morning
Should I not pause in the light to remember god?
Upright and firm I stand on a star unstable,
He is immense and lonely as a cloud.
I will dedicate this moment before my mirror
To him alone; for him I will comb my hair.
Accept these humble offerings, cloud of silence!
I will think of you as I descend the stair.

Vine leaves tap my window,
The snail-track shines on the stones,
Dew-drops flash from the chinaberry tree
Repeating two clear tones.

It is morning, I awake from a bed of silence,
Shining I rise from the starless waters of sleep.
The walls are about me still as in the evening,
I am the same, and the same name still I keep.
The earth revolves with me, yet makes no motion,
The stars pale silently in a coral sky.
In a whistling void I stand before my mirror,
Unconcerned, and tie my tie.

There are horses neighing on far-off hills
Tossing their long white manes,
And mountains flash in the rose-white dusk,
Their shoulders black with rains . . .
It is morning. I stand by the mirror
And surprise my soul once more;
The blue air rushes above my ceiling,
There are suns beneath my floor . . .

... It is morning, Senlin says, I ascend from darkness
And depart on the winds of space for I know not where,
My watch is wound, a key is in my pocket,
And the sky is darkened as I descend the stair.
There are shadows across the windows, clouds in heaven,
And a god among the stars; and I will go
Thinking of him as I might think of daybreak
And humming a tune I know ...

Vine leaves tap at the window,
Dew-drops sing to the garden stones,
The robin chirps in the chinaberry tree
Repeating three clear tones. *(1918)*

From *PRIAPUS AND THE POOL*

4

This is the shape of the leaf, and this of the flower,
And this the pale bole of the tree
Which watches its bough in a pool of unwavering water
In a land we never shall see.

The thrush on the bough is silent, the dew falls softly,
In the evening is hardly a sound.
And the three beautiful pilgrims who come here together
Touch lightly the dust of the ground,

Touch it with feet that trouble the dust but as wings do,
Come shyly together, are still,
Like dancers who wait, in a pause of the music, for music
The exquisite silence to fill.

This is the thought of the first, and this of the second,
And this the grave thought of the third:
"Linger we thus for a moment, palely expectant,
And silence will end, and the bird

"Sing the pure phrase, sweet phrase, clear phrase in the twilight
To fill the blue bell of the world;
And we, who on music so leaflike have drifted together,
Leaflike apart shall be whirled

"Into what but the beauty of silence, silence forever?" ...
... This is the shape of the tree,

And the flower, and the leaf, and the three pale beautiful pilgrims
This is what you are to me. (*1920–21, 1925*)

THE WEDDING

At noon, Tithonus, withered by his singing,
Climbing the oatstalk with his hairy legs,
Met grey Arachne, poisoned and shrunk down
By her own beauty; pride had shrivelled both.
In the white web—where seven flies hung wrapped—
She heard his footstep; hurried to him; bound him;
Enshrouded him in silk; then poisoned him.
Twice shrieked Tithonus, feebly; then was still.
Arachne loved him. Did he love Arachne?
She watched him with red eyes, venomous sparks,
And the furred claws outspread . . . "O sweet Tithonus!
Darling! Be kind, and sing that song again!
Shake the bright web again with that deep fiddling!
Are you much poisoned? sleeping? do you dream?
Darling Tithonus!"

        And Tithonus, weakly
Moving one hairy shin against the other
Within the silken sack, contrived to fiddle
A little tune, half-hearted: "Shrewd Arachne!
Whom pride in beauty withered to this shape
As pride in singing shrivelled me to mine—
Unwrap me, let me go—and let me limp,
With what poor strength your venom leaves me, down
This oatstalk, and away."

        Arachne, angry,
Stung him again, twirling him with rough paws,
The red eyes keen. "What! you would dare to leave me?
Unkind Tithonus! Sooner I'll kill and eat you
Than let you go. But sing that tune again—
So plaintive was it!"

        And Tithonus faintly
Moved the poor fiddles, which were growing cold,
And sang: "Arachne, goddess envied of gods,
Beauty's eclipse eclipsed by angry beauty,
Have pity, do not ask the withered heart
To sing too long for you! My strength goes out,

Too late we meet for love. O be content
With friendship, which the noon sun once may kindle
To give one flash of passion, like a dewdrop,
Before it goes! . . . Be reasonable, Arachne!"

Arachne heard the song grow weaker, dwindle
To first a rustle, and then half a rustle,
And last a tick, so small no ear could hear it
Save hers, a spider's ear. And her small heart,
(Rusted away, like his, to a pinch of dust,)
Gleamed once, like his, and died. She clasped him tightly
And sunk her fangs in him. Tithonus dead,
She slept awhile, her last sensation gone;
Woke from the nap, forgetting him; and ate him.   (*1925*)

[WATCH LONG ENOUGH, AND YOU WILL SEE]

Watch long enough, and you will see the leaf
Fall from the bough. Without a sound it falls:
And soundless meets the grass. . . . And so you have
A bare bough, and a dead leaf in dead grass.
Something has come and gone. And that is all.

But what were all the tumults in this action?
What wars of atoms in the twig, what ruins,
Fiery and disastrous, in the leaf?
Timeless the tumult was, but gave no sign.
Only, the leaf fell, and the bough is bare.

This is the world: there is no more than this.
The unseen and disastrous prelude, shaking
The trivial act from the terrific action.
Speak: and the ghosts of change, past and to come,
Throng the brief word. The maelstrom has us all.   (*1931*)

[KEEP IN THE HEART THE JOURNAL]

Keep in the heart the journal nature keeps;
Mark down the limp nasturtium leaf with frost;
See that the hawthorn bough is ice-embossed,
And that the snail, in season, has his grief;
Design the winter on the window pane;
Admit pale sun through cobwebs left from autumn;

Remember summer when the flies are stilled;
Remember spring, when the cold spider sleeps.

Such diary, too, set down as this: the heart
Beat twice or thrice this day for no good reason;
For friends and sweethearts dead before their season;
For wisdom come too late, and come to naught.
Put down "the hand that shakes," "the eye that glazes";
The "step that falters betwixt thence and hence";
Observe that hips and haws burn brightest red
When the North Pole and sun are most apart.

Note that the moon is here, as cold as ever,
With ages on her face, and ice and snow;
Such as the freezing mind alone can know,
When loves and hates are only twigs that shiver.
Add in a postscript that the rain is over,
The wind from southwest backing to the south,
Disasters all forgotten, hurts forgiven;
And that the North Star, altered, shines forever.

Then say: I was a part of nature's plan;
Knew her cold heart, for I was consciousness;
Came first to hate her, and at last to bless;
Believed in her; doubted; believed again.
My love the lichen had such roots as I,—
The snowflake was my father; I return,
After this interval of faith and question,
To nature's heart, in pain, as I began. *(1931)*

[BEND AS THE BOW BENDS]

Bend as the bow bends, and let fly the shaft,
the strong cord loose its words as light as flame;
speak without cunning, love, as without craft,
careless of answer, as of shame or blame.
This to be known, that love is love, despite
knowledge or ignorance, truth, untruth, despair;
careless of all things, if that love be bright,
careless of hate and fate, careless of care.
Spring the word as it must, the leaf or flower,
broken or bruised, yet let it, broken, speak
of time transcending this too transient hour,

and space that finds the beating heart too weak.
Thus, and thus only, will our tempest come
by continents of snow to find a home. *(1940)*

[SNOWFLAKE ON ASPHODEL]

Snowflake on asphodel, clear ice on rose,
frost over thistledown, the instant death
that speaks Time's judgment, turning verse to prose,
or withering June to blackness in a breath—
icicle, cheek by jowl with goldenrod,
and on the purple aster silver rime,
a web of death, bright as the web of god,
spun on these simple themes and schemes by time:
snowflake on asphodel—how clear, how bright
the blue burns through the melting star! how brave
the dying flower, and the snow how light
that on the dying flower makes his grave!
Snow's death on dying flower, yet both immortal—
love, these are you and I—enter this portal. *(1940)*

SOUTH END

The benches are broken, the grassplots brown and bare,
the laurels dejected, in this neglected square.
Dogs couple undisturbed. The roots of trees
heave up the bricks in the sidewalk as they please.

Nobody collects the papers from the grass,
nor the dead matches, nor the broken glass.
The elms are old and shabby; the houses, around,
stare lazily through paintless shutters at forgotten ground.

Out of the dusty fountain, with the dust,
the leaves fly up like birds on a sudden gust.
The leaves fly up like birds, and the papers flap,
or round the legs of benches wrap and unwrap.

Here, for the benefit of some secret sense,
warm-autumn-afternoon finds permanence.
No one will hurry, or wait too long, or die:
all is serenity, under a serene sky.

Dignity shines in old brick and old dirt,
in elms and houses now hurt beyond all hurt.

A broken square, where little lives or moves;
these are the city's earliest and tenderest loves. *(1942)*

THE WINDOW

She looks out in the blue morning
and sees a whole wonderful world
she looks out in the morning
and sees a whole world

she leans out of the window
and this is what she sees
a wet rose singing to the sun
with a chorus of red bees

she leans out of the window
and laughs for the window is high
she is in it like a bird on a perch
and they scoop the blue sky

she and the window scooping
the morning as if it were air
scooping a green wave of leaves
above a stone stair

and an urn hung with leaden garlands
and girls holding hands in a ring
and raindrops on an iron railing
shining like a harp string

an old man draws with his ferrule
in wet sand a map of Spain
the marble soldier on his pedestal
draws a stiff diagram of pain

but the walls around her tremble
with the speed of the earth the floor
curves to the terrestrial center
and behind her the door

opens darkly down to the beginning
far down to the first simple cry
and the animal waking in water
and the opening of the eye

she looks out in the blue morning
and sees a whole wonderful world
she looks out in the morning
and sees a whole world.   *(1949)*

Edna St. Vincent Millay
(1892–1950)

GOD'S WORLD

O World, I cannot hold thee close enough!
  Thy winds, thy wide grey skies!
  Thy mists, that roll and rise!
Thy woods, this autumn day, that ache and sag
And all but cry with color! That gaunt crag
To crush! To lift the lean of that black bluff!
World, World, I cannot get thee close enough!

Long have I known a glory in it all,
  But never knew I this;
  Here such a passion is
As stretcheth me apart,—Lord, I do fear
Thou'st made the world too beautiful this year;
My soul is all but out of me,—let fall
No burning leaf; prithee, let no bird call. *(1917)*

THE PHILOSOPHER

And what are you that, wanting you,
  I should be kept awake
As many nights as there are days
  With weeping for your sake?

And what are you that, missing you,
  As many days as crawl
I should be listening to the wind
  And looking at the wall?

I know a man that's a braver man
  And twenty men as kind,
And what are you, that you should be
  The one man in my mind?

II-297

Yet women's ways are witless ways,
    As any sage will tell,—
And what am I, that I should love
    So wisely and so well? (*1920*)

ELEGY BEFORE DEATH

There will be rose and rhododendron
    When you are dead and under ground;
Still will be heard from white syringas
    Heavy with bees, a sunny sound;

Still will the tamaracks be raining
    After the rain has ceased, and still
Will there be robins in the stubble,
    Brown sheep upon the warm green hill.

Spring will not ail nor autumn falter;
    Nothing will know that you are gone,
Saving alone some sullen plough-land
    None but yourself sets foot upon;

Saving the may-weed and the pig-weed
    Nothing will know that you are dead,—
These, and perhaps a useless wagon
    Standing beside some tumbled shed.

Oh, there will pass with your great passing
    Little of beauty not your own,—
Only the light from common water,
    Only the grace from simple stone! (*1921*)

PASSER MORTUUS EST

Death devours all lovely things:
    Lesbia with her sparrow
Shares the darkness,—presently
    Every bed is narrow.

Unremembered as old rain
    Dries the sheer libation;
And the little petulant hand
    Is an annotation.

After all, my erstwhile dear,
   My no longer cherished,
Need we say it was not love,
   Just because it perished?   *(1921)*

SONG OF A SECOND APRIL

April this year, not otherwise
   Than April of a year ago,
Is full of whispers, full of sighs,
   Of dazzling mud and dingy snow;
   Hepaticas that pleased you so
Are here again, and butterflies.

There rings a hammering all day,
   And shingles lie about the doors;
In orchards near and far away
   The grey wood-pecker taps and bores;
   And men are merry at their chores,
And children earnest at their play.

The larger streams run still and deep,
   Noisy and swift the small brooks run;
Among the mullein stalks the sheep
   Go up the hillside in the sun,
   Pensively,—only you are gone,
You that alone I cared to keep.   *(1921)*

ELEGY

Let them bury your big eyes
In the secret earth securely,
Your thin fingers, and your fair,
Soft, indefinite-coloured hair,—
All of these in some way, surely,
From the secret earth shall rise;
Not for these I sit and stare,
Broken and bereft completely:
Your young flesh that sat so neatly
On your little bones will sweetly
Blossom in the air.

But your voice . . . never the rushing
Of a river underground,

Not the rising of the wind
In the trees before the rain,
Not the woodcock's watery call,
Not the note the white-throat utters,
Not the feet of children pushing
Yellow leaves along the gutters
In the blue and bitter fall,
Shall content my musing mind
For the beauty of that sound
That in no new way at all
Ever will be heard again.

Sweetly through the sappy stalk
Of the vigorous weed,
Holding all it held before,
Cherished by the faithful sun,
On and on eternally
Shall your altered fluid run,
Bud and bloom and go to seed:
But your singing days are done;
But the music of your talk
Never shall the chemistry
Of the secret earth restore.
All your lovely words are spoken.
Once the ivory box is broken,
Beats the golden bird no more. *(1921)*

WILD SWANS

I looked in my heart while the wild swans went over.
And what did I see I had not seen before?
Only a question less or a question more;
Nothing to match the flight of wild birds flying.
Tiresome heart, forever living and dying,
House without air, I leave you and lock your door.
Wild swans, come over the town, come over
The town again, trailing your legs and crying! *(1921)*

[PITY ME NOT BECAUSE THE LIGHT OF DAY]

Pity me not because the light of day
At close of day no longer walks the sky;
Pity me not for beauties passed away

From field and thicket as the year goes by;
Pity me not the waning of the moon,
Nor that the ebbing tide goes out to sea,
Nor that a man's desire is hushed so soon,
And you no longer look with love on me.
This have I known always: Love is no more
Than the wide blossom which the wind assails,
Than the great tide that treads the shifting shore,
Strewing fresh wreckage gathered in the gales:
Pity me that the heart is slow to learn
What the swift mind beholds at every turn.   *(1923)*

[EUCLID ALONE HAS LOOKED ON BEAUTY BARE]

Euclid alone has looked on Beauty bare.
Let all who prate of Beauty hold their peace,
And lay them prone upon the earth and cease
To ponder on themselves, the while they stare
At nothing, intricately drawn nowhere
In shapes of shifting lineage; let geese
Gabble and hiss, but heroes seek release
From dusty bondage into luminous air.
O blinding hour, O holy, terrible day,
When first the shaft into his vision shone
Of light anatomized! Euclid alone
Has looked on Beauty bare. Fortunate they
Who, though once only and then but far away,
Have heard her massive sandal set on stone.   *(1923)*

DIRGE WITHOUT MUSIC

I am not resigned to the shutting away of loving hearts in the hard
   ground.
So it is, and so it will be, for so it has been, time out of mind:
Into the darkness they go, the wise and the lovely. Crowned
With lilies and with laurel they go; but I am not resigned.

Lovers and thinkers, into the earth with you.
Be one with the dull, the indiscriminate dust.
A fragment of what you felt, of what you knew,
A formula, a phrase remains,—but the best is lost.

The answers quick and keen, the honest look, the laughter, the love,—
They are gone. They are gone to feed the roses. Elegant and curled
Is the blossom. Fragrant is the blossom. I know. But I do not approve.
More precious was the light in your eyes than all the roses in the world.

Down, down, down into the darkness of the grave
Gently they go, the beautiful, the tender, the kind;
Quietly they go, the intelligent, the witty, the brave.
I know. But I do not approve. And I am not resigned. *(1928)*

SONNET TO GATH

Country of hunchbacks!—where the strong, straight spine,
Jeered at by crooked children, makes his way
Through by-streets at the kindest hour of day,
Till he deplore his stature, and incline
To measure manhood with a gibbous line;
Till out of loneliness, being flawed with clay,
He stoop into his neighbour's house and say,
"Your roof is low for me—the fault is mine."
Dust in an urn long since, dispersed and dead
Is great Apollo; and the happier he;
Since who amongst you all would lift a head
At a god's radiance on the mean door-tree,
Saving to run and hide your dates and bread,
And cluck your children in about your knee? *(1928)*

From FATAL INTERVIEW

11

Not in a silver casket cool with pearls
Or rich with red corundum or with blue,
Locked, and the key withheld, as other girls
Have given their loves, I give my love to you;
Not in a lovers'-knot, not in a ring
Worked in such fashion, and the legend plain—
Semper fidelis, where a secret spring
Kennels a drop of mischief for the brain:
Love in the open hand, no thing but that,
Ungemmed, unhidden, wishing not to hurt,
As one should bring you cowslips in a hat
Swung from the hand, or apples in her skirt,

I bring you, calling out as children do:
"Look what I have!—And these are all for you."

30

Love is not all; it is not meat nor drink
Nor slumber nor a roof against the rain,
Nor yet a floating spar to men that sink
And rise and sink and rise and sink again;
Love can not fill the thickened lung with breath,
Nor clean the blood, nor set the fractured bone;
Yet many a man is making friends with death
Even as I speak, for lack of love alone.
It well may be that in a difficult hour,
Pinned down by pain and moaning for release,
Or nagged by want past resolution's power,
I might be driven to sell your love for peace,
　Or trade the memory of this night for food.
　It well may be. I do not think I would.

36

Hearing your words, and not a word among them
Tuned to my liking, on a salty day
When inland woods were pushed by winds that flung them
Hissing to leeward like a ton of spray,
I thought how off Matinicus the tide
Came pounding in, came running through the Gut,
While from the Rock the warning whistle cried,
And children whimpered, and the doors blew shut;
There in the autumn when the men go forth,
With slapping skirts the island women stand
In gardens stripped and scattered, peering north,
With dahlia tubers dripping from the hand:
The wind of their endurance, driving south,
Flattened your words against your speaking mouth.

52

Oh, sleep forever in the Latmian cave,
Mortal Endymion, darling of the Moon!
Her silver garments by the senseless wave
Shouldered and dropped and on the shingle strewn,
Her fluttering hand against her forehead pressed,
Her scattered looks that trouble all the sky,
Her rapid footsteps running down the west—

Of all her altered state, oblivious lie!
Whom earthen you, by deathless lips adored,
Wild-eyed and stammering to the grasses thrust,
And deep into her crystal body poured
The hot and sorrowful sweetness of the dust:
Whereof she wanders mad, being all unfit
For mortal love, that might not die of it. *(1931)*

From EPITAPH FOR THE RACE OF MAN

6

See where Capella with her golden kids
Grazes the slope between the east and north:
Thus when the builders of the pyramids
Flung down their tools at nightfall and poured forth
Homeward to supper and a poor man's bed,
Shortening the road with friendly jest and slur,
The risen She-Goat showing blue and red
Climbed the clear dusk, and three stars followed her.
Safe in their linen and their spices lie
The kings of Egypt; even as long ago
Under these constellations, with long eye
And scented limbs they slept, and feared no foe.
Their will was law; their will was not to die:
And so they had their way; or nearly so. *(1934)*

ON THE WIDE HEATH

On the wide heath at evening overtaken,
    When the fast-reddening sun
Drops, and against the sky the looming bracken
    Waves, and the day is done,

Though no unfriendly nostril snuffs his bone,
    Though English wolves be dead,
The fox abroad on errands of his own,
    The adder gone to bed,

The weary traveler from his aching hip
    Lengthens his long stride;
Though Home be but a humming on his lip,
    No happiness, no pride,

He does not drop him under the yellow whin
    To sleep the darkness through;

Home to the yellow light that shines within
    The kitchen of a loud shrew.

Home over stones and sand, through stagnant water
    He goes, mile after mile
Home to a wordless poaching son and a daughter
    With a disdainful smile,

Home to the worn reproach, the disagreeing,
    The shelter, the stale air; content to be
Pecked at, confined, encroached upon,—it being
    Too lonely, to be free. *(1934)*

THE STRAWBERRY SHRUB

Strawberry Shrub, old-fashioned, quaint as quinces,
Hard to find in a world where neon and noise
Have flattened the ends of the three more subtle senses;
And blare and magenta are all that a child enjoys.

More brown than red the bloom—it is a dense colour;
Colour of dried blood; colour of the key of F.
Tie it in your handkerchief, Dorcas, take it to school
To smell. But no, as I said, it is browner than red; it is duller
Than history, tinnier than algebra; and you are colour-deaf.

Purple, a little, the bloom, like musty chocolate;
Purpler than the purple avens of the wet fields;
But brown and red and hard and hiding its fragrance;
More like an herb it is: it is not exuberant.
You must bruise it a bit: it does not exude; it yields.

Clinker-built, the bloom, over-lapped its petals
Like clapboards; like a boat I had; like the feathers of a wing;
Not graceful, not at all Grecian, something from the provinces:
A chunky, ruddy, beautiful Boeotian thing.

Take it to school, knotted in your handkerchief, Dorcas,
Corner of your handkerchief, take it to school, and see
What your teacher says; show your pretty teacher the curious
Strawberry Shrub you took to school for me. *(1954)*

Archibald MacLeish
(1892–   )

THE SILENT SLAIN

We too, we too, descending once again
The hills of our own land, we too have heard
Far off—Ah, *que ce cor a longue haleine*—
The horn of Roland in the passages of Spain,
The first, the second blast, the failing third,
And with the third turned back and climbed once more
The steep road southward, and heard faint the sound
Of swords, of horses, the disastrous war,
And crossed the dark defile at last, and found
At Roncevaux upon the darkening plain
The dead against the dead and on the silent ground
The silent slain—   (*1926*)

MEMORIAL RAIN

Ambassador Puser the ambassador
Reminds himself in French, felicitous tongue,
What these (young men no longer) lie here for
In rows that once, and somewhere else, were young—

All night in Brussels the wind had tugged at my door:
I had heard the wind at my door and the trees strung
Taut, and to me who had never been before
In that country it was a strange wind, blowing
Steadily, stiffening the walls, the floor,
The roof of my room. I had not slept for knowing
He too, dead, was a stranger in that land
And felt beneath the earth in the wind's flowing
A tightening of roots and would not understand,
Remembering lake winds in Illinois,
That strange wind. I had felt his bones in the sand
Listening.

—Reflects that these enjoy
Their country's gratitude, that deep repose,
That peace no pain can break, no hurt destroy,
That rest, that sleep—

     At Ghent the wind rose.
There was a smell of rain and a heavy drag
Of wind in the hedges but not as the wind blows
Over fresh water when the waves lag
Foaming and the willows huddle and it will rain:
I felt him waiting.

   —Indicates the flag
Which (may he say) enisles in Flanders' plain
This little field these happy, happy dead
Have made America—

     In the ripe grain
The wind coiled glistening, darted, fled,
Dragging its heavy body: at Waereghem
The wind coiled in the grass above his head:
Waiting—listening—

   —Dedicates to them
This earth their bones have hallowed, this last gift
A grateful country—

     Under the dry grass stem
The words are blurred, are thickened, the words sift
Confused by the rasp of the wind, by the thin grating
Of ants under the grass, the minute shift
And tumble of dusty sand separating
From dusty sand. The roots of the grass strain,
Tighten, the earth is rigid, waits—he is waiting—

And suddenly, and all at once, the rain!

The living scatter, they run into houses, the wind
Is trampled under the rain, shakes free, is again
Trampled. The rain gathers, running in thinned
Spurts of water that ravel in the dry sand
Seeping in the sand under the grass roots, seeping
Between cracked boards to the bones of a clenched hand:

The earth relaxes, loosens; he is sleeping,
He rests, he is quiet, he sleeps in a strange land. *(1926)*

THE END OF THE WORLD

Quite unexpectedly as Vasserot
The armless ambidextrian was lighting
A match between his great and second toe
And Ralph the lion was engaged in biting
The neck of Madame Sossman while the drum
Pointed, and Teeny was about to cough
In waltz-time swinging Jocko by the thumb—
Quite unexpectedly the top blew off:

And there, there overhead, there, there, hung over
Those thousands of white faces, those dazed eyes,
There in the starless dark the poise, the hover,
There with vast wings across the canceled skies,
There in the sudden blackness the black pall
Of nothing, nothing, nothing—nothing at all. *(1926)*

ARS POETICA

A poem should be palpable and mute
As a globed fruit,

Dumb
As old medallions to the thumb,

Silent as the sleeve-worn stone
Of casement ledges where the moss has grown—

A poem should be wordless
As the flight of birds.

*

A poem should be motionless in time
As the moon climbs,

Leaving, as the moon releases
Twig by twig the night-entangled trees,

Leaving, as the moon behind the winter leaves,
Memory by memory the mind—

A poem should be motionless in time
As the moon climbs

*

A poem should be equal to:
Not true.

For all the history of grief
An empty doorway and a maple leaf.

For love
The leaning grasses and the two lights above the sea—

A poem should not mean
But be   *(1926)*

"NOT MARBLE NOR THE GILDED MONUMENTS"

The praisers of women in their proud and beautiful poems
Naming the grave mouth and the hair and the eyes
Boasted those they loved should be forever remembered
These were lies

The words sound but the face in the Istrian sun is forgotten
The poet speaks but to her dead ears no more
The sleek throat is gone—and the breast that was troubled to listen
Shadow from door

Therefore I will not praise your knees nor your fine walking
Telling you men shall remember your name as long
As lips move or breath is spent or the iron of English
Rings from a tongue

I shall say you were young and your arms straight and your mouth
    scarlet
I shall say you will die and none will remember you
Your arms change and none remember the swish of your garments
Nor the click of your shoe

Not with my hand's strength not with difficult labor
Springing the obstinate words to the bones of your breast
And the stubborn line to your young stride and the breath to your
    breathing

And the beat to your haste
Shall I prevail on the hearts of unborn men to remember

(What is a dead girl but a shadowy ghost
Or a dead man's voice but a distant and vain affirmation
Like dream words most)

Therefore I will not speak of the undying glory of women
I will say you were young and straight and your skin fair
And you stood in the door and the sun was a shadow of leaves on your
    shoulders
And a leaf on your hair

I will not speak of the famous beauty of dead women
I will say the shape of a leaf lay once on your hair
Till the world ends and the eyes are out and the mouths broken
Look! It is there! (*1930*)

YOU, ANDREW MARVELL

And here face down beneath the sun
And here upon earth's noonward height
To feel the always coming on
The always rising of the night

To feel creep up the curving east
The earthy chill of dusk and slow
Upon those under lands the vast
And ever climbing shadow grow

And strange at Ecbatan the trees
Take leaf by leaf the evening strange
The flooding dark about their knees
The mountains over Persia change

And now at Kermanshah the gate
Dark empty and the withered grass
And through the twilight now the late
Few travelers in the westward pass

And Baghdad darken and the bridge
Across the silent river gone
And through Arabia the edge
Of evening widen and steal on

And deepen on Palmyra's street
The wheel rut in the ruined stone
And Lebanon fade out and Crete
High through the clouds and overblown

And over Sicily the air
Still flashing with the landward gulls
And loom and slowly disappear
The sails above the shadowy hulls

And Spain go under and the shore
Of Africa the gilded sand
And evening vanish and no more
The low pale light across that land

Nor now the long light on the sea

And here face downward in the sun
To feel how swift how secretly
The shadow of the night comes on ...   *(1930)*

IMMORTAL AUTUMN

I speak this poem now with grave and level voice
In praise of autumn of the far-horn-winding fall
I praise the flower-barren fields the clouds the tall
Unanswering branches where the wind makes sullen noise

I praise the fall it is the human season
                          now
No more the foreign sun does meddle at our earth
Enforce the green and bring the fallow land to birth
Nor winter yet weigh all with silence the pine bough

But now in autumn with the black and outcast crows
Share we the spacious world the whispering year is gone
There is more room to live now the once secret dawn
Comes late by daylight and the dark unguarded goes

Between the mutinous brave burning of the leaves
And winter's covering of our hearts with his deep snow
We are alone there are no evening birds we know
The naked moon the tame stars circle at our eaves

It is the human season on this sterile air
Do words outcarry breath the sound goes on and on.
I hear a dead man's cry from autumn long since gone.

I cry to you beyond upon this bitter air.   *(1930)*

EPISTLE TO BE LEFT IN THE EARTH

. . . It is colder now
                    there are many stars
                                    we are drifting
North by the Great Bear
                    the leaves are falling
The water is stone in the scooped rocks
                                    to southward
Red sun grey air
                    the crows are
Slow on their crooked wings
                            the jays have left us
Long since we passed the flares of Orion
Each man believes in his heart he will die
Many have written last thoughts and last letters
None know if our deaths are now or forever
None know if this wandering earth will be found

We lie down and the snow covers our garments
I pray you
            you (if any open this writing)
Make in your mouths the words that were our names
I will tell you all we have learned
                            I will tell you everything
The earth is round
                    there are springs under the orchards
The loam cuts with a blunt knife
                            beware of
Elms in thunder
                    the lights in the sky are stars
We think they do not see
                        we think also
The trees do not know nor the leaves of the grasses
                                            hear us
The birds too are ignorant
                    Do not listen

Do not stand at dark in the open windows
We before you have heard this
                    they are voices
They are not words at all but the wind rising
Also none among us has seen God
(. . . We have thought often
The flaws of sun in the late and driving weather
Pointed to one tree but it was not so.)
As for the nights I warn you the nights are dangerous
The wind changes at night and the dreams come

It is very cold
                    there are strange stars near Arcturus

Voices are crying an unknown name in the sky   *(1930)*

LINES FOR AN INTERMENT

Now it is fifteen years you have lain in the meadow:
The boards at your face have gone through: the earth is
Packed down and the sound of the rain is fainter:
The roots of the first grass are dead:

It's a long time to lie in the earth with your honor:
The world, Soldier, the world has been moving on:

The girls wouldn't look at you twice in the cloth cap:
Six years old they were when it happened:

It bores them even in books: "Soissons besieged!"
As for the gents they have joined the American Legion:

Belts and a brass band and the ladies' auxiliaries:
The Californians march in the OD silk:

We are all acting again like civilized beings:
People mention it at tea . . .

The Facts of Life we have learned are Economic:
You were deceived by the detonations of bombs:

You thought of courage and death when you thought of warfare:
Hadn't they taught you the fine words were unfortunate?

Now that we understand we judge without bias:
We feel of course for those who had to die:

Women have written us novels of great passion
Proving the useless death of the dead was a tragedy:

Nevertheless it is foolish to chew gall:
The foremost writers on both sides have apologized:

The Germans are back in the Midi with cropped hair:
The English are drinking the better beer in Bavaria:

You can rest now in the rain in the Belgian meadow—
Now that it's all explained away and forgotten:
Now that the earth is hard and the wood rots:

Now you are dead . . . (*1933*)

LANDSCAPE AS A NUDE

She lies on her left side her flank golden:
Her hair is burned black with the strong sun:
The scent of her hair is of rain in the dust on her shoulders:
She has brown breasts and the mouth of no other country:

Ah she is beautiful here in the sun where she lies—
Not like the soft girls naked in vineyards
Nor the soft naked girls of the English islands
Where the rain comes in with the surf on an east wind:

Hers is the west wind and the sunlight: the west
Wind is the long clean wind of the continents—
The wind turning with earth: the wind descending
Steadily out of the evening and following on:

The wind here where she lies is west: the trees
Oak ironwood cottonwood hickory: standing in
Great groves they roll on the wind as the sea would:
The grasses of Iowa Illinois Indiana

Run with the plunge of the wind as a wave tumbling:

Under her knees there is no green lawn of the Florentines:
Under her dusty knees is the corn stubble:
Her belly is flecked with the flickering light of the corn:

She lies on her left side her flank golden:
Her hair is burned black with the strong sun:
The scent of her hair is of dust and of smoke on her shoulders:
She has brown breasts and the mouth of no other country.   (*1933*)

E. E. Cummings
(1894–1962)

[ALL IN GREEN WENT MY LOVE RIDING]

All in green went my love riding
on a great horse of gold
into the silver dawn.

four lean hounds crouched low and smiling
the merry deer ran before.

Fleeter be they than dappled dreams
the swift sweet deer
the red rare deer.

Four red roebuck at a white water
the cruel bugle sang before.

Horn at hip went my love riding
riding the echo down
into the silver dawn.

four lean hounds crouched low and smiling
the level meadows ran before.

Softer be they than slippered sleep
the lean lithe deer
the fleet flown deer.

Four fleet does at a gold valley
the famished arrow sang before.

Bow at belt went my love riding
riding the mountain down
into the silver dawn.

four lean hounds crouched low and smiling
the sheer peaks ran before.

Paler be they than daunting death
the sleek slim deer
the tall tense deer.

Four tall stags at a green mountain
the lucky hunter sang before.

All in green went my love riding
on a great horse of gold
into the silver dawn.

four lean hounds crouched low and smiling
my heart fell dead before.   *(1923)*

[BUFFALO BILL'S]

Buffalo Bill's
defunct
          who used to
          ride a watersmooth-silver
                              stallion
and break onetwothreefourfive pigeonsjustlikethat
                                             Jesus

he was a handsome man
                    and what i want to know is
how do you like your blueeyed boy
Mister Death   *(1923)*

[GOODBY BETTY, DON'T REMEMBER ME]

goodby Betty, don't remember me
pencil your eyes dear and have a good time
with the tall tight boys at Tabari'
s, keep your teeth snowy, stick to beer and lime,
wear dark, and where your meeting breasts are round
have roses darling, it's all i ask of you—
but that when light fails and this sweet profound
Paris moves with lovers, two and two
bound for themselves, when passionately dusk

brings softly down the perfume of the world
(and just as smaller stars begin to husk
heaven) you, you exactly paled and curled

with mystic lips take twilight where i know:
proving to Death that Love is so and so.   *(1923)*

[LADIES AND GENTLEMEN THIS LITTLE GIRL]

ladies and gentlemen this little girl
with the good teeth and small important breasts
(is it the Frolic or the Century whirl?
one's memory indignantly protests)
this little dancer with the tightened eyes
crisp ogling shoulders and the ripe quite too
large lips always clenched faintly, wishes you
with all her fragile might to not surmise
she dreamed one afternoon
                    . . . . or maybe read?

of a time when the beautiful most of her
(this here and This, do you get me?)
will maybe dance and maybe sing and be
abslatively posolutely dead,
like Coney Island in winter   *(1923)*

[WHO'S MOST AFRAID OF DEATH?]

who's most afraid of death? thou
                    art of him
utterly afraid, i love of thee
(beloved) this

          and truly i would be
near when his scythe takes crisply the whim
of thy smoothness. and mark the fainting
murdered petals. with the caving stem.

But of all most would i be one of them

round the hurt heart which do so frailly cling . . . .)
i who am but imperfect in my fear

Or with thy mind against my mind, to hear
nearing our hearts' irrevocable play—
through the mysterious high futile day

an enormous stride
                    (and drawing thy mouth toward

my mouth, steer our lost bodies carefully downward) *(1925)*

[NOBODY LOSES ALL THE TIME]

nobody loses all the time

i had an uncle named
Sol who was a born failure and
nearly everybody said he should have gone
into vaudeville perhaps because my Uncle Sol could
sing McCann He Was A Diver on Xmas Eve like Hell Itself which
may or may not account for the fact that my Uncle

Sol indulged in that possibly most inexcusable
of all to use a highfalootin phrase
luxuries that is or to
wit farming and be
it needlessly
added

my Uncle Sol's farm
failed because the chickens
ate the vegetables so
my Uncle Sol had a
chicken farm till the
skunks ate the chickens when

my Uncle Sol
had a skunk farm but
the skunks caught cold and
died and so
my Uncle Sol imitated the
skunks in a subtle manner

or by drowning himself in the watertank
but somebody who'd given my Uncle Sol a Victor

Victrola and records while he lived presented to
him upon the auspicious occasion of his decease a
scrumptious not to mention splendiferous funeral with
tall boys in black gloves and flowers and everything and

i remember we all cried like the Missouri
when my Uncle Sol's coffin lurched because
somebody pressed a button
(and down went
my Uncle
Sol

and started a worm farm)   (1926)

[PONDER,DARLING,THESE BUSTED STATUES]

(ponder,darling,these busted statues
of yon motheaten forum be aware
notice what hath remained
—the stone cringes
clinging to the stone, how obsolete

lips utter their extant smile . . . .
remark

a few deleted of texture
or meaning monuments and dolls

resist Them Greediest Paws of careful
time all of which is extremely
unimportant) whereas Life

matters if or

when the your- and my-
idle vertical worthless
self unite in a peculiarly
momentary

partnership (to instigate
constructive
            Horizontal
business . . . . even so, let us make haste
—consider well this ruined aqueduct

lady,
which used to lead something into somewhere) *(1926)*

[MY SWEET OLD ETCETERA]

my sweet old etcetera
aunt lucy during the recent

war could and what
is more did tell you just
what everybody was fighting

for,
my sister

isabel created hundreds
(and
hundreds) of socks not to
mention shirts fleaproof earwarmers

etcetera wristers etcetera, my
mother hoped that

i would die etcetera
bravely of course my father used
to become hoarse talking about how it was
a privilege and if only he
could meanwhile my

self etcetera lay quietly
in the deep mud et

cetera
(dreaming,
et
   cetera, of
Your smile
eyes knees and of your Etcetera) *(1926)*

[IF I HAVE MADE,MY LADY,INTRICATE]

if i have made,my lady,intricate
imperfect various things chiefly which wrong
your eyes(frailer than most deep dreams are frail)

songs less firm than your body's whitest song
upon my mind—if i have failed to snare
the glance too shy—if through my singing slips
the very skillful strangeness of your smile
the keen primeval silence of your hair

—let the world say "his most wise music stole
nothing from death"—

you only will create
(who are so perfectly alive)my shame:
lady through whose profound and fragile lips
the sweet small clumsy feet of April came

into the ragged meadow of my soul. (*1926*)

[IF YOU CAN'T EAT YOU GOT TO]

If you can't eat you got to

smoke and we aint got
nothing to smoke:come on kid

let's go to sleep
if you can't smoke you got to

Sing and we aint got

nothing to sing;come on kid
let's go to sleep

if you can't sing you got to
die and we aint got

Nothing to die,come on kid

let's go to sleep
if you can't die you got to

dream and we aint got
nothing to dream(come on kid

Let's go to sleep) (*1940*)

[A PRETTY A DAY]

a pretty a day
(and every fades)
is here and away
(but born are maids
to flower an hour
in all,all)

o yes to flower
until so blithe
a doer a wooer
some limber and lithe
some very fine mower
a tall;tall

some jerry so very
(and nellie and fan)
some handsomest harry
(and sally and nan
they tremble and cower
so pale:pale)

for betty was born
to never say nay
but lucy could learn
and lily could pray
and fewer were shyer
than doll.   doll   *(1940)*

[AS FREEDOM IS A BREAKFASTFOOD]

as freedom is a breakfastfood
or truth can live with right and wrong
or molehills are from mountains made
—long enough and just so long
will being pay the rent of seem
and genius please the talentgang
and water most encourage flame

as hatracks into peachtrees grow
or hopes dance best on bald men's hair

and every finger is a toe
and any courage is a fear
—long enough and just so long
will the impure think all things pure
and hornets wail by children stung

or as the seeing are the blind
and robins never welcome spring
nor flatfolk prove their world is round
nor dingsters die at break of dong
and common's rare and millstones float
—long enough and just so long
tomorrow will not be too late

worms are the words but joy's the voice
down shall go which and up come who
breasts will be breasts thighs will be thighs
deeds cannot dream what dreams can do
—time is a tree(this life one leaf)
but love is the sky and i am for you
just so long and long enough   *(1940)*

[ANYONE LIVED IN A PRETTY HOW TOWN]

anyone lived in a pretty how town
(with up so floating many bells down)
spring summer autumn winter
he sang his didn't he danced his did.

Women and men(both little and small)
cared for anyone not at all
they sowed their isn't they reaped their same
sun moon stars rain

children guessed(but only a few
and down they forgot as up they grew
autumn winter spring summer)
that noone loved him more by more

when by now and tree by leaf
she laughed his joy she cried his grief
bird by snow and stir by still
anyone's any was all to her

someones married their everyones
laughed their cryings and did their dance
(sleep wake hope and then)they
said their nevers they slept their dream

stars rain sun moon
(and only the snow can begin to explain
how children are apt to forget to remember
with up so floating many bells down)

one day anyone died i guess
(and noone stooped to kiss his face)
busy folk buried them side by side
little by little and was by was

all by all and deep by deep
and more by more they dream their sleep
noone and anyone earth by april
wish by spirit and if by yes.

Women and men(both dong and ding)
summer autumn winter spring
reaped their sowing and went their came
sun moon stars rain   (*1940*)

[MY FATHER MOVED THROUGH DOOMS OF LOVE]

my father moved through dooms of love
through sames of am through haves of give,
singing each morning out of each night
my father moved through depths of height

this motionless forgetful where
turned at his glance to shining here;
that if(so timid air is firm)
under his eyes would stir and squirm

newly as from unburied which
floats the first who,his april touch
drove sleeping selves to swarm their fates
woke dreamers to their ghostly roots

and should some why completely weep
my father's fingers brought her sleep:

vainly no smallest voice might cry
for he could feel the mountains grow.

Lifting the valleys of the sea
my father moved through griefs of joy;
praising a forehead called the moon
singing desire into begin

joy was his song and joy so pure
a heart of star by him could steer
and pure so now and now so yes
the wrists of twilight would rejoice

keen as midsummer's keen beyond
conceiving mind of sun will stand,
so strictly(over utmost him
so hugely)stood my father's dream

his flesh was flesh his blood was blood:
no hungry man but wished him food;
no cripple wouldn't creep one mile
uphill to only see him smile.

Scorning the pomp of must and shall
my father moved through dooms of feel;
his anger was as right as rain
his pity was as green as grain

septembering arms of year extend
less humbly wealth to foe and friend
than he to foolish and to wise
offered immeasurable is

proudly and(by octobering flame
beckoned)as earth will downward climb,
so naked for immortal work
his shoulders marched against the dark

his sorrow was as true as bread:
no liar looked him in the head;
if every friend became his foe
he'd laugh and build a world with snow.

My father moved through theys of we,
singing each new leaf out of each tree
(and every child was sure that spring
danced when she heard my father sing)

then let men kill which cannot share,
let blood and flesh be mud and mire,
scheming imagine,passion willed,
freedom a drug that's bought and sold

giving to steal and cruel kind,
a heart to fear,to doubt a mind,
to differ a disease of same,
conform the pinnacle of am

though dull were all we taste as bright,
bitter all utterly things sweet,
maggoty minus and dumb death
all we inherit,all bequeath

and nothing quite so least as truth
—i say though hate were why men breathe—
because my father lived his soul
love is the whole and more than all   *(1940)*

[I AM SO GLAD AND VERY]

i am so glad and very
merely my fourth will cure
the laziest self of weary
the hugest sea of shore

so far your nearness reaches
a lucky fifth of you
turns people into eachs
and cowards into grow

our can'ts were born to happen
our mosts have died in more
our twentieth will open
wide a wide open door

we are so both and oneful
night cannot be so sky
sky cannot be so sunful
i am through you so i   (1940)

[SILENCE]

silence

.is
a
looking

bird:the

turn
ing;edge,of
life

(inquiry before snow   (1958)

Hart Crane
(1899–1932)

MY GRANDMOTHER'S LOVE LETTERS

There are no stars to-night
But those of memory.
Yet how much room for memory there is
In the loose girdle of soft rain.

There is even room enough
For the letters of my mother's mother,
Elizabeth,
That have been pressed so long
Into a corner of the roof
That they are brown and soft,
And liable to melt as snow.

Over the greatness of such space
Steps must be gentle.
It is all hung by an invisible white hair.
It trembles as birch limbs webbing the air.

And I ask myself:

"Are your fingers long enough to play
Old keys that are but echoes:
Is the silence strong enough
To carry back the music to its source
And back to you again
As though to her?"

Yet I would lead my grandmother by the hand
Through much of what she would not understand;
And so I stumble. And the rain continues on the roof
With such a sound of gently pitying laughter.   (1926)

PRAISE FOR AN URN
In Memoriam: Ernest Nelson

It was a kind and northern face
That mingled in such exile guise
The everlasting eyes of Pierrot
And, of Gargantua, the laughter.

His thoughts, delivered to me
From the white coverlet and pillow,
I see now, were inheritances—
Delicate riders of the storm.

The slant moon on the slanting hill
Once moved us toward presentiments
Of what the dead keep, living still,
And such assessments of the soul

As, perched in the crematory lobby,
The insistent clock commented on,
Touching as well upon our praise
Of glories proper to the time.

Still, having in mind gold hair,
I cannot see that broken brow
And miss the dry sound of bees
Stretching across a lucid space.

Scatter these well-meant idioms
Into the smoky spring that fills
The suburbs, where they will be lost.
They are no trophies of the sun.   (*1926*)

CHAPLINESQUE

We make our meek adjustments,
Contented with such random consolations
As the wind deposits
In slithered and too ample pockets.

For we can still love the world, who find
A famished kitten on the step, and know

Recesses for it from the fury of the street,
Or warm torn elbow coverts.

We will sidestep, and to the final smirk
Dally the doom of that inevitable thumb
That slowly chafes its puckered index toward us,
Facing the dull squint with what innocence
And what surprise!

And yet these fine collapses are not lies
More than the pirouettes of any pliant cane;
Our obsequies are, in a way, no enterprise.
We can evade you, and all else but the heart:
What blame to us if the heart live on.

The game enforces smirks; but we have seen
The moon in lonely alleys make
A grail of laughter of an empty ash can,
And through all sound of gaiety and quest
Have heard a kitten in the wilderness.   *(1926)*

NORTH LABRADOR

A land of leaning ice
Hugged by plaster-grey arches of sky,
Flings itself silently
Into eternity.

"Has no one come here to win you,
Or left you with the faintest blush
Upon your glittering breasts?
Have you no memories, O Darkly Bright?"

Cold-hushed, there is only the shifting of moments
That journey toward no Spring—
No birth, no death, no time nor sun
In answer.   *(1926)*

VOYAGES

1

Above the fresh ruffles of the surf
Bright striped urchins flay each other with sand.

They have contrived a conquest for shell shucks,
And their fingers crumble fragments of baked weed
Gaily digging and scattering.

And in answer to their treble interjections
The sun beats lightning on the waves,
The waves fold thunder on the sand;
And could they hear me I would tell them:

O brilliant kids, frisk with your dog,
Fondle your shells and sticks, bleached
By time and the elements; but there is a line
You must not cross nor ever trust beyond it
Spry cordage of your bodies to caresses
Too lichen-faithful from too wide a breast.
The bottom of the sea is cruel.

2

—And yet this great wink of eternity,
Of rimless floods, unfettered leewardings,
Samite sheeted and processioned where
Her undinal vast belly moonward bends,
Laughing the wrapt inflections of our love;

Take this Sea, whose diapason knells
On scrolls of silver snowy sentences,
The sceptred terror of whose sessions rends
As her demeanors motion well or ill,
All but the pieties of lovers' hands.

And onward, as bells off San Salvador
Salute the crocus lustres of the stars,
In these poinsettia meadows of her tides,—
Adagios of islands, O my Prodigal,
Complete the dark confessions her veins spell.

Mark how her turning shoulders wind the hours,
And hasten while her penniless rich palms
Pass superscription of bent foam and wave,—
Hasten, while they are true,—sleep, death, desire,
Close round one instant in one floating flower.

Bind us in time, O Seasons clear, and awe.
O minstrel galleons of Carib fire,
Bequeath us to no earthly shore until

Is answered in the vortex of our grave
The seal's wide spindrift gaze toward paradise.

3

Infinite consanguinity it bears—
This tendered theme of you that light
Retrieves from sea plains where the sky
Resigns a breast that every wave enthrones;
While ribboned water lanes I wind
Are laved and scattered with no stroke
Wide from your side, whereto this hour
The sea lifts, also, reliquary hands.

And so, admitted through black swollen gates
That must arrest all distance otherwise,—
Past whirling pillars and lithe pediments,
Light wrestling there incessantly with light,
Star kissing star through wave on wave unto
Your body rocking!
                    and where death, if shed,
Presumes no carnage, but this single change,—
Upon the steep floor flung from dawn to dawn
The silken skilled transmemberment of song;

Permit me voyage, love, into your hands. . .

4

Whose counted smile of hours and days, suppose
I know as spectrum of the sea and pledge
Vastly now parting gulf on gulf of wings
Whose circles bridge, I know, (from palms to the severe
Chilled albatross's white immutability)
No stream of greater love advancing now
Than, singing, this mortality alone
Through clay aflow immortally to you.

All fragrance irrefragably, and claim
Madly meeting logically in this hour
And region that is ours to wreathe again,
Portending eyes and lips and making told
The chancel port and portion of our June—

Shall they not stem and close in our own steps
Bright staves of flowers and quills to-day as I
Must first be lost in fatal tides to tell?

In signature of the incarnate word
The harbor shoulders to resign in mingling
Mutual blood, transpiring as foreknown
And widening noon within your breast for gathering
All bright insinuations that my years have caught
For islands where must lead inviolably
Blue latitudes and levels of your eyes,—

In this expectant, still exclaim receive
The secret oar and petals of all love.

5

Meticulous, past midnight in clear rime,
Infrangible and lonely, smooth as though cast
Together in one merciless white blade—
The bay estuaries fleck the hard sky limits.

—As if too brittle or too clear to touch!
The cables of our sleep so swiftly filed,
Already hang, shred ends from remembered stars.
One frozen tractless smile . . . What words
Can strangle this deaf moonlight? For we

Are overtaken. Now no cry, no sword
Can fasten or deflect this tidal wedge,
Slow tyranny of moonlight, moonlight loved
And changed . . . "There's

Nothing like this in the world," you say,
Knowing I cannot touch your hand and look
Too, into that godless cleft of sky
Where nothing turns but dead sands flashing.

"—And never to quite understand!" No,
In all the argosy of your bright hair I dreamed
Nothing so flagless as this piracy.

                                But now
Draw in your head, alone and too tall here.
Your eyes already in the slant of drifting foam;
Your breath sealed by the ghosts I do not know:
Draw in your head and sleep the long way home.

6

Where icy and bright dungeons lift
Of swimmers their lost morning eyes,

And ocean rivers, churning, shift
Green borders under stranger skies,

Steadily as a shell secretes
Its beating leagues of monotone,
Or as many waters trough the sun's
Red kelson past the cape's wet stone;

O rivers mingling toward the sky
And harbor of the phœnix' breast—
My eyes pressed black against the prow,
—Thy derelict and blinded guest

Waiting, afire, what name, unspoke,
I cannot claim: let thy waves rear
More savage than the death of kings,
Some splintered garland for the seer.

Beyond siroccos harvesting
The solstice thunders, crept away,
Like a cliff swinging or a sail
Flung into April's inmost day—

Creation's blithe and petalled word
To the lounged goddess when she rose
Conceding dialogue with eyes
That smile unsearchable repose—

Still fervid covenant, Belle Isle,
—Unfolded floating dais before
Which rainbows twine continual hair—
Belle Isle, white echo of the oar!

The imaged Word, it is, that holds
Hushed willows anchored in its glow.
It is the unbetrayable reply
Whose accent no farewell can know. (1926)

PASSAGE

Where the cedar leaf divides the sky
I heard the sea.
In sapphire arenas of the hills
I was promised an improved infancy.

Sulking, sanctioning the sun,
My memory I left in a ravine,—
Casual louse that tissues the buckwheat,
Aprons rocks, congregates pears
In moonlit bushels
And wakens alleys with a hidden cough.

Dangerously the summer burned
(I had joined the entrainments of the wind).
The shadows of boulders lengthened my back:
In the bronze gongs of my cheeks
The rain dried without odour.

"It is not long, it is not long;
See where the red and black
Vine-stanchioned valleys—": but the wind
Died speaking through the ages that you know
And hug, chimney-sooted heart of man!
So was I turned about and back, much as your smoke
Compiles a too well-known biography.

The evening was spear in the ravine
That throve through very oak. And had I walked
The dozen particular decimals of time?
Touching an opening laurel, I found
A thief beneath, my stolen book in hand.

"Why are you back here—smiling an iron coffin?"
"To argue with the laurel," I replied:
"Am justified in transience, fleeing
Under the constant wonder of your eyes—."

He closed the book. And from the Ptolemies
Sand troughed us in a glittering abyss.
A serpent swam a vertex to the sun
—On unpaced beaches leaned its tongue and drummed.
What fountains did I hear? what icy speeches?
Memory, committed to the page, had broke.   (1926)

REPOSE OF RIVERS

The willows carried a slow sound,
A sarabande the wind mowed on the mead.
I could never remember

That seething, steady leveling of the marshes
Till age had brought me to the sea.

Flags, weeds. And remembrance of steep alcoves
Where cypresses shared the noon's
Tyranny; they drew me into hades almost.
And mammoth turtles climbing sulphur dreams
Yielded, while sun-silt rippled them
Asunder. . .

How much I would have bartered! the black gorge
And all the singular nestings in the hills
Where beavers learn stitch and tooth.
The pond I entered once and quickly fled—
I remember now its singing willow rim.

And finally, in that memory all things nurse;
After the city that I finally passed
With scalding unguents spread and smoking darts
The monsoon cut across the delta
At gulf gates . . . There, beyond the dykes

I heard wind flaking sapphire, like this summer,
And willows could not hold more steady sound.   (*1926*)

From THE BRIDGE

PROEM: TO BROOKLYN BRIDGE

How many dawns, chill from his rippling rest
The seagull's wings shall dip and pivot him,
Shedding white rings of tumult, building high
Over the chained bay waters Liberty—

Then, with inviolate curve, forsake our eyes
As apparitional as sails that cross
Some page of figures to be filed away;
—Till elevators drop us from our day . . .

I think of cinemas, panoramic sleights
With multitudes bent toward some flashing scene
Never disclosed, but hastened to again,
Foretold to other eyes on the same screen;

And Thee, across the harbor, silver-paced
As though the sun took step of thee, yet left

Some motion ever unspent in thy stride,—
Implicitly thy freedom staying thee!

Out of some subway scuttle, cell or loft
A bedlamite speeds to thy parapets,
Tilting there momently, shrill shirt ballooning,
A jest falls from the speechless caravan.

Down Wall, from girder into street noon leaks,
A rip-tooth of the sky's acetylene;
All afternoon the cloud-flown derricks turn . . .
Thy cables breathe the North Atlantic still.

And obscure as that heaven of the Jews,
Thy guerdon . . . Accolade thou dost bestow
Of anonymity time cannot raise:
Vibrant reprieve and pardon thou dost show.

O harp and altar, of the fury fused,
(How could mere toil align thy choiring strings!)
Terrific threshold of the prophet's pledge,
Prayer of pariah, and the lover's cry,—

Again the traffic lights that skim thy swift
Unfractioned idiom, immaculate sigh of stars,
Beading thy path—condense eternity:
And we have seen night lifted in thine arms.

Under thy shadow by the piers I waited;
Only in darkness is thy shadow clear.
The City's fiery parcels all undone,
Already snow submerges an iron year . . .

O Sleepless as the river under thee,
Vaulting the sea, the prairies' dreaming sod,
Unto us lowliest sometime sweep, descend
And of the curveship lend a myth to God.

From II. POWHATAN'S DAUGHTER

The River

[. . . *and past the din and slogans of the year*—]
Stick your patent name on a signboard
brother—all over—going west—young man

Tintex—Japalac—Certain-teed Overalls ads
and lands sakes! under the new playbill ripped
in the guaranteed corner—see Bert Williams what?
Minstrels when you steal a chicken just
save me the wing for if it isn't
Erie it ain't for miles around a
Mazda—and the telegraphic night coming on Thomas

a Ediford—and whistling down the tracks
a headlight rushing with the sound—can you
imagine—while an EXPRESS makes time like
SCIENCE—COMMERCE and the HOLYGHOST
RADIO ROARS IN EVERY HOME WE HAVE THE NORTHPOLE
WALLSTREET AND VIRGINBIRTH WITHOUT STONES OR
WIRES OR EVEN RUNNing brooks connecting ears
and no more sermons windows flashing roar
Breathtaking—as you like it . . . eh?

                    So the 20th Century—so
whizzed the Limited—roared by and left
three men, still hungry on the tracks, ploddingly
watching the tail lights wizen and converge, slip·
ping gimleted and neatly out of sight.

                    *   *   *

                    [to those whose addresses are never near]
The last bear, shot drinking in the Dakotas
Loped under wires that span the mountain stream.
Keen instruments, strung to a vast precision
Bind town to town and dream to ticking dream.
But some men take their liquor slow—and count
—Though they'll confess no rosary nor clue—
The river's minute by the far brook's year.
Under a world of whistles, wires and steam
Caboose-like they go ruminating through
Ohio, Indiana—blind baggage—
To Cheyenne tagging . . . Maybe Kalamazoo.

Time's rendings, time's blendings they construe
As final reckonings of fire and snow;
Strange bird-wit, like the elemental gist
Of unwalled winds they offer, singing low
My Old Kentucky Home and Casey Jones,
Some Sunny Day. I heard a road-gang chanting so.

And afterwards, who had a colt's eyes—one said,
"Jesus! Oh I remember watermelon days!" And sped
High in a cloud of merriment, recalled
"—And when my Aunt Sally Simpson smiled," he drawled—
"It was almost Louisiana, long ago."
"There's no place like Booneville though, Buddy,"
One said, excising a last burr from his vest,
"—For early trouting." Then peering in the can,
"—But I kept on the tracks." Possessed, resigned,
He trod the fire down pensively and grinned,
Spreading dry shingles of a beard. . . .

                                        Behind
My father's cannery works I used to see
Rail-squatters ranged in nomad raillery,
The ancient men—wifeless or runaway
Hobo-trekkers that forever search
An empire wilderness of freight and rails.
Each seemed a child, like me, on a loose perch,
Holding to childhood like some termless play.
John, Jake or Charley, hopping the slow freight
—Memphis to Tallahassee—riding the rods,
Blind fists of nothing, humpty-dumpty clods.
          [*but who have touched her, knowing her without name*]
Yet they touch something like a key perhaps.
From pole to pole across the hills, the states
—They know a body under the wide rain;
Youngsters with eyes like fjords, old reprobates
With racetrack jargon,—dotting immensity
They lurk across her, knowing her yonder breast
Snow-silvered, sumac-stained or smoky blue—
Is past the valley-sleepers, south or west.
—As I have trod the rumorous midnights, too,

And past the circuit of the lamp's thin flame
(O Nights that brought me to her body bare!)
Have dreamed beyond the print that bound her name.
Trains sounding the long blizzards out—I heard
Wail into distances I knew were hers.
Papooses crying on the wind's long mane
Screamed redskin dynasties that fled the brain,
—Dead echoes! But I knew her body there,
Time like a serpent down her shoulder, dark,
And space, an eaglet's wing, laid on her hair.

[*nor the myths of her fathers . . .*]

Under the Ozarks, domed by Iron Mountain,
The old gods of the rain lie wrapped in pools
Where eyeless fish curvet a sunken fountain
And re-descend with corn from querulous crows.
Such pilferings make up their timeless eatage,
Propitiate them for their timber torn
By iron, iron—always the iron dealt cleavage!
They doze now, below axe and powder horn.

And Pullman breakfasters glide glistening steel
From tunnel into field—iron strides the dew—
Straddles the hill, a dance of wheel on wheel.
You have a half-hour's wait at Siskiyou,
Or stay the night and take the next train through.
Southward, near Cairo passing, you can see
The Ohio merging,—borne down Tennessee;
And if it's summer and the sun's in dusk
Maybe the breeze will lift the River's musk
—As though the waters breathed that you might know
Memphis Johnny, Steamboat Bill, Missouri Joe.
Oh, lean from the window, if the train slows down,
As though you touched hands with some ancient clown,
—A little while gaze absently below
And hum *Deep River* with them while they go.

Yes, turn again and sniff once more—look see,
O Sheriff, Brakeman and Authority—
Hitch up your pants and crunch another quid,
For you, too, feed the River timelessly.
And few evade full measure of their fate;
Always they smile out eerily what they seem.
I could believe he joked at heaven's gate—
Dan Midland—jolted from the cold brake-beam.

Down, down—born pioneers in time's despite,
Grimed tributaries to an ancient flow—
They win no frontier by their wayward plight,
But drift in stillness, as from Jordan's brow.

You will not hear it as the sea, even stone
Is not more hushed by gravity . . . But slow,

As loth to take more tribute—sliding prone
Like one whose eyes were buried long ago

The River, spreading, flows—and spends your dream.
What are you, lost within this tideless spell?
You are your father's father, and the stream—
A liquid theme that floating niggers swell.

Damp tonnage and alluvial march of days—
Nights turbid, vascular with silted shale
And roots surrendered down of moraine clays:
The Mississippi drinks the farthest dale.

O quarrying passion, undertowed sunlight!
The basalt surface drags a jungle grace
Ochreous and lynx-barred in lengthening might;
Patience! and you shall reach the biding place!

Over De Soto's bones the freighted floors
Throb past the City storied of three thrones.
Down two more turns the Mississippi pours
(Anon tall ironsides up from salt lagoons)

And flows within itself, heaps itself free.
All fades but one thin skyline 'round . . . Ahead
No embrace opens but the stinging sea;
The River lifts itself from its long bed,

Poised wholly on its dream, a mustard glow
Tortured with history, its one will—flow!
—The Passion spreads in wide tongues, choked and slow,
Meeting the Gulf, hosannas silently below.

VII. THE TUNNEL

*To Find the Western path
Right thro' the Gates of Wrath.*
                    —Blake.

Performances, assortments, résumés—
Up Times Square to Columbus Circle lights
Channel the congresses, nightly sessions,
Refractions of the thousand theatres, faces—
Mysterious kitchens. . . . You shall search them all.
Some day by heart you'll learn each famous sight

And watch the curtain lift in hell's despite;
You'll find the garden in the third act dead,
Finger your knees—and wish yourself in bed
With tabloid crime-sheets perched in easy sight.

    Then let you reach your hat
    and go.
    As usual, let you—also
    walking down—exclaim
    to twelve upward leaving
    a subscription praise
    for what time slays.

Or can't you quite make up your mind to ride;
A walk is better underneath the L a brisk
Ten blocks or so before? But you find yourself
Preparing penguin flexions of the arms,—
As usual you will meet the scuttle yawn:
The subway yawns the quickest promise home.

Be minimum, then, to swim the hiving swarms
Out of the Square, the Circle burning bright—
Avoid the glass doors gyring at your right,
Where boxed alone a second, eyes take fright
—Quite unprepared rush naked back to light:
And down beside the turnstile press the coin
Into the slot. The gongs already rattle.

    And so
    of cities you bespeak
    subways, rivered under streets
    and rivers. . . . In the car
    the overtone of motion
    underground, the monotone
    of motion is the sound
    of other faces, also underground—

"Let's have a pencil Jimmy—living now
at Floral Park
Flatbush—on the Fourth of July—
like a pigeon's muddy dream—potatoes
to dig in the field—travlin the town—too—

night after night—the Culver line—the
girls all shaping up—it used to be—"

Our tongues recant like beaten weather vanes.
This answer lives like verdigris, like hair
Beyond extinction, surcease of the bone;
And repetition freezes—"What

"what do you want? getting weak on the links?
fandaddle daddy don't ask for change—IS THIS
FOURTEENTH? it's half past six she said—if
you don't like my gate why did you
swing on it, why *didja*
swing on it
anyhow—"

And somehow anyhow swing—

The phonographs of hades in the brain
Are tunnels that re-wind themselves, and love
A burnt match skating in a urinal—
Somewhere above Fourteenth TAKE THE EXPRESS
To brush some new presentiment of pain—

"But I want service in this office SERVICE
I said—after
the show she cried a little afterwards but—"

Whose head is swinging from the swollen strap?
Whose body smokes along the bitten rails,
Bursts from a smoldering bundle far behind
In back forks of the chasms of the brain,—
Puffs from a riven stump far out behind
In interborough fissures of the mind . . . ?

And why do I often meet your visage here,
Your eyes like agate lanterns—on and on
Below the toothpaste and the dandruff ads?
—And did their riding eyes right through your side,
And did their eyes like unwashed platters ride?
And Death, aloft,—gigantically down
Probing through you—toward me, O evermore!
And when they dragged your retching flesh,

Your trembling hands that night through Baltimore—
That last night on the ballot rounds, did you
Shaking, did you deny the ticket, Poe?

For Gravesend Manor change at Chambers Street.
The platform hurries along to a dead stop.

The intent escalator lifts a serenade
Stilly
Of shoes, umbrellas, each eye attending its shoe, then
Bolting outright somewhere above where streets
Burst suddenly in rain. . . . The gongs recur:
Elbows and levers, guard and hissing door.
Thunder is galvothermic here below. . . . The car
Wheels off. The train rounds, bending to a scream,
Taking the final level for the dive
Under the river—
And somewhat emptier than before,
Demented, for a hitching second, humps; then
Lets go. . . . Toward corners of the floor
Newspapers wing, revolve and wing.
Blank windows gargle signals through the roar.

And does the Dæmon take you home, also,
Wop washerwoman, with the bandaged hair?
After the corridors are swept, the cuspidors—
The gaunt sky-barracks cleanly now, and bare,
O Genoese, do you bring mother eyes and hands
Back home to children and to golden hair?

Dæmon, demurring and eventful yawn!
Whose hideous laughter is a bellows mirth
—Or the muffled slaughter of a day in birth—
O cruelly to inoculate the brinking dawn
With antennæ toward worlds that glow and sink;—
To spoon us out more liquid than the dim
Locution of the eldest star, and pack
The conscience navelled in the plunging wind,
Umbilical to call—and straightway die!

O caught like pennies beneath soot and steam,
Kiss of our agony thou gatherest;
Condensed, thou takest all—shrill ganglia
Impassioned with some song we fail to keep.

And yet, like Lazarus, to feel the slope,
The sod and billow breaking,—lifting ground,
—A sound of waters bending astride the sky
Unceasing with some Word that will not die . . . !

* * *

A tugboat, wheezing wreaths of steam,
Lunged past, with one galvanic blare stove up the River.
I counted the echoes assembling, one after one,
Searching, thumbing the midnight on the piers.
Lights, coasting, left the oily tympanum of waters;
The blackness somewhere gouged glass on a sky.
And this thy harbor, O my City, I have driven under,
Tossed from the coil of ticking towers. . . . Tomorrow,
And to be. . . . Here by the River that is East—
Here at the waters' edge the hands drop memory;
Shadowless in that abyss they unaccounting lie.
How far away the star has pooled the sea—
Or shall the hands be drawn away, to die?

Kiss of our agony Thou gatherest,
                    O Hand of Fire
                            gatherest— (1930)

KEY WEST

Here has my salient faith annealed me.
Out of the valley, past the ample crib
To skies impartial, that do not disown me
Nor claim me, either, by Adam's spine—nor rib.

The oar plash, and the meteorite's white arch
Concur with wrist and bicep. In the moon
That now has sunk I strike a single march
To heaven or hades—to an equally frugal noon.

Because these millions reap a dead conclusion
Need I presume the same fruit of my bone
As draws them towards a doubly mocked confusion
Of apish nightmares into steel-strung stone?

O, steel and stone! But gold was, scarcity before.
And here is water, and a little wind. . . .
There is no breath of friends and no more shore
Where gold has not been sold and conscience tinned. (1933)

ROYAL PALM

For Grace Hart Crane

Green rustlings, more than regal charities
Drift coolly from that tower of whispered light.
Amid the noontide's blazed asperities
I watched the sun's most gracious anchorite

Climb up as by communings, year on year
Uneaten of the earth or aught earth holds,
And the grey trunk, that's elephantine, rear
Its frondings sighing in ætherial folds.

Forever fruitless, and beyond that yield
Of sweat the jungle presses with hot love
And tendril till our deathward breath is sealed—
It grazes the horizons, launched above

Mortality—ascending emerald-bright,
A fountain at salute, a crown in view—
Unshackled, casual of its azured height
As though it soared suchwise through heaven too.   (*1933*)

THE HURRICANE

Lo, Lord, Thou ridest!
Lord, Lord, Thy swifting heart

Naught stayeth, naught now bideth
But's smithereened apart!

Ay! Scripture flee'th stone!
Milk-bright, Thy chisel wind

Rescindeth flesh from bone
To quivering whittlings thinned—

Swept—whistling straw! Battered,
Lord, e'en boulders now out-leap

Rock sockets, levin lathered!
Nor, Lord, may worm out-deep

Thy drum's gambade, its plunge abscond!
Lord God, while summits crashing

Whip sea-kelp screaming on blond
Sky-seethe, high heaven dashing—

Thou ridest to the door, Lord!
Thou bidest wall nor floor, Lord!   (1933)

TO EMILY DICKINSON

You who desired so much—in vain to ask—
Yet fed your hunger like an endless task,
Dared dignify the labor, bless the quest—
Achieved that stillness ultimately best,

Being, of all, least sought for: Emily, hear!
O sweet, dead Silencer, most suddenly clear
When singing that Eternity possessed
And plundered momently in every breast;

—Truly no flower yet withers in your hand,
The harvest you descried and understand
Needs more than wit to gather, love to bind.
Some reconcilement of remotest mind—

Leaves Ormus rubyless, and Ophir chill.
Else tears heap all within one clay-cold hill.   (1933)

THE PHANTOM BARK

So dream thy sails, O phantom bark
That I thy drownèd man may speak again
Perhaps as once Will Collins spoke the lark,
And leave me half a-dream upon the main.

For who shall lift head up to funnel smoke,
And who trick back the leisured winds again
As they were fought—and wooed? They now but stoke
Their vanity, and dream no land in vain.

Of old there was a promise, and thy sails
Have kept no faith but wind, the cold stream

—The hot fickle wind, the breath of males
Imprisoned never, no not soot or rain.   (*1933*)

THE BROKEN TOWER

The bell-rope that gathers God at dawn
Dispatches me as though I dropped down the knell
Of a spent day—to wander the cathedral lawn
From pit to crucifix, feet chill on steps from hell.

Have you not heard, have you not seen that corps
Of shadows in the tower, whose shoulders sway
Antiphonal carillons launched before
The stars are caught and hived in the sun's ray?

The bells, I say, the bells break down their tower;
And swing I know not where. Their tongues engrave
Membrane through marrow, my long-scattered score
Of broken intervals. . . . And I, their sexton slave!

Oval encyclicals in canyons heaping
The impasse high with choir. Banked voices slain!
Pagodas, campaniles with reveilles outleaping—
O terraced echoes prostrate on the plain! . . .

And so it was I entered the broken world
To trace the visionary company of love, its voice
An instant in the wind (I know not whither hurled)
But not for long to hold each desperate choice.

My word I poured. But was it cognate, scored
Of that tribunal monarch of the air
Whose thigh embronzes earth, strikes crystal Word
In wounds pledged once to hope—cleft to despair?

The steep encroachments of my blood left me
No answer (could blood hold such a lofty tower
As flings the question true?)—or is it she
Whose sweet mortality stirs latent power?—

And through whose pulse I hear, counting the strokes
My veins recall and add, revived and sure
The angelus of wars my chest evokes:
What I hold healed, original now, and pure . . .

And builds, within, a tower that is not stone
(Not stone can jacket heaven)—but slip
Of pebbles—visible wings of silence sown
In azure circles, widening as they dip

The matrix of the heart, lift down the eye
That shrines the quiet lake and swells a tower . . .
The commodious, tall decorum of that sky
Unseals her earth, and lifts love in its shower.   (*1933*)

Kenneth Fearing

(1902–1961)

CULTURAL NOTES

Professor Burke's symphony, "Colorado Vistas,"
In four movements,
I Mountains, II Canyons, III Dusk, IV Dawn,
Was played recently by the Philharmonic.
Snapshots of the localities described in music were passed around and
the audience checked for accuracy.
All O.K.
After the performance Maurice Epstein, 29, tuberculosis, stoker on the
S.S. *Tarboy*, rose to his feet and shouted,
"He's crazy, them artists are all crazy,
I can prove it by Max Nordau. They poison the minds of young girls."
Otto Svoboda, 500 Avenue A, butcher, Pole, husband, philosopher,
argued in rebuttal,
"Shut your trap, you.
The question is, does the symphony fit in with Karl Marx?"

At the Friday evening meeting of the Browning Writing League, Mrs.
Whittamore Ralston-Beckett,
Traveler, lecturer, novelist, critic, poet, playwright, editor, mother,
idealist,
Fascinated her audience with a brief talk, whimsical and caustic,
Appealing to the younger generation to take a brighter, happier, more
sunny and less morbid view of life's eternal fundamentals.
Mrs. Ralston-Beckett quoted Sir Henry Parke-Bennett: "O Beauty,"
she said,
"Take your fingers off my throat, take your elbow out of my eye,
Take your sorrow off my sorrow,
Take your hat, take your gloves, take your feet down off the table,
Take your beauty off my beauty, and go."

In the open discussion that followed, Maurice Epstein, 29, tuberculosis,
stoker on the S.S. *Tarboy*, arose and queried the speaker,

II-351

"Is it true, as certain scientists assert, that them artists are all of them
crazy?"
A Mr. Otto Svoboda present spoke in reply,
"Shut your trap, you. The question is, what about Karl Marx?" *(1929)*

RESURRECTION

You will remember the kisses, real or imagined;
You will remember the faces that were before you, and the words
exchanged;
You will remember the minute crowded with meaning, the moment of
pain, the aimless hour;
You will remember the cities, and the plains, and the mountains, and
the sea,

And recall the friendly voice of the killer, or the voice of the priest,
inhumanly sweet;
Recall the triumphant smile of the duped;
You will not forget compassion that glittered in the eyes of the money-
lender, refusing you, not forget the purpose that lay beneath the
merchant's warmth;
You will not forget the voice of the bought magistrate quivering in
horror through the courtroom above prostitute and pimp,
The majesty of the statesman at the microphone, the sober majesty of
the listening clerk,
The face of the fool, radiant on newspaper and screen;

You will remember hope that crawled up the bar-room tap and spoke
through the confident speech of the lost,
Happiness clearly displayed on the glaring billboards,
Love casually revealed in the magazines and novels, or stated in the
trembling limbs of ancient millionaires;
You will remember the triumph easily defined by the rebel messiah,
by the breadloaf in the hand of the ghetto wife, by the inscription
on the patriot tomb;
You will remember your laughter that rose with the steam from the
carcass on the street
In hatred and pity exactly matched.

These are the things that will return to you,
To mingle with the days and nights, with the sound of motors and
the sun's warmth,

With fatigue and desire,
As you work, and sleep, and talk, and laugh, and die. *(1935)*

NO CREDIT

Whether dinner was pleasant, with the windows lit by gunfire, and no
one disagreed; or whether, later, we argued in the park, and there
was a touch of vomit gas in the evening air;
Whether we found a greater, deeper, more perfect love, by courtesy of
Camels, over NBC; whether the comics amused us, or the news-
papers carried a hunger death and a White House prayer for
Mother's Day;
Whether the bills were paid or not, whether or not we had our doubts,
whether we spoke our minds at Joe's, and the receipt said "Not
Returnable," and the cash-register rang up "No Sale,"
Whether the truth was then, or later, or whether the best had already
gone—

Nevertheless, we know; as every turn is measured; as every unavoidable
risk is known;
As nevertheless, the flesh grows old, dies, dies in its only life, is gone;
The reflection goes from the mirror; as the shadow, of even a rebel, is
gone from the wall;
As nevertheless, the current is thrown and the wheels revolve; and
nevertheless, as the word is spoken and the wheat grows tall and
the ships sail on—

None but the fool is paid in full; none but the broker, none but the
scab is certain of profit;
The sheriff alone may attend a third degree in formal attire; alone, the
academy artists multiply in dignity as trooper's bayonet guards the
door;
Only Steve, the side-show robot, knows content; only Steve, the
mechanical man in love with a photo-electric beam, remains aloof;
only Steve, who sits and smokes or stands in salute, is secure;
Steve, whose shoebutton eyes are blind to terror, whose painted ears
are deaf to appeal, whose welded breast will never be slashed by
bullets, whose armature soul can hold no fear. *(1935)*

LULLABY

Wide as this night, old as this night is old and young as it is young,
still as this, strange as this;

Filled as this night is filled with the light of a moon as gray;
Dark as these trees, heavy as this scented air from the fields, warm as
this hand;
As warm, as strong;

Is the night that wraps all the huts of the south and folds the empty
barns of the west;
Is the wind that fans the roadside fire;
Are the trees that line the country estates, tall as the lynch trees, as
straight, as black;
Is the moon that lights the mining towns, dim as the light upon tene-
ment roofs, gray upon the hands at the bars of Moabit, cold as
the bars of the Tombs. *(1935)*

TWENTIETH-CENTURY BLUES

What do you call it, bobsled champion, and you, too, Olympic roller-
coaster ace,
High-diving queen, what is the word,
Number one man on the Saturday poker squad, motion-picture star
incognito as a home girl, life of the party or you, the serious type,
what is it, what is it,

When it's just like a fever shooting up and up and up but there are
no chills and there is no fever,
Just exactly like a song, like a knockout, like a dream, like a book,

What is the word, when you know that all the lights of all the cities
of all the world are burning bright as day, and you know that some
time they all go out for you,
Or your taxi rolls and rolls through streets made of velvet, what is the
feeling, what is the feeling when the radio never ends, but the hour,
the swift, the electric, the invisible hour does not stop and does not
turn,
What does it mean, when the get-away money burns in dollars big as
moons, but where is there to go that's just exactly right,
What have you won, plunger, when the 20-to-1 comes in; what have
you won, salesman, when the dotted line is signed; irresistible lover,
when her eyelids flutter shut at last, what have you really, finally
won;
And what is gone soldier, soldier, step-and-a-half marine who saw the
whole world; hot-tip addict, what is always just missed; picker of

crumbs, how much has been lost, denied, what are all the things
destroyed,
Question mark, question mark, question mark, question mark,
And you, fantasy Frank, and dreamworld Dora and hallucination
Harold, and delusion Dick, and nightmare Ned,

What is it, how do you say it, what does it mean, what's the word,
That miracle thing, the thing that can't be so, quote, unquote, but just
the same it's true,
That third-rail, million-volt exclamation mark, that ditto, ditto, ditto,
That stop, stop, go. (*1935*)

MEMO

Is there still any shadow there, on the rainwet window of the coffee pot,
Between the haberdasher's and the pinball arcade,
There, where we stood one night in the warm, fine rain, and smoked
and laughed and talked.

Is there now any sound at all,
Other than the sound of tires, and motors, and hurrying feet,
Is there on tonight's damp, heelpocked pavement somewhere the mark
of a certain toe, an especial nail, or the butt of a particular dropped
cigarette?—

(There must be, there has to be, no heart could beat if this were not so,
That was an hour, a glittering hour, an important hour in a tremendous
year)

Where we talked for a while of life and love, of logic and the senses, of
you and of me, character and fate, pain, revolution, victory and
death,

Is there tonight any shadow, at all,
Other than the shadows that stop for a moment and then hurry past
the windows blurred by the same warm, slow, still rain? (*1938*)

TOMORROW

Now that the others are gone, all of them, forever,
And they have your answer, and you have theirs, and the decision is
made,

And the river of minutes between you widens to a tide of hours, a flood
of days, a gulf of years and a sea of silence;

If, now, there are any questions you would like to ask of the shapes that
still move and speak inaudibly in the empty room,
If there are any different arrangements you would like to suggest,

Make them to the river boats, whose echoing whistle will be a clear
reply,
Speak to the seagulls, their effortless flight will provide any answer you
may wish to hear,
Ask the corner chestnut vendor, ask the tireless hammer and pulse of
the subway,
Speak to the family on the illuminated billboard, forever friendly, or
to the wind, or to the sign that sways and creaks above the sta-
tioner's door. (*1938*)

REQUIEM

Will they stop,
Will they stand there for a moment, perhaps before some shop where
you have gone so many times
(Stand with the same blue sky above them and the stones, so often
walked, beneath)

Will it be a day like this—
As though there could be such a day again—

And will their own concerns still be about the same,
And will the feeling still be this that you have felt so many times,
Will they meet and stop and speak, one perplexed and one aloof,

Saying: Have you heard,
Have you heard,
Have you heard about the death?

Yes, choosing the words, tragic, yes, a shock,
One who had so much of this, they will say, a life so filled with that,
Then will one say that the days are growing crisp again, the other that
the leaves are turning,
And will they say good-bye, good-bye, you must look me up some time,
good-bye,
Then turn and go, each of them thinking, and yet, and yet,

Each feeling, if it were I, instead, would that be all,
Each wondering, suddenly alone, if that is all, in fact—
And will that be all?
On a day like this, with motors streaming through the fresh parks, the
streets alive with casual people,
And everywhere, on all of it, the brightness of the sun. *(1938)*

PACT

It is written in the skyline of the city (you have seen it, that bold and
accurate inscription), where the gray and gold and soot-black roofs
project against the rising or the setting sun,
It is written in the ranges of the farthest mountains, and written by the
lightning bolt,
Written, too, in the winding rivers of the prairies, and in the strangely
familiar effigies of the clouds,

That there will be other days and remoter times, by far, than these,
still more prodigious people and still less credible events,
When there will be a haze, as there is today, not quite blue and not
quite purple, upon the river, a green mist upon the valley below,
as now,

And we will build, upon that day, another hope (because these cities
are young and strong),
And we will raise another dream (because these hills and fields are rich
and green),

And we will fight for all of this again, and if need be again,
And on that day, and in that place, we will try again, and this time we
shall win. *(1940)*

ANY MAN'S ADVICE TO HIS SON

If you have lost the radio beam, then guide yourself by the sun or the
stars.
(By the North Star at night, and in daytime by the compass and the
sun.)
Should the sky be overcast and there are neither stars nor a sun, then
steer by dead reckoning.
If the wind and direction and speed are not known, then trust to your
wits and your luck.

Do you follow me? Do you understand? Or is this too difficult to learn?
But you must and you will, it is important that you do,
Because there may be troubles even greater than these that I have said.

Because, remember this: Trust no man fully.
Remember: If you must shoot at another man squeeze, do not jerk the
   trigger. Otherwise you may miss and die, yourself, at the hand of
   some other man's son.
And remember: In all this world there is nothing so easily squandered,
   or once gone, so completely lost as life.

I tell you this because I remember you when you were small,
And because I remember all your monstrous infant boasts and lies,
And the way you smiled, and how you ran and climbed, as no one else
   quite did, and how you fell and were bruised,
And because there is no other person, anywhere on earth, who remem-
   bers these things as clearly as I do now.   (1940)

PAY-OFF

Do you, now, as the news becomes known,
And you have the telegram still in your hand, here in the familiar room
   where there is no sound but the ticking of the clock,
Or there on the street, where you see the first headlines, and it is true
   this time, really true, actual as the green and red of the traffic lights,
   as real as the fruit vendor's rhythmic cry,

Do you recall any being other than this, before your world suddenly
   shook and settled to this new, strange axis upon which it will turn,
   now, always while you live?
Does it seem possible, now, you were ever bored? Or drunk and confident? Or sober and afraid?
Will the sound of the clock ever fade, or the voice of the vendor sometime stop?   (1940)

Richard Eberhart
(1904–   )

FOR A LAMB

I saw on the slant hill a putrid lamb,
Propped with daisies. The sleep looked deep,
The face nudged in the green pillow
But the guts were out for crows to eat.

Where's the lamb? whose tender plaint
Said all for the mute breezes.
Say he's in the wind somewhere,
Say, there's a lamb in the daisies.   (1936)

THE GROUNDHOG

In June, amid the golden fields,
I saw a groundhog lying dead.
Dead lay he; my senses shook,
And mind outshot our naked frailty.
There lowly in the vigorous summer
His form began its senseless change,
And made my senses waver dim
Seeing nature ferocious in him.
Inspecting close his maggots' might
And seething cauldron of his being,
Half with loathing, half with a strange love,
I poked him with an angry stick.
The fever arose, became a flame
And Vigour circumscribed the skies,
Immense energy in the sun,
And through my frame a sunless trembling.
My stick had done nor good nor harm.
Then stood I silent in the day
Watching the object, as before;
And kept my reverence for knowledge

II-359

Trying for control, to be still,
To quell the passion of the blood;
Until I had bent down on my knees
Praying for joy in the sight of decay.
And so I left; and I returned
In Autumn strict of eye, to see
The sap gone out of the groundhog,
But the bony sodden hulk remained.
But the year had lost its meaning,
And in intellectual chains
I lost both love and loathing,
Mured up in the wall of wisdom.
Another summer took the fields again
Massive and burning, full of life,
But when I chanced upon the spot
There was only a little hair left,
And bones bleaching in the sunlight
Beautiful as architecture;
I watched them like a geometer,
And cut a walking stick from a birch.
It has been three years, now.
There is no sign of the groundhog.
I stood there in the whirling summer,
My hand capped a withered heart,
And thought of China and of Greece,
Of Alexander in his tent;
Of Montaigne in his tower,
Of Saint Theresa in her wild lament. *(1936)*

"IN A HARD INTELLECTUAL LIGHT"

In a hard intellectual light
I will kill all delight,
And I will build a citadel
Too beautiful to tell

O too austere to tell
And far too beautiful to see,
Whose evident distance
I will call the best of me.

And this light of intellect
Will shine on all my desires,

It will my flesh protect
And flare my bold constant fires,

For the hard intellectual light
Will lay the flesh with nails.
And it will keep the world bright
And closed the body's soft jails.

And from this fair edifice
I shall see, as my eyes blaze,
The moral grandeur of man
Animating all his days.

And peace will marry purpose,
And purity married to grace
Will make the human absolute
As sweet as the human face.

Until my hard vision blears,
And Poverty and Death return
In organ music like the years,
Making the spirit leap, and burn

For the hard intellectual light
That kills all delight
And brings the solemn, inward pain
Of truth into the heart again.   (1936)

THE SOUL LONGS TO RETURN WHENCE IT CAME

I drove up to the graveyard, which
Used to frighten me as a boy,
When I walked down the river past it,
And evening was coming on. I'd make sure
I came home from the woods early enough.
I drove in, I found to the place, I
Left the motor running. My eyes hurried,
To recognize the great oak tree
On the little slope, among the stones.
It was a high day, a crisp day,
The cleanest kind of Autumn day,
With brisk intoxicating air, a
Little wind that frisked, yet there was

Old age in the atmosphere, nostalgia,
The subtle heaviness of the Fall.
I stilled the motor. I walked a few paces;
It was good, the tree; the friendliness of it.
I touched it, I thought of the roots;
They would have pierced her seven years.
O all peoples! O mighty shadows!
My eyes opened along the avenue
Of tombstones, the common land of death.
Humiliation of all loves lost,
That might have had full meaning in any
Plot of ground, come, hear the silence,
See the quivering light. My mind worked
Almost imperceptibly, I
In the command, I the wilful ponderer.
I must have stood silent and thoughtful
There. A host of dry leaves
Danced on the ground in the wind.
They startled, they curved up from the ground,
There was a dry rustling, rattling.
The sun was motionless and brittle.
I felt the blood darken in my cheeks
And burn. Like running. My eyes
Telescoped on decay, I out of command.
Fear, tenderness, they seized me.
My eyes were hot, I dared not look
At the leaves. A pagan urge swept me.
Multitudes, O multitudes in one.
The urge of the earth, the titan
Wild and primitive lust, fused
On the ground of her grave.
I was a being of feeling alone.
I flung myself down on the earth
Full length on the great earth, full length,
I wept out the dark load of human love.
In pagan adoration I adored her.
I felt the actual earth of her.
Victor and victim of humility,
I closed in the wordless ecstasy
Of mystery: where there is no thought
But feeling lost in itself forever,
Profound, remote, immediate, and calm.
Frightened, I stood up, I looked about

Suspiciously, hurriedly (a rustling),
As if the sun, the air, the trees
Were human, might not understand.
I drew breath, it made a sound,
I stepped gingerly away. Then
The mind came like a fire, it
Tortured man, I thought of madness.
The mind will not accept the blood.
The sun and sky, the trees and grasses,
And the whispering leaves, took on
Their usual characters. I went away,
Slowly, tingling, elated, saying, saying
Mother, Great Being, O Source of Life
To whom in wisdom we return,
Accept this humble servant evermore. (*1940*)

TWO LOVES

That her serene influence should spread
An afternoon of soft autumnal light
Is to my heart not unaccountable
For she was young, and is not dead.
And still her cheek is red and white.

But that this stealthy still insistent power
Pervades my mind and will not slumber me
Is delicate woe and glory hard to bear;
Her life lives in a ghost-wrought hour,
From whose chill spirit I am not free.

The one was willow to an ardent touch
And she was mood that had a right to die.
But she, the other, the passion of my mind
Long-living still, does overmuch
Come from the dead, and from the sky. (*1940*)

"WHEN DORIS DANCED"

When Doris danced under the oak tree
The sun himself might wish to see,
Might bend beneath those lovers, leaves,
While her her virgin step she weaves

And envious cast his famous hue
To make her daft, yet win her too

When Doris danced under the oak tree
Slow John, so stormed in heart, at sea
Gone all his store, a wreck he lay.
But on the ground the sun-beams play.
They lit his face in such degree
Doris lay down, all out of pity. *(1940)*

THE FURY OF AERIAL BOMBARDMENT

You would think the fury of aerial bombardment
Would rouse God to relent; the infinite spaces
Are still silent. He looks on shock-pried faces.
History, even, does not know what is meant.

You would feel that after so many centuries
God would give man to repent; yet he can kill
As Cain could, but with multitudinous will,
No farther advanced than in his ancient furies.

Was man made stupid to see his own stupidity?
Is God by definition indifferent, beyond us all?
Is the eternal truth man's fighting soul
Wherein the Beast ravens in its own avidity?

Of Van Wettering I speak, and Averill,
Names on a list, whose faces I do not recall
But they are gone to early death, who late in school
Distinguished the belt feed lever from the belt holding pawl.

(1944)

THE HORSE CHESTNUT TREE

Boys in sporadic but tenacious droves
Come with sticks, as certainly as Autumn,
To assault the great horse chestnut tree.

There is a law governs their lawlessness.
Desire is in them for a shining amulet
And the best are those that are highest up

They will not pick them easily from the ground.
With shrill arms they fling to the higher branches,
To hurry the work of nature for their pleasure.

I have seen them trooping down the street
Their pockets stuffed with chestnuts shucked, unshucked.
It is only evening keeps them from their wish.

Sometimes I run out in a kind of rage
To chase the boys away: I catch an arm,
Maybe, and laugh to think of being the lawgiver.

I was once such a young sprout myself
And fingered in my pocket the prize and trophy.
But still I moralize upon the day

And see that we, outlaws on God's property,
Fling out imagination beyond the skies,
Wishing a tangible good from the unknown.

And likewise death will drive us from the scene
With the great flowering world unbroken yet,
Which we held in idea, a little handful. (*1953*)

THE ROC

The perfervid Roc, sitting on candle light,
The moon's, inaccessible to night,
Thrusting invention, as if he were human,
Thought he could do anything in the world.

Sidereal emblem, come from far away,
This Roc had made amends with flight; and thought,
As men lean upward on the shaft of God,
He'd lean to mankind's aspirations, downward.

Thus is a stance of heavenly approbation,
Sitting in silence where the moonbeams glow,
Fluffing, not taking, the winds of other worlds,
The Roc's imagination grew, a perfect bird

For being beyond his native limitations.
The planets were in order marked, but nebulous;

He sat upon the edges of the world
And sorted the rhythms of the Field stars.

How small they are, down on that sphere,
The good Roc said, becoming a mental power.
I who know all of flight and fight and light
Will tell these creatures what they need to know.

They are afraid. See how each in his heart
Recoils from vistas of revenging evil.
They thrust their chests out cobalt bomb-wise
And bruit the big wars with their minds like boys'.

They are accursed. And what has cursed them is
The forcing gods they have themselves created,
The inability to look at anything
Explicitly, or straight enough to see it straight,

But they look with their old blood-dimmed feelings
And they feel with their old avenging muscles;
They are surprised at all access of wit,
And intellectual laughter they endure but little.

They fear their death because they do not understand it.
They fear insecurity, which lacks philosophy,
Presuming that so timed a creature could be safe.
And they fear injustice, a lack of reality.

The Roc began his acclamation thus.
He preened, and he aspired, and he espied,
And thought that he would move the world,
But the bedrock seemed to give, to fly.

It was the bedrock that buckled and roared.
He, who had defeated flight, a flying bird
Beyond birdhood, an angel of a newer motion,
Felt, in looking down, a crepitation:

The gravid base gave out; tumultuous waters
Crested black upheavals: the groined earth
Rocked spasmodically and lurched in space,
Its mankind clinging to the crust unknowingly.

He could not reach them. His new dimension
Affronted the clear light of the old moon.
The Roc then lifted up his ancient wings
And flew, instinctively, toward the dawn. *(1957)*

VAST LIGHT

The fighting nature of the intellect,
The loving nature of the heart,
The head that hits, the blood that lets,
The lift, and the abandonment,

Concern us not fitfully, in no abatement,
Speak to us not evenly, advance
Our good in no equal certainties,
Prevail without finalities,

As when we dare not speak out for justice
Having too fine a sense of discrimination,
Or as we do not know what to do
Speculating upon the imprecision of action,

While time rolls over the richest meadows.
It is now the soul rolls over us.
It is the soul between the head and the heart
Is our air-borne master and our hair-shirt.

It is the soul that cannot be put into words
Is the word of control. Like it or not,
The soul is all that is left of time:
We see through it: we breathe it out.

I have come back to old streets at nightfall
After journeys among volcanoes and icebergs.
I have been up in sidereal glows,
I have eaten of the chill taunt of the spirit.

Whether I apply to the light of reason,
Or feed on insatiable night,
I am aware of light and of vastness,
It is the vague of the soul that I know. *(1957)*

Theodore Roethke
(1908-1963)

ORCHIDS

They lean over the path
Adder-mouthed,
Swaying close to the face,
Coming out, soft and deceptive,
Limp and damp, delicate as a young bird's tongue;
Their fluttery fledgling lips
Move slowly,
Drawing in the warm air.

And at night,
The faint moon falling through whitewashed glass,
The heat going down
So their musky smell comes even stronger,
Drifting down from their mossy cradles:
So many devouring infants!
Soft luminescent fingers,
Lips neither dead nor alive,
Loose ghostly mouths
Breathing. *(1948)*

BIG WIND

Where were the greenhouses going,
Lunging into the lashing
Wind driving water
So far down the river
All the faucets stopped?—
So we drained the manure-machine
For the steam plant,
Pumping the stale mixture
Into the rusty boilers,
Watching the pressure gauge
Waver over to red,

As the seams hissed
And the live steam
Drove to the far
End of the rose-house,
Where the worst wind was,
Creaking the cypress window-frames,
Cracking so much thin glass
We stayed all night,
Stuffing the holes with burlap;
But she rode it out,
That old rose-house,
She hove into the teeth of it,
The core and pith of that ugly storm,
Ploughing with her stiff prow,
Bucking into the wind-waves
That broke over the whole of her,
Flailing her sides with spray,
Flinging long strings of wet across the roof-top,
Finally veering, wearing themselves out, merely
Whistling thinly under the wind-vents;
She sailed until the calm morning
Carrying her full cargo of roses.   *(1948)*

MY PAPA'S WALTZ

The whiskey on your breath
Could make a small boy dizzy;
But I held on like death:
Such waltzing was not easy.

We romped until the pans
Slid from the kitchen shelf;
My mother's countenance
Could not unfrown itself.

The hand that held my wrist
Was battered on one knuckle;
At every step I missed
My right ear scraped a buckle.

You beat time on my head
With a palm caked hard by dirt,

Then waltzed me off to bed
Still clinging to your shirt. *(1942, 1948)*

DOLOR

I have known the inexorable sadness of pencils,
Neat in their boxes, dolor of pad and paper-weight,
All the misery of manilla folders and mucilage,
Desolation in immaculate public places,
Lonely reception room, lavatory, switchboard,
The unalterable pathos of basin and pitcher,
Ritual of multigraph, paper-clip, comma,
Endless duplication of lives and objects.
And I have seen dust from the walls of institutions,
Finer than flour, alive, more dangerous than silica,
Sift, almost invisible, through long afternoons of tedium,
Dropping a fine film on nails and delicate eyebrows,
Glazing the pale hair, the duplicate gray standard faces. *(1948)*

GIVE WAY, YE GATES

1

Believe me, knot of gristle, I bleed like a tree;
I dream of nothing but boards;
I could love a duck.

Such music in a skin!
A bird sings in the bush of your bones.
Tufty, the water's loose.
Bring me a finger. This dirt's lonesome for grass.
Are the rats dancing? The cats are.
And you, cat after great milk and vasty fishes,
A moon loosened from a stag's eye,
Twiced me nicely,—
In the green of my sleep,
In the green.

2

Mother of blue and the many changes of hay,
This tail hates a flat path.
I've let my nose out;
I could melt down a stone,—

How is it with the long birds?
May I look too, loved eye?
It's a wink beyond the world.
In the slow rain, who's afraid?
We're king and queen of the right ground.
I'll risk the winter for you.

You tree beginning to know,
You whisper of kidneys,
We'll swinge the instant!—
With jots and jogs and cinders on the floor:
The sea will be there, the great squashy shadows,
Biting themselves perhaps;
The shrillest frogs;
And the ghost of some great howl
Dead in a wall.
In the high-noon of thighs,
In the springtime of stones,
We'll stretch with the great stems.
We'll be at the business of what might be
Looking toward what we are.

3

You child with a beast's heart,
Make me a bird or a bear!
I've played with the fishes
Among the unwrinkling ferns
In the wake of a ship of wind;
But now the instant ages,
And my thought hunts another body.
I'm sad with the little owls.

4

Touch and arouse. Suck and sob. Curse and mourn.
It's a cold scrape in a low place.
The dead crow dries on a pole.
Shapes in the shade
Watch.

The mouth asks. The hand takes.
These wings are from the wrong nest
Who stands in a hole
Never spills.

I hear the clap of an old wind.
The cold knows when to come.
What beats in me
I still bear.

The deep stream remembers:
Once I was a pond.
What slides away
Provides. *(1951)*

THE SHAPE OF THE FIRE

1

What's this? A dish for fat lips.
Who says? A nameless stranger.
Is he a bird or a tree? Not everyone can tell.

Water recedes to the crying of spiders.
An old scow bumps over black rocks.
A cracked pod calls.

Mother me out of here. What more will the bones allow?
Will the sea give the wind suck? A toad folds into a stone.
These flowers are all fangs. Comfort me, fury.
Wake me, witch, we'll do the dance of rotten sticks.

Shale loosens. Marl reaches into the field. Small birds pass over water.
Spirit, come near. This is only the edge of whiteness.
I can't laugh at a procession of dogs.

In the hour of ripeness, the tree is barren.
The she-bear mopes under the hill.
Mother, mother, stir from your cave of sorrow.

A low mouth laps water. Weeds, weeds, how I love you.
The arbor is cooler. Farewell, farewell, fond worm.
The warm comes without sound.

2

Where's the eye?
The eye's in the sty.
The ear's not here

Beneath the hair,
When I took off my clothes
To find a nose,
There was only one shoe
For the waltz of To,
The pinch of Where.

Time for the flat-headed man. I recognize that listener,
Him with the platitudes and rubber doughnuts,
Melting at the knees, a varicose horror.
Hello, hello. My nerves knew you, dear boy.
Have you come to unhinge my shadow?
Last night I slept in the pits of a tongue.
The silver fish ran in and out of my special bindings;
I grew tired of the ritual of names and the assistant keeper of the mol-
  lusks:
Up over a viaduct I came, to the snakes and sticks of another winter,
A two-legged dog hunting a new horizon of howls.
The wind sharpened itself on a rock;
A voice sang:

    Pleasure on ground
    Has no sound,
    Easily maddens
    The uneasy man.

    Who, careless, slips
    In coiling ooze
    Is trapped to the lips,
    Leaves more than shoes;

    Must pull off clothes
    To jerk like a frog
    On belly and nose
    From the sucking bog.

My meat eats me. Who waits at the gate?
Mother of quartz, your words writhe into my ear.
Renew the light, lewd whisper.

3

The wasp waits.
    The edge cannot eat the center.

The grape glistens.
    The path tells little to the serpent.
An eye comes out of the wave.
    The journey from flesh is longest.
A rose sways least.
    The redeemer comes a dark way.

4

Morning-fair, follow me further back
Into that minnowy world of weeds and ditches,
When the herons floated high over the white houses,
And the little crabs slipped into silvery craters.
When the sun for me glinted the sides of a sand grain,
And my intent stretched over the buds at their first trembling.

That air and shine: and the flicker's loud summer call:
The bearded boards in the stream and the all of apples;
The glad hen on the hill; and the trellis humming.
Death was not. I lived in a simple drowse:
Hands and hair moved through a dream of wakening blossoms.
Rain sweetened the cave and the dove still called;
The flowers leaned on themselves, the flowers in hollows;
And love, love sang toward.

5

To have the whole air!
The light, the full sun
Coming down on the flowerheads,
The tendrils turning slowly,
A slow snail-lifting, liquescent;
To be by the rose
Rising slowly out of its bed,
Still as a child in its first loneliness;
To see cyclamen veins become clearer in early sunlight,
And mist lifting out of the brown cattails;
To stare into the after-light, the glitter left on the lake's surface,
When the sun has fallen behind a wooded island;
To follow the drops sliding from a lifted oar,
Held up, while the rower breathes, and the small boat drifts quietly
    shoreward;
To know that light falls and fills, often without our knowing,
As an opaque vase fills to the brim from a quick pouring,
Fills and trembles at the edge yet does not flow over,
Still holding and feeding the stem of the contained flower. (*1951*)

THE VISITANT

1

A cloud moved close. The bulk of the wind shifted.
A tree swayed over water.
A voice said:
Stay. Stay by the slip-ooze. Stay.

Dearest tree, I said, may I rest here?
A ripple made a soft reply.
I waited, alert as a dog.
The leech clinging to a stone waited;
And the crab, the quiet breather.

2

Slow, slow as a fish she came,
Slow as a fish coming forward,
Swaying in a long wave;
Her skirts not touching a leaf,
Her white arms reaching towards me.

She came without sound,
Without brushing the wet stones,
In the soft dark of early evening,
She came,
The wind in her hair,
The moon beginning.

3

I woke in the first of morning.
Staring at a tree, I felt the pulse of a stone.
Where's she now, I kept saying.
Where's she now, the mountain's downy girl?

But the bright day had no answer.
A wind stirred in a web of appleworms;
The tree, the close willow, swayed. *(1953)*

MEDITATION AT OYSTER RIVER

1

Over the low, barnacled, elephant-colored rocks,
Come the first tide-ripples, moving, almost without sound, toward me,

Running along the narrow furrows of the shore, the rows of dead clam
  shells;
Then a runnel behind me, creeping closer,
Alive with tiny striped fish, and young crabs climbing in and out of the
  water.

No sound from the bay. No violence.
Even the gulls quiet on the far rocks,
Silent, in the deepening light,
Their cat-mewing over,
Their child-whimpering.

At last one long undulant ripple,
Blue-black from where I am sitting,
Makes almost a wave over a barrier of small stones,
Slapping lightly against a sunken log.
I dabble my toes in the brackish foam sliding forward,
Then retire to a rock higher up on the cliff-side.
The wind slackens, light as a moth fanning a stone:
A twilight wind, light as a child's breath
Turning not a leaf, not a ripple.
The dew revives on the beach-grass;
The salt-soaked wood of a fire crackles;
A fish raven turns on its perch (a dead tree in the rivermouth),
Its wings catching a last glint of the reflected sunlight.

2

The self persists like a dying star,
In sleep, afraid. Death's face rises afresh,
Among the shy beasts, the deer at the salt-lick,
The doe with its sloped shoulders loping across the highway,
The young snake, poised in green leaves, waiting for its fly,
The hummingbird, whirring from quince-blossom to morning-glory—
With these I would be.

And with water: the waves coming forward, without cessation,
The waves, altered by sand-bars, beds of kelp, miscellaneous driftwood,
Topped by cross-winds, tugged at by sinuous undercurrents
The tide rustling in, sliding between the ridges of stone,
The tongues of water, creeping in, quietly.

3

In this hour,
In this first heaven of knowing,

The flesh takes on the pure poise of the spirit,
Acquires, for a time, the sandpiper's insouciance,
The hummingbird's surety, the kingfisher's cunning—
I shift on my rock, and I think:
Of the first trembling of a Michigan brook in April,
Over a lip of stone, the tiny rivulet;
And that wrist-thick cascade tumbling from a cleft rock,
Its spray holding a double rain-bow in early morning,
Small enough to be taken in, embraced, by two arms,—
Or the Tittebawasee, in the time between winter and spring,
When the ice melts along the edges in early afternoon.
And the midchannel begins cracking and heaving from the pressure
    beneath,
The ice piling high against the iron-bound spiles,
Gleaming, freezing hard again, creaking at midnight—
And I long for the blast of dynamite,
The sudden sucking roar as the culvert loosens its debris of branches and
    sticks,
Welter of tin cans, pails, old bird nests, a child's shoe riding a log,
As the piled ice breaks away from the battered spiles,
And the whole river begins to move forward, its bridges shaking.

4

Now, in this waning of light,
I rock with the motion of morning;
In the cradle of all that is,
I'm lulled into half-sleep
By the lapping of water,
Cries of the sandpiper.
Water's my will, and my way,
And the spirit runs, intermittently,
In and out of the small waves,
Runs with the intrepid shorebirds—
How graceful the small before danger!

In the first of the moon,
All's a scattering,
A shining. (1964)

THE THING

Suddenly they came flying, like a long scarf of smoke,
Trailing a thing—what was it?—small as a lark
Above the blue air, in the slight haze beyond,

A thing in and out of sight,
Flashing between gold levels of the late sun,
Then throwing itself up and away from the implacable swift pursuers,
Confusing them once flying straight into the sun
So they circled aimlessly for almost a minute,
Only to find, with their long terrible eyes
The small thing diving down toward a hill,
Where they dropped again
In one streak of pursuit.

Then the first bird
Struck;
Then another, another,
Until there was nothing left,
Not even feathers from so far away.

And we turned to our picnic
Of veal soaked in marsala and little larks arranged on a long platter,
And we drank the dry harsh wine
While I poked with a stick at a stone near a four-pronged flower,
And a black bull nudged at a wall in the valley below,
And the blue air darkened. *(1964)*

Charles Olson
(1910-1970)

THE KINGFISHERS

1

What does not change / is the will to change

He woke, fully clothed, in his bed. He
remembered only one thing, the birds, how
when he came in, he had gone around the rooms
and got them back in their cage, the green one first,
she with the bad leg, and then the blue,
the one they had hoped was a male

Otherwise? Yes, Fernand, who had talked lispingly of Albers & Angkor
    Vat.
He had left the party without a word. How he got up, got into his coat,
I do not know. When I saw him, he was at the door, but it did not
    matter,
he was already sliding along the wall of the night, losing himself
in some crack of the ruins. That it should have been he who said,
    "The kingfishers!
who cares
for their feathers
now?"

His last words had been, "The pool is slime." Suddenly everyone,
ceasing their talk, sat in a row around him, watched
they did not so much hear, or pay attention, they
wondered, looked at each other, smirked, but listened,
he repeated and repeated, could not go beyond his thought
"The pool   the kingfishers' feathers were wealth   why
did the export stop?"

It was then he left

II-379

2

I thought of the E on the stone, and of what Mao said
la lumière"
        but the kingfisher
de l'aurore"
        but the kingfisher flew west
est devant nous!
        he got the color of his breast
        from the heat of the setting sun!

The features are, the feebleness of the feet (syndactylism of the 3rd &
    4th digit)
the bill, serrated, sometimes a pronounced beak, the wings
where the color is, short and round, the tail
inconspicuous.

But not these things were the factors. Not the birds.
The legends are
legends. Dead, hung up indoors, the kingfisher
will not indicate a favoring wind,
or avert the thunderbolt. Nor, by its nesting,
still the waters, with the new year, for seven days.
It is true, it does nest with the opening year, but not on the waters
It nests at the end of a tunnel bored by itself in a bank. There,
six or eight white and translucent eggs are laid, on fishbones
not on bare clay, on bones thrown up in pellets by the birds.

                On these rejectamenta
(as they accumulate they form a cup-shaped structure) the young are
    born.
And, as they are fed and grow, this nest of excrement and decayed fish
    becomes
                a dripping, fetid mass
Mao concluded:
        nous devons
                nous lever
                    et agir!

3

When the attentions change / the jungle
leaps in
        even the stones are split
                they rive

Or,
enter
that other conqueror we more naturally recognize
he so resembles ourselves

But the E
cut so rudely on that oldest stone
sounded otherwise,
was differently heard

as, in another time, were treasures used:

(and, later, much later, a fine ear thought
a scarlet coat)

       "of green feathers   feet, beaks and eyes
       of gold

       "animals likewise,
       resembling snails

       "a large wheel, gold, with figures of unknown four-foots,
       and worked with tufts of leaves, weight
       3800 ounces

       "last, two birds, of thread and featherwork, the quills
       gold, the feet
       gold, the two birds perched on two reeds
       gold, the reeds arising from two embroidered mounds,
       one yellow, the other
       white.
                "And from each reed hung
                seven feathered tassels.

In this instance, the priests
(in dark cotton robes, and dirty,
their dishevelled hair matted with blood, and flowing wildly
over their shoulders)
rush in among the people, calling on them
to protect their gods

And all now is war
where so lately there was peace,

and the sweet brotherhood, the use
of tilled fields.

4

Not one death but many,
not accumulation but change, the feed-back proves, the feed-back is
the law

> Into the same river no man steps twice
> When fire dies air dies
> No one remains, nor is, one

Around an appearance, one common model, we grow up
many. Else how is it,
if we remain the same,
we take pleasure now
in what we did not take pleasure before? love
contrary objects? admire and/or find fault? use
other words, feel other passions, have
nor figure, appearance, disposition, tissue
the same?

> To be in different states without a change
> is not a possibility

We can be precise. The factors are
in the animal and/or the machine the factors are
communication and/or control, both involve
the message. And what is the message? The message is
a discrete or continuous sequence of measurable events distributed in
    time

is the birth of air, is
the birth of water, is
a state between
the origin and
the end, between
birth and the beginning of
another fetid nest

is change, presents
no more than itself

And the too strong grasping of it,
when it is pressed together and condensed,
loses it

This very thing you are

II

    They buried their dead in a sitting posture
    serpent   cane   razor   ray of the sun

    And she sprinkled water on the head of the child, crying
    "Cioa-coatl! Cioa-coatl!"
    with her face to the west

    Where the bones are found, in each personal heap
    with what each enjoyed, there is always
    the Mongolian louse

The light is in the east. Yes. And we must rise, act. Yet
in the west, despite the apparent darkness (the whiteness
which covers all), if you look, if you can bear, if you can, long enough

        as long as it was necessary for him, my guide
        to look into the yellow of that longest lasting rose

so you must, and, in that whiteness, into that face, with what candor,
    look
and, considering the dryness of the place
    the long absence of an adequate race

        (of the two who first came, each a conquistador, one healed, the
            other
        tore the eastern idols down, toppled
        the temple walls, which, says the excuser
        were black from human gore)

hear
hear, where the dry blood talks
    where the old appetite walks

            la più saporita e migliore
            che si possa trovar al mondo

where it hides, look
in the eye how it runs
in the flesh / chalk

> but under these petals
> in the emptiness
> regard the light, contemplate
> the flower

whence it arose

> with what violence benevolence is bought
> what cost in gesture justice brings
> what wrongs domestic rights involve
> what stalks
> this silence

> what pudor pejorocracy affronts
> how awe, night-rest and neighborhood can rot
> what breeds where dirtiness is law
> what crawls
> below

III

> I am no Greek, hath not th'advantage.
> And of course, no Roman:
> he can take no risk that matters,
> the risk of beauty least of all.

> But I have my kin, if for no other reason than
> (as he said, next of kin) I commit myself, and,
> given my freedom, I'd be a cad
> if I didn't. Which is most true.

> It works out this way, despite the disadvantage.
> I offer, in explanation, a quote:
> si j'ai du goût, ce n'est guère
> que pour la terre et les pierres

> Despite the discrepancy (an ocean   courage   age)
> this is also true: if I have any taste
> it is only because I have interested myself
> in what was slain in the sun

I pose you your question:

shall you uncover honey / where maggots are?

I hunt among stones   *(1960)*

MAXIMUS, TO HIMSELF

I have had to learn the simplest things
last. Which made for difficulties.
Even at sea I was slow, to get the hand out, or to cross
a wet deck.
          The sea was not, finally, my trade.
But even my trade, at it, I stood estranged
from that which was most familiar. Was delayed,
and not content with the man's argument
that such postponement
is now the nature of
obedience,
          that we are all late
          in a slow time,
          that we grow up many
          And the single
          is not easily
          known

It could be, though the sharpness (the *achiote*)
I note in others,
makes more sense
than my own distances. The agilities

          they show daily
          who do the world's
          businesses
          And who ao nature's
          as I have no sense
          I have done either

I have made dialogues,
have discussed ancient texts,
have thrown what light I could, offered
what pleasures
doceat allows

But the known?
This, I have had to be given,
a life, love, and from one man
the world.

Tokens.
But sitting here
I look out as a wind
and water man, testing
And missing
some proof

I know the quarters
of the weather, where it comes from,
where it goes. But the stem of me,
this I took from their welcome,
or their rejection, of me

And my arrogance
was neither diminished
nor increased,
by the communication

2

It is undone business
I speak of, this morning,
with the sea
stretching out
from my feet   *(1960)*

MAXIMUS, TO GLOUCESTER, LETTER 19
(A PASTORAL LETTER

relating
to the care of souls,
it says)

He had smiled at us,
each time we were in town, inquired
how the baby was, had two cents
for the weather,wore
(besides his automobile)

good clothes.
                    And a pink face.

It was yesterday
it all came out. The gambit
(as he crossed the street,
after us):"I don't believe
I know your name."Given.
How do you do,
how do you do.And then:
"Pardon me, but
what church
do you belong to,
may I ask?"

And the whole street, the town, the cities, the nation
blinked, in the afternoon sun, as the gun
was held at them. And I wavered
in the thought.

            I sd, you may, sir.
            He sd, what, sir.
            I sd, none,
            sir.

And the light was back.
For I am no merchant.
Nor so young I need to take a stance
to a loaded
smile.

            I have known the face
            of God.
            And turned away,
            turned,
            as He did,
            his backside

                    2

And now it is noon
of a cloudy sunday.
And a bird sings
loudly

And my daughter, naked
on the porch, sings
as best she can, and loudly,
back

> She wears her own face
> as we do not,
> until we cease to wear
> the clouds
> of all confusion,
>
> of all confusers
> who wear the false face
> He never wore, Whose
> is terrible. Is
> perfection   (1960)

THE MOON IS THE NUMBER 18

is a monstrance,
the blue dogs bay,
and the son sits,
grieving

is a grinning god, is
the mouth of, is
the dripping moon

while in the tower the cat
preens
and all motion
is a crab

and there is nothing he can do but what they do, watch
the face of waters, and fire

> The blue dogs paw,
> lick the droppings, dew
> or blood, whatever
> results are. And night,
> the crab, rays round
> attentive as the cat to catch
> human sound

The blue dogs rue,
as he does, as he would howl, confronting
the wind which rocks what was her, while prayers
striate the snow, words blow
as questions cross fast, fast
as flames, as flames form, melt
along any darkness

Birth is an instance as is a host, namely, death

The moon has no air

In the red tower
in that tower where she also sat
in that particular tower where watching & moving
    are,
there,
there where what triumph there is, is: there
is all substance, all creature
all there is against the dirty moon, against
number, image, sortilege—

alone with cat & crab,
and sound is, is, his
conjecture   (1960)

Karl Shapiro
(1913–   )

AUTO WRECK

Its quick soft silver bell beating, beating,
And down the dark one ruby flare
Pulsing out red light like an artery,
The ambulance at top speed floating down
Past beacons and illuminated clocks
Wings in a heavy curve, dips down,
And brakes speed, entering the crowd.
The doors leap open, emptying light;
Stretchers are laid out, the mangled lifted
And stowed into the little hospital.
Then the bell, breaking the hush, tolls once,
And the ambulance with its terrible cargo
Rocking, slightly rocking, moves away,
As the doors, an afterthought, are closed.

We are deranged, walking among the cops
Who sweep glass and are large and composed.
One is still making notes under the light.
One with a bucket douches ponds of blood
Into the street and gutter.
One hangs lanterns on the wrecks that cling,
Empty husks of locusts, to iron poles.

Our throats were tight as tourniquets,
Our feet were bound with splints, but now,
Like convalescents intimate and gauche,
We speak through sickly smiles and warn
With the stubborn saw of common sense,
The grim joke and the banal resolution.
The traffic moves around with care,
But we remain, touching a wound
That opens to our richest horror.

Already old, the question Who shall die?
Becomes unspoken Who is innocent?
For death in war is done by hands;
Suicide has cause and stillbirth, logic;
And cancer, simple as a flower, blooms.
But this invites the occult mind,
Cancels our physics with a sneer,
And spatters all we knew of denouement
Across the expedient and wicked stones.   (*1942*)

BUICK

As a sloop with a sweep of immaculate wing on her delicate spine
And a keel as steel as a root that holds in the sea as she leans,
Leaning and laughing, my warm-hearted beauty, you ride, you ride,
You tack on the curves with parabola speed and a kiss of goodbye,
Like a thoroughbred sloop, my new high-spirited spirit, my kiss.

As my foot suggests that you leap in the air with your hips of a girl,
My finger that praises your wheel and announces your voices of song,
Flouncing your skirts, you blueness of joy, you flirt of politeness,
You leap, you intelligence, essence of wheelness with silvery nose,
And your platinum clocks of excitement stir like the hairs of a fern.

But how alien you are from the booming belts of your birth and the
   smoke
Where you turned on the stinging lathes of Detroit and Lansing at night
And shrieked at the torch in your secret parts and the amorous tests,
But now with your eyes that enter the future of roads you forget;
You are all instinct with your phosphorous glow and your streaking hair.

And now when we stop it is not as the bird from the shell that I leave
Or the leathery pilot who steps from his bird with a sneer of delight,
And not as the ignorant beast do you squat and watch me depart,
But with exquisite breathing you smile, with satisfaction of love,
And I touch you again as you tick in the silence and settle in sleep.
                                                          (*1942*)

THE DOME OF SUNDAY

With focus sharp as Flemish-painted face
In film of varnish brightly fixed
And through a polished hand-lens deeply seen,

Sunday at noon through hyaline thin air
Sees down the street,
And in the camera of my eye depicts
Row-houses and row-lives:
Glass after glass, door after door the same,
Face after face the same, the same,
The brutal visibility the same;

As if one life emerging from one house
Would pause, a single image caught between
Two facing mirrors where vision multiplies
Beyond perspective,
A silent clatter in the high-speed eye
Spinning out photo-circulars of sight.

I see slip to the curb the long machines
Out of whose warm and windowed rooms pirouette
Shellacked with silk and light
The hard legs of our women.
Our women are one woman, dressed in black.
The carmine printed mouth
And cheeks as soft as muslin-glass belong
Outright to one dark dressy man,
Merely a swagger at her curvy side.
This is their visit to themselves:
All day from porch to porch they weave
A nonsense pattern through the even glare,
Stealing in surfaces
Cold vulgar glances at themselves.

And high up in the heated room all day
I wait behind the plate glass pane for one,
Hot as a voyeur for a glimpse of one,
The vision to blot out this woman's sheen;
All day my sight records expensively
Row-houses and row-lives.

But nothing happens; no diagonal
With melting shadow falls across the curb:
Neither the blinded negress lurching through fatigue,
Nor exiles bleeding from their pores,
Nor that bright bomb slipped lightly from its rack
To splinter every silvered glass and crystal prism,
Witch-bowl and perfume bottle

And billion candle-power dressing-bulb,
No direct hit to smash the shatter-proof
And lodge at last the quivering needle
Clean in the eye of one who stands transfixed
In fascination of her brightness. *(1942)*

DRUG STORE

*I do remember an apothecary,
And hereabouts 'a dwells*

It baffles the foreigner like an idiom,
And he is right to adopt it as a form
Less serious than the living-room or bar;
    For it disestablishes the café,
Is a collective, and on basic country.

Not that it praises hygiene and corrupts
The ice-cream parlor and the tobacconist's
Is it a center; but that the attractive symbols
    Watch over puberty and leer
Like rubber bottles waiting for sick-use.

Youth comes to jingle nickels and crack wise;
The baseball scores are his, the magazines
Devoted to lust, the jazz, the Coca-Cola,
    The lending-library of love's latest.
He is the customer; he is heroized.

And every nook and cranny of the flesh
Is spoken to by packages with wiles.
"Buy me, buy me," they whimper and cajole;
    The hectic range of lipstick pouts,
Revealing the wicked and the simple mouth.

With scarcely any evasion in their eye
They smoke, undress their girls, exact a stance;
But only for a moment. The clock goes round;
    Crude fellowships are made and lost;
They slump in booths like rags, not even drunk. *(1942)*

NOSTALGIA

My soul stands at the window of my room,
    And I ten thousand miles away;

My days are filled with Ocean's sound of doom,
Salt and cloud and the bitter spray.
Let the wind blow, for many a man shall die.

My selfish youth, my books with gilded edge,
Knowledge and all gaze down the street;
The potted plants upon the window ledge
Gaze down with selfish lives and sweet.
Let the wind blow, for many a man shall die.

My night is now her day, my day her night,
So I lie down, and so I rise;
The sun burns close, the star is losing height,
The clock is hunted down the skies.
Let the wind blow, for many a man shall die.

Truly a pin can make the memory bleed,
A world explode the inward mind
And turn the skulls and flowers never freed
Into the air, no longer blind.
Let the wind blow, for many a man shall die.

Laughter and grief join hands. Always the heart
Clumps in the breast with heavy stride;
The face grows lined and wrinkled like a chart,
The eyes bloodshot with tears and tide.
Let the wind blow, for many a man shall die.   (1942)

POET

Il arrive que l'esprit demande la poésie

Left leg flung out, head cocked to the right,
Tweed coat or army uniform, with book,
Beautiful eyes, who is this walking down?
Who, glancing at the pane of glass looks sharp
And thinks it is not he—as when a poet
Comes swiftly on some half-forgotten poem
And loosely holds the page, steady of mind,
Thinking it is not his?

And when will *you* exist?—Oh, it is I,
Incredibly skinny, stooped, and neat as pie,

Ignorant as dirt, erotic as an ape,
Dreamy as puberty—with dirty hair!
Into the room like kangaroo he bounds,
Ears flopping like the most expensive hound's;
His chin receives all questions as he bows
Mouthing a green bon-bon.

Has no more memory than rubber. Stands
Waist-deep in heavy mud of thought and broods
At his own wetness. When he would get out,
To his surprise he lifts in air a phrase
As whole and clean and silvery as a fish
Which jumps and dangles on his damned hooked grin,
But like a name-card on a man's lapel
Calls him a conscious fool.

And child-like he remembers all his life
And cannily constructs it, fact by fact,
As boys paste postage stamps in careful books,
Denoting pence and legends and profiles,
Nothing more valuable.—And like a thief,
His eyes glassed over and congealed with guilt,
Fondles his secrets like a case of tools,
And waits in empty doors.

By men despised for knowing what he is,
And by himself. But he exists for women.
As dolls to girls, as perfect wives to men,
So he to women. And to himself a thing,
All ages, epicene, without a trade.
To girls and wives always alive and fated;
To men and scholars always dead like Greek
And always mistranslated.

Towards exile and towards shame he lures himself,
Tongue winding on his arm, and thinks like Eve
By biting apple will become most wise.
Sentio ergo sum: he feels his way
And words themselves stand up for him like Braille
And punch and perforate his parchment ear.
All language falls like Chinese on his soul,
Image of song unsounded.

This is the coward's coward that in his dreams
Sees shapes of pain grow tall. Awake at night
He peers at sounds and stumbles at a breeze.
And none holds life less dear. For as a youth
Who by some accident observes his love
Naked and in some natural ugly act,
He turns with loathing and with flaming hands,
    Seared and betrayed by sight.

He is the business man, on beauty trades,
Dealer in arts and thoughts who, like the Jew,
Shall rise from slums and hated dialects
A tower of bitterness. Shall be always strange,
Hunted and then sought after. Shall be sat
Like an ambassador from another race
At tables rich with music. He shall eat flowers,
Chew honey and spit out gall. They shall all smile
    And love and pity him.

His death shall be by drowning. In that hour
When the last bubble of pure heaven's air
Hovers within his throat, safe on his bed,
A small eternal figurehead in terror,
He shall cry out and clutch his days of straw
Before the blackest wave. Lastly, his tomb
Shall list and founder in the troughs of grass
    And none shall speak his name. (1942)

From SIX RELIGIOUS LYRICS: I

I sing the simplest flower,
    The earliest quest of day,
That wears in its white corolla
    The signet of breathing May.

For the envelope of beauty
    Discloses the female part,
The bending and swollen stigma,
    The sly tongue of the heart.

And the dusty bee for nectar
    Enters and drinks his fill,
And the wind comes freely, freshly
    To assist the season's will.

I give you the simplest flower,
The color of air, a dress
Self-woven and frail and holy,
The signet of love's distress.   (1942)

THE INTELLECTUAL

What should the wars do with these jigging fools?

The man behind the book may not be man,
His own man or the book's or yet the time's,
But still be whole, deciding what he can
In praise of politics or German rimes;

But the intellectual lights a cigarette
And offers it lit to the lady, whose odd smile
Is the merest hyphen—lest he should forget
What he has been resuming all the while.

He talks to overhear, she to withdraw
To some interior feminine fireside
Where the back arches, beauty puts forth a paw
Like a black puma stretching in velvet pride,

Making him think of cats, a stray of which
Some days sets up a howling in his brain,
Pure interference such as this neat bitch
Seems to create from listening disdain.

But talk is all the value, the release,
Talk is the very fillip of an act,
The frame and subject of the masterpiece
Under whose film of age the face is cracked.

His own forehead glows like expensive wood,
But back of it the mind is disengaged,
Self-sealing clock recording bad and good
At constant temperature, intact, unaged.

But strange, his body is an open house
Inviting every passerby to stay;
The city to and fro beneath his brows
Wanders and drinks and chats from night to day

Think of a private thought, indecent room
Where one might kiss his daughter before bed!
Life is embarrassed; shut the family tomb,
Console your neighbor for his recent dead;

Do something! die in Spain or paint a green
Gouache, go into business (Rimbaud did),
Or start another Little Magazine,
Or move in with a woman, have a kid.

Invulnerable, impossible, immune,
Do what you will, your will will not be done
But dissipate the light of afternoon
Till evening flickers like the midnight sun,

And midnight shouts and dies: I'd rather be
A milkman walking in his sleep at dawn
Bearing fat quarts of cream, and so be free,
Crossing alone and cold from lawn to lawn.

I'd rather be a barber and cut hair
Than walk with you in gilt museum halls,
You and the puma-lady, she so rare
Exhaling her silk soul upon the walls.

Go take yourselves apart, but let me be
The fault you find with everyman. I spit,
I laugh, I fight; and you, *l'homme qui rît,*
Swallow your stale saliva, and still sit.   *(1944)*

THE PHENOMENON

How lovely it was, after the official fright,
To walk in the shadowy drifts, as if the clouds
Saturated with the obscurity of night
Had died and fallen piecemeal into shrouds.

What crepes there were, what sables heaped on stones,
What soft shakos on posts, tragically gay!
And oil-pool flooded fields that blackly shone
The more black under the liquid eye of day!

It was almost warmer to the touch than sands
And sweeter-tasting than the white, and yet,

Walking, the children held their fathers' hands
Like visitors to a mine or parapet.

Then black it snowed again and while it fell
You could see the sun, an irritated rim
Wheeling through smoke; each from his shallow hell
Experienced injured vision growing dim.

But one day all was clear, and one day soon,
Sooner than those who witnessed it had died,
Nature herself forgot the phenomenon,
Her faulty snowfall brilliantly denied. (1953)

Randall Jarrell
(1914–1965)

2ND AIR FORCE

Far off, above the plain the summer dries,
The great loops of the hangars sway like hills.
Buses and weariness and loss, the nodding soldiers
Are wire, the bare frame building, and a pass
To what was hers; her head hides his square patch
And she thinks heavily: My son is grown.
She sees a world: sand roads, tar-paper barracks,
The bubbling asphalt of the runways, sage,
The dunes rising to the interminable ranges,
The dim flights moving over clouds like clouds.
The armorers in their patched faded green,
Sweat-stiffened, banded with brass cartridges,
Walk to the line; their Fortresses, all tail,
Stand wrong and flimsy on their skinny legs,
And the crews climb to them clumsily as bears.
The head withdraws into its hatch (a boy's),
The engines rise to their blind laboring roar,
And the green, made beasts run home to air.
Now in each aspect death is pure.
(At twilight they wink over men like stars
And hour by hour, through the night, some see
The great lights floating in—from Mars, from Mars.)
How emptily the watchers see them gone.

They go, there is silence; the woman and her son
Stand in the forest of the shadows, and the light
Washes them like water. In the long-sunken city
Of evening, the sunlight stills like sleep
The faint wonder of the drowned; in the evening,
In the last dreaming light, so fresh, so old,
The soldiers pass like beasts, unquestioning,
And the watcher for an instant understands

What there is then no need to understand;
But she wakes from her knowledge, and her stare,
A shadow now, moves emptily among
The shadows learning in their shadowy fields
The empty missions.
                Remembering,
She hears the bomber calling, *Little Friend!*
To the fighter hanging in the hostile sky,
And sees the ragged flame eat, rib by rib,
Along the metal of the wing into her heart:
The lives stream out, blossom, and float steadily
To the flames of the earth, the flames
That burn like stars above the lands of men.

She saves from the twilight that takes everything
A squadron shipping, in its last parade—
Its dogs run by it, barking at the band—
A gunner walking to his barracks, half-asleep,
Starting at something, stumbling (above, invisible,
The crews in the steady winter of the sky
Tremble in their wired fur); and feels for them
The love of life for life. The hopeful cells
Heavy with someone else's death, cold carriers
Of someone else's victory, grope past their lives
Into her own bewilderment: The years meant *this?*

But for them the bombers answer everything. *(1945)*

THE DEATH OF THE BALL TURRET GUNNER

From my mother's sleep I fell into the State,
And I hunched in its belly till my wet fur froze.
Six miles from earth, loosed from its dream of life,
I woke to black flak and the nightmare fighters.
When I died they washed me out of the turret with a hose.
                                (1945)

A CAMP IN THE PRUSSIAN FOREST

I walk beside the prisoners to the road.
Load on puffed load,
Their corpses, stacked like sodden wood,
Lie barred or galled with blood

By the charred warehouse. No one comes today
In the old way
To knock the fillings from their teeth;
The dark, coned, common wreath

Is plaited for their grave—a kind of grief.
The living leaf
Clings to the planted profitable
Pine if it is able;

The boughs sigh, mile on green, calm, breathing mile,
From this dead file
The planners ruled for them. . . . One year
They sent a million here:

Here men were drunk like water, burnt like wood.
The fat of good
And evil, the breast's star of hope
Were rendered into soap.

I paint the star I sawed from yellow pine—
And plant the sign
In soil that does not yet refuse
Its usual Jews

Their first asylum. But the white, dwarfed star—
This dead white star—
Hides nothing, pays for nothing; smoke
Fouls it, a yellow joke,

The needles of the wreath are chalked with ash,
A filmy trash
Litters the black woods with the death
Of men; and one last breath

Curls from the monstrous chimney. . . . I laugh aloud
Again and again;
The star laughs from its rotting shroud
Of flesh. O star of men!   (*1948*)

THE MÄRCHEN

(GRIMM'S TALES)

Listening, listening; it is never still.
This is the forest: long ago the lives

Edged armed into its tides (the axes were its stone
Lashed with the skins of dwellers to its boughs);
We felled our islands there, at last, with iron.
The sunlight fell to them, according to our wish,
And we believed, till nightfall, in that wish;
And we believed, till nightfall, in our lives.

The bird is silent; but its cold breast stirs
Raggedly, and the gloom the moonlight bars
Is blurred with the fluff its long death strewed
In the crumpled fern; and far off something falls.
If the firs forget their breath, if the leaf that perishes
Holds, a bud, to spring; sleeps, fallen, under snow—
It is never still. The darkness quakes with blood;
From its pulse the dark eyes of the hunter glow
Green as their forest, fading images
Of the dream in the firelight: shudder of the coals
In their short Hell, vined skeleton
Of the charcoal-burner dozing in the snow.
Hänsel, to map the hard way, cast his bones
Up clouds to Paradise; His sparrows ate
And he plunged home, past peat and measures, to his kin
Furred in the sooty darkness of the cave
Where the old gods nodded. How the devil's beard
Coiled round the dreaming Hänsel, till his limbs
Grew gnarled as a fakir's on the spindling Cross
The missions rowed from Asia: eternal corpse
Of the Scapegoat, gay with His blood's watered beads,
Red wax in the new snow (strange to His warmed stare);
The wooden mother and the choir of saints, His stars;
And God and His barons, always, iron behind.
Gorged Hänsel felt His blood burn thin as air
In a belly swollen with the airy kine;
How many ages boiled Christ's bark for soup!
Giddy with emptiness, a second wife
Scolding the great-eyed children of a ghost,
He sends them, in his tale, not out to death
(Godfather Death, the reaping messenger),
Nor to the devil cringing in the gloom,
Shifting his barred hooves with a crunch like snow—
But to a king: the blind untroubled Might
Renting a destiny to men on terms—
Come, mend me and wed half of me, my son!
Behind, the headsman fondles his gnawn block.

So men have won a kingdom—there are kings;
Are giants, warlocks, the unburied dead
Invulnerable to any power—the Necessity
Men spring from, die under: the unbroken wood.

Noon, the gold sun of hens and aldermen
Inked black as India, on the green ground,
Our patterns, homely, mercenary, magnified—
Bewitching as the water of Friar Bacon's glass.
(*Our* farmer fooled the devil with a turnip,
Our tailor won a queen with seven flies;
Mouser and mousie and a tub of fat
Kept house together—and a louse, a louse
Brewed small beer in an eggshell with a flea.)
But at evening the poor light, far-off, fantastic—
Sun of misers and of mermen, the last foolish gold
Of soldiers wandering through the country with a crutch—
Scattered its leagues of shadows on the plots
Where life, horned sooty lantern patched with eyes,
Hides more than it illumines, dreams the hordes
Of imps and angels, all of its own hue.
In the great world everything is just the same
Or just the opposite, we found (we never went).
The tinkers, peddlers brought their pinch of salt:
In our mouths the mill of the unresting sea
Ground till their very sores were thirsty.
Quaking below like quicksand, there is fire—
The dowser's twig dips not to water but to Hell;
And the Father, uncomfortable overseer,
Shakes from the rain-clouds Heaven's branding bolt.
Beyond, the Alps ring, avalanche on avalanche,
And the lost palmers freeze to bliss, a smile
Baring their poor teeth, blackened as the skulls
Of sanctuaries—splinters of the Cross, the Ark, the Tree
Jut from a saint's set jawbone, to put out
With one bought vision many a purging fire.
As the circles spread, the stone hopes like a child.
The weak look to the helpless for their aid—
The beasts who, ruled by their god, Death,
Bury the son with their enchanted thanks
For the act outside their possibility:
The victim spared, the labors sweated through, for love
Neither for mate nor litter, but for—anything.

When had it mattered whom we helped? It always paid.
When the dead man's heart broke they found written there
(He could not write): *The wish has made it so.*
Or so he wished. The platter appliquéd
With meals for parents, scraps for children, gristle
For Towser, a poor dog; the walnut jetting wine;
The broom that, fretting for a master, swept a world;
The spear that, weeping for a master, killed a child;
And gold to bury, from the deepest mines—
These neither to wisdom nor to virtue, but to Grace,
The son remembered in the will of God—
These were wishes. The glass in which I saw ·
Somewhere else, someone else: the field upon which sprawled
Dead, and the ruler of the dead, my twin—
Were wishes? Hänsel, by the eternal sea,
Said to the flounder for his first wish, *Let me wish
And let my wish be granted;* it was granted.
Granted, granted. . . . Poor Hänsel, once too powerless
To shelter your own children from the cold
Or quiet their bellies with the thinnest gruel,
It was not power that you lacked, but wishes.
Had you not learned—have we not learned, from tales
Neither of beasts nor kingdoms nor their Lord,
But of our own hearts, the realm of death—
Neither to rule nor die? to change, to change! *(1948)*

THE ORIENT EXPRESS

One looks from the train
Almost as one looked as a child. In the sunlight
What I see still seems to me plain,
I am safe; but at evening
As the lands darken, a questioning
Precariousness comes over everything.

Once after a day of rain
I lay longing to be cold; and after a while
I was cold again, and hunched shivering
Under the quilt's many colors, gray
With the dull ending of the winter day.
Outside me there were a few shapes
Of chairs and tables, things from a primer;
Outside the window

There were the chairs and tables of the world. . . .
I saw that the world
That had seemed to me the plain
Gray mask of all that was strange
Behind it—of all that *was*—was all.

But it is beyond belief.
One thinks, "Behind everything
An unforced joy, an unwilling
Sadness (a willing sadness, a forced joy)
Moves changelessly"; one looks from the train
And there is something, the same thing
Behind everything: all these little villages,
A passing woman, a field of grain,
The man who says good-bye to his wife—
A path through a wood full of lives, and the train
Passing, after all unchangeable
And not now ever to stop, like a heart—

It is like any other work of art.
It is and never can be changed.
Behind everything there is always
The unknown unwanted life. *(1951)*

A SOUL

It is evening. One bat dances
Alone, where there were swallows.
The waterlilies are shadowed
With cattails, the cattails with willows.

The moon sets; after a little
The reeds sigh from the shore.
Then silence. There is a whisper,
"Thou art here once more."

In the castle someone is singing.
"Thou art warm and dry as the sun."
You whisper, and laugh with joy.
"Yes, here is one,

"Here is the other . . . *Legs* . . .
And they move so?"

I stroke the scales of your breast, and answer:
"Yes, as you know."

But you murmur, "How many years
Thou hast wandered there above!
Many times I had thought thee lost
Forever, my poor love.

"How many years, how many years
Thou hast wandered in air, thin air!
Many times I had thought thee lost,
My poor soul, forever." *(1951)*

THE BLACK SWAN

When the swans turned my sister into a swan
   I would go to the lake, at night, from milking:
The sun would look out through the reeds like a swan,
   A swan's red beak; and the beak would open
And inside there was darkness, the stars and the moon.

Out on the lake a girl would laugh.
   "Sister, here is your porridge, sister,"
I could call; and the reeds would whisper,
   "Go to sleep, go to sleep, little swan."
My legs were all hard and webbed, and the silky

Hairs of my wings sank away like stars
   In the ripples that ran in and out of the reeds:
I heard through the lap and hiss of water
   Someone's "Sister . . . sister," far away on the shore,
And then as I opened my beak to answer

I heard my harsh laugh go out to the shore
   And saw—saw at last, swimming up from the green
Low mounds of the lake, the white stone swans:
   The white, named swans . . "It is all a dream,"
I whispered, and reached from the down of the pallet

To the lap and hiss of the floor.
   And "Sleep, little sister," the swans all sang
From the moon and stars and frogs of the floor.
   But the swan my sister called, "Sleep at last, little sister,"
And stroked all night, with a black wing, my wings. *(1951)*

THE ELEMENTARY SCENE

Looking back in my mind I can see
The white sun like a tin plate
Over the wooden turning of the weeds;
The street jerking—a wet swing—
To end by the wall the children sang.

The thin grass by the girls' door,
Trodden on, straggling, yellow and rotten,
And the gaunt field with its one tied cow—
The dead land waking sadly to my life—
Stir, and curl deeper in the eyes of time.

The rotting pumpkin under the stairs
Bundled with switches and the cold ashes
Still holds for me, in its unwavering eyes,
The stinking shapes of cranes and witches,
Their path slanting down the pumpkin's sky.

Its stars beckon through the frost like cottages
(Homes of the Bear, the Hunter—of that absent star,
The dark where the flushed child struggles into sleep)
Till, leaning a lifetime to the comforter,
I float above the small limbs like their dream:

I, I, The future that mends everything. (*1960*)

Robert Lowell
(1917–   )

CHILDREN OF LIGHT

Our fathers wrung their bread from stocks and stones
And fenced their gardens with the Redman's bones;
Embarking from the Nether Land of Holland,
Pilgrims unhouseled by Geneva's night,
They planted here the Serpent's seeds of light;
And here the pivoting searchlights probe to shock
The riotous glass houses built on rock,
And candles gutter by an empty altar,
And light is where the landless blood of Cain
Is burning, burning the unburied grain.   *(1944)*

THE DRUNKEN FISHERMAN

Wallowing in this bloody sty,
I cast for fish that pleased my eye
(Truly Jehovah's bow suspends
No pots of gold to weight its ends);
Only the blood-mouthed rainbow trout
Rose to my bait. They flopped about
My canvas creel until the moth
Corrupted its unstable cloth.

A calendar to tell the day;
A handkerchief to wave away
The gnats; a couch unstuffed with storm
Pouching a bottle in one arm;
A whiskey bottle full of worms;
And bedroom slacks: are these fit terms
To mete the worm whose molten rage
Boils in the belly of old age?

Once fishing was a rabbit's foot—
O wind blow cold, O wind blow hot,

Let suns stay in or suns step out:
Life danced a jig on the sperm-whale's spout—
The fisher's fluent and obscene
Catches kept his conscience clean.
Children, the raging memory drools
Over the glory of past pools.

Now the hot river, ebbing, hauls
Its bloody waters into holes;
A grain of sand inside my shoe
Mimics the moon that might undo
Man and Creation too; remorse,
Stinking, has puddled up its source;
Here tantrums thrash to a whale's rage.
This is the pot-hole of old age.

Is there no way to cast my hook
Out of this dynamited brook?
The Fisher's sons must cast about
When shallow waters peter out.
I will catch Christ with a greased worm,
And when the Prince of Darkness stalks
My bloodstream to its Stygian term . . .
On water the Man-Fisher walks. (*1944*)

MR. EDWARDS AND THE SPIDER

I saw the spiders marching through the air,
Swimming from tree to tree that mildewed day
    In latter August when the hay
    Came creaking to the barn. But where
        The wind is westerly,
Where gnarled November makes the spiders fly
Into the apparitions of the sky,
    They purpose nothing but their ease and die
Urgently beating east to sunrise and the sea;

What are we in the hands of the great God?
It was in vain you set up thorn and briar
    In battle array against the fire
    And treason crackling in your blood;
        For the wild thorns grow tame
And will do nothing to oppose the flame;

Your lacerations tell the losing game
You play against a sickness past your cure.
How will the hands be strong? How will the heart endure?

A very little thing, a little worm,
Or hourglass-blazoned spider, it is said,
   Can kill a tiger. Will the dead
   Hold up his mirror and affirm
     To the four winds the smell
And flash of his authority? It's well
If God who holds you to the pit of hell,
Much as one holds a spider, will destroy,
Baffle and dissipate your soul. As a small boy

On Windsor Marsh, I saw the spider die
When thrown into the bowels of fierce fire:
   There's no long struggle, no desire
   To get up on its feet and fly—
     It stretches out its feet
And dies. This is the sinner's last retreat;
Yes, and no strength exerted on the heat
Then sinews the abolished will, when sick
And full of burning, it will whistle on a brick.

But who can plumb the sinking of that soul?
Josiah Hawley, picture yourself cast
   Into a brick-kiln where the blast
   Fans your quick vitals to a coal—
     If measured by a glass,
How long would it seem burning! Let there pass
A minute, ten, ten trillion; but the blaze
Is infinite, eternal: this is death,
To die and know it. This is the Black Widow, death. *(1946)*

AS A PLANE TREE BY THE WATER

Darkness has called to darkness, and disgrace
Elbows about our windows in this planned
Babel of Boston where our money talks
And multiplies the darkness of a land
Of preparation where the Virgin walks
And roses spiral her enamelled face
Or fall to splinters on unwatered streets.

Our Lady of Babylon, go by, go by,
I was once the apple of your eye;
Flies, flies are on the plane tree, on the streets.

The flies, the flies, the flies of Babylon
Buzz in my ear-drums while the devil's long
Dirge of the people detonates the hour
For floating cities where his golden tongue
Enchants the masons of the Babel Tower
To raise tomorrow's city to the sun
That never sets upon these hell-fire streets
Of Boston, where the sunlight is a sword
Striking at the withholder of the Lord:
Flies, flies are on the plane tree, on the streets.

Flies strike the miraculous waters of the iced
Atlantic and the eyes of Bernadette
Who saw Our Lady standing in the cave
At Massabielle, saw her so squarely that
Her vision put out reason's eyes. The grave
Is open-mouthed and swallowed up in Christ.
O walls of Jericho! And all the streets
To our Atlantic wall are singing: "Sing,
Sing for the resurrection of the King,"
Flies, flies are on the plane tree, on the streets.   *(1946)*

THE DEAD IN EUROPE

After the planes unloaded, we fell down
Buried together, unmarried men and women;
Not crown of thorns, not iron, not Lombard crown,
Not grilled and spindle spires pointing to heaven
Could save us. Raise us, Mother, we fell down
Here hugger-mugger in the jellied fire:
Our sacred earth in our day was our curse.

Our Mother, shall we rise on Mary's day
In Maryland, wherever corpses married
Under the rubble, bundled together? Pray
For us whom the blockbusters marred and buried;
When Satan scatters us on Rising-day,
O Mother, snatch our bodies from the fire:
Our sacred earth in our day was our curse.

Mother, my bones are trembling and I hear
The earth's reverberations and the trumpet
Bleating into my shambles. Shall I bear,
(O Mary!) unmarried man and powder-puppet,
Witness to the Devil? Mary, hear,
O Mary, marry earth, sea, air and fire;
Our sacred earth in our day is our curse. (*1946*)

THE QUAKER GRAVEYARD IN NANTUCKET

(for Warren Winslow, Dead at Sea)

*Let man have dominion over the fishes of the sea and the fowls of the air
and the beasts and the whole earth, and every creeping creature that moveth
upon the earth.*

1

A brackish reach of shoal off Madaket,—
The sea was still breaking violently and night
Had steamed into our North Atlantic Fleet,
When the drowned sailor clutched the drag-net. Light
Flashed from his matted head and marble feet,
He grappled at the net
With the coiled, hurdling muscles of his thighs:
The corpse was bloodless, a botch of reds and whites,
Its open, staring eyes
Were lustreless dead-lights
Or cabin-windows on a stranded hulk
Heavy with sand. We weight the body, close
Its eyes and heave it seaward whence it came,
Where the heel-headed dogfish barks its nose
On Ahab's void and forehead; and the name
Is blocked in yellow chalk.
Sailors, who pitch this portent at the sea
Where dreadnaughts shall confess
Its hell-bent deity,
When you are powerless
To sand-bag this Atlantic bulwark, faced
By the earth-shaker, green, unwearied, chaste
In his steel scales: ask for no Orphean lute
To pluck life back. The guns of the steeled fleet
Recoil and then repeat
The hoarse salute.

2

Whenever winds are moving and their breath
Heaves at the roped-in bulwarks of this pier,
The terns and sea-gulls tremble at your death
In these home waters. Sailor, can you hear
The Pequod's sea wings, beating landward, fall·
Headlong and break on our Atlantic wall
Off 'Sconset, where the yawing S-boats splash
The bellbuoy, with ballooning spinnakers,
As the entangled, screeching mainsheet clears
The blocks: off Madaket, where lubbers lash
The heavy surf and throw their long lead squids
For blue-fish? Sea-gulls blink their heavy lids
Seaward. The winds' wings beat upon the stones,
Cousin, and scream for you and the claws rush
At the sea's throat and wring it in the slush
Of this old Quaker graveyard where the bones
Cry out in the long night for the hurt beast
Bobbing by Ahab's whaleboats in the East.

3

All you recovered from Poseidon died
With you, my cousin, and the harrowed brine
Is fruitless on the blue beard of the god,
Stretching beyond us to the castles in Spain,
Nantucket's westward haven. To Cape Cod
Guns, cradled on the tide,
Blast the eelgrass about a waterclock
Of bilge and backwash, roil the salt and sand
Lashing earth's scaffold, rock
Our warships in the hand
Of the great God, where time's contrition blues
Whatever it was these Quaker sailors lost
In the mad scramble of their lives. They died
When time was open-eyed,
Wooden and childish; only bones abide
There, in the nowhere, where their boats were tossed
Sky-high, where mariners had fabled news
Of IS, the whited monster. What it cost
Them is their secret. In the sperm-whale's slick
I see the Quakers drown and hear their cry:
"If God himself had not been on our side,

If God himself had not been on our side,
When the Atlantic rose against us, why,
Then it had swallowed us up quick."

4

This is the end of the whaleroad and the whale
Who spewed Nantucket bones on the thrashed swell
And stirrred the troubled waters to whirlpools
To send the Pequod packing off to hell:
This is the end of them, three-quarters fools,
Snatching at straws to sail
Seaward and seaward on the turntail whale,
Spouting out blood and water as it rolls,
Sick as a dog to these Atlantic shoals:
Clamavimus, O depths. Let the sea-gulls wail

For water, for the deep where the high tide
Mutters to its hurt self, mutters and ebbs.
Waves wallow in their wash, go out and out,
Leave only the death-rattle of the crabs,
The beach increasing, its enormous snout
Sucking the ocean's side.
This is the end of running on the waves;
We are poured out like water. Who will dance
The mast-lashed master of Leviathans
Up from this field of Quakers in their unstoned graves?

5

When the whale's viscera go and the roll
Of its corruption overruns this world
Beyond tree-swept Nantucket and Wood's Hole
And Martha's Vineyard, Sailor, will your sword
Whistle and fall and sink into the fat?
In the great ash-pit of Jehoshaphat
The bones cry for the blood of the white whale,
The fat flukes arch and whack about its ears,
The death-lance churns into the sanctuary, tears
The gun-blue swingle, heaving like a flail,
And hacks the coiling life out: it works and drags
And rips the sperm-whale's midriff into rags,
Gobbets of blubber spill to wind and weather,
Sailor, and gulls go round the stoven timbers
Where the morning stars sing out together

And thunder shakes the white surf and dismembers
The red flag hammered in the mast-head. Hide,
Our steel, Jonas Messias, in Thy side.

6

OUR LADY OF WALSINGHAM

There once the penitents took off their shoes
And then walked barefoot the remaining mile;
And the small trees, a stream and hedgerows file
Slowly along the munching English lane,
Like cows to the old shrine, until you lose
Track of your dragging pain.
The stream flows down under the druid tree,
Shiloah's whirlpools gurgle and make glad
The castle of God. Sailor, you were glad
And whistled Sion by that stream. But see:

Our Lady, too small for her canopy,
Sits near the altar. There's no comeliness
At all or charm in that expressionless
Face with its heavy eyelids. As before,
This face, for centuries a memory,
Non est species, neque decor,
Expressionless, expresses God: it goes
Past castled Sion. She knows what God knows,
Not Calvary's Cross nor crib at Bethlehem
Now, and the world shall come to Walsingham.

7

The empty winds are creaking and the oak
Splatters and splatters on the cenotaph,
The boughs are trembling and a gaff
Bobs on the untimely stroke
Of the greased wash exploding on a shoal-bell
In the old mouth of the Atlantic. It's well;
Atlantic, you are fouled with the blue sailors,
Sea-monsters, upward angel, downward fish:
Unmarried and corroding, spare of flesh
Mart once of supercilious, wing'd clippers,
Atlantic, where your bell-trap guts its spoil
You could cut the brackish winds with a knife
Here in Nantucket, and cast up the time

When the Lord God formed man from the sea's slime
And breathed into his face the breath of life,
And blue-lung'd combers lumbered to the kill.
The Lord survives the rainbow of His will.   (*1946*)

FOR GEORGE SANTAYANA

1863–1952

In the heydays of 'forty-five,
bus-loads of souvenir-deranged
G.I.'s and officer-professors of philosophy
came crashing through your cell,
puzzled to find you still alive,
free-thinking Catholic infidel,
stray spirit, who'd found
the Church too good to be believed.
Later I used to dawdle
past Circus and Mithraic Temple
to *Santo Stefano* grown paper-thin
like you from waiting. . . .
There at the monastery hospital,
you wished those geese-girl sisters wouldn't bother
their heads and yours by praying for your soul:
"There is no God and Mary is His Mother."

Lying outside the consecrated ground
forever now, you smile
like Ser Brunetto running for the green
cloth at Verona—not like one
who loses, but like one who'd won . . .
as if your long pursuit of Socrates'
demon, man-slaying Alcibiades,
the demon of philosophy, at last had changed
those fleeting virgins into friendly laurel trees
at *Santo Stefano Rotondo,* when you died
near ninety,
still unbelieving, unconfessed and unreceived,
true to your boyish shyness of the Bride.
Old trooper, I see your child's red crayon pass,
bleeding deletions on the galleys you hold
under your throbbing magnifying glass,
that worn arena, where the whirling sand

and broken-hearted lions lick your hand
refined by bile as yellow as a lump of gold. (*1959*)

WORDS FOR HART CRANE

"When the Pulitzers showered on some dope
or screw who flushed our dry mouths out with soap,
few people would consider why I took
to stalking sailors, and scattered Uncle Sam's
phoney gold-plated laurels to the birds.
Because I knew my Whitman like a book,
stranger in America, tell my country: I,
Catullus redivivus, once the rage
of the Village and Paris, used to play my role
of homosexual, wolfing the stray lambs
who hungered by the Place de la Concorde.
My profit was a pocket with a hole.
Who asks for me, the Shelley of my age,
must lay his heart out for my bed and board."

MEMORIES OF WEST STREET AND LEPKE

Only teaching on Tuesdays, book-worming
in pajamas fresh from the washer each morning,
I hog a whole house on Boston's
"hardly passionate Marlborough Street,"
where even the man
scavenging filth in the back alley trash cans,
has two children, a beach wagon, a helpmate,
and is a "young Republican."
I have a nine months' daughter,
young enough to be my granddaughter.
Like the sun she rises in her flame-flamingo infants' wear.

These are the tranquillized *Fifties*,
and I am forty. Ought I to regret my seedtime?
I was a fire-breathing Catholic C. O.,
and made my manic statement,
telling off the state and president, and then
sat waiting sentence in the bull pen
beside a Negro boy with curlicues
of marijuana in his hair.

Given a year,
I walked on the roof of the West Street Jail, a short
enclosure like my school soccer court,
and saw the Hudson River once a day
through sooty clothesline entanglements
and bleaching khaki tenements.
Strolling, I yammered metaphysics with Abramowitz,
a jaundice-yellow ("it's really tan")
and fly-weight pacifist,
so vegetarian,
he wore rope shoes and preferred fallen fruit.
He tried to convert Bioff and Brown,
the Hollywood pimps, to his diet.
Hairy, muscular, suburban,
wearing chocolate double-breasted suits,
they blew their tops and beat him black and blue.

I was so out of things, I'd never heard
of the Jehovah's Witnesses.
"Are you a C. O.?" I asked a fellow jailbird.
"No," he answered, "I'm a J.W."
He taught me the "hospital tuck,"
and pointed out the T shirted back
of *Murder Incorporated's* Czar Lepke,
there piling towels on a rack,
or dawdling off to his little segregated cell full
of things forbidden the common man:
a portable radio, a dresser, two toy American
flags tied together with a ribbon of Eastern palm.
Flabby, bald, lobotomized,
he drifted in a sheepish calm,
where no agonizing reappraisal
jarred his concentration on the electric chair—
hanging like an oasis in his air
of lost connections. . . .   *(1959)*

SKUNK HOUR

(For Elizabeth Bishop)

Nautilus Island's hermit
heiress still lives through winter in her Spartan cottage;
her sheep still graze above the sea.

Her son's a bishop. Her farmer
is first selectman in our village;
she's in her dotage.

Thirsting for
the hierarchic privacy
of Queen Victoria's century,
she buys up all
the eyesores facing her shore,
and lets them fall.

The season's ill—
we've lost our summer millionaire,
who seemed to leap from an L. L. Bean
catalogue. His nine-knot yawl
was auctioned off to lobstermen.
A red fox stain covers Blue Hill.

And now our fairy
decorator brightens his shop for fall;
his fishnet's filled with orange cork,
orange, his cobbler's bench and awl;
there is no money in his work,
he'd rather marry.

One dark night,
my Tudor Ford climbed the hill's skull;
I watched for love-cars. Lights turned down,
they lay together, hull to hull,
where the graveyard shelves on the town. . . .
My mind's not right.

A car radio bleats,
"Love, O careless Love. . . ." I hear
my ill-spirit sob in each blood cell,
as if my hand were at its throat. . . .
I myself am hell;
nobody's here—

only skunks, that search
in the moonlight for a bite to eat.
They march on their soles up Main Street:
white stripes, moonstruck eyes' red fire

under the chalk-dry and spar spire
of the Trinitarian Church.

I stand on top
of our back steps and breathe the rich air—
a mother skunk with her column of kittens swills the garbage pail.
She jabs her wedge-head in a cup
of sour cream, drops her ostrich tail,
and will not scare. (*1959*)

WATER

It was a Maine lobster town—
each morning boatloads of hands
pushed off for granite
quarries on the islands,

and left dozens of bleak
white frame houses stuck
like oyster shells
on a hill of rock,

and below us, the sea lapped
the raw little match-stick
mazes of a weir,
where the fish for bait were trapped.

Remember? We sat on a slab of rock.
From this distance in time,
it seems the color
of iris, rotting and turning purpler,

but it was only
the usual gray rock
turning the usual green
when drenched by the sea.

The sea drenched the rock
at our feet all day,
and kept tearing away
flake after flake.

One night you dreamed
you were a mermaid clinging to a wharf-pile,

and trying to pull
off the barnacles with your hands.

We wished our two souls
might return like gulls
to the rock. In the end,
the water was too cold for us. *(1964)*

THE LESSON

No longer to lie reading "Tess of the d'Urbervilles,"
while the high, mysterious squirrels
rain small green branches on our sleep!

All that landscape, one likes to think it died
or slept with us, that we ourselves died
or slept then in the age and second of our habitation.

The green leaf cushions the same dry footprint,
or the child's boat luffs in the same dry chop,
and we are where we were. We were!

Perhaps the trees stopped growing in summer amnesia;
their day that gave them veins is rooted down—
and the nights? They are for sleeping now as then.

Ah the light lights the window of my young night,
and you never turn off the light,
while the books lie in the library, and go on reading.

The barberry fruit sticks on the small hedge,
cold slices the same crease in the finger,
the same thorn hurts. The leaf repeats the lesson. *(1964)*

THE OPPOSITE HOUSE

All day the opposite house,
an abandoned police stable,
just an opposite house,
is square enough—six floors,
six windows to a floor,
pigeons ganging through
broken windows and cooing

like gangs of children tooting
empty bottles.

Tonight, though, I see it shine
in the Azores of my open window.
Its manly, old-fashioned lines
are gorgeously rectilinear.
It's like some firework to be fired
at the end of the garden party,
some Spanish *casa,* luminous
with heraldry and murder,
marooned in New York.

A stringy policeman is crooked
in the doorway, one hand on his revolver.
He counts his bullets like beads.
Two on horseback sidle
the crowd to the curb. A red light
whirls on the roof of an armed car,
plodding slower than a turtle.
Deterrent terror!
Viva la muerte! *(1967)*

Robert Duncan
(1919–   )

OFTEN I AM PERMITTED TO RETURN TO A MEADOW

as if it were a scene made-up by the mind,
that is not mine, but is a made place,

that is mine, it is so near to the heart,
an eternal pasture folded in all thought
so that there is a hall therein

that is a made place, created by light
wherefrom the shadows that are forms fall.

Wherefrom fall all architectures I am
I say are likenesses of the First Beloved
whose flowers are flames lit to the Lady.

She is Queen Under The Hill
whose hosts are a disturbance of words within words
that is a field folded.

It is only a dream of the grass blowing
east against the source of the sun
in an hour before the sun's going down

whose secret we see in a children's game
of ring a round of roses told.

Often I am permitted to return to a meadow
as if it were a given property of the mind
that certain bounds hold against chaos,

that is a place of first permission,
everlasting omen of what is. (1960)

II-424

AFTER A PASSAGE IN BAUDELAIRE

Ship, leaving or arriving, of my lover,
my soul, leaving or coming into this harbor,
among your lights and shadows   shelterd,
at home in your bulk, the cunning
regularity and symmetry thruout
of love's design, of will, of your
attractive cells and chambers .

riding forward, darkest of shades
over the shadowd waters .
in the light, neat, symmetrically
arranged above your watery reflections
disturbing your own image, moving as you are

What passenger, what sailor,
looks out into the swirling currents round you
as if into those depths into a mirror?

What lights in what port-holes
raise in my mind again   hunger and impatience?
to make my bed down again, there, beyond me,
as if this room too, my bedroom, my lamp at my side,
were among those lights sailing out
                    away from me.

We too, among the others, passengers
in that *charme infini et mystérieux,*
in that suitable symmetry, that precision
everywhere, the shining fittings, the fit
of lights and polisht surfaces to the dark,
to the flickering shadows of them,
we too, unfaithful to me, sailing away,
leaving me.

L'idée poétique, the idea of a poetry,
that rises from the movement, from the
outswirling curves and imaginary figures
round this ship, this fate, this sure thing,

est l'hypothèse d'une être vaste, immense,

compliqué, mais eurythmique. (*1964*)

SHELLEY'S ARETHUSA *SET TO NEW MEASURES*

1

Now Arethusa from her snow couches arises,
Hi! from her Acroceraunian heights springs,
down leaping, from cloud and crag
jagged shepherds her bright fountains.
She bounds from rock-face to rock-face streaming
her uncombd rainbows of hair round her.
    Green paves her way-fare.
    Where she goes there
    dark ravine serves her
    downward towards the West-gleam.
As if still asleep she goes, glides or
    lingers in deep pools.

2

        Now bold Alpheus
    aroused from his cold glacier
strikes the mountains and opens
    a chasm in the rock so that
all Erymanthus shakes, and the black
    south wind is unseald,
from urns of silent snow comes. Earthquake
    rends asunder
thunderous the bars of the springs below.

    Beard and hair of the River-god
    show through the torrent's sweep
where he follows the fleeting-light of the nymph
    to the brink of the Dorian,
    margins of deep Ocean.

3

    Oh save me! Take me untoucht, she cries.
    Hide me,
for Alpheus already grasps at my hair!
    The loud Ocean heard,
to its blue depth stirrd and divided,
taking her into the roar of its surf.
    And under the water she flees,
    white Arethusa,

the sunlight still virginal in her courses,
    Earth's daughter, descends,
billowing, unblended in the Dorian
    brackish waters.

             Where Alpheus,
    close upon her, in gloom,
    staining the salt dark tides comes,
black clouds overtaking the white
    in an emerald sky, Alpheus
eagle-eyed down streams of the wind pursues
    dove-winged Arethusa.

4

    Under those bowers they go
    where the ocean powers
brood on their thrones. Thru these coral woods,
    shades in the weltering flood,
    maiden and raging
    Alpheus swirl.

Over forgotten heap, stone upon stone,
    thru dim beams
    which amid streams
weave a network of colord lights they go,
    girl-stream and man-river after her.

    Pearl amid shadows
    of the deep caves
that are green as the forest's night,
    swift they fly,
with the shark and the swordfish pass into the wave
    —he overtaking her,
    as if wedding, surrounding her,
spray rifts in clefts of the shore cliffs rising.

    Alpheus,
        Arethusa,
            come home.

5

When now from Enna's mountains they spring,
    afresh in her innocence
Arethusa to Alpheus gladly comes.

Into one morning two hearts awake,
at sunrise leap from sleep's caves to return
   to the vale where they meet,
drawn by yearning from night into day.

Down into the noontide flow,
   into the full of life winding again, they find
their way thru the woods
   and the meadows of asphodel below.
Wedded, one deep current leading,
   they follow to dream
in the rocking deep at the Ortygian shore.

   Spirits drawn upward,
   they are divided
into the azure from which the rain falls,
   life from life,
seeking their way to love once more. *(1964)*

STRAINS OF SIGHT

1

He brought a light so she could see
Adam move nakedly in the lighted room
It was a window in the tree.
It was a shelter where there was none.

She saw his naked back and thigh
and heard the notes of a melody
where Adam out of his nature came
into four walls, roof and floor.

He turnd on the light and turnd back,
moving with grace to match her eye.
She saw his naked loneliness.

Now I shall never rest, she sighd,
until he strips his heart for me.
The body flashes such thoughts of death
so that time leaps up, and a man's hand

seen naked catches upon my breath
the risk we took in Paradise.

The serpent thought before the tomb
laid naked, naked, naked before the eyes,

reflects upon itself in a bare room.

2

In the questioning phrase the voice
—he raises his eyes from the page—
follows towards some last
curve of the air, suspended above

its sign, that point, that
And asks, Who am I then?
Where am I going? There is no time
like now that is not like now.

Who? turns upon some body where
the hand striving to tune
curves of the first lute whose strings are nerves
see in the touch the phrase will

rise . break
as the voice does? above some moving obscurity

ripples out in the disturbd pool,
shadows and showings where we would read
—raising his eyes from the body's lure—

what the question is,
where the heart reflects. *(1964)*

AN INTERLUDE

My heart beats to the feet of the first faithful,
    long ago dancing in Broceliande's forest,
And my mind when it ceases to contend with the
    lies and dreams of Generalissimo Franco
delites in the company of defeated but glorious men
    who have taken to the highlands or,
in love with the people, striven to keep secret ways
    of brotherhood and compassion alive,
        spreading Truth
like seeds of a forbidden hallucinogen, marijuana or morning glory
    hidden away among the grasses of the field.

Love long conceald!   Love long suffering!
Love we never knew   moved us from the beginning!
Now it may be we are driven to your high
        pasture.   Hard presst,
my heart opens as if there were a pass in the rock,
        unknown, a by-pass,
close enough to be very like death.

Solitary door, road of solitudes,
the mute song at last sung in the veins among strangers!
I must go to the old inn in the canyon beyond us,
to the roller-skating rink among the pine trees.

For the dancers have come down from the mountains,
and the piano player strikes up such a sound the fiddler
sails away in the waving and waist-clasping rounds of it.
The people, then, are the people of a summer's night over and gone,
the people of a Polish dance hall before the last war,
in the sweat and reek of Limburger cheese and Bermuda onions,
sweltering in beer and music, Kansas country evangels,
or summer people in the Catskills
who have taken up square-dancing   as the poet takes up
measures of an old intoxication that leads into poetry,
not "square" dancing, but moving figures,
the ages and various personae of an old drama . . .

coupling and released from coupling,
        moving and removing themselves, bowing
and escaping into new and yet old
        configurations,
the word "*old*" appearing and reappearing
        in the minds of the youths dancing

. . . so that I remember I was an ancient man in that
part of the dance, *Granpaw,* I was nineteen and yet ninety,
taking the hand of Little Nell, dolce-doeing,

and the dance, the grand seance of romancing feet in their numbers,
        forward and back—we were the medium
for Folk of the Old Days in their ever returning.

                    *   *   *

In the great figure of many figures the four
        directions and empires

change into four times, and opposites of
  opposites meet and mate,
separating and joining, ascending a ladder of litanies
  until they are "sent"—
losing themselves in each other's being
  found again.

Now, because I am Fire and you are Water,
Water and Fire kiss and embrace.
Water and Fire dance together.   This,
  the grand mimesis,
imitates the wholeness we feel true to What Is.

*   *   *

We must go back to sets of simple things,
hill and stream, woods and the sea beyond,
the time of day—dawn, noon, bright or clouded,
five o'clock in November five o'clock of the year—
changing definitions of the light.

And say the dancers take the six unbroken lines of the Chinese
  hexagram,
and six dance for the six broken lines, the six gates or openings
in the otherwise stable figure: there are twelve in all.
Dividing into groups of three, they dance in four groups.

What twelve things of your world will you appoint guardians,
  Truth's signators?
Salt, Cordelia said. Gold and lead.
  The poet, the great maker of wars and states, and
the saint, Burckhardt names as the three creative
  masters of history.
But now, let the twelve be unnamed.

The dancers come forward to represent unclaimd things.   *(1968)*

Howard Nemerov
(1920–)

THE GOOSE FISH

On the long shore, lit by the moon
To show them properly alone,
Two lovers suddenly embraced
So that their shadows were as one.
The ordinary night was graced
For them by the swift tide of blood
That silently they took at flood,
And for a little time they prized
        Themselves emparadised.

Then, as if shaken by stage-fright
Beneath the hard moon's bony light,
They stood together on the sand
Embarrassed in each other's sight
But still conspiring hand in hand,
Until they saw, there underfoot,
As though the world had found them out,
The goose fish turning up, though dead,
        His hugely grinning head.

There in the china light he lay,
Most ancient and corrupt and grey.
They hesitated at his smile,
Wondering what it seemed to say
To lovers who a little while
Before had thought to understand,
By violence upon the sand,
The only way that could be known
        To make a world their own.

It was a wide and moony grin
Together peaceful and obscene;
They knew not what he would express,

So finished a comedian
He might mean failure or success,
But took it for an emblem of
Their sudden, new and guilty love
To be observed by, when they kissed,
    That rigid optimist.

So he became their patriarch,
Dreadfully mild in the half-dark.
His throat that the sand seemed to choke,
His picket teeth, these left their mark
But never did explain the joke
That so amused him, lying there
While the moon went down to disappear
Along the still and tilted track
    That bears the zodiac.   *(1955)*

THE SCALES OF THE EYES

A POEM IN THE FORM OF A TEXT AND VARIATIONS

1

To fleece the Fleece from golden sheep,
Or prey, or get—is it not lewd
That we be eaten by our food
And slept by sleepers in our sleep?

2

Sleep in the zero, sleep in the spore
Beyond the fires of Orion's hair,
Hard by the spiral burning dust;
Time being Always going west,
Let it be your dream.

Sleep sound in the spaceless lost
Curve running a blind coast;
Number and name, stretch the line
Out on the liquid of the brain,
Begin a falling dream.

The eye will flower in your night
A monstrous bulb, the broth of light
Stew in the marshes of a star;

Death is the wages of what you are,
Life is your long dream.

3

Around the city where I live
Dead men in their stone towns
Wait out the weather lying down,
And spread widely underground
The salt vines of blood.

Trains run a roaming sound
Under the wired shine of sun and rain.
Black sticks stand up in the sky
Where the wild rails cross and sprawl
Fast and still.

Out there beyond the island
The sea pounds a free way through,
Her wide tides spread on the sand
Stick and brine and rolling stone
The long weather long.

4

Beneath my foot the secret beast
Whispers, and its stone sinews
Tremble with strength. In the dark earth
Iron winds its tangled nerves,
And the worm eats of the rock
There by the old waters.

Down in dark the rich comb
Gathers wrath out of the light,
The dead ploughed down in their graves
Record the canceled seed its doom.
City, white lion among waters,
Who settest thy claw upon the time,

Measure the tape, wind the clock,
Keep track of weather, watch water
And the work of trains. The bees hum
The honeyed doom of time and time
Again, and riddle this underground
How sweetness comes from the great strength.

5

(A CAN OF DUTCH CLEANSER)

The blind maid shaking a stick,
Chasing dirt endlessly around
A yellow wall, was the very she
To violate my oldest nights;
I frighten of her still.

Her faceless bonnet flaps in wind
I cannot feel, she rages on,
The mad Margery of my sleep;
The socks wrinkle about her shoes
As she drats a maiden dream.

So shines her bleached virginity
On underground conveniences
That roar at once in porcelain hunger;
Her anger leaves me without stain
And white grits in the tub.

6

The angry voice has sought me out,
Loud-speakers shout among the trees.
What use to hide? He made it all,
Already old when I began.

He held it all upon his knee
And spoke it soft in a big voice
Not so much loud as everywhere,
And all things had to answer him.

This world is not my oyster, nor
No slow socratic pearl grows here.
But the blind valves are closing
On only one grain of sand.

7

The low sky was mute and white
And the sun a white hole in the sky
That morning when it came on to snow;
The hushed flakes fell all day.

The hills were hidden in a white air
And every bearing went away,
Landmarks being but white and white
For anyone going anywhere.

All lines were lost, a noon bell
I heard sunk in a sullen pool
Miles off. And yet this patient snow,
When later I walked out in it,

Had lodged itself in tips of grass
And made its mantle bridging so
It lay upon the air and not the earth
So light it hardly bent a blade.

8

From the road looking to the hill I saw
One hollow house hunched in the shoulder.
Windows blinded in a level sun
Stared with not random malice,
Though I had not been in that place.

But I have seen, at the white shore,
The crab eaten in the house of self
And the torn dog shark gutted in sand;
The whole sky goes white with silence
And bears on a few brazen flies.

As though the ground sighed under the foot
And the heart refused its blood; there is
No place I do not taste again
When I choke back the deeper sleep
Beneath the mined world I walk.

9

Striding and turning, the caged sea
Knocks at the stone and falls away,
Will not rest night or day
Pacing to be free.

The spiral shell, held at the ear,
Hums the ocean or the blood
A distant cry, misunderstood
Of the mind in the coiled air.

10

Roads lead to the sea, and then?
The signs drown in the blowing sand,
The breathing and smoothing tide.
It has been a long journey so far.
Gull, where do I go now?

No matter what girls have been laid
In this sand, or far-wandering birds
Died here, I think I will not know
What no galling road has told,
Why to be here or how.

Question the crab, the wasted moon,
The spume blown of the smashed wave,
Ask Polaris about the fish.
No good. I could go home, but there is
No way to go but back.

11

Plunged the tunnel with the wet wall
Through, sounding with sea space
And the shaken earth, I fell below
The shark diving and the wry worm.
Blindly I nudged a gasping sky.

Against drowning to be born in a caul
Is well. But all free engines
Race to burn themselves out, tear up
The earth and the air and choke on a mouth
Of dirt, throwing their oil.

In long halls of hospital, the white
Eye peeled beneath the pool of light;
Then the blinded, masked and stifled sky
Screamed silver when it grated bone
Beaching a stained keel.

But at last the moon swung dark and away
And waters withered to a salt.
Parched and shaken on a weaned world
I was in wonder burning cold
And in darkness did rest.

12

In the water cave, below the root,
The blind fish knew my veins.
I heard ticking the water drop,
The sighing where the wind fell,
When the bat laddered the black air.

Chalk and bone and salt and stone.
Let mother water begin me again,
For I am blackened with burning, gone
From the vain fire of the air,
The one salamander weather.

Slow cold salt, weeds washed
Under crumbling rock ledges
In the water cave below the root,
Quiet the crystal in the dark,
Let the blind way shine out.

13

Gone the armies on the white roads,
The priests blessing and denouncing,
Gone the aircraft speaking power
Through the ruined and echoing air;
And life and death are here.

The quiet pool, if you will listen,
Hisses with your blood, winds
Together vine and vein and thorn,
The thin twisted threads red
With the rust of breath.

Now is the hour in the wild garden
Grown blessed. Tears blinding the eyes,
The martyr's wound and the hurt heart
Seal and are dumb, the ram waits
In the thicket of nerves.

14

In the last hour of the dream
The eye turned upon itself
And stood at bay, peering among
The salt fibers of its blood.

String of the cradle and the kite,
Vine twisted against the bone,
Salt tears washing the sinews,
The spider strangled in her web.

I stood in the last wilderness
Watching the grass at the sea's edge
Bend as to the breathing touch
Of a blind slither at the stalk.

String of the navel and the net,
Vein threading the still pool,
Dumb fingers in the wet sand
Where the heart bled its secret food.

Salt of the flesh, I knew the world
For the white veil over the eye,
The eye for the caged water of light;
The beast asleep in the bleeding snare.

15

And the rabbis have said the last word
And the iron gates they have slammed shut
Closing my body from the world.
Around me all Long Island lies
Smouldering and still.

Cold winter, the roller coasters
Stand in the swamps by the sea, and bend
The lizards of their bones alone,
August of lust and the hot dog
Frozen in their fat.

But the sea goes her own way,
Around and down her barren green
Sliding and sucking the cold flesh
Of the wrinkled world, with no bone
To such mother-makings.

I have sept through the wide seine.
From Coney Island to Phlegethon
Is no great way by ferris wheel,
And we informal liquors may
Easily despise your bones.

16

Snow on the beaches, briny ice,
Grass white and cracking with the cold.
The light is from the ocean moon
Hanging in the dead height.

Gull rises in the snowy marsh
A shale of light flaked from a star,
The white hair of the breaking wave
Splashes the night sky.

Down at the root, in the warm dream,
The lily bows among the ruins.
Kingdoms rise and are blown down
While the summer fly hums.

17

When black water breaks the ice
The moon is milk and chalk of tooth.
The star is bleeding in the still pool
And the horny skin is left behind
When journey must be new-begun.

Teiresias watching in the wood
A wheel of snakes, gave his sight
To know the coupled work of time,
How pale woman and fiery man
Married their disguise away.

Then all was the self, but self was none;
Knowing itself in the fiery dark
The blind pool of the eye became
The sailing of the moon and sun
Through brightness melted into sky.

18

Of leaf and branch and rain and light,
The spider's web glistered with wet,
The robin's breast washed red in sun
After the rapid storm goes on;

Of long light level on the lake
And white on the side of lonely houses,

The thunder going toward the hill,
The last lightning cracking the sky;

New happiness of everything!
The blind worm lifts up his head
And the sparrow shakes a wet wing
In the home of little while. *(1955)*

THE MURDER OF WILLIAM REMINGTON

It is true, that even in the best-run state
Such things will happen; it is true,
What's done is done. The law, whereby we hate
Our hatred, sees no fire in the flue.
But by the smoke, and not for thought alone
It punishes, but for the thing that's done.

And yet there is the horror of the fact,
Though we knew not the man. To die in jail,
To be beaten to death, to know the act
Of personal fury before the eyes can fail
And the man die against the cold last wall
Of the lonely world—and neither is that all·

There is the terror too of each man's thought,
That knows not, but must quietly suspect
His neighbor, friend, or self of being taught
To take an attitude merely correct;
Being frightened of his own cold image in
The glass of government, and his own sin,

Frightened lest senate house and prison wall
Be quarried of one stone, lest righteous and high
Look faintly smiling down and seem to call
A crime the welcome chance of liberty,
And any man an outlaw who aggrieves
The patriotism of a pair of thieves. *(1958)*

THE TOWN DUMP

"The art of our necessities is strange,
That can make vile things precious."

A mile out in the marshes, under a sky
Which seems to be always going away

In a hurry, on that Venetian land threaded
With hidden canals, you will find the city
Which seconds ours (so cemeteries, too,
Reflect a town from hillsides out of town),
Where Being most Becomingly ends up
Becoming some more. From cardboard tenements,
Windowed with cellophane, or simply tenting
In paper bags, the angry mackerel eyes
Glare at you out of stove-in, sunken heads
Far from the sea; the lobster, also, lifts
An empty claw in his most minatory
Of gestures; oyster, crab, and mussel shells
Lie here in heaps, savage as money hurled
Away at the gate of hell. If you want results,
These are results.
                    Objects of value or virtue,
However, are also to be picked up here,
Though rarely, lying with bones and rotten meat,
Eggshells and mouldy bread, banana peels
No one will skid on, apple cores that caused
Neither the fall of man nor a theory
Of gravitation. People do throw out
The family pearls by accident, sometimes,
Not often; I've known dealers in antiques
To prowl this place by night, with flashlights, on
The off-chance of somebody's having left
Derelict chairs which will turn out to be
By Hepplewhite, a perfect set of six
Going to show, I guess, that in any sty
Someone's heaven may open and shower down
Riches responsive to the right dream; though
It is a small chance, certainly, that sends
The ghostly dealer, heavy with fly-netting
Over his head, across these hills in darkness,
Stumbling in cut-glass goblets, lacquered cups,
And other products of his dreamy midden
Penciled with light and guarded by the flies.

For there are flies, of course. A dynamo
Composed, by thousands, of our ancient black
Retainers, hums here day and night, steady
As someone telling beads, the hum becoming
A high whine at any disturbance; then,

Settled again, they shine under the sun
Like oil-drops, or are invisible as night,
By night.
        All this continually smoulders,
Crackles, and smokes with mostly invisible fires
Which, working deep, rarely flash out and flare,
And never finish. Nothing finishes;
The flies, feeling the heat, keep on the move.

Among the flies, the purifying fires,
The hunters by night, acquainted with the art
Of our necessities, and the new deposits
That each day wastes with treasure, you may say
There should be ratios. You may sum up
The results, if you want results. But I will add
That wild birds, drawn to the carrion and flies,
Assemble in some numbers here, their wings
Shining with light, their flight enviably free,
Their music marvelous, though sad, and strange. (*1958*)

Richard Wilbur
(1921–   )

TYWATER

Death of Sir Nihil, book the *nth,*
Upon the charred and clotted sward,
Lacking the lily of our Lord,
Alases of the hyacinth.

Could flicker from behind his ear
A whistling silver throwing knife
And with a holler punch the life
Out of a swallow in the air.

Behind the lariat's butterfly
Shuttled his white and gritted grin,
And cuts of sky would roll within
The noose-hole, when he spun it high.

The violent, neat and practiced skill
Was all he loved and all he learned;
When he was hit, his body turned
To clumsy dirt before it fell.

And what to say of him, God knows.
Such violence. And such repose.   *(1947)*

A SIMPLIFICATION

Those great rough ranters, Branns
And catarrhal Colonels, who hurled
Terrible taunts at the vault, ripped down Jesus' banns
And widowed the world

With Inquisitorial thunder, dammed-
Up Biblical damnations, were

The last with tongues to topple heaven; they hammed
Jahweh away and here

We are. The decorous god
Simply withdrew. If you hear
A good round rhetoric anywhere give me the nod.
I'd like to hear

Bryan lying and quoting sic
Transit nux vomica. These foetal-
Voiced people lack eloquence to blow a sick
Maggot off a dead beetle. *(1947)*

THE BEAUTIFUL CHANGES

One wading a Fall meadow finds on all sides
The Queen Anne's Lace lying like lilies
On water; it glides
So from the walker, it turns
Dry grass to a lake, as the slightest shade of you
Valleys my mind in fabulous blue Lucernes.

The beautiful changes as a forest is changed
By a chameleon's tuning his skin to it;
As a mantis, arranged
On a green leaf, grows
Into it, makes the leaf leafier, and proves
Any greenness is deeper than anyone knows.

Your hands hold roses always in a way that says
They are not only yours; the beautiful changes
In such kind ways,
Wishing ever to sunder
Things and things' selves for a second finding, to lose
For a moment all that it touches back to wonder. *(1947)*

PART OF A LETTER

Easy as cove-water rustles its pebbles and shells
In the slosh, spread, seethe, and the backsliding
Wallop and tuck of the wave, and just that cheerful,
      Tables and earth were riding

Back and forth in the minting shades of the trees.
There were whiffs of anise, a clear clinking
Of coins and glasses, a still crepitant sound
        Of the earth in the garden drinking

The late rain. Rousing again, the wind
Was swashing the shadows in relay races
Of sun-spangles over the hands and clothes
        And the drinkers' dazzled faces,

So that when somebody spoke, and asked the question
Comment s'appelle cet arbre-là?
A girl had gold on her tongue, and gave this answer:
        Ça, c'est l'acacia. (*1950*)

MUSEUM PIECE

The good gray guardians of art
Patrol the halls on spongy shoes,
Impartially protective, though
Perhaps suspicious of Toulouse.

Here dozes one against the wall,
Disposed upon a funeral chair.
A Degas dancer pirouettes
Upon the parting of his hair.

See how she spins! The grace is there,
But strain as well is plain to see.
Degas loved the two together:
Beauty joined to energy.

Edgar Degas purchased once
A fine El Greco, which he kept
Against the wall beside his bed
To hang his pants on while he slept. (*1950*)

JUGGLER

A ball will bounce, but less and less. It's not
A light-hearted thing, resents its own resilience.
Falling is what it loves, and the earth falls
So in our hearts from brilliance,

Settles and is forgot.
It takes a skyblue juggler with five red balls

To shake our gravity up. Whee, in the air
The balls roll round, wheel on his wheeling hands,
Learning the ways of lightness, alter to spheres
Grazing his finger ends,
Cling to their courses there,
Swinging a small heaven about his ears.

But a heaven is easier made of nothing at all
Than the earth regained, and still and sole within
The spin of worlds, with a gesture sure and noble
He reels that heaven in,
Landing it ball by ball,
And trades it all for a broom, a plate, a table.

Oh, on his toe the table is turning, the broom's
Balancing up on his nose, and the plate whirls
On the tip of the broom! Damn, what a show, we cry:
The boys stamp, and the girls
Shriek, and the drum booms
And all comes down, and he bows and says good-bye.

If the juggler is tired now, if the broom stands
In the dust again, if the table starts to drop
Through the daily dark again, and though the plate
Lies flat on the table top,
For him we batter our hands
Who has won for once over the world's weight. (1950)

STILL, CITIZEN SPARROW

Still, citizen sparrow, this vulture which you call
Unnatural, let him but lumber again to air
Over the rotten office, let him bear
The carrion ballast up, and at the tall

Tip of the sky lie cruising. Then you'll see
That no more beautiful bird is in heaven's height,
No wider more placid wings, no watchfuller flight;
He shoulders nature there, the frightfully free,

The naked-headed one. Pardon him, you
Who dart in the orchard aisles, for it is he
Devours death, mocks mutability,
Has heart to make an end, keeps nature new.

Thinking of Noah, childheart, try to forget
How for so many bedlam hours his saw
Soured the song of birds with its wheezy gnaw,
And the slam of his hammer all the day beset

The people's ears. Forget that he could bear
To see the towns like coral under the keel,
And the fields so dismal deep. Try rather to feel
How high and weary it was, on the waters where

He rocked his only world, and everyone's.
Forgive the hero, you who would have died
Gladly with all you knew; he rode that tide
To Ararat; all men are Noah's sons. (1950)

THE DEATH OF A TOAD

A toad the power mower caught,
Chewed and clipped of a leg, with a hobbling hop has got
To the garden verge, and sanctuaried him
Under the cineraria leaves, in the shade
Of the ashen heart-shaped leaves, in a dim,
Low, and a final glade.

The rare original heartsblood goes,
Spends on the earthen hide, in the folds and wizenings, flows
In the gutters of the banked and staring eyes. He lies
As still as if he would return to stone,
And soundlessly attending, dies
Toward some deep monotone,

Toward misted and ebullient seas
And cooling shores, toward lost Amphibia's emperies.
Day dwindles, drowning, and at length is gone
In the wide and antique eyes, which still appear
To watch, across the castrate lawn,
The haggard daylight steer. (1950)

ALTITUDES

1

Look up into the dome:
It is a great salon, a brilliant place,
    Yet not too splendid for the race
Whom we imagine there, wholly at home

    With the gold-rosetted white
Wainscot, the oval windows, and the fault-
    Less figures of the painted vault.
Strolling, conversing in that precious light,

    They chat no doubt of love,
The pleasant burden of their courtesy
    Borne down at times to you and me
Where, in this dark, we stand and gaze above.

    For all they cannot share,
All that the world cannot in fact afford,
    Their lofty premises are floored
With the massed voices of continual prayer.

2

    How far it is from here
To Emily Dickinson's father's house in America;
    Think of her climbing a spiral stair
Up to the little cupola with its clear

    Small panes, its room for one.
Like the dark house below, so full of eyes
    In mirrors and of shut-in flies,
This chamber furnished only with the sun

    Is she and she alone,
A mood to which she rises, in which she sees
    Bird-choristers in all the trees
And a wild shining of the pure unknown

    On Amherst. This is caught
In the dormers of a neighbor, who, no doubt,

Will before long be coming out
To pace about his garden, lost in thought.   (*1956*)

LOVE CALLS US TO THE THINGS OF THIS WORLD

The eyes open to a cry of pulleys,
And spirited from sleep, the astounded soul
Hangs for a moment bodiless and simple
As false dawn.
                    Outside the open window
The morning air is all awash with angels.

Some are in bed-sheets, some are in blouses,
Some are in smocks: but truly there they are.
Now they are rising together in calm swells
Of halcyon feeling, filling whatever they wear
With the deep joy of their impersonal breathing;

Now they are flying in place, conveying
The terrible speed of their omnipresence, moving
And staying like white water; and now of a sudden
They swoon down into so rapt a quiet
That nobody seems to be there.
                    The soul shrinks

From all that it is about to remember,
From the punctual rape of every blessèd day,
And cries,
          "Oh, let there be nothing on earth but laundry,
Nothing but rosy hands in the rising steam
And clear dances done in the sight of heaven."

Yet, as the sun acknowledges
With a warm look the world's hunks and colors,
The soul descends once more in bitter love
To accept the waking body, saying now
In a changed voice as the man yawns and rises,

"Bring them down from their ruddy gallows;
Let there be clean linen for the backs of thieves;
Let lovers go fresh and sweet to be undone,
And the heaviest nuns walk in a pure floating
Of dark habits,
                    keeping their difficult balance."   (*1956*)

MIND

Mind in the purest play is like some bat
That beats about in caverns all alone,
Contriving by a kind of senseless wit
Not to conclude against a wall of stone.

It has no need to falter or explore;
Darkly it knows what obstacles are there,
And so may weave and flitter, dip and soar
In perfect courses through the blackest air.

And has this simile a like perfection?
The mind is like a bat. Precisely. Save
That in the very happiest intellection
A graceful error may correct the cave. (1956)

MERLIN ENTHRALLED

In a while they rose and went out aimlessly riding,
Leaving their drained cups on the table round.
Merlin, Merlin, their hearts cried, where are you hiding?
In all the world was no unnatural sound.

Mystery watched them riding glade by glade;
They saw it darkle from under leafy brows;
But leaves were all its voice, and squirrels made
An alien fracas in the ancient boughs.

Once by a lake-edge something made them stop.
Yet what they found was the thumping of a frog,
Bugs skating on the shut water-top,
Some hairlike algae bleaching on a log.

Gawen thought for a moment that he heard
A whitethorn breathe *Niniane*. That Siren's daughter
Rose in a fort of dreams and spoke the word
Sleep, her voice like dark diving water;

And Merlin slept, who had imagined her
Of water-sounds and the deep unsoundable swell
A creature to bewitch a sorcerer,
And lay there now within her towering spell

Slowly the shapes of searching men and horses
Escaped him as he dreamt on that high bed:
History died; he gathered in its forces;
The mists of time condensed in the still head

Until his mind, as clear as mountain water,
Went raveling toward the deep transparent dream
Who bade him sleep. And then the Siren's daughter
Received him as the sea receives a stream.

Fate would be fated; dreams desire to sleep.
This the forsaken will not understand.
Arthur upon the road began to weep
And said to Gawen *Remember when this hand*

*Once haled a sword from stone; now no less strong
It cannot dream of such a thing to do.*
Their mail grew quainter as they clopped along.
The sky became a still and woven blue. *(1956)*

MARGINALIA

Things concentrate at the edges; the pond-surface
Is bourne to fish and man and it is spread
In textile scum and damask light, on which
The lily-pads are set; and there are also
    Inlaid ruddy twigs, becalmed pine-leaves,
    Air-baubles, and the chain mail of froth.

Descending into sleep (as when the night-lift
Falls past a brilliant floor), we glimpse a sublime
Décor and hear, perhaps, a complete music,
But this evades us, as in the night meadows
    The cricket's million roundsong dies away
    From all advances, rising in every distance.

Our riches are centrifugal; men compose
Daily, unwittingly, their final dreams,
And those are our own voices whose remote
Consummate chorus rides on the whirlpool's rim,
    Past which we flog our sails, toward which we drift,
    Plying our trades, in hopes of good drowning. *(1956)*

SPEECH FOR THE REPEAL OF THE McCARRAN ACT

As Wulfstan said on another occasion,
The strong net bellies in the wind and the spider rides it out;
But history, that sure blunderer,
Ruins the unkempt web, however silver.

I am not speaking of rose windows
Shattered by bomb-shock; the leads touselled; the glass-grains broadcast;
If the rose be living at all
A gay gravel shall be pollen of churches.

Nor do I mean railway networks.
Torn-up tracks are no great trouble. As Wulfstan said,
It is oathbreach, faithbreach, lovebreach
Bring the invaders into the estuaries.

Shall one man drive before him ten
Unstrung from sea to sea? Let thought be free. I speak
Of the spirit's weaving, the neural
Web, the self-true mind, the trusty reflex. *(1956)*

Sylvia Plath
(1932–1963)

TWO VIEWS OF A CADAVER ROOM

1

The day she visited the dissecting room
They had four men laid out, black as burnt turkey,
Already half unstrung. A vinegary fume
Of the death vats clung to them;
The white-smocked boys started working.
The head of his cadaver had caved in,
And she could scarcely make out anything
In that rubble of skull plates and old leather.
A sallow piece of string held it together.

In their jars the snail-nosed babies moon and glow.
He hands her the cut-out heart like a cracked heirloom.

2

In Brueghel's panorama of smoke and slaughter
Two people only are blind to the carrion army:
He, afloat in the sea of her blue satin
Skirts, sings in the direction
Of her bare shoulder, while she bends,
Fingering a leaflet of music, over him,
Both of them deaf to the fiddle in the hands
Of the death's-head shadowing their song.
These Flemish lovers flourish; not for long.

Yet desolation, stalled in paint, spares the little country
Foolish, delicate, in the lower right-hand corner. *(1960)*

DADDY

You do not do, you do not do
Any more, black shoe

In which I have lived like a foot
For thirty years, poor and white,
Barely daring to breathe or Achoo!

Daddy, I have had to kill you.
You died before I had time—
Marble-heavy, a bag full of God,
Ghastly statue with one grey toe
Big as a Frisco seal

And a head in the freakish Atlantic
Where it pours bean green over blue
In the waters off beautiful Nauset.
I used to pray to recover you.
Ach, du!

In the German tongue, in the Polish town
Scraped flat by the roller
Of wars, wars, wars.
But the name of the town is common.
My Polack friend

Says there are a dozen or two.
So I never could tell where you
Put your foot, your root,
I never could talk to you.
The tongue stuck in my jaw.

It stuck in a barb wire snare.
Ich, ich, ich, ich!
I could hardly speak.
I thought every German was you.
And the language obscene

An engine, an engine
Chuffing me off like a Jew.
A Jew to Dachau, Auschwitz, Belsen.
I began to talk like a Jew.
I think I may well be a Jew.

The snows of the Tyrol, the clear beer of Vienna
Are not very pure or true.
With my gypsy ancestress and my weird luck

And my Tarot pack and my Tarot pack
I may be a bit of a Jew.

I have always been scared of *you*,
With your Luftwaffe, your gobbledygoo.
And your neat moustache
And your Aryan eye, bright blue.
Panzer-man, panzer-man, o You!

Not God but a swastika
So black no sky could squeak through.
Every woman adores a Fascist,
The boot in the face, the brute
Brute heart of a brute like you.

You stand at the blackboard, daddy,
In the picture I have of you,
A cleft in your chin instead of your foot
But no less a devil for that, no not
Any less the black man who

Bit my pretty red heart in two.
I was ten when they buried you.
At twenty I tried to die
And get back, back, back to you.
I thought even the bones would do.

But they pulled me out of the sack,
And they stuck me together with glue.
And then I knew what to do.
I made a model of you,
A man in black with a Meinkampf look

And a love of the rack and the screw.
And I said I do, I do.
So daddy, I'm finally through.
The black telephone's off at the root,
The voices just can't worm through.

If I've killed one man, I've killed two—
The vampire who said he was you
And drank my blood for a year—
Seven years, if you want to know.
Daddy, you can lie back now.

There's a stake in your fat black heart
And the villagers never liked you.
They are dancing and stamping on you.
They always *knew* it was you.
Daddy, daddy, you bastard, I'm through. *(1965)*

ARIEL

Stasis in darkness.
Then the substanceless blue
Pour of tor and distances.

God's lioness,
How one we grow,
Pivot of heels and knees!—The furrow

Splits and passes, sister to
The brown arc
Of the neck I cannot catch,

Nigger-eye
Berries cast dark
Hooks—

Black sweet blood mouthfuls,
Shadows.
Something else

Hauls me through air—
Thighs, hair;
Flakes from my heels.

White
Godiva, I unpeel—
Dead hands, dead stringencies.

And now I
Foam to wheat, a glitter of seas.
The child's cry

Melts in the wall.
And I
Am the arrow,

The dew that flies
Suicidal, at one with the drive
Into the red

Eye, the cauldron of morning. (1965)

FEVER 103°

Pure? What does it mean?
The tongues of hell
Are dull, dull as the triple

Tongues of dull, fat Cerberus
Who wheezes at the gate. Incapable
Of licking clean

The aguey tendon, the sin, the sin.
The tinder cries.
The indelible smell

Of a snuffed candle!
Love, love, the low smokes roll
From me like Isadora's scarves, I'm in a fright

One scarf will catch and anchor in the wheel,
Such yellow sullen smokes
Make their own element. They will not rise,

But trundle round the globe
Choking the aged and the meek,
The weak

Hothouse baby in its crib,
The ghastly orchid
Hanging its hanging garden in the air,

Devilish leopard!
Radiation turned it white
And killed it in an hour.

Greasing the bodies of adulterers
Like Hiroshima ash and eating in
The sin. The sin.

Darling, all night
I have been flickering, off, on, off, on.
The sheets grow heavy as a lecher's kiss.

Three days. Three nights.
Lemon water, chicken
Water, water makes me retch.

I am too pure for you or anyone.
Your body
Hurts me as the world hurts God. I am a lantern—

My head a moon
Of Japanese paper, my gold beaten skin
Infinitely delicate and infinitely expensive.

Does not my heat astound you! And my light!
All by myself I am a huge camellia
Glowing and coming and going, flush on flush.

I think I am going up,
I think I may rise—
The heads of hot metal fly, and I love, I

Am a pure acetylene
Virgin
Attended by roses,

By kisses, by cherubim,
By whatever these pink things mean!
Not you, nor him

Nor him, nor him
(My selves dissolving, old whore petticoats)—
To Paradise. (1965)

DEATH & Co.

Two, of course there are two.
It seems perfectly natural now—
The one who never looks up, whose eyes are lidded
And balled, like Blake's,
Who exhibits

The birthmarks that are his trademark—
The scald scar of water,
The nude
Verdigris of the condor.
I am red meat. His beak

Claps sidewise: I am not his yet.
He tells me how badly I photograph.
He tells me how sweet
The babies look in their hospital
Icebox, a simple

Frill at the neck,
Then the flutings of their Ionian
Death-gowns,
Then two little feet.
He does not smile or smoke.

The other does that,
His hair long and plausive.
Bastard
Masturbating a glitter,
He wants to be loved.

I do not stir.
The frost makes a flower,
The dew makes a star,
The dead bell,
The dead bell.

Somebody's done for.   *(1965)*

BIOGRAPHICAL AND BIBLIOGRAPHICAL NOTES:
POETS OF AMERICA

The following notes are intended only to provide the most basic identification of the poets represented in this anthology and a highly selective list of their books. Occasionally commentaries on their lives and work are noted, but only when these seem particularly useful to students.

Conrad Aiken (1889–   ). Educated Harvard University. Contributing editor *The Dial*, 1917–1919. Lived for many years in England. *Selected Poems*, 1929, 1961; *Preludes for Mennon*, 1931; *Collected Poems*, 1953; *The Morning Song of Lord Zero: Poems Old and New*, 1963. FICTION: *Collected Short Stories*, 1960; *The Collected Novels*, 1964. CRITICISM: *Scepticisms*, 1919; *A Reviewer's ABC*, 1958.

Hart Crane (1899–1932). The son of a candy manufacturer who was largely hostile to his literary interests. Educated in Ohio public schools and sent to New York to prepare for college, he devoted himself instead to writing, holding miscellaneous jobs during the war period and after. His reputation as a poet grew sufficiently by 1925 so that Otto Kahn supported him while he worked on *The Bridge*, published in 1930. Guggenheim fellowship, 1931, took him to Mexico to work on poem about Montezuma and the Spanish Conquest. After failure of this enterprise, committed suicide by leaping from ship in Gulf of Mexico on homeward voyage. Despite his alcoholism, homosexuality, and early disintegration, Crane (like Dylan Thomas) made an enormous impact in his few years of effective creativity. *White Buildings*, 1926; *The Bridge*, 1930; *The Collected Poems*, ed. Waldo Frank, 1933 (reprinted 1958 as *The Complete Poems*); *The Complete Poems and Selected Letters and Prose*, ed. Brom Weber, 1966; *The Letters*, ed. Brom Weber, 1952. COMMENTARY: Philip Horton, *Hart Crane, The Life of an American Poet*, 1937, 1957; Brom Weber, *Hart Crane*, 1948; L. Dembo, *Hart Crane's Sanskrit Charge: A Study of The Bridge*, 1960; John Unterecker, *Voyager: A Life of Hart Crane*, 1969.

E. E. Cummings (1894–1962). Son of a prominent Boston minister. Educated Harvard University. Served with Norton Harjes Ambulance Corps in World War I and was held for several months in a French detention camp through an error of the military censor (the experience is described with gusto in *The Enormous Room*, 1922). Interpreted a 1931 journey to USSR in *Eimi*, 1933. *Tulips and Chimneys*, 1923 (enlarged edition 1937); *XLI Poems*, 1925; *Is 5*, 1926; *Collected Poems*, 1938; *Poems 1923–1954*, 1954; *95 Poems*, 1958. COMMENTARY: Norman Friedman, *E. E. Cummings*, 1960.

Emily Dickinson (1830–1886). Educated Amherst Academy and Mount Holyoke Female Seminary. Outwardly the uneventful life of a spinster recluse, hers is revealed in her poetry as that of a passionate and vital person responsive to nature, brooding over the meaning of existence and of God and death, and deeply in love with an unnamed renounced person who figures in many of her poems—the subject of much speculation by her biographers. Virtually none of her work was published in her lifetime, but she left almost two thousand poems behind. *Poems*, ed. Mabel Loomis Todd and Thomas Wentworth Higginson, 1890; *Poems: Second Series*, ed. Todd and Higginson, 1891; *Poems: Third Series*, ed. Todd, 1896; *The Single Hound*, ed. Martha Dickinson Bianchi, 1914; *Selected Poems*, 1924; *Further Poems*, ed. Bianchi and Alfred Leete Hampson, 1929; *Unpublished Poems*, ed. Bianchi and Hampson, 1935; *Collected Poems*, 1937; *Bolts of Melody*, ed. Mabel L. Todd and Millicent Todd Bingham, 1945; *The Poems of Emily Dickinson*, "including variant readings critically compared with all known manuscripts," ed. Thomas Johnson, 1958; *Letters*, 1958, *Complete Poems*, 1960, and *Final Harvest*, 1961. See also *Complete Letters of Emily Dickinson*, ed. Mabel L. Todd, 1931, and *Letters of Emily Dickinson*, ed. Mabel L. Todd, 1951. COMMENTARY: Genevieve Taggard, *The Life and Mind of Emily Dickinson*, 1934; George F. Whicher, *This Was a Poet*, 1938; Millicent Todd Bingham, *Ancestors' Brocades*, 1945, and *Emily Dickinson: A Revelation*, 1954; Thomas H. Johnson, *Emily Dickinson*, 1955; Charles R. Anderson, *Emily Dickinson's Poetry*, 1960.

Hilda Doolittle (1886–1961). "H. D." Daughter of a professor of mathematics and astronomy. Educated Bryn Mawr College. With Ezra Pound became leader of Imagist movement. Married Richard Aldington, another of the original Imagists, in 1913; separated after World War I. Lived mainly in Europe, studying Greek civilization. Translator, editor of *The Egoist* during Mr. Aldington's war service. *Sea*

Garden, 1916; *Collected Poems,* 1925; *Selected Poems,* 1957; *Helen in Egypt,* 1961.

Robert Duncan (1919–   ). Educated in California schools and a leading San Francisco poet, critic, and editor. His half-mystical esthetic of "process" has helped define the work of the Black Mountain group, which includes Charles Olson, Denise Levertov, Robert Creeley, and others. *Heavenly City, Earthly City,* 1947; *Letters,* 1958; *Selected Poems,* 1959; *The Opening of the Field,* 1960; *Roots and Branches,* 1964; *The Years as Catches: First Poems* (*1939–1946*), 1966; *Bending the Bow,* 1968.

Richard Eberhart (1904–   ). Educated Dartmouth College and Cambridge University. Former schoolteacher; World War II Naval service; vice-president, Butcher Polish Company. Permanent Resident Poet, Dartmouth College since 1956. *A Bravery of Earth,* 1930; *Reading the Spirit,* 1937; *Song and Idea,* 1942; *Poems, New and Selected,* 1944; *Burr Oaks,* 1947; *Selected Poems,* 1951; *Undercliff,* 1953; *Great Praises,* 1957; *Collected Poems,* 1960; *The Quarry,* 1964; *Selected Poems,* 1965; *Shifts of Being,* 1968.

T. S. Eliot (1888–1965). Born St. Louis, Missouri. Educated Harvard, the Sorbonne, Oxford. After 1913 lived in London, where he was a bank clerk, taught school, and became assistant editor of *The Egoist* and founded and edited *The Criterion.* Naturalized a British citizen, 1927, and became a member of the Anglican Church. For many years a director of Faber and Faber. With Yeats and Ezra Pound the strongest single influence in modern poetry (and criticism) in the English language. *Prufrock and Other Observations,* 1917; *The Waste Land,* 1922; *Poems, 1909–1925,* 1925; *Ash-Wednesday,* 1930; *Collected Poems, 1909–1935,* 1936; *Four Quartets,* 1944; *The Complete Poems and Plays,* 1952. (ADDITIONAL PLAYS: *The Confidential Clerk,* 1954; *The Elder Statesman,* 1959); *Collected Poems, 1909–1962,* 1963; *Poems Written in Early Youth,* 1967. CRITICISM: *Selected Essays,* 1950; *On Poetry and Poets,* 1957. COMMENTARY: F. O. Matthiessen, *The Achievement of T. S. Eliot,* 1935, 1947 (rev. and enlarged), 1958 (with a chapter on Eliot's later work by C. L. Barber); Elizabeth Drew, *T. S. Eliot: The Design of His Poetry,* 1949; Helen Gardner, *The Art of T. S. Eliot,* 1949; Grover Smith, *T. S. Eliot's Poetry and Plays,* 1956; Hugh Kenner, *The Invisible Poet: T. S. Eliot,* 1959, and ed., *T. S. Eliot: A Collection of Critical Essays,* 1962.

Kenneth Fearing (1902–1961). Educated University of Wisconsin Outstanding Left poetic satirist of the American Depression, and later of the age of mass communication. Free-lance writer, reviewer, novelist. *Angel Arms*, 1929; *Poems*, 1935; *Dead Reckoning*, 1938; *Collected Poems*, 1940; *New and Selected Poems*, 1956.

Robert Frost (1874–1963). Born of schoolteacher parents. Education incomplete, though he studied at Dartmouth College and at Harvard University. Various jobs—mill work, shoe factory, newspaper, teaching—as well as farming to sustain him while writing poetry, but his work went unrecognized in this country. Moved with family to England in 1912, where he was published almost at once, becoming a part of the Georgian movement with his rural Hertfordshire neighbors Wilfrid Gibson, Lascelles Abercrombie, and Edward Thomas. Returned to U.S. in 1915, and had ever-growing recognition and success thereafter. Professor of English at Amherst 1916–1938, and periods at other colleges and universities. *A Boy's Will*, 1913; *North of Boston*, 1914; *West-Running Brook*, 1928; *Collected Poems*, 1930, 1939 (enlarged); *Complete Poems of Robert Frost*, 1949; *Selected Poems*, 1963; *Selected Letters*, ed. Lawrance Thompson, 1964; *Selected Prose*, 1966. COMMENTARY: Reuben A. Brower, *The Poetry of Robert Frost*, 1963; Lawrance R. Thompson, *Robert Frost: The Early Years 1874–1915*, 1966.

Randall Jarrell (1914–1965). Educated Vanderbilt University. Served in Army Air Force during World War II. Taught in various colleges, and then for a number of years at the Woman's College of the University of North Carolina. *Blood for a Stranger*, 1942; *Little Friend, Little Friend*, 1945; *Losses*, 1948; *The Seven-League Crutches*, 1951; *Selected Poems*, 1955; *The Woman at the Washington Zoo*, 1960; *The Lost World*, 1965; *Collected Poems*, 1969. CRITICISM: *Poetry and the Age*, 1953; *A Sad Heart at the Supermarket*, 1962. NOVEL: *Pictures from an Institution*, 1954.

Robinson Jeffers (1887–1962). Son of a linguist and theology teacher who gave him a thorough training in classical languages. Educated in European schools and at the University of Pennsylvania and Occidental College, with further studies at other universities including medical training at the University of Southern California. A legacy enabled him in 1912 to become financially independent and devote his life to poetry. Built Tor House, a stone tower in which he did much of his writing, on a bluff near the Pacific in Carmel, California. A vigorous opponent of many of the characteristics of modern civilization. *Tamar*, 1924; *Roan Stallion, Tamar, and Other Poems,* 1925; *The Selected Poetry,* 1938.

Vachel Lindsay (1879–1931). Educated Hiram College, Chicago Art Institute, Chase School of Art. Viewing himself as an apostle of beauty, he made several walking tours during which he would trade pamphlets containing his verse and drawings for food and shelter. After his first important volume (1913) became a great success, he traveled widely as a popular lecturer on poetry and reader of his own work. Toward the end of his life this popularity waned greatly; sick and in debt, he committed suicide. *General William Booth Enters Heaven,* 1913; *The Congo,* 1914; *The Chinese Nightingale,* 1917; *Collected Poems,* 1923, 1925 (revised); *Johnny Appleseed,* 1928; *Selected Poems,* 1931.

Robert Lowell (1917–   ). Educated Harvard University and Kenyon College. Conscientious objector in World War II, confined for five months to a federal penitentiary. Has taught in various universities. A descendant of a famous literary family, he is often considered the outstanding American poet of his generation. *Land of Unlikeness,* 1944; *Lord Weary's Castle,* 1946; *Poems, 1938–1949,* 1950; *The Mills of the Kavanaughs,* 1951; *Life Studies,* 1959; *Imitations,* 1961; *For the Union Dead,* 1964; *Near the Ocean,* 1967; *Notebook, 1967–68,* 1969. DRAMA: *The Old Glory,* 1965.

Archibald MacLeish (1892–   ). Educated Yale University and Harvard Law School. Artillery captain, World War I. Brief law career, 1920–1923. As Assistant Secretary of State (1944–1945), helped draft the UNESCO constitution. Librarian of Congress 1939–1944. Appointed Boylston Professor of Rhetoric, Harvard University, 1949. Experimented with radio drama and documentary use of poetry. *Tower of Ivory,* 1917; *The Hamlet of A. MacLeish,* 1928; *New Found Land,* 1930; *Conquistador,* 1932; *Poems, 1924–1933,* 1933; *Collected Poems, 1917–1952,* 1952; *"The Wild Old Wicked Man,"* 1968. PLAYS: *Panic,* 1935; *The Fall of the City,* 1937; *Air Raid,* 1938; *J. B.,* 1959.

Edgar Lee Masters (1869–1950). Educated German private school, Petersburg, Illinois, in Illinois public schools, Knox College (one year), and law offices. Admitted to bar 1891 and pursued a successful law career, mainly in Chicago, until 1923. Much self-education, and an unusual poetic career in that most of his early work appeared in newspapers. The Spoon River poems appeared first in *Reedy's Mirror,* attracting so much attention that the series was reprinted in 1915 in a book which at once became a national best seller. Novelist; biographer of Lincoln, Lindsay, Whitman, and Mark Twain; local historian. *Spoon River Anthology*, 1915, 1916 (expanded edition), 1942; *Domesday Book*, 1920; *The New Spoon River*, 1924; *Selected Poems*, 1925. AUTOBIOGRAPHY: *Across Spoon River*, 1936.

Edna St. Vincent Millay (1892–1950). Educated Barnard and Vassar Colleges. Won early recognition with her poem "Renascence" (1912). Acted with and had plays produced by Provincetown Players; translated songs and wrote short stories (under pseudonym Nancy Boyd); libretto for Deems Taylor's opera *The King's Henchman*, 1925. Married Eugen Boissevain 1923, lived thereafter on Berkshire Hills farm (see Vincent Sheean's *The Indigo Bunting*, 1951, for a beautiful memoir of her later years). *Renascence*, 1917; *A Few Figs from Thistles*, 1920; *Second April*, 1921; *The Harp Weaver*, 1923; *The Buck in the Snow*, 1928; *Fatal Interview*, 1931; *Wine from These Grapes*, 1934; *Collected Poems*, 1956. See also *Letters*, 1952, ed. Allan Ross Macdougall.

Marianne Moore (1887–   ). Educated Bryn Mawr College and Carlisle Commercial College (Pennsylvania). Taught stenography 1911–1915 government Indian school, Carlisle. Assistant, New York Public Library, 1921–1925. Editor *The Dial*, 1926–1929. *Poems*, 1921; *Observations*, 1924 (reprint with additions of the English edition of *Poems*, 1921); *Selected Poems*, 1935 (introduction by T. S. Eliot); *The Pangolin*, 1936; *What Are Years*, 1941; *Nevertheless*, 1944; *Collected Poems*, 1951; *Fables of La Fontaine* (translation), 1954; *Like a Bulwark*, 1956; *O To Be a Dragon*, 1959; *The Arctic Ox*, 1964; *Complete Poems*, 1967. CRITICISM: *Predilections*, 1955.

Howard Nemerov (1920–   ). Educated Harvard University. Coeditor *Furioso* for a time. Pilot in World War II with RCAF and USAAF. Professor, Brandeis University. Novelist and critic as well as poet. *The Image and the Law*, 1947; *Guide to the Ruins*, 1950; *The Salt Garden*, 1955; *Mirrors & Windows*, 1958; *New and Selected Poems*, 1960;*The Next Room of the Dream*, 1962; *The Blue Swallow*, 1967. PROSE: *Poetry and Fiction*, 1963.

Charles Olson (1910–1970). Educated Wesleyan, Yale, and Harvard Universities; has taught at Clark and Harvard Universities, at Black Mountain College 1951–1956 (where the poetic school called "Black Mountain" came into being), and most recently at the State University of New York at Buffalo. Like Robert Duncan, a leading theorist of his group and an even more faithful disciple than Duncan of Pound and Williams. Has cultivated a deliberate nativism in historical depth based on Gloucester, Massachusetts, comparable to Williams's use of Paterson, New Jersey. His essay "Projective Verse," first published in *Poetry New York* in 1950, is perhaps the most influential single theoretical statement of this movement. *The Distances,* 1960; *The Maximus Poems,* 1960; *Selected Writings,* 1966; *Human Universe and Other Essays,* 1967.

Sylvia Plath (1932–1963). Educated Smith College; while on Fulbright Scholarship to Cambridge University in England, met the British poet Ted Hughes, whom she married in 1956. Taught briefly at Smith College, but returned to England, where she lived with her husband and children until her suicide in 1963. *The Colossus,* 1960, 1962 (first American edition, slightly changed), 1967 (reissue in original form); *Ariel,* 1965; *Uncollected Poems,* 1965. AUTOBIOGRAPHICAL NOVEL: *The Bell Jar,* 1963.

Ezra Pound (1885–   ). Educated Hamilton College and University of Pennsylvania, where he was graduate fellow in Romance Languages and Literature. After a brief period of teaching (four months at Wabash College, Indiana), lived in London 1908–1919, where he was European correspondent for *Poetry* until 1919, London editor *The Little Review,* 1917–1919, and founder and editor *Blast,* 1914, the "Vorticist" review. Paris correspondent *The Dial,* 1919–1923. After 1923 lived in Rapallo, Italy. His sympathies with the Mussolini regime and hostility to what he considered the corruption of the Western democracies because of their banking systems led him to broadcast propaganda to the American troops in World War II. Arrested for treason in 1945 by United States forces, he was never brought to trial because adjudged insane; committed to St. Elizabeth's Hospital, Washington, D.C., and released in 1958. The history of his ideas may readily be followed in his poetry, especially *Hugh Selwyn Mauberley,* the *Cantos,* and *Poems of Alfred Venison.* Pound's theories of translation, his critical views, and his active sponsorship of many of the most significant writers and artists of the age have carried tremendous influence. His political attitudes and psychological condition have made him the most controversial literary figure of the age. *Personae: The Collected Poems,* 1926, 1949 (expanded); *Selected Poems,* 1949; *The Translations,* 1954; *Section: Rock-Drill,* 1956 (*Cantos* 85–95); *Thrones,* 1959 (*Cantos* 96–109); *The Cantos,* "New Collected Edition," 1964; *Selected Cantos,* 1967. PROSE: *ABC of Reading,* 1934, 1951; *Jefferson and/or Mussolini,* 1935, *The Un-*

wobbling Pivot and The Great Digest (transl.), 1947; *The Letters,* ed. D. D. Paige, 1950; *Literary Essays,* 1954. COMMENTARY: Hugh Kenner, *The Poetry of Ezra Pound,* 1951; John Espey, *Ezra Pound's Mauberley,* 1955; John H. Edwards and William W. Vasse, *Annotated Index to the Cantos of Ezra Pound,* 1957; M. L. Rosenthal, *A Primer of Ezra Pound,* 1960; Walter Sutton, ed. *Ezra Pound: A Collection of Critical Essays,* 1963; Donald Davie, *Ezra Pound: Poet as Sculptor,* 1964.

John Crowe Ransom (1888–   ). Educated Vanderbilt University and Oxford University (Rhodes Scholar). English professor Vanderbilt University 1914–1937 except for 1917–1919. Helped found and edit *The Fugitive,* 1922–1925. Carnegie Professor of Poetry at Kenyon College and editor *Kenyon Review* 1939–1959. An outstanding "New Critic" (the phrase was coined by Mr. Ransom). *Poems about God,* 1919; *Chills and Fever,* 1924; *Two Gentlemen in Bonds,* 1927; *Selected Poems,* 1945, 1963 (rev. and enlarged); *Poems and Essays,* 1955. CRITICISM: *The World's Body,* 1938; *The New Criticism,* 1941; ed. *The Kenyon Critics,* 1951.

Edwin Arlington Robinson (1869–1935). Educated Harvard University. Lived most of his life before thirty in Gardiner, Maine, the "Tilbury Town" of the poems. Failing to win editors' attention, published his first book himself in 1896, then lived in New York City after 1898, for a while employed as a checker of materials for the new subway system. In 1905 President Roosevelt, who had become interested in his poetry, procured him a position in the New York Customs House that he retained until 1909. Thereafter devoted himself to his writing, spending summers from 1911 on in the MacDowell Colony, Peterborough, New Hampshire. *The Torrent and the Night Before,* 1896; *The Children of the Night,* 1897; *Captain Craig,* 1903; *The Man against the Sky,* 1916; *Collected Poems,* 1921, 1927, 1937 (complete edition, with additional poems). See also *Selected Letters,* 1940, ed. Ridgely Torrence. COMMENTARY: Yvor Winters, *Edwin Arlington Robinson,* 1946; Edwin S. Fussell, *Edwin Arlington Robinson,* 1954; Louis O. Coxe, *Edwin Arlington Robinson,* 1969.

Theodore Roethke (1908–1963). Educated University of Michigan and Harvard University. Son of a Prussian immigrant whose flourishing greenhouse in Saginaw, Michigan, provided the matrix of experience for many of his most interesting poems. Taught in various colleges before going to the University of Washington and gathering a number of disciples about him. *Open House,* 1941; *The Lost Son and Other Poems,* 1948; *Praise to the End!,* 1951; *The Waking:*

Poems 1933–1953, 1953; *Words for the Wind: The Collected Verse*, 1957; *Collected Poems*, 1966. PROSE: *On the Poet and His Craft*, ed. Ralph J. Mills, 1965. COMMENTARY: Karl Malkoff, *Theodore Roethke*, 1966; Allan Seager, *The Glass House: The Life of Theodore Roethke*, 1968.

Carl Sandburg (1878–1967). Son of Swedish immigrants. Educated Lombard College after working at various jobs and serving in Puerto Rico during the Spanish–American War. Organizer for the Social-Democratic Party, Wisconsin, 1907–1908, newspaper work for occasional periods, secretary to Emil Seidel, first Socialist mayor of Milwaukee 1910–1912. Ballad and American folksong collector and singer, author children's books, Lincoln biographer. *In Reckless Ecstasy*, 1904; *Chicago Poems*, 1916; *Cornhuskers*, 1918; *Smoke and Steel*, 1920; *Slabs of the Sunburnt West*, 1922; *Selected Poems*, 1926; *Good Morning, America*, 1928; *Early Moon*, 1930; *The People, Yes*, 1936; *Complete Poems*, 1950. AUTOBIOGRAPHY: *Always the Young Strangers*, 1953. BIOGRAPHY: *Abraham Lincoln: The Prairie Years*, 1929; *Abraham Lincoln: The War Years*, 1939.

Karl Shapiro (1913–   ). Educated University of Virginia and Johns Hopkins University, where later he taught writing (1946–1950). Has taught in various universities since then. First won recognition with a volume published in 1942, while he was with American forces in the South Pacific. Editor *Poetry* magazine 1950–1956. For some years attempted to lead revolt against Eliot–Pound influence. *Person, Place and Thing*, 1942; *V-Letter*, 1944; *Essay on Rime*, 1945; *Trial of a Poet*, 1947; *Poems 1940–1953*, 1953; *Poems of a Jew*, 1958; *The Bourgeois Poet*, 1964; *The White-Haired Lover*, 1968. CRITICISM: *Beyond Criticism*, 1953; *In Defense of Ignorance*, 1960.

Wallace Stevens (1879–1955). Educated Harvard University and New York Law School. Entered legal department Hartford Accident and Indemnity Company 1916; became vice-president of firm 1934. The most retiring of poets (from the literary world, at any rate), he published his first book at the age of forty-four. *Harmonium*, 1923; *Ideas of Order*, 1935; *Owl's Clover*, 1936; *The Man with the Blue Guitar*, 1937; *Parts of a World*, 1942; *Notes Toward a Supreme Fiction*, 1942; *Esthétique du Mal*, 1946; *Transport to Summer*, 1947; *The Auroras of Autumn*, 1950; *Collected Poems*, 1954; *Opus Posthumous*, 1957; *Letters*, ed. Holly Stevens, 1967. CRITICISM: *The Necessary Angel*, 1951 COMMENTARY: William Van O'Connor, *The Shaping Spirit*, 1950; Frank Kermode, *Wallace Stevens*, 1960.

Richard Wilbur (1921–   ). Educated Amherst College and Harvard University. Professor of English, Wellesley College. *The Beautiful Changes*, 1947; *Ceremony*, 1950; *Things of This World*, 1956; *Advice to a Prophet*, 1961; *Walking to Sleep*, 1969.

William Carlos Williams (1883–1963). Educated in Horace Mann High School, New York City, Chateau de Lancy, Switzerland, and University of Pennsylvania Medical School. Internship followed by graduate study abroad. After 1910 lived in Rutherford, New Jersey, where he practiced medicine until retirement; for a time head pediatrician at Paterson General Hospital. One of the most experimental of American free-verse poets, constantly in search of "the line" rhythmically most natural to American speech and feeling, Dr. Williams's career was in many ways parallel (though often counter, also) to that of his old friend Ezra Pound, whom he met when both were students at the University of Pennsylvania. His *In the American Grain*, 1925, attempts to fix the main figures and motifs of the American myth. *The Complete Collected Poems 1906–1938*, 1938; *Selected Poems*, ed. Randall Jarrell, 1949; *Collected Later Poems*, 1950, rev. 1963; *Collected Earlier Poems*, 1951; *The Desert Music*, 1954; *Journey to Love*, 1955; *Paterson*, Books I–IV, 1946–1951; Book V, 1958; Books I–V, with a fragment of a projected Book VI, 1963. *The Autobiography of William Carlos Williams*, 1951; *Selected Essays*, 1954; *Selected Letters*, ed. J. Thirlwall, 1957; *The Farmers' Daughters: Collected Stories*, 1961; *Pictures from Brueghel: Collected Poems 1954–1962*, 1962; *The William Carlos Williams Reader*, ed. M. L. Rosenthal, 1966. COMMENTARY: J. Hillis Miller, ed., *William Carlos Williams*, 1966; Emily Mitchell Wallace, *A Bibliography of William Carlos Williams*, 1968.

INDEX

of authors, titles, and first lines

Titles are in italics, first lines in roman type. When a title and first line are the same, usually only the first line is indexed. *A, an,* or *the* at the beginning of a title is placed at the end, but in first lines these words are indexed in their normal order. When first lines are long, only the first few words may be given.